T0313705

Slow Print

Slow Print

Literary Radicalism and
Late Victorian Print Culture

Elizabeth Carolyn Miller

Stanford University Press
Stanford, California

Stanford University Press
Stanford, California

Printed in the United States of America on acid-free, archival-quality paper

Library of Congress Cataloging-in-Publication Data
Miller, Elizabeth Carolyn, 1974– author.
  Slow print : literary radicalism and late Victorian print culture / Elizabeth Carolyn Miller.
    pages cm
  Includes bibliographical references and index.
  ISBN 978-0-8047-8408-5 (cloth : alk. paper)
    1. Radicalism and the press—Great Britain—History—19th century. 2. Journalism—Political aspects—Great Britain—History—19th century. 3. Press and politics—Great Britain—History—19th century. 4. Printing—Great Britain—History—19th century. 5 Mass media—Great Britain—History—19th century. 6. English literature—19th century—Political aspects. I. Title.
  PN5124.R295M55 2013
  302.23—dc23
                          2012020621

Portions of the following chapters have been appeared in earlier publications:

Chapter 1, "William Morris, Print Culture, and the Politics of Aestheticism," *Modernism/modernity* 15.3 (2008): 477–502. Copyright 2008 The Johns Hopkins University Press. Reprinted with permission by The Johns Hopkins University Press."

Chapter 4, "Tom Maguire: 'An Under-Paid Agitator' in the Late-Victorian Socialist Press," *Philological Quarterly* 91.1 (2012). Reprinted with permission.

Chapter 5, "Body, Spirit, Print: The Radical Autobiographies of Annie Besant and Helen and Olivia Rossetti," *Feminist Studies* 35.2 (Summer 2009): 243–273. Reprinted with permission of the publisher, Feminist Studies, Inc.

Typeset by Bruce Lundquist in 11/15 Bell MT

Contents

Acknowledgments

When one informational medium is superseded by another, the transfer of an archive from the old format to the new usually entails a great deal of lost or rejected material. Such loss is movingly documented in Sean Dunne's *The Archive* (2009), a short film about the world's largest vinyl record collection and why most of that music will never make it to digital format. In the world of nineteenth- and early twentieth-century periodicals, we are currently witnessing a shift from print and microfilm archives to far more accessible digital archives; yet one wonders what kind of sources will be left out of this digitization boom. The radical newspapers and magazines that are the focus of my study will continue to be, I expect, of lowest priority in digitization projects, because of small circulations and, in many cases, short runs. While I was writing *Slow Print*, only two of the periodicals I discuss (*Commonweal* and *New Age*) were available digitally, thanks to the University of Michigan Library and the Modernist Journals Project. This is a project that has required, therefore, a great deal of research in brick and mortar libraries, and I would like to begin by thanking all those custodians of radical print who made this project possible. I am grateful to librarians at the following collections, roughly in order of importance to the project: the Labadie Collection, University of Michigan; the International Institute of Social History, Amsterdam; the British Library, London (especially the Colindale Newspaper Library); the Working Class Movement Library, Salford; Central Library, Manchester; John Rylands Library, University of Manchester; Leeds University Library; the Beinecke Rare Book and Manuscript Library, Yale University; the London School of Economics

Archives; the Bodleian Library, Oxford; University Library, Cambridge; and Churchill Archives Center, Cambridge. I would also like to thank the librarians at the University of California, Davis, for tracking down countless books and reels of microfilm through interlibrary loan.

I was able to spend so much time in these brick and mortar archives thanks to support from a number of different organizations. My first thanks go to the American Council of Learned Societies: The Charles A. Ryskamp Fellowship enabled crucial research time in Manchester and Leeds and a research year during which I wrote much of *Slow Print*. I am also grateful to have received the Curran Fellowship from the Research Society of Victorian Periodicals and the Joseph R. Dunlap Fellowship from the William Morris Society in the United States, which helped to fund a research trip to London and a research trip to Amsterdam, respectively. In addition, I feel very fortunate indeed to have had my research travel supported by my current and former employers, the University of California, Davis and Ohio University, and to have received a publication subsidy from the Division of Humanities, Arts, and Cultural Studies and the Office of Research at the University of California, Davis.

I am thankful, too, for my wonderful colleagues in the English Department at UC–Davis, especially Fran Dolan and Margaret Ferguson, who have been exceptionally generous with their guidance and interest in my work. Kathleen Frederickson, Hsuan Hsu, and John Marx all read portions of this project, and my work is better for their perceptive feedback. Other colleagues offered suggestions at our faculty research colloquium or in more informal settings; my thanks go to Gina Bloom, Nathan Brown, Seeta Chaganti, Greg Dobbins, Beth Freeman, Alessa Johns, Colin Milburn, Tim Morton, Parama Roy, Scott Shershow, David Simpson, and Mike Ziser. I owe extra special thanks to our department chair, Scott Simmon, for his support and kindness.

Many other friends, colleagues, and mentors have been instrumental in this project's development. I am especially indebted to Florence Boos, Joseph Bristow, John Kucich, and Rebecca Walkowitz for generously offering advice and encouragement. From Angela Berkley, Susan Bernstein, William Cohen, Jonathan Freedman, Taryn Hakala, Casie LeGette, Morna O'Neill, Mario Ortiz Robles, Todd Shepard, and Jenny Sorensen I received helpful responses to my work and key research leads.

Many thanks to my friend Laura Vroomen, who let me stay with her on a research trip to London, and to my friends Jane Rickard and Richard Meek, who put me up in Leeds. I presented portions of this project in draft form to the University of Michigan Nineteenth Century Forum and to the UCLA Nineteenth Century Group, and my work benefited greatly from these experiences. Thanks, too, to my former colleagues at Ohio University, who offered helpful suggestions at an early stage of the project, especially Andrew Escobedo, Paul Jones, Joe McLaughlin, Beth Quitsland, and Carey Snyder. I am deeply grateful to Emily-Jane Cohen and everyone at Stanford University Press for their expert stewardship of my project. Stanford also chose two exceptional readers whose work I very much admire, Ann Ardis and Matthew Beaumont; they gave invaluable suggestions for improvement and kindly made their identities known to me. I would also like to thank my three wonderfully resourceful graduate student research assistants: Ryan Fong, Greg Giles, and Michael Martel.

My last acknowledgments go to my family. My parents, sisters, and grandparents have always encouraged my intellectual work, for which I thank them: Giacomo and Phyllis Ghiardi; Cathy, Cristina, Frank, and Rhea Miller; Sarah Miller and Jon Konrath; and Mary Ellen Powers. Hearing tales of my parents' personal involvement with radical print in the 1960s and 1970s, and coming across my mother's name on a masthead in the Labadie Collection, was, I'm sure, part of what led to my interest in slow print. I am also grateful to Vickie Simpson and the Stratton family. Saving the most important person for the end: I owe more than I can ever say to Matthew Stratton, and I feel exceptionally fortunate to have his love and intellectual companionship. I would also like to thank our imminent twin sons, Ambrose and Giacomo. As I put the finishing touches on *Slow Print*, they are due to arrive within weeks, and I thank them for staying put long enough for me to finish the book (and for livening up my final revisions with all their kicks and rolls)!

Slow Print

Introduction

H. G. WELLS'S 1906 utopian novel *In the Days of the Comet* takes place in a socialist future where newspapers have become "strange to us—like the 'Empires,' the 'Nations,' the Trusts, and all the other great monstrous shapes" of the past (75). The narrator, an old man who remembers the capitalist days before "the Great Change," describes late Victorian commercial print culture to an audience of postprint socialists, and he emphasizes above all its speed.

[Imagine] a hastily erected and still more hastily designed building in a dirty, paper-littered back street of old London, and a number of shabbily dressed men coming and going in this with projectile swiftness, and within this factory companies of printers, tensely active with nimble fingers—they were always speeding up the printers—ply their type-setting machines, and cast and arrange masses of metal in a sort of kitchen inferno, above which, in a beehive of little brightly lit rooms, dishevelled men sit and scribble. There is a throbbing of telephones and a clicking of telegraph needles, a rushing of messengers, a running to and fro of heated men, clutching proofs and copy. Then begins a clatter roar of machinery catching the infection, going faster and faster, and whizzing and banging—engineers, who have never had time to wash since their birth, flying about with oil-cans, while paper runs off its rolls with a shudder of haste. The proprietor you must suppose arriving explosively on a swift motor-car, leaping out before the thing is at a standstill, with letters and documents clutched in his hand, rushing in, resolute to "hustle." . . . You imagine all the parts of this complex lunatic machine working hysterically towards a crescendo of haste and excitement as the night wears on. (76)

The passage is a study in velocity. Words such as "haste," "projectile," "swift," "speed," "rush," "fast," and "run" fly as the narrator exhausts his supply of speedy synonyms. Here Wells's socialist novel expresses a radical consensus of the era: that the speed- and profit-oriented print marketplace had become a synecdoche for capitalism, an automatic machine for reproducing the logic of mass production.[1]

Radical writers sought to counter this development. Hence the final decades of the nineteenth century witnessed not only a flood of print production aimed at mass audiences but also a corresponding surge in small-scale radical periodicals, or "slow print." What I call slow print is print that actively opposed literary and journalistic mass production; it was often explicitly political in objective, as socialist, anarchist, and other radical groups came to believe that large-scale mass-oriented print was no way to bring about revolutionary social change. On issuing the first printed number of their anarchist newspaper *The Torch*, for example, Olivia and Helen Rossetti, who produced the paper from their parents' basement, apologized for its late appearance: "We have comp'd it ourselves and as we are but novices in the noble art of printing we are as yet slow" (15 July 1892: 2). With the emergence of a mass public came manifold countercurrents, erupting against a broad trend toward the rapid mass production of literature and print for larger and larger audiences. In this book I investigate anticapitalist print and literary countercultures in this key moment of literary, print, and media history.

From the onset of the socialist revival around 1880 to the early years of the twentieth century, Britain saw a flourishing of radical political activity as well as an explosion of print production.[2] Although the rise of mass print was a long historical process, the final decades of the nineteenth century were a watershed moment because of such innovations as mechanized composition, cheaper paper, and photomechanical reproduction and such cultural shifts as universal education and widespread literacy.[3] Economic factors were also key. Print in the second half of the nineteenth century went from being a predominantly "authoritarian" to a predominantly "commercial" communication system, to use Raymond Williams's terminology; the printing industry was consolidated, publishers became ever more profit oriented, and advertising became for the first time the major source of revenue in periodical publishing.[4] Key to this shift was the late nineteenth-century "Northcliffe revolution," when Lord Northcliffe (Alfred Harmsworth) "and similar figures saw increased revenue from the new display advertising as the key to modern newspaper finance, and in particular as a means to reduction in price per copy so as to gain a large circulation" (Williams 18). As circulations became larger and larger, ownership became narrower and narrower; newspaper capitalists such as Lord Northcliffe, Arthur Pearson, and George Newnes built publishing empires by launching and acquiring many periodicals, a mode of ownership that resembled "the major forms of ownership in general industrial production. The methods and attitudes of capitalist business . . . established themselves at the centre of public communications" (24).

On the heels of such changes, Britain saw a dramatic rise in the number of printed periodicals: from 643 magazines published in 1875 to 1,298 in 1885, 2,081 in 1895, and 2,531 in 1903 (Keating 32–34). Literary historians have focused on such numbers as evidence of a new mass market in publishing, but many of the new periodicals were small, specialized, and independent organs oriented toward alternative publics. For example, hundreds of British radical papers originated in this era, and this microsurge in the radical press paralleled the macrosurge of periodical publishing in general.[5] The term *slow print*, which I use throughout this book, suggests that late nineteenth-century radical literature's challenge to mainstream print culture was largely temporal—slow as opposed to fast—but the radical literary countermove to print mass production was as much about scale as it was about speed. The print community that emerged in British radical circles during these years directed itself, for better or worse, to a small-scale audience, a political and aesthetic counterculture, a public that defined itself against a mass-oriented, mainstream print culture.

Such an orientation developed, in part, from the ideas of John Ruskin, whose critique of modern labor, industry, and information networks is everywhere apparent in the late-century radical press, although his name is not often invoked.[6] By the 1870s Ruskin had become, as Judith Stoddart puts it, "increasingly cynical about the benefits of free discussion. In 1865 he had criticized Mill's liberty of thought as little more than liberty of 'clamour'" (7–8). According to Brian Maidment, Ruskin deplored the commercial press and "above all the *quantity* of Victorian popular journalism" because it "created a baffling proliferation of information" (36). In 1871 Ruskin began to publish his letters to work-men, *Fors Clavigera*, which were issued in monthly installments for a yearly subscription and continued with some interruptions until 1884. He sought to bypass the infrastructure of commercial publication alto-gether by issuing the pamphlets himself at a fixed (and expensive) price, with no advertisements or trade discounts. As he wrote in his Decem-ber 1873 letter: "I find it . . . necessary to defy the entire principle of advertisement; and to make no concession of any kind whatsoever to the public press—even in the minutest particular" (Ruskin 167). Inter-spersed with the letters were clippings from the periodical press, meant to define Ruskin's work against the mass press through juxtaposition. In their cost and their style, Ruskin's letters were mostly inaccessible to the "workmen and labourers of Great Britain" to whom they were ostensibly directed, but as Dinah Birch comments, "Those who did re-ceive the letters on their first appearance . . . could feel themselves to be members of a privileged and distinguished coterie" (xxxv). Ruskin's attempt to opt out of the commercial publishing industry, where an an-ticapitalist gesture became the mark of a privileged coterie, anticipates the key dilemma of the late-century radical press.

Some late-century radical writers were more conscious than others of the dangers of coterie authorship, but across radical writing, at the heart of the move toward slow print, was widespread doubt about whether a mass public could exist outside capitalism. Was the mass public merely a reflection of capitalism's drive toward ever-widening, ever-quickening global expansion? Was it possible to imagine a wide, anonymous pub-lic outside capitalist ideology? Many socialist utopian novels of the era imagine an international postrevolutionary socialism, but in England the most influential visions of the socialist future—such as William Mor-ris's *News from Nowhere* (1890) or Robert Blatchford's *Merrie England* (1893)—were intensely local, a reaction against the expansive capitalist ideology that seemed to be the grounds for an emerging mass media. The radical turn away from mass audiences was thus not merely elitist or bourgeois, although it sometimes was that. It was, at heart, anticapi-talist. The duality inherent in the rejection of the mass market—that it seemingly required a degree of elitism or exclusivity, a betrayal of the democratic ideal, in the service of rejecting capitalist networks of production—was the central challenge for radical writers, and it created the literary and cultural dynamic from which literary modernism would emerge.

This dynamic little resembled the situation of radical print and radical communities in the first half of the nineteenth century. The first chapter of E. P. Thompson's classic history *The Making of the English Working Class* is titled "Members Unlimited," referencing the London Corresponding Society's cardinal rule "that the number of our Members be unlimited." For Thompson this rule, instituted in the pivotal political moment of the 1790s, is "one of the hinges upon which history turns. It signified the end to any notion of exclusiveness, of politics as the preserve of any hereditary *élite* or property group" (21). The rule of unlimited membership ascribed a democratic sensibility to the notion of limitless scale, evident in discussions of "free print" in the period Thompson analyzes, 1780–1832. As William St. Clair notes, these years saw "the last sustained attempt by the British state to control the minds of the British people by controlling the print to which they had access" (12). Under such conditions the radical press became, as David Vincent puts it, "both the vehicle and the object of political protest" (128). "There is perhaps no country in the world," Thompson says, "in which the contest for the rights of the press was so sharp, so emphatically victorious, and so peculiarly identified with the cause of the artisans and labourers" (720). Ian Haywood describes "the sense of optimism, self-confidence and ambition which fuelled radical periodicals. Spreading the gospel of the radical enlightenment could only be achieved by constant proliferation and expansion" (*Revolution* 76).

Thus early nineteenth-century radical print culture associated successful class-oriented protest with rapid and large-scale expansion into a potentially limitless print frontier. It was a moment when, in Oskar Negt and Alexander Kluge's phrasing, English radicals created something akin to a "proletarian public sphere that embraces the nation as a whole" (199).[7] In the following chapters I consider another print cultural context, some fifty to a hundred years later, but this later context was shaped in part by the history of a radical investment in the dream of limitless print. As Thompson notes, early nineteenth-century radicals "thought that the only limit imposed to the diffusion of reason and knowledge was that imposed by the inadequacy of the means." He calls this the "rationalist illusion," the mechanistic confidence that "the art of Printing is a multiplication of mind'" (*English Working Class* 732–33). The phrase "multiplication of mind," coined by radical journalist Richard Carlile, epitomizes the "celebratory tone of a techno-determinist account" in early nineteenth-century conceptions of radical print, as Kevin Gilmartin puts it (26). By the end of the century, however, the tone had changed; radical thinkers came to believe that print's endless reproducibility made it especially subject, as a technology, to the expansive market ideology of industrial capitalism.

Did print function as a synecdoche for capitalism, wordlessly conveying the values of mass production, homogeneity, and invisible labor? Could this capitalist technology—which in its very form implies standardization and the mechanization of manual labor (handwriting)—be used to produce anticapitalist political effects? These were the questions of the day for radical writers at the end of the nineteenth century, and the answer, for many of them, involved purposefully reducing the scale of print by appealing to a small, countercultural audience.[8] Some radicals still reiterated the "rationalist illusion," but many others had been disabused of it; they came to think that the large scale that had been achieved by mass print was possible only within a commercial infrastructure of production and distribution that inevitably tainted the print that was produced. By redirecting independent small-scale print toward a limited community, these writers hoped to resist the political failings of a mass-produced medium.

By focusing on the literary culture of the radical press—the literature published within and around radical periodicals—I suggest that literature was a crucial means by which the turn-of-the-century radical counterpublic defined itself against capitalist mass print culture. In a wide survey of radical journals of the era, I have found that all of them included literature, to varying extents: poetry, serialized novels, short fiction, drama, and dialogues in addition to reviews and criticism of contemporary theater, fiction, and literary culture. As Peter Kropotkin remarks in his *Memoirs of a Revolutionist*, the socialist cause "has never been rich in books. . . . Its main force lies in its small pamphlets and its newspapers" (275). The same is true of its literary culture. Within this radical sphere, we find a series of debates concerning how to use literature as an agent of radical change, how to make and distribute print literature without compromising anticapitalist values, and how to situate radical values within an evolving media ecology—a nascent mass media sphere characterized by New Journalism, ghostwriting, celebrity authorship, and other shifts in the modern author function. These debates engaged some of the most famous writers of the era, such as William Morris and George Bernard Shaw; a host of lesser-known writers, such as Annie Besant and Edward Carpenter; and countless obscure, working-class, and/or anonymous contributors to the radical press.

Working within the radical print sphere, these writers sought to explore medium as a conveyor of meaning, and they struggled with the common challenge of how to start a mass movement without using what they understood to be aesthetically and politically compromised mass media. Despite a shared aversion to literary mass production, they rarely agreed on how best to use literature or print to effect radical change, and their work exhibits a considerable variety of media strategies and literary modes. William Morris, for example, would produce artisanal, handcrafted books through the Kelmscott Press, while George Bernard Shaw sought to vivify the radical public by merging radical print with the radical stage. At the same time, such writers were participating in major literary and aesthetic debates raging outside the radical sphere: aestheticism and the autonomy of art, naturalism, the decline of the Victorian novel, the dramatic revival, and the protomodernist rejection of Victorian literary convention.

The literary culture that emerged from turn-of-the-century radical print complicates and contextualizes critical understandings of a modernist rupture from Victorian literary sensibilities. Although critics such as Jonathan Rose have argued "that the fundamental motive behind the modernist movement was a corrosive hostility toward the common reader" and that modernist writers strove "to maintain social distinctions in an increasingly democratic and educated society" because they "felt threatened by the prospect of a more equal distribution of culture" (393), literature of the late-century radical press reminds us that the protomodernist backlash against mass print culture was also anticapitalist, an expression of class critique.[9] Radical writers were often unsuccessful in balancing anticommercialism against elitism, as we will see, but to reduce their reaction against mass print to elitism is to misinterpret a social movement that intended to decapitalize print literature. Ian Haywood has cautioned against "essentialist thinking about the relationship between radicalism and commercialism," arguing that although "it may be difficult for the anti-populist instincts of the political left to accept the fact," the Victorian popular press, especially *Reynolds's Newspaper* and *Lloyd's Weekly Newspaper*, was the true inheritor of early nineteenth-century print radicalism ("Encountering Time" 80). However, this was not the way the late-century radical press saw it; *Reynolds's* slogan, after all, was "Largest, Cheapest, and Best." Henry Hyde Champion's socialist paper, *Labour Elector*, called the mass print *Reynolds's* "a mere Liberal Will-o'-the wisp, whose flickering and expiring flame would lure the British workers to their destruction" (14 January 1893: 7).[10]

Appraising the relative radicalism of a popular paper like *Reynolds's* begs a larger question of terminology. The term *radical*, which I use throughout this book, denoted in the early nineteenth century an anti-government or limited-government perspective. Class-oriented social protest literature at the end of the century does not sit easily under the term *radical*, both because of internal conflict over the role of state structures in achieving classlessness (e.g., socialist vs. anarchist, big-state vs. small-state collectivism) and because by the end of the century the term *Radical* had been effectively appropriated by the left wing of the Liberal Party, making it less useful in describing anti-establishment groups (hence Charles Bradlaugh was a Radical, but he was far less radical than the writers under consideration here).[11] I will nonetheless use the uncapitalized term *radical* as shorthand for "wholesale class-oriented social protest," drawing on its etymological sense of "the root" to describe late-century activism with the aim of "root and branch" political and economic change.[12] As one writer put it in the *Workman's Times*, "Radicalism, we all know, means going to the root of things. And there can be no radical reform of the present hateful condition of society without advancing Social Democracy" (25 November 1893: 1). This focus on attacking the root of social dysfunction was characteristic of turn-of-the-century class radicalism.

The term *radical* is not a perfect terminological solution, but neither are other potential descriptors such as *socialist* (which would exclude anarchist and labor groups that actively rejected that label), *labor* or *working-class* (which would include some apolitical or politically tepid print organs and would exclude middle-class groups such as the Fabians or the Fellowship of the New Life that shared the objective of a classless society), or *left-wing* (which might include left-wing Liberals who did not advocate thoroughgoing economic change). The commodious term *radical* suits a print community that defined itself against mainstream culture yet left ideological divisions among groups loose and unenforced. Indeed, although much has been written about "hair-splitting over doctrine" in the late Victorian left (MacKenzie and MacKenzie 71)—rifts emerged, for example, between reformist and revolutionary, nationalist and internationalist approaches—a strong collective spirit also led diverse groups to work together.

For example, Charlotte Wilson edited the most important British anarchist paper of the era, *Freedom*, but in the 1880s she was a member of the Fabian Society, a group that advocated incremental reform on the path to state socialism. Shaw, a fellow Fabian, collegially wrote an anarchist essay for her to publish in *Freedom*, "more to shew Mrs Wilson my idea of the line an anarchist paper should take in England than as an expression of my own convictions" (*Collected Letters* 1: 109). Initially, *Freedom* was printed by Annie Besant and Charles Bradlaugh's secularist Free Thought Publishing Company, although Bradlaugh was antisocialist and anti-anarchist. Wilson, in her notes on the history of *Freedom*, writes that at the time of the Chicago Haymarket affair, the paper was "obliged, in deference to the strongly anti-anarchist views of Mr. Bradlaugh, to remove from its original office on the premises of the Free Thought Publishing Company." *Freedom* then "set up at the Socialist League printing office, by the kind permission of William Morris." Morris was no anarchist either, although his tolerance for anarchism ultimately led to its takeover of the Socialist League organization. After leaving the Socialist League press and before finally securing a press of its own, *Freedom* was also printed by the Fellowship of the New Life, an "ethical socialist" group that advocated individual ethical transformation but not anarchism.[13] As *Freedom's* promiscuous migration among diverse leftist presses demonstrates, printing equipment was literally common ground connecting all these movements: anarchist, revolutionary socialist, state socialist, ethical socialist, secularist, and so on.[14] Even among groups with clear ideological differences, there was an impetus to work together: to speak on one another's platforms, to reprint material from one another's papers, and to develop a shared literary canon and a mutual print community.

This sense of community was created in large part by a united effort to define a radical print sphere in opposition to the capitalist print sphere. In the following chapters I describe literary efforts in this direction, but in this introduction I want to first establish how strongly this sense of print opposition characterized radical press discourse. For example, *Justice*, the newspaper of the Social Democratic Federation and the first major socialist paper in England, was perhaps the first British paper to define a socialist public by means of vehement opposition to the capitalist press.[15] The paper declared, "Capitalists own almost all the whole Press; they are masters of the ordinary means of distribution. We must consequently organise a distribution of our own" (5 July 1884: 4). A letter in its correspondence column, from Mr. Reeves of Liverpool, expresses views typical of the paper's readership: "Any Social Democrat who is in the habit of writing to the newspaper press knows that nothing detrimental to the interests of capital is allowed. . . . Profit is the great aim of speculators in magazines and newspapers, hence the lying advertisements of quacks which flood the advertising columns, hence the sickening accounts of royal shows and the revels of aristocratic flunkydom" (16 February 1884: 6). When another reader wrote to complain about press coverage of a West Midlands strike, the editor commented, "The working classes must expect this. The whole capitalist press is but one huge machine in the hands of their enemies" (18 October 1884: 5).

Justice's attitude toward mass print anticipated the tone of many papers that came in its wake. Glossing and correcting the conclusions of mainstream newspapers became a favorite pastime of radical writers and editors, and cut-and-paste montage took on a revolutionary cast long before the advent of Soviet film. In its first issue *Justice* juxtaposed a clipping on "Yachting in the Mediterranean" with one on "The Homes of the Poor" under the headline "How We Live Now" (19 January 1884: 3). The technique recalls Sergei Eisenstein's argument that class difference is the social origin of the montage aesthetic, that the structure of montage reflects "the structure of bourgeois society . . . *a contrast between the haves and the have nots*" (234). In its July 1893 issue the *Labour Leader* similarly juxtaposed two columns of clippings under the heading "Our Un-Social Contrasts"—one on the rich and one on the poor—noting that the contrast was "sufficiently eloquent to need little comment or introduction" (8–9). Henry Hyde Champion's paper *Common Sense* was almost entirely composed of quotations and cuttings, edited in clever relation to make an argument; the paper nodded to Thomas Paine in its title, but its content implies a very different moment for radical print. Annie Besant's socialist magazine *Our Corner* said *Common Sense* "might almost be called *Socialist Tit-Bits*," comparing the paper to George Newnes's wildly popular exercise in New Journalistic mass print (1 June 1887: 375–76), but although *Common Sense*, like *Tit-Bits*, emphasized short cut-and-paste items, its use of this technique was satirical and dialectical. In the June 1887 issue the article "Why People Die: Class Mortality Statistics" reprinted information from government-produced blue books as a form of revolutionary propaganda (27). Juxtaposition also served in *Common Sense* as a formal reflection of class difference; side-by-side columns titled "Our National Wealth" and "Our National Poverty" visually instantiate the extreme gap between the social classes (May 1887: 3). The whole scheme of the paper suggests an age of overabundant print and a need for cutting and selecting from an overload of information.[16]

Despite this effort to draw a clear division between the capitalist press and the radical press, such distinctions were not always easy to maintain, as in the case of advertising. *Justice*, like most radical papers, was chronically underfinanced and never self-supporting. In its second issue the paper noted having received a number of complaints about its 2 penny price: "In reply we can only appeal to the workers to support a paper which is entirely independent of trade or capitalist advertisements or pecuniary support. A journal cannot permanently appear in the interest of the mass of the people which is not supported by the people and by the people alone" (26 January 1884: 1). The price was reduced to 1 penny in the third issue, but *Justice* was not always able to hold to the declaration that it would not accept advertisements. From early on it ran "trade advertisements" for other radical papers and publications, although its rejection of regular advertising remained central to its counterprint identity; the editor boasted on 13 March 1886 that *Justice* had survived thus far "without receiving a single capitalist advertisement" (1).[17] The *Commonweal*, the Socialist League newspaper edited by William Morris, likewise ran advertisements for books and other materials relating to the cause, yet even this limited concession to commercialism produced defensive apologies, as in its "Terms of Advertising" circular (see Figure 1): "The proprietors are confident that in taking this step they are alike benefiting their readers and advertisers." Many papers experienced a conflict between the desire to denounce the newspaper industry's reliance on advertising revenue and the necessity of running ads to stay afloat. *Labour Elector*, a paper that itself ran regular ads, not just those associated with the cause, argued in an attack on the *Daily Chronicle* that "the interests of the paper's clients—the propertied and *advertising* class—[are] necessarily opposed to the interests of the workers" (7 January 1893: 1).

Conditions of late nineteenth-century mass journalism were such that it was difficult for a paper to survive without advertising.[18] Newspapers and magazines had shifted to make more of their profit from advertising than from subscriptions; prices went down in consequence, and papers sold for a penny or even a half-penny. Radical papers kept the low prices but found surviving without advertising difficult. The *Clarion*, the most mass-oriented socialist paper of the era, ran many advertisements, often with the attention-grabbing fonts of New Journalism. Julia Dawson, a *Clarion* columnist, defended the paper on this score.

May I beg of my readers to complain to me on any subject except that of the advertisements which appear in our columns. I don't take exception to any one of them—because they are all necessary, at present. There may, nay, there *will* come a time when the support of Clarionettes will enable us to be as dainty as we like in these matters, and accept only those advertisements which correspond to our *highest* ideals. But that time is not yet. (17 April 1897: 128)

E. Belfort Bax, one of England's most influential early Marxists, launched a wholesale assault in *Justice* on the ideal of "free print," which had been the center of early nineteenth-century radicalism, arguing that the conditions of the modern print industry—such as dependence on advertising revenue—made a mockery of this ideal. The article,

THE COMMONWEAL

PUBLISHING OFFICE,
13 Farringdon Road, London, E.C.

WE beg to call your attention to the under-given Terms of Advertising in the *COMMONWEAL*, which, circulating as it does throughout Europe, America, and the Colonies, affords by far the best medium for bringing books—especially those which deal with Social questions—under the notice of probable purchasers. Among the subscribers and readers of the *COMMONWEAL* are numbered the most prominent Political and Social Reformers of this Country, as well as of the Continent and America; and the greater part of its *clientèle* are men continually upon the alert for the latest expressions of opinion or statements of fact upon the problems of the day.

Hitherto there has existed no medium capable of bringing the publisher of works upon Social questions into such close connexion with his special public; and the proprietors are confident that in taking this step they are alike benefiting their readers and advertisers.

For the Proprietors,

H. HALLIDAY SPARLING.

TERMS OF ADVERTISING.

On Back Page,	. . .	4d. *per Line each Insertion.*	SCALE OF BREVIER LINES.
Half Column (57 Lines),	.	18s. *each Insertion.*	
One Column (114 Lines),	.	35s. *each Insertion.*	
One Page (two Columns),	.	£3, 5s. *each Insertion.*	

Discount on Monthly Accounts amounting to £1, five per cent.; £5, ten per cent.

Advertisements must be acceptable in every respect. Copy received until Tuesdays, 3 p.m.

The COMMONWEAL *is sent free to those who advertise in it as long as their advertisement continues.*

—5

—10

Figure 1. Terms of Advertising circular, *Commonweal*. Socialist League Archives, International Institute of Social History (Amsterdam).

"A 'Free Press,'" disabuses readers of the liberal idea that a deregulated print sphere was necessarily an advantage for democracy: "Among the glories of latter-day liberty, the first place is commonly accorded to our 'free press.' That the newspaper press, at least in this country, is really free, few persons appear to have the faintest doubt." But, Bax argues, an unregulated press is far from a "free" press.

What are the conditions of the success of a newspaper? That it should have a good circulation of course, but first and foremost that it should obtain advertisements, the backbone of the newspaper publishing trade being the modern system of advertising. What are the conditions of a circulation and of obtaining advertisements? Obviously that the paper should appear to the interests of those who have money and leisure. . . . Is not the newspaper proprietor himself a capitalist, generally on the largest scale . . . ? But some may say surely there must be a large section of the workers who would give an independent organ a circulation. Unfortunately there is not in this country at present. The workers have received, where any at all, a class education, having been fed by class literature. . . . This is in the first place. In the second, the middle and upper classes having control of the *means of distribution* can generally succeed in smothering an organ which is offensive to them. . . . It follows then that our boasted freedom of the press is a "snare and a delusion". . . . "Free Press" indeed! Ye men of England, when will ye forsake these idols, these empty and vapid abstractions—"freedom," "toleration," "equality before the law" . . . for belief in a real, a concrete social order in which while the truth of these things will be embodied, their false and evanescent form will have vanished. (6 December 1884: 4)

To Bax the long-standing radical ideal of free print is not only misguided but also misguiding, a false ideal that inhibits widespread recognition of the real conditions of print media.

Justice recognized that appealing to the free print ideal could generate widespread sympathy for its program, but it was dubious of the wisdom of such a tactic. After several of the paper's promoters were prevented from selling it in the streets, on the charge of obstruction, *Justice* organized a successful demonstration and drew positive attention from the mainstream press (3 October 1885: 2–3). But even amid this victory the paper stressed the importance of fomenting economic reform, not settling for the old liberal "rights." A letter from correspondent J. J.

Dobbin voiced impatience with the liberal discourse of radicalisms past: "Freedom of speech we hold to be one of our inalienable birthrights, and naturally we cling to it . . . but we Socialists are not going to rest satisfied here. Free speech to millions of our starving fellow countrymen and women savours too much of middle-class mockery." Dobbin makes an "appeal to the workmen of England to unite with us to take hold of the land and the means of production . . . and, depend upon it, the next demonstration in Limehouse will be one for something more than the mere right of free speech" (17 October 1885: 3). Harry Quelch, who took over as editor of *Justice* after H. M. Hyndman, also felt the danger of a liberal agenda as a distraction from socialist change: "Englishmen have always prided themselves upon the enjoyment of rights and privileges which were denied to the people of other countries. We, as Englishmen, are constantly being congratulated on the possession of the right of combination, of public meeting, and of free speech." And yet "the classes which have controlled all the political as well as all the social forces have permitted the enjoyment of these rights only so long as they have been used either entirely in their interest or with the effect of checking instead of helping on the cause of the workers" (19 March 1887: 2). The liberal cause of free print no longer made sense as a galvanizing force within the radical sphere, depriving radical writers and editors of one of the most successful planks in the nineteenth-century radical tradition.

In lieu of the free print cause, attention to printing as a capitalist industry became a prominent topic across the radical press. For example, many of those who produced *Justice* labored in the printing trade; on a list of fifty-nine working men who helped turn out the paper in London, fifteen were compositors and three were otherwise employed in the trade (18 July 1885: 5). The paper depended on volunteer compositors and printers for its production: "This journal is written, set up, edited, and in great part distributed gratuitously. We are showing how even a newspaper may be produced under Socialism. Will not all workers and sympathisers help?" (21 March 1885: 5).[19] Other papers made similar appeals. *Home Links*, a short-lived communistic magazine, announced on the inside front cover of its February 1897 issue: "One or two compositors, willing to render voluntary services for the cause might find a genial home and vegetarian meals provided for them, on application to Mr. Gottschling [editor]."

The 15 June 1893 issue of the *Torch*, Olivia and Helen Rossetti's anarchist newspaper, called for volunteer assistance in print production: "We find our circulation has so rapidly increased that it entails a lot of extra work, so we have decided till further notice to be in our offices on Monday night (from 8-30 to 1-00) when any help that comrades care to give will be gratefully received."

Radical papers that did not run their own press had to ensure that the printing firms they used did not exploit workers. The *Labour Journal* out of Bradford responded in its 25 November 1892 issue to a charge made by the Typographical Society that the paper relied on an "unfair" firm: "The firm in question carried on business over 100 miles from Bradford, and therefore it was not easy to know much about it. . . . We had made a mistake through lack of information, and we frankly acknowledged that that was so, expressed our great regret, and very gladly promised not to order anything more from that firm or any other 'unfair' firm" (1). Likewise, the *Fabian News* warned in July 1891 that some socialists "who in their writings advocate Trade-Unionism, are not sufficiently careful that these very writings are printed in Fair Houses." For example, "a compositor was recently 'sacked' merely for belonging to his Trade Union by a firm who have printed the works of at least two Fabians; other Fabians contribute to or conduct Socialist magazines which are published by houses whose reputation is not spotless" (1).

Attention to such issues in radical papers demonstrates that at this time printing represented the endangering of skilled trades by industrial mechanization. Human labor was being pushed out in favor of speedier automation, and consequently print labor developed a special resonance, akin to that of Lancashire textile weavers earlier in the century. As Matthew Rubery notes, speed itself had become "a valuable commodity" for Victorian newspapers; widespread use of the term "Express" "registered the public's fascination with the rapid transmission of news that seemed to embody the experience of modernity" (160). However, this speed came at a cost to workers, which the radical press was at pains to document. The 15 May 1897 issue of *Labour Leader* ran a piece titled "Men vs. Machines" that focused on the mechanization of printing and the "trouble brewing in the printing trade" (164). A letter from a reader argued that the Linotype Users' Association's new recommendations on rates of pay for print workers were unjust: "Are we, as one of the most powerful trade unions in the kingdom, whose ranks have already been decimated by the adoption of mechanical devices during the past five or six years, to drive the last nail into the coffin of a once wealthy and powerful institution by the adoption of such unreasonable propositions[?]" (167). The mechanization of printing meant that it was becoming a less skilled trade; it was losing the status that had allowed printers' unions to become relatively powerful earlier in the century. In *Justice* James Blackwell wrote of "the displacement of labour by labour-saving machinery" in the print industry: "Some years ago the Hoe Cylinder machine took the lead amongst printing machines. Its speed was 8,000 perfect copies per hour. . . . The Victory Web Perfecting Machine now takes the lead . . . at a speed ranging from 12,000 to 25,000 copies per hour. . . . The Hoe machine required nineteen [attendants], including all the folders; the Victory has only two" (3 January 1885: 6). An update titled "Compositors' Trade Union" in *Justice* claimed, "The prospect of the London Society of Compositors is not a bright one, for it is felt throughout the trade that type-setting can and will soon be done by machinery" (3 April 1886: 2).[20]

It wasn't that radicals were opposed to technological innovation but that such developments under capitalism were bound to hurt workers, not help them: "An electrical type-setting machine is now to be seen at work at Beccles. What will be the effect of this labour-saving contrivance under present conditions? What *might* its effect be under a rational system of property holding?" (*Justice*, 6 September 1884: 2). James Blackwell tried to imagine what postrevolutionary print would be like in an article titled "Wasted Labour": "Of the enormous amount of utterly useless work which the present system necessitates the printer and his satellites do a great deal. Indeed, if it were not for advertising, which would be for the most part done away with in a Socialistic State, two-thirds of the printers would have nothing to do" (*Justice*, 13 June 1885: 4). He imagines that after the revolution "theatrical announcements, lists of new books and such like would alone be necessary in the way of advertisement" (5). "Denuded of advertisements, the newssheets of the future will undoubtedly assume a very different form to that which newspapers now possess." Robert Blatchford, editor of the *Clarion*, reiterated this line of thought in *Merrie England*, his 1893 series of fictional letters on

socialism, which sold upward of 2 million copies after its original serialization in the *Clarion*.

Commercial waste is something appalling. . . . Take the one item of advertisement
alone. There are draughtsmen, paper-makers, printers, bill-posters, painters, car-
penters, gilders, mechanics, and a perfect army of other people all employed in
making advertisement bills, pictures, hoardings, and other abominations—for
what? To enable one soap or patent medicine dealer to secure more orders than
his rival. (20)

A letter from James Smith in *Justice* took a similar line: "About half of
our labour has been taken up in helping to puff shoddy wares, quack
medicines, etc. . . . Another fourth of our time is taken up to provide
the gamblers in the necessaries of life with the latest news concerning the markets of the world. . . . I hope my fellow comps. will ponder
over the manner in which much of our labour is utilised by designing
capitalists" (27 November 1886: 3).

  Smith's letter asks workers in the printing industry to consider
their complicity in capitalist print production. A similar tension existed
around the question of readers' complicity in the mass print market, the
question of whether the press "reflects" the people's will or whether it
manifestly does not reflect it but creates it. For example, Tom Maguire's
paper *Labour Champion* was a Leeds socialist paper that often defined
itself against the mainstream *Yorkshire Post*, as in this article about reports on a miners' strike:

It is a grave and serious concern when a great class organ, carrying with it wide
and far-reaching influences, deliberately sets itself in direct and deadly antagonism to the lives and safety of tens of thousands of men, women, and children,
immediately within the circle of its power . . . but when, in order to justify such a
course, facts are distorted, statements exaggerated, and the whole case presented
in false lights and colours, the offence grows in magnitude and becomes a crime
against humanity. (11 November 1893: 3)

Maguire sees the *Post* as ruthlessly manipulative of the public, and he
sees wealth and capital at the root of this ruthlessness: "With the prac-
ticed ingenuity that wealth can always command, the *Post* proceeds to
excite public hostility against the miners and their leaders." But he also

calls out working-class readers for supporting the paper: "How long our stupid, unseeing brethren will continue to pay their ha'pence for snubs and kicks heaven alone knows! They, themselves, are responsible for the engine that destroys them." Maguire attributes readers' support of the capitalist press to their naïve faith in mainstream print. Such an argument also appears in Robert Tressell's socialist novel *The Ragged Trousered Philanthropists*, written between 1906 and 1910; Tressell depicts a group of mystified workers who read papers called *The Daily Obscurer* and *The Weekly Chloroform*, papers owned by wealthy capitalists who "controlled their policy and contents" (319). The workers nonetheless believe that "when you have a thing in print—in black and white—why there it is, and you can't get away from it! If it wasn't all right, a paper like that would never have printed it" (100). Other radical writers saw readers' desires, not their ingenuousness, as the problem. An 1890 penny pamphlet titled *Working Men Indeed!* by the Scottish socialist Bruce Glasier, complains that working-class readers only care about "whether the Duke of Clarence means to marry the daughter of an American millionaire; whether Mr. Gladstone prefers grain or lump sugar to his tea; . . . or what players will be selected for the next international football team" (5).

The term *public opinion* had by this time already occupied an unstable ground of reference between the consensus of the newspaper sphere and a supposedly real, measurable public sentiment.[21] At times some radical writers would blame readers for the conditions of mass print, as though the print marketplace was a straightforward reflection of their desires; but for the most part the radical press took the view that the capitalist press did not reflect public opinion but manufactured it. A leaflet titled "The Workers' Claims and 'Public Opinion,'" published by the Socialist League to promote sale of the *Commonweal*, argued:

Men of Labour! Whenever you show signs of impatience at your present degraded position . . . you are met not only by the stolid opposition of your Capitalist-Masters, but also by the censuring shouts of what is called "Public Opinion." But what is that "Public Opinion"? . . . Is it a common, wide-spread, a national feeling? Not at all! Public Opinion, that is, the Press, is, nowadays, like all private enterprise, a profit-mongering, mercenary concern. The Press of to-day is established, in the first instance, to make money out of the ignorance, curiosity and credulity of the public. . . . Beware of the Capitalist Press, and look out for and support those few papers that are working for your freedom! (Socialist League Archive, f. 587)

A piece in *Justice* titled "Press and People" similarly declared that "public opinion" means only "capitalist opinion": "Newspapers owned by capitalists, and depending for their existence upon capitalist advertisements cannot, of course, afford to quarrel with their means of livelihood. But then let us all understand, once for all, that the daily press of England expresses now and ever only the public opinion of the plundering class" (15 May 1886: 2).

The operating theory in most radical papers was that the mainstream press did not reflect readers' will but rather the economic structures of the print industry. At the same time, radical writers and editors wanted to believe that workers, once enlightened, would "choose" a radical paper as a "reflection" of their views. For example, *The Workers' Herald: A Socialist Weekly*, declared in its inaugural issue on 12 December 1891:

A notable strike is being carried on in our midst, and the local press has no word of advice to give to the men . . . the capitalist press remains silent. JUST BECAUSE IT IS THE CAPITALIST PRESS. . . . it is because of all this and much more that THE WORKERS' HERALD has been called into existence. . . . We believe Socialism has only to be known in order to find general acceptance. (6–7)

The choice was left to readers: "If the WORKERS' HERALD is wanted it will live. If, on the other hand, the people of Scotland have not yet sufficiently learned the meaning of the Class War to maintain in a healthy state the only paper which preaches the class war, the WORKERS' HERALD may die" (7). Many papers professed the Enlightenment ideal that "socialism only has to be known in order to find general acceptance," but they also confronted evidence against this all the time. The layers of complexity between the availability of print and the achievement of a readership had complicated the twinned "print-knowledge" formation at the heart of Chartism and other early nineteenth-century radical movements.[22]

For example, the London paper *The Radical* included in its 8 January 1881 issue an article titled "'Spread the Light.'" The title expresses a sense of skepticism toward familiar Enlightenment rhetoric: "In England it is not so easy to spread the light. Long centuries of grovelling in the low depths of ignorance and vice and semi-starvation . . . have dulled, almost to the extent of extinguishing, the minds of the people" (4). As a letter from Herbert Burrows in the paper's first issue declares, reformist ideas "have no chance of being discussed by the class journals of the day. The so-called Liberal press of London is a poor thing, hardly daring to call its soul its own, having to write up, or . . . down, to the views of the middle-class plutocrats, by whom it is supported" (4 December 1880: 7). Appeals to liberal Enlightenment values—such as the neutral pursuit of transparent truth—were losing their force in the late-century radical press.

The headline on the front page of the inaugural issue of the *Alarm*, a London anarchist paper, read "Our Paper. Why We Publish 'The Alarm,'" with the subheading, "Knowledge Is Power." The subheading sums up the argument of the article: "The main object of this paper will be to get the workers of the English-speaking world to understand the idea of Anarchy, to persuade them to unite their efforts and bring about a condition of affairs where men shall have his own and be happy" (26 July 1896: 1). Yet in subsequent issues of the paper the struggle to spread this knowledge became more and more untenable. The next issue was not printed until 13 September 1896, the delay owing to expense and equipment: "We could not get the paper out with the scanty means at our disposal so long as it was being printed by an ordinary commercial firm. In order to meet this difficulty we decided to get the requisite type and get it out from our own office, and this is the first issue 'on our own'" (4). Finances became more and more of an impediment by the third issue.

We Take Anything!!! Although money is handiest, stern necessity compels us to be universalist and we therefore wish to make known here that in payment for literature supplied by us we take *anything* which we can use for *The Alarm* or sell in support of it. Odd type, ink, furniture, wearing apparel, boots, jewellery, books, back numbers or sets of any paper, used or unused stamps, American paper currency, tea, sugar, cocoa, crockery ware, cutlery. (27 September 1896: 2)

The next issue declared: "Advertise in *The Alarm*: Cheapest Advertising Medium Known" (11 October 1896: 4).

In its third issue the *Alarm* announced that it would stop justifying lines, following Benjamin Tucker, editor of the American anarchist paper *Liberty*. Under the headline "Typography Turns over a New Leaf," the *Alarm* called Tucker "the first printer to break through hide-bound conventionality and print his paper in the nonjustification style. . . . Apart from the added beauty imparted to the page . . . the time saved is equal to ten minutes in the hour" (4) (see Figure 2). This was an instance where radical print found a political value in a money-saving formal strategy. To avoid justification was to violate typological standardization, to "break through hide-bound conventionality," preparing readers through unconventional print form for unconventional ideas.[23] Yet despite the time saved by not justifying lines, by its seventh issue the *Alarm* was in dire straits: "We have thrown out many hints in these

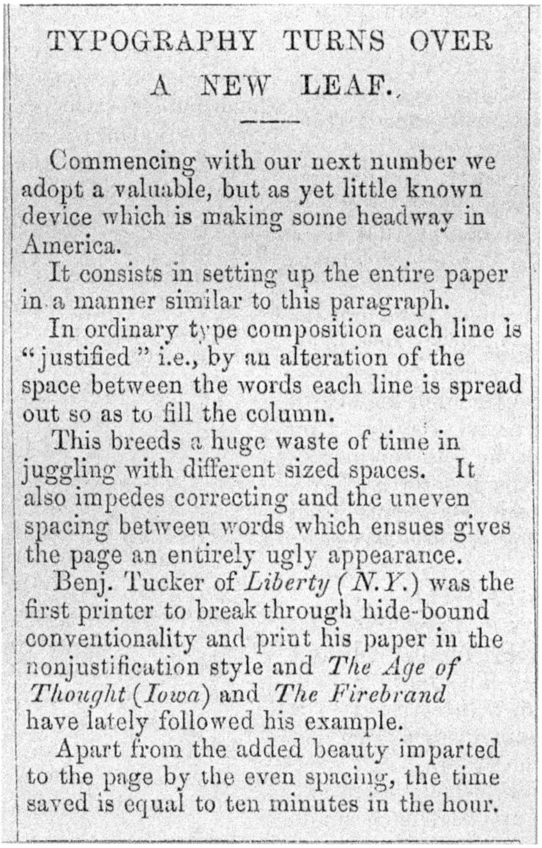

TYPOGRAPHY TURNS OVER

A NEW LEAF.

———

Commencing with our next number we adopt a valuable, but as yet little known device which is making some headway in America.

It consists in setting up the entire paper in a manner similar to this paragraph.

In ordinary type composition each line is "justified" i.e., by an alteration of the space between the words each line is spread out so as to fill the column.

This breeds a huge waste of time in juggling with different sized spaces. It also impedes correcting and the uneven spacing between words which ensues gives the page an entirely ugly appearance.

Benj. Tucker of *Liberty* (*N.Y.*) was the first printer to break through hide-bound conventionality and print his paper in the nonjustification style and *The Age of Thought* (*Iowa*) and *The Firebrand* have lately followed his example.

Apart from the added beauty imparted to the page by the even spacing, the time saved is equal to ten minutes in the hour.

Figure 2. "Typography Turns over a New Leaf" from the *Alarm* (1 November 1896: 4). Labadie Collection, University of Michigan.

columns for support to carry on the publication of the ALARM," but now "plain language must take the place of hints."

> It is now well known that we are only a small band of wage-slaves who devote the few moments allowed us by our exploiters to carry on the printing and pub-lication of what we consider is greatly needed in this country. . . . We have man-aged, by practicing the utmost economy in all things, to cut down our expense to £1 15s. per week! . . . This is cutting it very fine indeed; in fact as fine as possible. (1 November 1896: 3)

The *Alarm* folded after its tenth issue. This was a common fate for many radical papers. The *Labour Prophet*, a Northern socialist paper, described labor papers as "coming and going like the leaves on the trees of the forest" (January 1892: 4).[24]

The trajectory of the *Alarm* was depressingly familiar in the radical print sphere: The rhetoric of Enlightenment would shine through in the first issue, to be replaced soon after by disillusionment. *The Dawn*, a so-cialist paper out of Ilkeston, claimed in its first issue that the paper was "the outcome of a sincere conviction that the majority of our fellow-citizens . . . need only to have an intelligent exposition of Socialism laid before them to see the truth, the justice, the practicability, and the inevitability of our cause. . . . It is also intended as a channel through which the mis-representations of the Party Press can be corrected" (January 1902: 2). A year later, the paper had changed its tune: "It is a sad commentary on the intelligence of the British democracy that scarcely a single paper run in the sole interest of the working classes, can be made to pay its way. The pathway of progress is strewn with the relics of ventures in this direction which have to be abandoned . . . for lack of support" (January 1903: 3). Meanwhile, the mass print market was only growing larger: "The reflection is the more bitter when it is borne in mind that organs run on the most sensational lines and convicted of the most atrocious lies and the vilest misrepresentations, sell in their millions every week" (3).

A few radical papers responded to this situation by emulating the popular press even as they defined themselves against it. This tactic was characteristic of the *Clarion*, the most mass oriented and best sell-ing of the era's radical papers. Edited by Robert Blatchford (nicknamed Nunquam, for "Nunquam Dormio," or "I Never Sleep"), the *Clarion* was launched in Manchester in 1891, and its weekly circulation hit a high of 90,000, averaging between 40,000 and 50,000 a week (Brake and Demoor 583). Blatchford claimed that the *Clarion* was "the first Socialist paper that ever paid its way in this country" and that it provided socialism with "a literature of its own, and a Press of its own" (*New Religion* 2). The paper achieved this distinction by using elements of popular mass press journalism to present socialist material; it tended toward New Journalism, playing up the personalities of the paper's staff (all of whom had nicknames like The Bounder and Dangle), running human interest stories, and using typographical novelties. Matthew Arnold had coined the term New Journalism in 1887 as a deprecatory description of the "feather-brained" popular press, which was understood to have borrowed its "new" techniques from vulgar American journalism.[25] However, in the first issue of the *Clarion* Blatchford embraced New Journalism as the theme of his paper: "Be it remembered that those who would teach must please. . . . The essence of this new journalism; for it *is* a new journalism, and a journalism created by the men now risking this venture, is variety" (12 December 1891: 3). As noted earlier, the *Clarion* ran advertisements, a mode of revenue rejected by many socialist papers; it also ran sporting news and often emulated the language of the sporting press (Blatchford had gotten his start at *Bell's Life*); and it tended (increasingly over the years, resulting in a loss of readers around World War I) to strike a nationalistic tone and to appeal to workers' sense of race.

The *Clarion* brought together news and politics with a wide variety of literature (fiction, poetry, nonfictional essays) and features, such as a women's column and a bicycling column. In its pages Blatchford ran his series of socialist letters, *Merrie England*, a tract that was heavily indebted to William Morris and went on to sell millions of cheap pamphlet editions.[26] As a 1910 biography of Blatchford put it, Morris "was a greater poet than Mr. Blatchford," but "Morris was a literary exquisite. His appeal, in any true sense, was only to the few—the comparative few. 'R.B.' has put poetry and desire into the souls of thousands upon thousands of working people" (Lyons 110). The inaugural issue of the *Clarion* declared that its staff would "write not for faction; but for the people" (12 December 1891: 3), seemingly aligning the paper with mass-oriented publications such as Newnes's *Tit-Bits*, which ostensibly appealed to all classes and ages of readers everywhere in England.

Still, the *Clarion's* readership continued to be mostly Northern, and its specialty, which accounted for its long-running success, was a propensity for gathering together live subcultural communities of working-class socialists who called themselves Clarionettes. From the readership of the paper grew the Clarion Cycling Clubs, which took on a life of their own and still exist to this day, as well as Clarion Players' Dramatic Societies, Rambling Clubs, Swimming Clubs, Handicraft Guilds, Camera Clubs, Clarion Choirs, Clubhouses, and, in Liverpool and Manchester, Clarion Cafés.[27] These instances of live socialist community perfectly exemplify the kind of subcultural networks the radical press sought to generate. They represent a broader radical effort to develop a "politics of everyday life," as Chris Waters put it (*British Socialists* 14), that would allow socialists and other radicals to opt out of capitalist consumer culture by participating in alternative leisure and social networks as well as alternative print networks.[28] In this sense the *Clarion*, which was unusual among radical papers for its affinities with the popular press, was also typical in its efforts to define a separate radical counterpublic.

Deian Hopkin has claimed that the *Clarion* differed from other socialist papers that came before it in part because it serialized novels and stories (227), but in fact, the literary content of the *Clarion* closely resembled that of other radical papers. All radical papers of this era printed literature, in part to attract a wider audience of readers but also because literature was understood to have a political use beyond attractiveness. Literature and art were considered crucial components of a healthy socialist society, and developing a literary and cultural tradition for a future socialist society was a task that radical writers took seriously. However, the radical papers' use of and ideas about literature varied. In the following chapters I trace out a range of radical literary responses to the consolidation of the print industry and the emergence of a mass print market. What they share is an effort to generate an anticapitalist counterpublic through literature.

In Chapter 1, "No News Is Good News: William Morris's Utopian Print," I focus on perhaps the most influential radical writer of the era. Printers, artists, and radical thinkers of all stripes have been inspired by the Arts and Crafts movement that Morris spearheaded and by his vast body of work. In this chapter I discuss Morris's two major ventures into radical print: the *Commonweal* socialist newspaper, which he edited from 1885 to 1890, and the Kelmscott Press, which he founded in 1891. Pointedly removed from the general flow of mainstream print, these two print enterprises construct themselves as utopian spaces outside the "march of progress" narrative (predicting endless expansion) that had accrued to print and to capitalism. But whereas the *Commonweal* relied on a template of mass mediation, selling for 1 penny with a small circulation of 2,500–3,000 a week, the Kelmscott Press produced unique objects using preindustrial methods, handmade materials, and ornate typography and illustration. Literary critics often view Kelmscott as Morris's retreat from the active political work represented by the *Commonweal*, but important continuities exist between the two projects. In Chapter 1 I compare versions of Morris's novels *A Dream of John Ball* and *News from Nowhere*, both of which were initially published serially in the *Commonweal* and later in Kelmscott editions, to show how Morris exploited aspects of each print medium to critique the political effects of mass print culture. Morris's career in radical print demonstrates his perception of the failure of liberal notions of print as an agent of progress and his effort to reinvent print as an ideal practice at the level of production.

In Chapter 2, "The Black and White Veil: Shaw, Mass Print Culture, and the Antinovel Turn," I consider the radical turn against the realist novel at the end of the nineteenth century, which was also a turn against the literary mass market in its most developed mode. Against a broad account of the socialist turn against the novel, I examine George Bernard Shaw's four early novels, which were originally serialized in two 1880s socialist magazines, and his subsequent abandonment of the novelistic form in favor of the radical drama. During his early years in London, Shaw was a relentless contributor to the radical press, including his four novels. In later years he dismissed these "novels of his nonage," but at the time the works were read and admired by the radical public. I consider the novels' appearance within a context of broad debate about the realist novel within the radical press—Is it an inherently bourgeois form? What are the politics of naturalism?—and look at the careers of contemporary radical novelists such as C. Allen Clarke and Margaret Harkness ("John Law"). Critics have read Shaw's dramas, which he began to write in the 1890s and for which he is much better known, as novelistic or print centered in a way that was unprecedented in theater history, but less attention has been paid to the dramatic quality of his novels, which strive after the dialogic and public features of the theatrical sphere and strain against novelistic form. In this chapter and in Chapter 3 I connect the socialist turn away from the novel and toward the theater to a broader radical discontent with print and its seeming incapacity to generate a political counterpublic.

In Chapter 3, "Living Language: Print Drama, Live Drama, and the Socialist Theatrical Turn," I look at the domain of the theater and the radical investment in the dramatic revival of the 1890s. To many socialists the theater appeared to offer an oral, live, mutual experience, less mass oriented but more communal than print. Radical efforts to develop a theatrical counterpublic, however, were intensely reliant on the radical print community; in this sense, frustration with the political inadequacies of print media actually generated new points of contact between radical print and radical theater. Henrik Ibsen's plays *Ghosts* and *A Doll's House* were key texts in fomenting the radical turn to theater, and both were championed in the radical press; indeed, the first appearance of *Ghosts* in English was in the socialist magazine *To-Day*. Likewise, in 1886 the Shelley Society's successful private staging of Percy Bysshe Shelley's unlicensed play *The Cenci* proved a galvanizing event for the private theatrical societies that emerged from the radical sphere during the 1890s. Theater for late Victorian radicals suggested the possibility of fusing together artistic and political purpose, yet theater developed within the movement as a mode of containment against the outsized anonymous public being newly formed by means of mass print. Ultimately, Shaw and his fellow theatrical socialists drew an exclusive public in the theatrical sphere as the Kelmscott Press had done in the print sphere, and they continued in the outworn track of early nineteenth-century print radicalism by adopting an anticensorship, free-expression credo (foundationally liberal in principle) as their primary political strategy.

In Chapter 4, "Measured Revolution: Poetry and the Late Victorian Radical Press," I provide the first sustained analysis of poetry published in this era's radical press. Most journals valued traditional poetic forms and aural rhythmic songs over and above formal poetic innovation. Thus poetry served a unique purpose in this print context: to situate radical ideals within the familiar forms and rhythms of the past and to claim poetic tradition as a precapitalist formation. The implied political value of poetry was in its potential to draw together readers of the radical press into a separate alternative culture made familiar by appeals to the past and brought to life by appeals to oral forms. Print remained the most obvious means of forming and interpellating a public, but poetry and song held the promise of rendering the communion of print into the realm of live voice and live action. I include in Chapter 4 a wide survey of poetry from a number of radical journals and sections detailing the poetry of the *Commonweal* and the poetry of Tom Maguire, a working-class Leeds socialist and labor organizer who published in a range of radical journals, sometimes under the pen name Bardolph. Through its rendering of the relationship between tradition (language and poetic form) and change (the poems' revolutionary themes), radical press poetry theorized a particular vision of cultural change: that one can engage and transform dominant culture from within the forms of that culture. Anticipating modernist poetry's emphasis on rupture, poetry of the radical press developed its own theory of cultural rupture with a distinct politics of form.

In Chapter 5, "Enlightenment Beyond Reason: Theosophical Socialism and Radical Print Culture," I consider the proliferation of theosophy and related esoteric discourses in turn-of-the-century radical literature, arguing that these discourses functioned to critique the Enlightenment rationalism entrenched in radical conceptions of print literature and free print. Theosophy was an occultist philosophy loosely based in Eastern religion and was ideologically rampant within fin de siècle radicalism, despite the militant materialism of "scientific socialist" groups such as the Social Democratic Federation. Annie Besant, the most significant of the socialist theosophists, eventually became a worldwide leader of the Theosophical Society after abandoning the scientific secularism with which she had long been associated. I consider Besant's career in socialist print alongside that of Alfred Orage, a prominent Leeds socialist theosophist who eventually became editor of the *New Age*. I position these two writers and editors within a broader context of mystical and theosophical socialism in print, including work by Edward Carpenter, Florence Farr, and John Trevor. For Besant and Orage theosophical conceptions of subjectivity produced a quasi-mystical view of the author-reader relation, providing a model of authorship that elided the capitalist, individualist implications of the author function as it operated under the new media conditions of mass publishing. Theosophical discourse was a space within radical print where esoteric exclusivity purportedly met communal union—an ostensible but not untroubled compromise between a radical desire for universal equality and a radical reaction against mass culture.

In the final chapter, "Free Love, Free Print: Sex Radicalism, Censorship, and the Biopolitical Turn," I consider the migration of the old liberal line on print enlightenment into the sphere of sexual radicalism at the end of the nineteenth century. In terms of class radicalism, turn-of-the-century radical print registers a widespread loss of confidence in the political effectiveness of the free print cause, but at the same time such rhetoric persisted in the corner of the radical press that focused on sexuality. This is particularly apparent in print activism around censorship and biopolitical issues such as free love, birth control, homosexuality, and sexual discourse in the public sphere. Michel Foucault has influentially argued, contra the repressive hypothesis, that "rather than a massive censorship" of sexual discourse in the Victorian era, there was "a regulated and polymorphous incitement to discourse" (*History* 34). We can see a version of the "repressive hypothesis" articulated in the late-century radical press's reaction against state censorship of sexually transgressive print, but I argue that the radical press took this line not simply out of an "incitement to discourse" but as a continuation of the tradition of libertarian rhetoric around free print in nineteenth-century radicalism. Examining a wide variety of texts—such as the free love journal *The Adult*, suppressed writing on homosexuality by Edward Carpenter and Havelock Ellis, radical press accounts of "free love novels" (such as Grant Allen's *The Woman Who Did*, Thomas Hardy's *Jude the Obscure*, and Edith Ellis's *Seaweed*), and the pro–birth control women's columns of the *Clarion*—I connect a radical turn to sexuality, usually attributed to modernism, to the evolving political charge of the old radical free print discourse.

Radical print has a history that long precedes the fin de siècle, but in *Slow Print*, I hope to demonstrate that it faced uniquely modern challenges at the turn of the twentieth century—challenges that are inherent in any effort to oppose commercial pressures rather than state pressures on the circulation of political information. These challenges have only grown since the advent of radio, television, and other mass media. In the early nineteenth century radical writers had to circumvent direct governmental controls over expression, and radical arguments about print tended to focus on the necessity of removing authoritarian constraints. Prohibited by laws, taxes, and duties from publishing freely, radical reformers tended to imagine free, plentiful print as a font of enlightenment tied to democratic representation, labor reform, and the eradication of poverty. Post-Enlightenment reformers set great sights on literacy and print as agents of equality, democracy, and classlessness, but the last decades of the nineteenth century saw this seemingly intuitive truth increasingly questioned. Liberal notions of free print as an agent of rational Enlightenment became less tenable for social reformers after the 1860s, who began to see print as dangerously embedded in commercial capitalism.

Radical writers were acutely aware that in the context of a sharp increase in late Victorian print production, print literature was losing much of the authority that it had previously held over speech. Although some welcomed this timely challenge to established discursive authority, others worried that with the profusion of mass print, the printed word was becoming disposable, incidental, and ephemeral. To many writers the situation resembled a return to an oral rather than textual society, which was underscored by new sound technologies, such as the telephone and the phonograph, which were creating a culture of "secondary orality," to use Walter Ong's term. Visual innovations such as moving pictures further complicated the status of print by offering an entirely new medium of visual communication.[29]

How did radical writers imagine that the literary text would function within the new media ecology of the modern era? What literary, political, and social factors contributed to their imaginative vision? And how did new conditions of media, form, and textuality open up new political and literary possibilities at the same time that they shut down others?

To get at these questions, I have found it necessary to look closely at radical periodicals and to put radical literature back into the context of the radical press. Not all turn-of-the-century radical periodicals have survived, but enough have been preserved in archives and research collections to offer a considerable challenge to received notions of the era's literary politics.

CHAPTER 1 # No News Is Good News
William Morris's Utopian Print

THE 7 JANUARY 1893 ISSUE of the *Workman's Times*, a socialist newspaper aimed at working-class trade unionists, features an illustration of a manual artisan in an apron who has carved in stone: "Life without industry is guilt. Industry without art is brutality" (Figure 3). The artist-worker, depicted with a mallet and chisel, is burly yet sensitive, muscular yet mustached, with downcast eyes and a jaunty cap. A second illustration depicts another artist-worker—similarly brawny but now bearded and wielding a sledge-hammer—standing beneath a banner that reads, "By hammer and hand all arts do stand" (Figure 4).[1] The illustrations and their accompanying sentiments are clearly indebted to a Ruskinian ideal of manual labor as a form of artistic expression and a manifestation of the worker's innate dignity, yet they also refer to Walter Pater in their underlying perception of art as the pinnacle of human experience and individual pleasure. Such a philosophy of "socialist aestheticism" was everywhere apparent in radical papers aimed at working-class audiences. In the 2 May 1891 issue of *Workers' Cry*, J. Runciman argued in "Art for the Workers" that, although some may scoff "at the notion of Art of any sort for the workers, . . . it seems to me that the cry for leisure is an expression of the longing for a life of fuller and intenser enjoyments—that is to say, of enjoyments such as can only be found in Art, and will ultimately be found there by all" (13). This idea was also expressed in "Art and the Mob" from the 4 October 1884 issue of *Justice*: "With labour free, when every man has to do his share of the world's work, and there is leisure for all, then and then only will the cultivation of art be within the reach of all, when art is followed for its own sake and not for gain" (1). The idiom of art for its own sake summons the project of aestheticism, but in service of democratizing and universalizing art.[2]

The *Workman's Times, Workers' Cry,* and *Justice* all target a radical working-class audience and express a vision of art—as the source of purest pleasure, as an object of highest value for its own sake—clearly

Figure 3. From the *Workman's Times* (7 January 1893).

Figure 4. From the *Workman's Times* (7 January 1893).

indebted to Pater and the aesthetic movement. But the socialist aestheticism of the radical press derived from William Morris, not Pater, and the passage of such ideas into working-class-oriented papers is a historical rejoinder to the prevailing notion of fin de siècle aestheticism as politically disengaged.[3] Morris has long posed definitional difficulties for theorists of fin de siècle aestheticism.[4] As a Pre-Raphaelite, he was considered an aesthete—"the idle singer of an empty day"—but the revolutionary aesthetics of his later career are often taken as being opposed to aestheticism.[5] Oscar Wilde's articulation of "The House Beautiful" and "The Decorative Arts" on his 1880s lecture tour of America was deeply influenced by Morris's Arts and Crafts ethos, and in this sense Morris was the font of a popular 1880s aestheticism of which Wilde was emblematic. But beginning in the early 1880s, Morris was a revolutionary socialist who spent the last thirteen years of his life formulating what Caroline Arscott has called "the first English-language attempt to produce a Marxist theory of art" ("William Morris" 9). I would suggest that recognizing the interconnections between Morris's aestheticism and his revolutionary socialism is crucial to understanding Morris's print politics.

Morris's revolutionary response to mass print culture is discernible in his two major experiments in what I call slow print: the *Commonweal* newspaper and the Kelmscott Press. Socialist aestheticism, as formulated by Morris in these print projects, is a utopian aestheticism, understood to be incomplete until after the revolution. The difference between a conventional aestheticism—"art for art's sake," art as a system of value, art as preeminent human experience—and Morris's socialist aestheticism is chiefly a matter of timing: All these things *will* be true of art after the revolution. Until that time, real art is impossible, but there are things that art can do to hasten the revolution. Realism is not one of these things. Instead, Morris draws on the forms and sensibilities of aestheticism to print literature that allows readers to imagine what art might be like in the socialist future to come. Morris's print ventures in the 1880s and 1890s expose and critique the political effects of mass print culture, but they also establish print literature as a utopian space in which one can imagine the possibility of a future detached from present conditions.

Morris, Print, and Utopia

Morris's print work reveals a political resonance to aestheticism's insistence on a schism between art and social reality: that this schism is what allows art to think outside the capitalist "march of progress." Writing and printing in the 1880s and 1890s, Morris confronts the failure of liberal notions of print as an agent of progress and tries to reinvent print at the level of production. This inward recoil has been viewed by many as evidence of naïveté or hypocrisy on Morris's part, because it resulted in print products with a limited audience, such as the *Commonweal* and Kelmscott editions. At the same time, however, the move renders print literature as a utopian space in which to imagine postrevolutionary art and politics.

Fredric Jameson's book on Utopia, *Archaeologies of the Future*, suggests how a text can at once be seemingly freestanding from the social world as such and yet still be politically revolutionary. Beginning with the long-standing problem of how "works that posit the end of history can offer any usable historical impulses" (*Archaeologies* xiv), Jameson argues that the creation of utopian space involves "the momentary formation of a kind of eddy or self-contained backwater within . . . seemingly irresistible forward momentum" (15). This "pocket of stasis within the ferment and rushing forces of social change may be thought of as a kind of enclave within which Utopian fantasy can operate" (15). This fantasy work is politically productive, because it "allows the imagination to overleap the moment of revolution itself and posit a radically different 'postrevolutionary' society" (16). Paradoxically, this aligns utopianism with revolutionary rather than reformist thought: "One cannot . . . change individual features of current reality. A reform which singles out . . . this or that flaw or error in the system . . . quickly discovers that any given feature entertains a multitude of unexpected yet constitutive links with all the other features in the system" (39). Thus "the modification of reality must be absolute and totalizing: and this impulsion of the Utopian text is at one with a revolutionary and systemic concept of change rather than a reformist one."

It is no revelation to say that Morris was a utopian thinker. His 1890 novel *News from Nowhere* is a classic of the genre, and many of his political essays and lectures have a utopian flavor, focusing on what life would be like after the revolution.⁶ But Morris's theory of print literature was itself utopian, productive of a kind of utopian space on the page. Morris thought that print in his day was politically incapacitated by capitalism, putting writers like himself at an impasse; this is precisely the sort of condition, according to Jameson, under which utopianism thrives, moments when change seems impracticable and the status quo entrenched. At such moments "the very principle of the radical break as such, its possibility . . . is reinforced by the Utopian form. . . . The Utopian form itself is the answer to the universal ideological conviction that no alternative is possible, that there is no alternative to the system" (*Archaeologies* 231–32). Morris's *Commonweal* and Kelmscott Press enact the utopian strategy that Jameson calls disruption: The print pages become self-contained, enclosed spaces irrevocably separated from present-day reality. Locating this utopianism within Morris's literary practice allows us to see how he used medium and production to articulate a revolutionary rather than a progressive politics of print.

Morris's print interventions emerged at a moment of seemingly inevitable, invulnerable capitalist print progress—progress toward a bigger, faster, more commercial, and more profitable print marketplace. As discussed in the Introduction, early nineteenth-century debates about print politics tended to polarize into two positions: a radical position that viewed an abundance of print as necessarily democratic and progressive, and a conservative position in which abundant print was an anarchic and dangerous force.⁷ However, the nature of this debate changed over the course of the Victorian era, as mass print became aligned with capitalist, not just democratic, ideology. With the surge in cheap print and periodicals that followed the dissolution of the stamp tax, the newspaper tax, and the paper duty, the years between 1860 and 1890 fomented a genuine mass reading public. By the end of the century left-wing reformers like Morris were less inclined to see plentiful print in and of itself as a progressive social force and more inclined to see it as an effect of unrestrained capitalism.

Morris at times wondered whether print itself was part of the problem, that is, whether a reproducible medium tied to industrial modernity could be expected to produce anything *but* apologies for capitalism. In an unpublished essay titled "Some Thoughts on the Ornamented Manuscripts of the Middle Ages," written around 1892, Morris reflects on "the present age of superabundance of books" and argues that "the utilitarian production of makeshifts, which is the especial curse of modern times, has swept away the book producer in its current" (1). He contrasts this condition of modern print with bookmaking in the Middle Ages, when a book was "a palpable work of art, a comely body fit for the habitation of the dead man who was speaking to them: the craftsman, scribe, limner, printer, who had produced it had worked on it directly as an artist, not turned it out as the machine of a tradesman" (2). Morris's suspicion of print reproducibility prefigures Max Horkheimer and Theodor Adorno, who often use images and metaphors associated with printing to express the homogeny and uniformity of the culture industry—for example, "Culture now impresses the same stamp on everything" (Horkheimer and Adorno 120)—as though the mechanism of removable type determines the conditions of its cultural realization. Morris also prefigures the conclusions of critics such as Walter Ong, who would argue that the advent of print "created a new sense of the private ownership of words. . . . Typography had made the word into a commodity. The old communal world had split up into privately claimed freeholdings" (131).

Morris's horror at the "superabundance" of books echoes Marx and Engels's disgust at the "epidemic of overproduction" that characterizes capitalist modernity (*Communist Manifesto* 163), the waste and superfluity that coexist with want and privation. Yet books proved to be a problematic commodity for such analysis. Progressive reformers had long presumed that widespread desire for books reflected a natural hunger for knowledge rather than a created need or, as Marx and Engels put it, a "new want" summoned forth by capitalism (162). Advocates of democracy and classlessness had argued that literacy and widespread reading materials went hand in hand with social and economic equality, forming the very basis of an equitable society. As the *Democrat*, a radical but not socialist journal, argued in 1887, "In past days literature has been for the cultured view, and in the eyes of the Quarterly Reviewer and men of that ilk, such is the ideal state of affairs. The people, forsooth, are to wallow in ignorance and darkness lest haply they should offend the muses by their vulgar gaze" (1 September 1887: 310). Under such conditions, how could a socialist object to the overproduction of print?

Morris was often caught on the horns of this dilemma. In an 1891 interview with the *Pall Mall Gazette*, his hostility toward small type prompted the interviewer to ask, "But, Mr. Morris, is it not better to give [the millions] books with small type, which they can buy cheap, than to prevent them from reading at all, which would be the case if there were no small type and consequent cheap editions?" (Morris, "Poet as Printer" 92). In many ways Morris's ambivalent relationship with print and mass print culture reflected his growing sense that books and periodicals were not passive vessels of ideas, as progressive campaigners preceding him had conceived of them, but media commodities subject to the logic of their mediation. For Morris print was not a transparent delivery system for knowledge and information, and he questioned whether the mass print marketplace had not undermined the political gains of widespread print. Indeed, remarkably for someone so famed as a printer, Morris often spoke disparagingly of print.[8] He claimed in an 1895 lecture that when movable type was first invented, it did not serve a fundamentally different cultural role than writing: "The difference between the printed book and the written one was very little. . . . The results of printing, although considerable, were nothing like so considerable as people tried to make out" ("Early Illustration" 20).[9] Morris believed that print as a medium was historically synthesized with capitalism. In an 1895 interview he said that print's "history, as a whole, has practically coincided with the growth of the commercial system, the requirements of which have been fatal, so far as beauty is concerned, to anything which has come within its scope" ("Mr. William Morris" 102). The implicit question here is whether the medium itself is indelibly marked by the economic or political structures that facilitate the circulation and production of print.

Morris's response to this chicken-or-egg scenario was not to abandon print altogether but to turn inward, in the manner of aestheticism, and reform print at the level of production with two "backwaters" of utopian print: the socialist newspaper *Commonweal* in the 1880s and the Kelmscott Press in the 1890s. In these venues and in his novels *News from Nowhere* and *A Dream of John Ball*, both of which were published in *Commonweal* and Kelmscott editions, Morris's antiprint sentiment became productive of new print and literary forms. These print works construct themselves as utopian spaces outside the "march of progress" narrative that had accrued to print and to capitalism and pointedly remove themselves from the general flow of mainstream print. The *Commonweal* was printed cheaply in large quantities, whereas the Kelmscott books were printed in limited numbers of handmade materials and were quite expensive—reaching the exorbitant price of £20 for the famous Kelmscott Chaucer. Yet both ventures appeal to small, specialized audiences, and both are characterized by a utopian impulse to create whole cloth a new print reality, outside the existing culture of print.

The Commonweal

One of Morris's duties as editor of the *Commonweal*, the official journal of the Socialist League, was to write the weekly "Notes on News" leader for the newspaper's front page. On 17 March 1888 Morris devoted this column to the recent death of Wilhelm I, emperor of Germany, and titled the week's segment "Dead at Last." The piece is typical of the radical press in that its upshot is a biting critique of the "bourgeois press," and its general effect is to separate the *Commonweal* and other socialist newspapers into an oppositional, alternative print sphere.

The flood of cant and servility which has been poured out by the bourgeois press during the last few days, because [of] the long-expected death of a tyrant ... disgusts one so much that at first one is tempted to keep silence in contempt for such degraded nonsense. . . . Yet though silence may be best in the abstract it may be misunderstood at a time when even democratic papers . . . profess to share more or less in the sham sentiment of the day which weeps strange tears indeed over [his] death-bed. . . . As a Socialist print, the *Commonweal* is an outlaw from the press, and its poverty and desolate freedom compels it to speech, though but of a few words. (81)

Rather than directing his anger at the antisocialist policies of the emperor himself, Morris addresses the emperor's idealized afterlife in the sycophantic mainstream press, including ordinary "democratic" papers such as the *Daily News*. The *Commonweal*, in contrast, is "outlaw" from the capitalist press, cut off in a space of "desolate freedom." The piece demonstrates Morris's pervasive conception of socialist print as a separate sphere apart from mainstream print.

Morris's turn toward print production corresponded nearly exactly with his turn toward revolutionary socialism. He had been thinking about print production at least since his unrealized plan to publish an illustrated version of *Earthly Paradise* in the 1860s, but he did not actually dive into print until he became a socialist.[10] Shortly after his political conversion in the early 1880s, Morris helped launch *Justice*, the newspaper for the Social Democratic Federation. He would declare in its pages, "I am determined not to contribute articles to any capitalist paper whatsoever" (11 October 1884: 6). When Morris and the Socialist League broke from the Social Democratic Federation for being too compromised in its tactics and too autocratic under H. M. Hyndman, Morris became editor of the *Commonweal*, which launched in 1885. This was Morris's first major printing project, and he later attributed his rising interest in print, which culminated in the Kelmscott Press, to his time spent on the paper: "In the course of my life I had obtained a good deal of knowledge of type. Particularly I was much among type when I was the editor of the *Commonweal*" ("Master Printer" 96).

The Socialist League operated its own printing press, producing the *Commonweal*, political pamphlets for the League, and material for other radical writers and groups. Circulating in a crowded field of radical journals founded in a spirit of opposition to the capitalist press, the *Commonweal* is often singled out as the best in terms of composition and style.[11] It sold cheaply for 1 penny and had a circulation of 2,500 to 3,000 a week, which was less than Morris hoped and not enough to cover the paper's costs.[12] "The Manifesto of the Socialist League," which ran in the first issue, explained the mission of the League and its paper: "Fellow Citizens, We come before you as a body advocating the principles of Revolutionary International Socialism; that is, we seek a change in the basis of Society—a change which would destroy the distinctions of classes and nationalities" (February 1885: 1).

As the "Manifesto" indicates, the *Commonweal* had a specific agenda and in that sense was less utopian than directly engaged in politics; yet the paper's political agenda was itself utopian, not in the sense of impossibly fantastic but in Jameson's structural sense of wholesale reinvention. The Socialist Leaguers were anti-Parliamentarian socialists; they did not believe that running socialist candidates or participating in electoral politics would bring about radical social change. The paper dissuaded readers from voting or from participating in political activities aimed at incremental change, including trade unionism. For example, Morris's article "Anti-Parliamentary" urged readers to boycott the ballot box: "The *Commonweal* advocates abstention from Parliamentary action. . . . The Socialist League neither puts forward candidates, nor advises its members to vote for this or that or the other candidate. . . . The true weapon of the workers as against Parliament is not the ballot-box but the *Boycott*" (7 June 1890: 180). In a supplement to the May 1885 issue, Thomas Binning appealed to fellow trade unionists not to "waste our strength and resources in isolated, costly, and futile attempts to better ourselves by striking for a few pence additional to our scanty wages . . . but, recognising the Solidarity of Labour, let us unite with our brethren throughout the world, steadily organising our forces, and patiently waiting the time till a supreme effort shall once for all burst our bonds asunder" (39). According to E. P. Thompson, the League's tendency during the 1880s miner strikes to exhort the miners to aim at this sort of unified revolution of all workers—not the small changes secured by sporadic local strikes—"was decisive in causing its failure in 1887 and 1888 to organize the opinion in favour of Socialism which was spreading among the workers," because the League never grasped the "impossibility of preaching purism to workers engaged in bitter class struggles" (*William Morris* 438). The *Commonweal* regularly reported on strikes, and the Socialist League did maintain a strike fund (Figure 5 reproduces a flyer advertising an evening of entertainments to benefit the strike fund), but the League insisted that only wholesale revolution could eradicate capitalism, and reforms that slightly improved some workers' lot did nothing to hasten socialism's advent. The mission was to educate in preparation for eventual revolution, as Morris and E. B. Bax put it in an editorial: "Our function is to educate the people by criticizing all attempts at so-called reforms . . . and by encouraging the union of the working classes towards Revolution" (1 May 1886: 33). This all-or-nothing insistence on a complete break from existing social reality mirrors the formal features of Utopia.

Even beyond its political ideology, however, the *Commonweal* constructed itself as a utopian print space by way of art and literature. Beginning with its second issue, the paper featured a decorative heading designed

SOCIALIST LEAGUE,

13 FARRINGDON ROAD, E.C.

THE STRIKE COMMITTEE

ANNOUNCE THAT

ON SATURDAY, MARCH 24th, 1888,

A SERIES OF WEEKLY

ENTERTAINMENTS

WILL BE COMMENCED,

Beginning at 8 P.M. sharp,

IN AID OF THE STRIKE FUND.

The following talented Artistes have promised their services :

Messrs. Moreson, William Morris, John Burns, W. Blundell, H. A. Barker, W. H. Utley, C. D. Richardson, Arthur Gough, J. Thorne, Owen Lloyd, H. Halliday Sparling, Wm. Stuart, A. Hicks, W. Barker, T. Binning, J. Fox, T. Turner, and others.

Mesdames McKenzie, Nita Freori, Mary Gostling, Nelly Gostling, Letitia Storr, and Eleanor Fryers.

The Choir of the Socialist League and the Hammersmith Branch Choir will sing Glees, Madrigals, etc.

After each of the Entertainments DANCING LESSONS will be given gratuitously by competent Professors.

The Refreshment Stall will be superintended by Nelly Parker.

Scenery and Appointments by C. Barker.

Manager, ... W. B. PARKER.

ADMISSION BY PROGRAMME, THREEPENCE.

This Programme will admit Bearer to either Entertainment during March or April.

Note.—*The Entertainment will commence promptly at the time announced.*

Figure 5. Handbill advertising weekly entertainments to benefit the Socialist League Strike Fund (1888). Socialist League Archives, International Institute of Social History (Amsterdam).

by Morris and engraved by George Campfield, intertwining print letters with botanical imagery, promising a harmony of nature and craft
after the socialist revolution (Figure 6). In addition, a significant part of
the paper's mission was the imaginative creation of a postrevolutionary
utopian future through poetry and prose. Morris published *News from
Nowhere* serially in the paper, and other of his works published there,
such as *A Dream of John Ball*, "The Society of the Future," and "How
We Live and How We Might Live," have strongly utopian elements.
His essay "The Worker's Share of Art," printed in the *Commonweal* in
1885, argued that socialism "is the only hope of the arts." Art will be
"born again" in the socialist future: "The leisure which Socialism above
all things aims at obtaining for the worker is also the very thing that
breeds desire—desire for beauty, for knowledge, for more abundant life.
. . . Leisure and desire are sure to produce art, and without them nothing but sham art . . . can be produced" (April 1885: 18). A vision of art in
the socialist future is also drawn in "How We Live and How We Might
Live," published in the *Commonweal* in June 1887; Morris imagines "the
noble communal hall[s] of the future, unsparing of materials, generous
in worthy ornament, alive with the noblest thoughts of our time and
the past, embodied in the best art which a free and manly people could
produce; such an abode of man as no private enterprise could come anywhere near for beauty and fitness" (155).[13]

In the stated need for a separation between the beauty of art and
the ugliness of life under capitalism, Morris prefigures by several years
Wilde's aesthetic manifesto "The Decay of Lying": "All bad art comes
from returning to Life and Nature, and elevating them into ideals. . . .

Figure 6. Heading for the *Commonweal*. Designed by William Morris and engraved by
George Campfield. Labadie Collection, University of Michigan.

As a method Realism is a complete failure" (991). Wilde asserts a political rationale for this rift between art and life in "The Critic as Artist": "We are trying at present to stave off the coming crisis, the coming revolution, as my friends the Fabianists call it, by means of doles and alms.... England will never be civilized till she has added Utopia to her dominions.... What we want are unpractical people who see beyond the moment, and think beyond the day" (1140). Like Morris and the Socialist League, Wilde rejects the use value of piecemeal reform—he argues against charity in "The Soul of Man Under Socialism," for example—and instead endorses a complete utopian separation of art from the political reality of the present. Wilde's interest in Morris's theories and in the *Commonweal* is evidenced by his 1887 letter to the Socialist League: "Please send Mr. Morris's tract on 'Socialism and Art' to Mr. Oscar Wilde, 16 Tite Street, Chelsea. Also the 'Commonweal' for the year beginning with the November no."[14]

The art of the *Commonweal*, a resolutely socialist journal, is surprisingly faithful to Wilde's aesthetic vision and yet is not apolitical, as Wilde's work is often accused of being.[15] The *Commonweal* published at least one poem in nearly every issue, and typically the political form of this poetry was explicitly utopian. Wilde expressed England's need for people "who think beyond the day," and, as discussed at greater length in Chapter 4, the *Commonweal* poets did this quite literally by endlessly drawing on imagery of the dawn and the morning of the day after the revolution. Of course they did not invent this poetic association between sunrise and the postrevolutionary future—Algernon Swinburne had used it quite recently in *Songs Before Sunrise* (1871)—but the effect of this persistent trope within the pages of the *Commonweal* was to position its textual space in a discrete chronology, historically broken from the present day. A poet named C. W. Beckett, for example, contributed more poems to the *Commonweal* than anyone else and made generous use of matutinal imagery. Beckett's "It Is the Day" metaphorically conjoins the sun and Christ to depict the dawning of the postrevolutionary future.

O Son of Man, at last, at last,
over the wide and waiting earth
the herald beams are spreading fast,
glad earnest of the daylight's birth.

The night is spent, the stars are wan,
rose are the peaks that late were grey;
lift up thyself, O Son of Man,
arise, awake, it is the day! (3 September 1887: 283)

Another Beckett poem in the *Commonweal*, "For Fellowship," uses the image of the dawn to position itself in a utopian chronology.

For we live in the future already,
We live in the ages gone by,

    . . .

We are one with the world of tomorrow,
We are one with our children unborn,

    . . .

Come follow the Socialist banner,
Come fight for the Spirit of Time. (3 March 1888: 67)

The final line might more appropriately say, "Come fight against the Spirit of Time," given that the poem invites readers to "live in the future already." Beckett's poem "A New World," the title of which indicates its utopianism, similarly uses a time-defying refrain: "Hasten we, hasten the happy morn!" Arguing for a utopian collapse of time, a chronological fold that would unite the present and the future, the poetry of the *Commonweal* is riddled with such references to the "hastening" of time (28 April 1888: 135).

The visual art of Walter Crane, the "artist of socialism," also renders the *Commonweal* as utopian print space, severed chronologically and spatially from the historical present. Crane, a member of the Socialist League, designed subheadings for the *Commonweal* (one of which appears in Figure 7) and printed original political cartoons in its pages. The title of his cartoon "Vive la Commune!" (Figure 8) insists that the past event of the 1871 Paris Commune is still alive. Included as a supplement to the paper in March 1888 and March 1889, the cartoon honors the anniversary of the Commune by depicting victorious workers flanking an abstracted female figure of freedom. The image functions to merge the past and the future, skipping over the present altogether by simultaneously memorializing the Commune and imagining the future revolution. Its abstracted female figure transcends history or exists outside it; with a vacant expression and a wreath garland in her hair,

Figure 7. Subheading for the *Commonweal*. Designed by Walter Crane. Labadie Collection, University of Michigan.

she is not historically bound to the Commune like the male figures in the picture but rather evokes a timeless idea.[16] Brandishing the printed banner, she operates as a figure of print itself, a reminder of the power of printed words to transcend time and represent abstract ideas outside their historical moment. The cartoon thus positions the print space of the *Commonweal* as detached from the present and as utopian.

Similarly, Crane's "Solidarity of Labour" cartoon ran in the 24 May 1890 issue of the *Commonweal*, during the serialization of *News from Nowhere* (Figure 9). This image is set in the future and depicts a world of global harmony after the revolution. Just as the Paris Commune cartoon features an abstracted female figure of freedom atop a base of two workers, this cartoon depicts a female angel of freedom hovering over the workers of the world, a visual image of idealized transcendence. Each of the men in the cartoon is identified with a particular continent, but the angel of freedom is geographically unspecific, embodying an abstract concept apart from geographic or historical contexts. Again, she is the word holder. The banner she brandishes reads "Fraternity," "Equality," and "Freedom," and it contains the names of all the continents. The globe itself is festooned with a banner that reads "Solidarity of Labour." In this cartoon and in the Paris Commune cartoon, we can read the banners and the women who hold them as figures for the *Commonweal*, word bearers that transcend national and temporal boundaries in a self-consciously utopian manner.[17]

Figure 8. Walter Crane cartoon, "Vive La Commune!" Originally printed in the *Commonweal* (March 1888). Reprinted in Crane, *Cartoons for the Cause.*

THE COMMONWEAL

The Official Journal of the

SOCIALIST LEAGUE.

VOL. 6.—No. 228. SATURDAY, MAY 24, 1890. WEEKLY; ONE PENNY.

NEWS FROM NOWHERE:

OR,

AN EPOCH OF REST.

BEING SOME CHAPTERS FROM A UTOPIAN ROMANCE.

CHAP. XVII. (continued).—HOW THE CHANGE CAME.

"WHAT stood in the way of this?" said I.

"Why, of course," said he, "just that instinct for freedom aforesaid. It is true that the slave-class could not conceive the happiness of a free life. Yet they grew to understand (and very speedily too) that they were oppressed by their masters, and they assumed, you see how justly, that they could do without them, though perhaps they scarce knew how; so that it came to this, that though they could not look forward to the happiness or the peace of the freeman, they did at least look forward to the war which should bring that peace about."

"Could you tell me rather more closely what actually took place?" said I; for I thought him rather vague here.

"Yes," he said, "I can. That machinery of life for the use of people who didn't know what they wanted of it, and which was known as State Socialism, was partly put in motion, though in a very piecemeal way. But it did not work smoothly; it was, of course, resisted at every turn by the capitalists; and no wonder, for it tended more and more to upset the commercial system I have told you of, without providing anything really effective in its place. The result was growing confusion, great suffering amongst the working classes, and, as a consequence, great discontent. For a long time matters went on like this. The power of the upper classes had lessened as their command over wealth lessened, and they could not carry things wholly by the high hand as they had been used to in earlier days. On the other hand, the working classes were ill-organised, and growing poorer in reality, in spite of the gains (also real in the long run) which they had forced from the masters. Thus matters hung in the balance; the masters could not reduce their slaves to complete subjection, though they put down some feeble and partial riots easily enough. The workers forced their masters to grant them ameliorations, real or imaginary, of their condition, but could not force freedom from them. At last came a great crash. On some trifling occasion a great meeting was summoned by the workmen leaders to meet in Trafalgar Square (about the right to meet in which place there had for long been bickering). The civic bourgeois guard (called the police) attacked the said meeting with bludgeons, according to their custom; many people were hurt in the mêlée, of whom five in all died, either trampled to death on the spot, or from the effects of their cudgelling; the meeting was scattered, and some hundred of prisoners cast into gaol. A similar meeting had been treated in the same way a few days before at a place called Manchester, which has now disappeared. The whole country was thrown into a ferment by this; meetings were held which attempted some rough organisation for the holding of another meeting to retort on the authorities. A huge crowd assembled in Trafalgar Square and the neighbourhood (then a place of crowded streets), and was too big for the bludgeon-armed police to cope with; there was a good deal of dry-blow fighting; three or four of the people were killed, and half a score of policemen were crushed to death in the throng, and the rest got away as they could. The next day all London (remember what it was in those days) was in a state of turmoil. Many of the rich fled into the country; the executive got together soldiery, but did not dare to use them; and the police could not be massed in any one place, because riots or threats of riots were everywhere. But in Manchester, where the people were not so courageous or not so desperate as in London, several of the popular leaders were arrested. In London a convention of leaders was got together, and sat under the old revolutionary name of the Committee of Public Safety; but as they had no organised body of men to direct, they attempted no aggressive measures, but only placarded the walls with somewhat vague appeals to the workmen not to allow themselves to be trampled upon. However, they called a meeting in Trafalgar Square for the day fortnight of the last-mentioned skirmish.

"Meantime the town grew no quieter, and business came pretty much to an end. The newspapers—then, as always hitherto, almost entirely in the hands of the masters—clamoured to the Government for repressive measures; the rich citizens were enrolled as an extra body of police, and armed with bludgeons like them; many of these were strong, well-fed, full-blooded young men, and had plenty of stomach for fighting; but the government did not dare to use them, and contented itself with getting full powers voted to it by the Parliament for suppressing any revolt, and bringing up more and more soldiers to London. Thus passed the week after the great meeting; almost as large a one was held on the Sunday, which went off peaceably on the whole, as no opposition to it was offered. But on the Monday the people woke up to find that they were hungry. During the last few days there had been groups of men parading the streets asking (or, if you please, demanding) money to buy food; and what for goodwill, what for fear, the richer people gave them a good deal. The authorities of the parishes also (I haven't time to explain that phrase at present) gave willy-nilly what provisions they could to wandering people; and the Government, which by that time had established some feeble national workshops, also fed a good number of half-starved folk. But in addition to this, several bakers' shops and other provision stores had been emptied without a great deal of disturbance. So far, so good. But on the Monday in question the Committee of Public Safety, on the one hand afraid of general unorganised pillage, and on the other emboldened by the wavering conduct of the authorities, sent a deputation provided with carts and all necessary gear to clear out two or three big provision stores in the centre of the town, leaving blank

LABOUR'S MAY DAY
DEDICATED TO THE WORKERS OF THE WORLD

SOLIDARITY OF LABOUR

Figure 9. "Solidarity of Labour" cartoon by Walter Crane. Originally appeared in the *Commonweal* (24 May 1890), embedded in serialization of *News from Nowhere*. Labadie Collection, University of Michigan.

Crane was a leader in designing the visual imagery of socialism, and, like Morris, his theory of art's relation to political reality was aestheticist and utopian. In 1898 Crane described the "general theory of Art which has influenced my practice," distinguishing between "art which springs directly out of nature . . . more or less imitative in aim" and art which is "the record or re-creation of ideas, which selects or invents only such forms as may express a preconceived idea, as a poet uses words" (Introduction 29). Crane's work exemplifies this second form of art, which strives to represent an abstract idea, or "inner vision" as he puts it, rather than an outward reality. For Crane art deals in abstract signifiers and forms rather than in realist particulars; it constitutes a utopian language that refers to what could be rather than what is.

Of course, the word *Utopia* also has negative political connotations, and many of the *Commonweal*'s readers would have been conscious of Friedrich Engels's 1880 study *Socialism: Utopian and Scientific*, although it was not translated into English until 1892. The *Commonweal* had its "scientific socialist" side—evident, for example, in Edward Aveling's 1885 series "Scientific Socialism," which held "that Socialism is based on grounds as scientific and as irrefragable as the theory of Evolution" (April 1885: 21)—but the paper does not hew to Marx and Engels's anti-utopian line. Instead, it provides a spirited defense of Utopia's political use. Engels, who was living in London at this time, was famously displeased with the British socialist leaders because of their utopian and idealist tendencies. He dubbed Morris "a pure sentimental dreamer" in an 1886 letter and sarcastically commented in 1887 that "as a poet [Morris] is above science" (Marx and Engels, "Marx and Engels," pt. IV, 120, 123). The Socialist League, Engels said, "has no time to take an interest in the living movement going on under its nose" (pt. IV, 121) and "look[s] down on everything that is not immediately revolutionary" ("Marx and Engels," pt. VII, 309). The *Commonweal*'s utopian bent suggests that its writers identified with an indigenous, utopian socialist tradition—associated in Britain with the legacy of Robert Owen and Percy Bysshe Shelley—as much as a Marxist, scientific one. Rebuffing the idea that Utopia is apolitical because it rejects historical process, the *Commonweal* often references Thomas More's sixteenth-century *Utopia* as if to provide historical precedent for its own utopian discontinuity with history. The 27 April 1889 issue collects three pertinent passages from More, and a January 1886 article presents More as a man out of time: "As a social reformer, More was even in advance of our own times" (5).

In its efforts to depict its pages as a space apart from and historically discontinuous with capitalist society, the *Commonweal* created not so much a subculture as an alternative culture based in the print space of the paper. It preached a revolutionary vision that called for disengagement with contemporary politics in service of total social transformation; such a comprehensive program demanded the creation of a new culture. Consequently, the Socialist League hosted plays, meetings, lectures, musical entertainments, and variety shows. The paper and the events were mutually dependent; events were advertised and recounted in the *Commonweal*, and music and words for the socialist songs sung at such events regularly appeared in the paper. Figure 10 depicts a flyer advertising a "'Commonweal' Concert," a night of entertainment including music and a performance of Morris's play *The Tables Turned; or, Nupkins Awakened*, which depicts life after the revolution as a pastoral Utopia. The event instantiates in physical space the utopianism of the *Commonweal* print space. Describing the play's "vision of an idyllic, agrarian, post-revolutionary society," Pamela Bracken Wiens points to an 1881 letter by Morris: "Those who want to make art educational must accept the necessity of showing people things decidedly above their daily life" (24). The letter encapsulates his idea of how a conception of art as a thing above and separate from everyday reality could serve political ends.

Kelmscott Press

Morris left the *Commonweal* in 1890, when the Socialist League's anarchist contingent took over and voted him out, and he never again took on a print project of this nature. His next paper, the *Hammersmith Socialist Record* (1891–1893), was a free four-page monthly newsletter for members of the Hammersmith Socialist Society; it had humbler aspirations and a much smaller circulation than the *Commonweal*, serving mainly as a vehicle to announce upcoming lectures at Kelmscott House and to express Morris's and Bruce Glasier's thoughts on current events.[18] In December 1890, when Hyndman asked Morris to write again for the

3456

"COMMONWEAL" CONCERT.

13 FARRINGDON ROAD, E.C.

SATURDAY, OCTOBER 15th, 1887.

〜〜〜〜〜〜〜〜〜〜〜〜〜〜〜〜〜〜〜〜〜〜〜〜〜〜

PROGRAMME.

Part 1.

OVERTURE, PIANO.		
SONG	"The Forge" ...	... OWEN LLOYD.
VIOLIN SOLO	De Beriot	... HARVEY J. MILES.
SONG	... ...	... G. BROCHER.
PIANOFORTE, SELECTION.		

DRAMATIC SKETCH, BY WILLIAM MORRIS,

THE TABLES TURNED;

OR, NUPKINS AWAKENED.

Scene I. . . A COURT OF JUSTICE.
(By C. and H. A. Barker.)

Scene II. . . FIELDS NEAR A COUNTRY VILLAGE.
(By Mr. Campfield.)

(The properties and fittings by J. Flockton.)

For the Cast, see the other side.

Part 2.

PIANOFORTE, SELECTION.		
DUET	From "Ruddigore"	... { MISS V. PAUL AND JOHN BURNS.
SONG	"Father O'Flynn" ...	... E. SNELLING.
ZITHER SOLO ...	... ...	... MR. FYFE.
SONG	... "We'll Never be Slaves." ...	MARK FRANKLIN.
SONG	... ...	... W. LEWIS.
SONG, Serio-Comic ...	... ...	MISS ROSE SUTHERLAND
SONG	... ...	... A. SCHEU.
SONG	... ...	... MR. SHORTER.
SONG	... ...	... WILLIAM ROSE.

Marseillaise.

Figure 10. Program for a "'Commonweal' Concert." Socialist League Archives, International Institute of Social History (Amsterdam).

Social Democratic Federation paper *Justice,* Morris replied, "I have come to the conclusion that no form of journalism is suited to me" (*Collected Letters* 3: 247). Instead, he went on to establish the Kelmscott Press, a different kind of print project characterized by preindustrial methods, handmade materials, and ornate typography and illustration. Kelmscott Press deeply influenced many fine and radical printers that came in its wake, yet the project was much opposed to the spirit and inclination of print of its day. As Pat Francis notes,

Morris died in 1896, and the Kelmscott Press came to an end two years later. Ironically, it was at precisely this time that Monotype was perfected and made commercially viable. . . . If 1890 had already been too late for a major revival of the hand press, the twentieth century seemed about to choke the world with reading matter produced by people with little direct control over the appearance of the end-product. Speed was all. (155)[19]

Morris's late-life venture into "slow publishing" has prompted many critics to question the connection between his politics and his aesthetics. In his 1899 study *Theory of the Leisure Class,* Thorstein Veblen issued a damning indictment of Kelmscott Press, calling it a prime example of the "conspicuous waste" that characterized modern consumption: "These products, since they require hand labour, are more expensive; they are also less convenient for use. . . . They therefore argue ability on the part of the purchaser to consume freely, as well as ability to waste time and effort" (163). That the Kelmscott books were "edited with the obsolete spelling, printed in black-letter, and bound in limp vellum fitted with thongs" (163) suggested to Veblen greater concern with the beauty of the autonomous art object than with print's political impact. Arthur Pendenys likewise published an open letter to Morris: "If you were consistent your Printing Press would exist for the sake of spreading knowledge. As it is your publications appeal to capitalists and others of the wealthy classes" (qtd. in Clair 246). Even critics sympathetic to Morris have not traditionally viewed the Kelmscott books as exemplifying Morris's political principles. William Peterson's history of the Press notes that the Kelmscott books were "intended to symbolize a protest against the ethos of Victorian industrial capitalism [but] became themselves, in all their opulent splendour, an example of conspicuous consumption"

(*Kelmscott Press* 275). In his biography of Morris, E. P. Thompson figures Kelmscott as a fundamentally apolitical enterprise, "founded in a different spirit from that in which the original Firm had been launched thirty years before. Morris now had no thought of reforming the world through his art" (*William Morris* 583). In short, Kelmscott Press has been viewed as an apolitical outlier in Morris's socialist oeuvre.[20]

Yet other recent critics have identified a distinctly modernist and distinctly Marxist sensibility in Kelmscott's deliberate attention to materials. Jerome McGann argues that in the Kelmscott books "the distinction between physical medium and conceptual message breaks down completely" (*Textual Condition* 77); in the Kelmscott edition of Morris's *Earthly Paradise*, "the effect is to foreground textuality as such, turning words from means to ends-in-themselves. The text is . . . thick with its own materialities. It resists any processing that would simply treat it as a set of referential signs . . . [and] declares its radical self-identity" (*Black Riders* 74). This radical self-identity positions art on a transcendent plane beyond its referential faculty, but it also enacts, as Jeffrey Skoblow puts it, "a rigorously materialist impulse," part of "a great Romantic-Marxist continuum" involving "the exploration of objectification, sensory alienation, commodification, and the negative dialectics of resistance" (241). These analyses of Morris's materialized language draw on Jameson's ideas in *Marxism and Form*: "It is enough to evoke the fad for rapid reading and the habitual conscious or unconscious skimming of newspaper and advertising slogans, for us to understand the deeper social reasons for the stubborn insistence of modern poetry on the materiality and density of language, on words felt not as transparency but rather as things in themselves" (24).

In its pointed attention to the materiality of the book, then, Kelmscott Press unexpectedly unites utopian idealism with Marxist materialism. Certainly, Morris's effort to marry a Ruskinian philosophy of art and labor with a Marxian analysis of class and capitalism presented a difficult task, yet this union is at the heart of his aesthetic and his political project. He imagined a fervently anti-utilitarian form of socialism, one that valued individual distinction among persons and in production, such that rare and unique commodities would be the norm in a healthy socialist society. In "Useful Work Versus Useless Toil," a lecture originally published as a Socialist League pamphlet in 1885, Morris argues that "men who have just waded through a period of strife and revolution will be the last to put up long with a life of mere utilitarianism, though Socialists are sometimes accused by ignorant persons of aiming at such a life" (99–100).[21] The Kelmscott books can be said to encapsulate this struggle against utilitarianism, which Morris saw as a by-product of capitalism, not a corollary of socialism. The point is illustrated in Morris's *A Dream of John Ball*, which depicts a precapitalist society "untouched by the degradation of the sordid utilitarianism that cares not and knows not of beauty and history" (35). Likewise, in *News from Nowhere* a denizen of the future describes how "reactionists of past times" had predicted that "a dull level of utilitarian comfort" would result from socialist revolution. Instead, the opposite happened. Labor became pleasurable, a means for workers to express an innate "craving for beauty" for its own sake (176–77).

The Kelmscott Press edition of Ruskin's *Nature of Gothic: A Chapter of the Stones of Venice*, printed in 1892, pays homage to Ruskin's influence on the Press, and Morris's preface to the volume claims Ruskin for the socialist tradition: "John Ruskin the teacher of morals and politics . . . has done serious and solid work towards that new-birth of Society, without which genuine art, the expression of man's pleasure in his handiwork, must inevitably cease altogether, and with it the hopes of the happiness of mankind" (v).[22] The Kelmscott project was influenced not only by Ruskin's aesthetics and politics but also by his strategy of self-publishing *Fors Clavigera* to avoid commercial print, discussed in the Introduction. Ruskin's quarrel with the mass print marketplace and the alternative model of publishing he consequently developed anticipated many features of Morris's print radicalism. Ruskin "controlled the quality not only of the writing but of the ultimate product, 'paper, binding, eloquence, and all' ([*Fors Clavigera*] 27: 100), and he determined its fixed value. His commodity would not be hawked by advertisement in the penny papers like the latest quack medicine ([*Fors Clavigera*] 27: 353). Rather, it would circulate among a community with shared values, passing 'from friend to friend' (28:42)" (Stoddart 17).

With Kelmscott Press, Morris, like Ruskin, seized control of print production and distribution for himself and attempted to remake print from the ground up, root and branch. For all the advantages afforded by this mode of print production, however, Kelmscott and *Fors Clavigera* had the same deficiency: limited access as a result of high price.[23] As Judith Stoddart points out, "Ruskin's rhetorical use of his publishing strategies to foreground the material circumstances of discourse" was "frustrated by the practical effect of such a move" (11). But in reclaiming print at the level of production, Morris went further than Ruskin in remaking the *form* of print materiality, enacting dramatic changes to defamiliarize the print interface. As Joseph Dunlap argues, a fundamental premise of Kelmscott was that adding illustration and decoration to a book would do nothing to improve a basically flawed typeface and design; in its form the Press was revolutionary, not reformist, from the very font, the very paper of its books. This explains why Kelmscott printed so many titles originally published by William Caxton, the first English printer, although Morris was not an admirer of his work and did not collect it in his personal book collection (*In Fine Print* i). Morris printed five Caxton titles at Kelmscott Press; he was trying to go back to the beginning of the print industry in Britain, to reclaim print from its subsequent capitalist history.

In different ways both the *Commonweal* and Kelmscott Press make, in Jameson's formulation, "a Utopian leap, between our empirical present and the Utopian arrangements of [an] imaginary future" (*Archaeologies* 147). The *Commonweal,* in its art and its politics, focuses on the morning after the revolution, and Kelmscott tries to instantiate a postcapitalist mode of production better suited for the morning after the revolution than for a print culture where "speed is all." Kelmscott combines this utopian leap, however, with a resolutely materialist insistence on attention to production. As Morris describes in "A Note by William Morris on His Aims in Founding the Kelmscott Press," he worked hard at the Press to create beautiful objects under humane labor conditions. An Albion printing press was used—an iron hand press that had been developed around 1822, which printed at a rate of about 200 impressions an hour (Clair 211).[24] Thomas Binning, a stalwart trade unionist who had been the *Commonweal*'s foreman printer, became the head printer at Kelmscott—a direct link between the two ventures (Stansky 224). Kelmscott workers were unionized and received a living wage, although Morris sometimes struggled to balance optimal labor conditions with the use of the best materials.[25]

Morris could not, of course, truly extricate Kelmscott from its historical moment, but the Press can be viewed as a Utopia based on the premise
that the process of production is as politically significant as the product.
The Press attempts to estrange readers from the present day through its
highly visible production values, which are simultaneously archaic and
futuristic. As discussed in the Introduction, at the end of the nineteenth
century printing was an industry experiencing automation and restruc-
turing, with the effect of worsening conditions for print workers, so that
print itself, in its very form, was a reminder of the subjugation of workers
within the capitalist system. These conditions lent particular poignancy
to Morris's print work, as is evident in a 1911 issue of the *Daily Herald*,
the paper for the London Society of Compositors. The newspaper was
founded at the beginning of the Society's struggle for a 48-hour work-
week, and the epigraph on the front page of the first issue is a quotation
from Morris's poem "The March of the Workers," which originally appeared in the first issue of the *Commonweal*. Following the epigraph, the
paper asked its readers, "What nobler inspirer for the hour and the object—your modest, legitimate demand for a shorter working day—than
the author of the above, the noble Old English Master Printer, William
Morris, who treated his men as men, 'fellow craftsmen,' in that famous
Kelmscott Press, down Hammersmith Way?" (25 January 1911: 1).

Kelmscott's influence on the fine printing movement that emerged
at the turn of the twentieth century has been widely documented, but
its influence on such venues as the *Daily Herald* has been less noted. Although Kelmscott unquestionably produced expensive goods, inaccessible
to most consumers, it likewise represented a new art form that was recognized by radical working-class papers as anticapitalist in spirit. The
fine presses that sprouted in its wake, such as the Ashendene, Eragny,
Essex House, Doves, and Vale presses and the Dun Emer Press in Ireland, signified "a reaction to the Industrial Revolution, where the individual worker had become debased, his traditional role as craftsman
obliterated and replaced by machinery" (Genz 11). Many of these presses
were launched by men and women of socialist and/or anarchist opinions,
such as C. R. Ashbee, T. J. Cobden-Sanderson, and Lucien Pissarro.[26]
The Kelmscott books (and books from other such presses) were shown
in exhibitions and discussed in the radical press. Indeed, the Kelmscott

Figure 11. Use of Kelmscott-style initial letters in the *Labour Leader* (25 December 1897).

volume of Morris's lecture *Gothic Architecture* was printed in public at the 1893 Arts and Crafts Exhibition in front of large crowds and sold for 2s. 6d. (Peterson, *Kelmscott Press* 182, 318). The books were part of a broader anticapitalist counterculture, and their influence extended beyond those who could afford to purchase them. For example, the *Labour Leader* used Kelmscott-style initial letters in its special issue for Christmas 1897 (see Figure 11).[27] The Kelmscott books were artifacts from the future, material and aesthetic reminders that after the revolution labor and production would no longer be the alienating, repetitive industrial enterprise that mechanized mass print so neatly symbolized.

News from Nowhere *and* A Dream of John Ball: *The* Commonweal *and Kelmscott Editions*

To better conceptualize the continuities between the *Commonweal* and Kelmscott Press—which are not generally thought to have much in common—let us turn to Morris's dream vision novel *A Dream of John Ball* and his utopian novel *News from Nowhere*, both of which appeared in Kelmscott and *Commonweal* editions. Both works were written at the height of Morris's career as a socialist agitator, and both express an antiprint or even antitextual sensibility. In *A Dream of John Ball* the narrator goes back in time, or dreams that he goes back in time, to experience firsthand the primarily oral culture of fourteenth-century peasants; the book suggests that the oral means of communication that sparked the Peasants' Revolt were better equipped to channel revolutionary discourse than the print media of the nineteenth century. *News from Nowhere* depicts a peaceful, prosperous future society that has undergone a socialist revolution as well as an information revolution, having virtually abandoned print in favor of oral communication. Because utopias are unnecessary in Utopia and because Morris wants to render print as a utopian space, there is no print in the world of his utopias. Instead, the two works generate out of an antiprint sensibility new forms of print suited to their socialist moment. In this way both works exhibit the ironic reflexivity that is a formal feature of utopias. As Jameson argues, utopian novels' ironic "interrogation of the dilemmas involved in their own emergence as utopian texts" functions to remind us of their unreality, to secure their borders as a space apart (*Archaeologies* 293). When Morris critiques the medium of print within the context of print, ironically deconstructing his own critique in a manner that prefigures Derrida's reading of Plato, he reminds us that his fiction is not an attempt to predict the future and should not be read as such. Its unreality constitutes its revolutionary quality, breaking from historical possibility and destabilizing the future altogether.

The publishing histories of *News from Nowhere* and *A Dream of John Ball* reveal Morris's commitment to two distinct theories of radical printing. Both novels originally appeared in the *Commonweal* and were later reprinted as Kelmscott editions. *News from Nowhere* ran serially in the *Commonweal* from 11 January to 4 October 1890, alongside articles on such topics as the labor struggle, the abuse of Russian political prisoners in Siberia, and the brutality of African colonization. The serialized novel resonated with and against the newspaper items with which it was embedded. For example, the front page of the 29 March 1890 issue of the *Commonweal* delivered a blistering verbal and visual critique of Henry Morton Stanley (see Figure 12), whose hypocritical Christian piety, the paper suggested, had obscured his profit-driven exploitation of Africa. Stanley was widely reviled in the radical press, and the *Commonweal*, like other socialist papers, objected that "England has the hypocrisy to talk of civilising the African races," even though it has "hundreds dying yearly of partial and absolute starvation in her great cities and towns." On the very next page *News from Nowhere* picks up in the middle of Chapter Ten, a chapter that describes how the slums of London were cleared after the

The Official Journal of the

SOCIALIST LEAGUE.

VOL. 6.—No. 220.   SATURDAY, MARCH 29, 1890.   WEEKLY; ONE PENNY.

THE CHRISTIAN PIONEER.

IN a few days there will land in England a man whom all the Christians of the counter in this Christian nation of shopkeepers will rush

of another worker in the same sacred field of duty, "Christian Gordon." The same good authority assures us, further, that every heart in this great and glorious empire, upon which the sun even declines to set, will thrill with enthusiastic joy at the prospect of welcoming home to these shores the Modern Crusader. And then, after laying upon England, who is bound by her glorious traditions as a civilising power to accept it, the duty of carrying the blessings of her civilising influences into yearning Africa, until we shake hands across her equatorial forests with the colonists of the Cape, he hurls at us Hannibal, Charlemagne, Napoleon, Rome and Greece, in their palmiest days, mind, and lastly Christ, but modestly withholding his own name, retires into obscurity.

Across the road, where another branch of the "Great Industry" is carried on, the limner lends his aid to supplement the efforts of the scribe. And we see the presentment of a lion, real British you know, often used for similar purposes, and Britannia, clad in what appears to be a damp sheet, is standing in an inclement wind awaiting her Stanley: in her hand she holds a terrific wreath suggestive of Kensal Green cemetery, and this is also for Stanley.

The patriots of the stalls at music-halls and theatres are also on the war-path. We are treated to tin swords, red fire, and second-hand uniforms in honour of those who are ready, desh boys, to dare and die, or get it done by proxy. Scribe, limner, and bawler, all pressed into the service of doing honour to the homicide.

The scribe is most probably the same who anonymously satirises and vilifies the working-class and their aspirations for a fuller share of the pleasures of life.

The sketcher will, if a strike disturbs the classes, represent the workman with an ape-like countenance, with mouth of letter-box proportions, sottishly handling pot and pipe. The same will do, with slight alterations, for our Irish comrades when their turn comes to be abused. Such are the applauders of Stanley.

If the working class allow the loafers of society to misrepresent them in this matter of swashbuckling and butchering expeditions in the name of England and civilisation, and do not by emphatic protest

Figure 12. Front page of the 29 March 1890 issue of the *Commonweal* depicting Henry Morton Stanley as a Christian hypocrite. Labadie Collection, University of Michigan.

revolution, with the residents resettling in the roomy and comfortable buildings of what used to be London's "business quarter."

Similarly, *A Dream of John Ball* was serialized in the *Commonweal* from 13 November 1886 to 22 January 1887 and created a dialogue about utopianism through print context. Its opening chapter ran on the front page opposite Morris's regular column, "Notes on Passing Events," which focused in this issue on the Liberal Party's failure to sponsor effective legislation for Irish home rule: "That the assembled Liberals did not think of or wish for the results of the political freedom of Ireland is not a matter of guess, but is proved by the barrenness of the programme put forward by them—a programme about as valuable as a proposal for the re-enactment of Magna Charta" (13 November 1886). Morris's comment forms an ironic juxtaposition with the opening chapter of *John Ball*, a novel that could be said to "reenact" another medieval political event, the Peasants' Revolt of 1381, by sending the narrator back in time to witness it.[28] The section of the novel that ran in the 18 December 1886 issue appeared alongside the poem "Be Content" by the working-class Leeds poet Tom Maguire, who is discussed in Chapter 4. "Be Content," like *A Dream of John Ball*, challenges the idea that the poor must suffer on earth for a reward in heaven. It opens: "Said the parson, 'Be content, / Pay your tithe-dues, pay your rent; / They that earthly things despise / Shall have mansions in the skies.'" The closing stanza reads:

Be content! be content!
Till your dreary life is spent!
Lowly live and lowly die,
All for mansions in the sky.
Castles here are much too rare:
All may have them—in the air. (18 December 1886: 299)

The poem's point (also made by Joe Hill in the famous Industrial Workers of the World song "The Preacher and the Slave": "You'll get pie in the sky when you die—that's a lie!") is likewise articulated by John Ball, the excommunicated priest who helped foment the Peasants' Revolt, in a speech from Morris's novel: "Forsooth, ye have heard it said that ye shall do well in this world that in the world to come ye may live happily for ever; do ye well then, and have your reward both on earth and in heaven; for I say to you that earth and heaven are not two but one" (51). The novel and the poem remind us that Christianity and capitalism alike depend on a particular means of appropriating the future: of determining present conditions on the basis of speculations about the future (future profits or a future afterlife). Utopias, by contrast, call attention to their unreality to suggest the indeterminacy of the future, not its predictability à la Christian, capitalist, or rigidly Marxist notions of progress.

The *Commonweal* editions of *News from Nowhere* and *A Dream of John Ball* create a utopian print context for Morris's work by means of the resources conventionally available to periodicals: juxtaposition, editorial tone, and design. Still, these editions depend on industrial forms of literary production, such as cheap print (the paper sold for a penny) and the serialized novel (a nineteenth-century print form perhaps formally tied to capitalist ideology, as discussed in the next chapter) to provoke a changed consciousness *against* industrial capitalism. The *Commonweal* had a small countercultural readership but relied on the template of mass mediation; as Glasier notes, Morris did attempt "to make the paper in some degree a good example of typographical art, designing for it a simple but beautiful title block, and insisting on good, readable type and consistency of headings and spacing throughout" (*William Morris* 179), but nonetheless William Peterson calls it "a typographically unimpressive periodical" (*Kelmscott Press* 65). In transferring his labors from the *Commonweal* to Kelmscott, Morris refocused his attention on questions of mediation and production, with the effect of making his print works more expensive and less accessible. Yet as Crane has argued in Morris's defense, "The cheapness of the cheapest things of modern manufacture is generally at the cost of the cheapening of human labour and life, which is a costly kind of cheapness after all" (*William Morris* 39).[29]

After founding the Press, Morris published a Kelmscott edition of *A Dream of John Ball* in 1892 and a Kelmscott edition of *News from Nowhere* in 1893.[30] These editions embody a process-based rather than an outcome-based approach to radical print and textuality; production of the book becomes an end in itself rather than a means, exemplifying Morris's call for a Ruskinian anti-industrial revolution in labor and creativity. With Kelmscott Morris skipped over historical process altogether to make books "in the future already." Some of Kelmscott's titles suggest this utopian vision for the Press. For example, a Kelmscott edition of More's *Utopia* was published in 1893, and Morris even began designing a map of Utopia for it, although the book was published without the map (Peterson, *Kelmscott Press* 154). Kelmscott likewise produced all manner of antirealist texts, including Morris's romance tale *The Story of the Glittering Plain*, the first book produced at the Press. Such books are not transparent vehicles of political enlightenment or information but rather express their politics in their life and production as objects, embodying in the present a future disruption of industrial progress.

Kelmscott's *News from Nowhere* demands attention to its material presence beginning with the frontispiece illustration (Figure 13). The rigorous literalism of its caption forces the reader to pay attention to the object at hand: "This is the picture of the old house by the Thames to which the people of this story went. Hereafter follows the book itself which is called News from Nowhere or an Epoch of Rest & is written by William Morris." The caption calls attention to the picture and text as representations, even as it uses present tense to reinforce the immediacy and concreteness of "the picture" and "the book itself," which become artifacts from the future. The illustration of Kelmscott Manor that accompanies this caption, drawn by C. M. Gere and engraved by W. H. Hooper, echoes this literalism visually; the perspective seems to invite readers to walk right into the house.[31] Matthew Beaumont argues that *News from Nowhere* engages with "the perceptual problem of the present," which is "at some level the result of the reifying effects of commodity culture under capitalism," and that it "depicts a world wherein the

Figure 13. Frontispiece to the Kelmscott edition of *News from Nowhere* (1893). Illustration drawn by C. M. Gere and engraved by W. H. Hooper. Beinecke Rare Book and Manuscript Library, Yale University.

present is finally present to itself" ("*News*" 36–37). Although Beaumont does not address the print context of *News from Nowhere*, Morris's attempt to simulate the presence of the future is all the more obvious in the Kelmscott frontispiece, which reminds us of its alterity to highlight our own alienation from the present it depicts.

Similarly, the frontispiece for *A Dream of John Ball*, drawn by the Pre-Raphaelite artist Edward Burne-Jones, takes a famous catchphrase of John Ball as its caption: "When Adam delved and Eve span, who was then the gentleman" (Figure 14). In a radical commandeering of art for the working classes, the words and picture stress the book's materiality, challenging the reader to consider the labor at the heart of all production. The caption omits the question mark in a sentence that is obviously a question, rejecting orthographic signs of meaning in favor of an im-

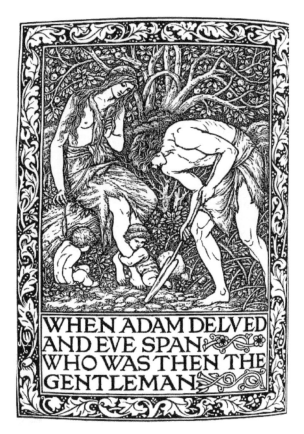

Figure 14. Frontispiece for the Kelmscott edition of *A Dream of John Ball* (1892). Drawn by Edward Burne-Jones and engraved by W. H. Hooper. Beinecke Rare Book and Manuscript Library, Yale University.

plied intonation, necessarily oral- rather than print-based. The image also denaturalizes leisure rather than obfuscating labor, in a manner quite uncharacteristic of aestheticism, but as Ruth Livesey suggests of much socialist art of the period, the image also renders the "masculine laboring body" as "an aesthetic site"—a central link between Morris's socialist aesthetics and homoerotic aestheticism ("Morris" 603). At the same time the image relies on traditional gender divisions to mount an ideological critique of class.[32]

Burne-Jones originally composed this illustration for the first book edition of *A Dream of John Ball* in 1888, and he revised the image for the Kelmscott edition, which was the first Kelmscott book to include woodblock illustrations.[33] W. H. Hooper engraved the Kelmscott illustration, and Morris designed the lettering and border. Figure 15 reproduces the

Figure 15. Frontispiece for the 1888 edition of *A Dream of John Ball*. Drawn by Edward Burne-Jones.

earlier frontispiece; note that it is a photogravure illustration, whereas the Kelmscott frontispiece is a wood-block print, just one of the key differences that reveal a great deal about Kelmscott's aesthetic project. Wood-block engraving had become obsolete "almost overnight" with the onset of photographic means of reproducing images in the 1880s (Peterson, *Kelmscott Press* 21).[34] The Kelmscott frontispiece uses capital letters and sharper, cleaner lines to insist on its material presence, even as it depicts a prelapsarian scene wholly detached from history.

The leafy border framing the Kelmscott frontispiece functions to integrate the work of art into organic nature, yet it also demarcates the image's artificiality by cordoning it off. Such frames and borders, exemplified in the frontispiece for *News* as well as *John Ball*, were characteristic of all Kelmscott books and are a feature of their utopian form. They signify that the image is not continuous with phenomenal reality but exists in a separate space and chronology. Responses in the socialist press suggest that critics read the works in this light. A review of *News* in the *Workers' Cry* claims that the depiction of the postrevolutionary commonwealth should not be taken as prophetic.

> Morris, alike with the true instinct of a poet and artist and the foresight of wise political judgment, does not attempt to frame together a cast-iron social structure fixing its height, width, and depth, and filling in all the details of its construction. He knows too well that we cannot quite foresee how all things may be done when the people's minds and bodies are set free from the sordid desires and the industrial servitude of to-day. (18 July 1891: 10)

Some socialists did appeal to *News* as a vision of what a socialist society might look like, but typically they did so to reinforce the point that a new social order *was* possible. A poem by R. L. Gorton titled "The Promised Land (As Shown by Morris's 'News from Nowhere')" ran in the 14 March 1896 issue of the *Clarion*: "I ofttimes wonder if 'twill ever be, / That future visioned by the Poet-seer, / When England's children shall in truth be *free*." The point of the poem is that the conditions of capitalism have the effect of making alternatives seems impossible: "Amidst the lovely vale now factory's wheel / Throbs, hammers clang; the struggle e'er is rife / For food and pelf: there is no Common Weal." Playing on the name of the newspaper where *News* originally appeared, "Common Weal" connects the space of radical print to the space of the "Promised Land" Morris's novel imagined. The poem's final stanza suggests, however, in a self-referential allusion to its own forum, that the populist, reformist socialism of the *Clarion* is better suited to make the promised land actually come true: "But dream not yet. Clear blows the clarion call / To don our armour. Comrades all, awake!" (81).

The *Clarion* again drew on Morris's model of socialist utopian narrative in its serial story "A Free Country," by M. B. ("Mont Blanc"), which ran from 27 April to 25 May 1895. The story begins in homage to Morris: "In William Morris's 'Dream of John Ball,' a modern Englishman is carried back to the fourteenth century of our glorious country. In 'News from Nowhere,' by the same author, a modern Englishman is lifted forward into the twenty-somethingth century." M. B. proposes a variation on these premises: "I daresay you have often wondered—as I have—what an English serf of the Middle Ages would think of that freedom which we are supposed to enjoy in this nineteenth century" (136). The story focuses on a medieval peasant, Wat Warton, who awakens in present-day England. Humorous difficulties of dress and language—like those met by William Guest in *News*—ensue, but soon Warton is imprisoned for stealing, after nearly starving from lack of money to purchase food. Eventually, after a suicide attempt and a workplace injury at an iron foundry, he dies destitute. The narrative art of "A Free Country" is rather clumsy—for example, the 11 May 1895 installment abandons story for exposition: "It would take too long to tell in detail how [Wat] discovered that freedom, the Englishman's birthright, is little more than a mockery to the majority of the English people" (149)—but the central imaginative move of the story suggests how Morris's fictional structure, built on the defamiliarization of social custom through chronological juxtaposition, was influential across radical press literature.

Critics of Morris often suggest that his neomedievalism was a form of political quietism, but a review of *A Dream of John Ball* by F. Keddell in the 14 April 1888 issue of *Justice* argues that the novel, despite its historical setting, will foment socialist feeling: "To-day . . . the more immediate work is the propaganda of Socialism and in this we think this little work of Mr. Morris will have a good part to play." Of John Ball's rousing speech to the peasants at the heart of the novel, Keddell writes,

"More pleasant and profitable reading can scarcely anywhere else be found in so small a compass as in these few pages." Still, the review, published just after the 1888 edition of *John Ball* first appeared in print, objects that the novel was not published in a cheaper edition.

The price is 4s. 8d., and this places it beyond the reach of those who would be most likely to buy it. It would be well if Mr. Morris could see his way to publish a shilling edition; if roughly printed and simply stitched together it would not interfere with the sale of the dearer volume which after all will be read by those who can spare 4s. 8d. chiefly for the charm of its style, rather than for the doctrines it puts forth. (2)

The Kelmscott edition of *John Ball* was even more expensive (30s.), but unlike the 1888 edition, it was able to emphasize the interconnectedness of its style and doctrine.

Orality and Print in News from Nowhere *and* A Dream of John Ball

In both of their print forms, *News from Nowhere* and *A Dream of John Ball* express an antiprint sensibility, as though the technology of print is hopelessly bound up in capitalist formations. These novels are saturated with subtle irony, but perhaps the deepest irony of all is their skepticism concerning their own form. The novels' denigration of books and newspapers seems to diverge from Morris's commitment to changing the politics of print, evident in his labors for the *Commonweal* and Kelmscott Press, but in both works Morris builds on antiprint sentiment to innovate new print forms and genres.

As the editor of the *Commonweal*, Morris argued that education through print and oral propaganda would precede the revolution, preparing the masses to assume power when the change came. He wrote in the newspaper's inaugural issue: "To awaken the sluggish, to strengthen the waverers, to instruct the seekers after truth; these are high aims, yet not too high for a journal that claims to be Socialistic, and we hope by patience and zeal to accomplish them" (February 1885: 1). Print, in this hopeful proclamation, does crucial preparatory work for the revolution. Given such a theory of print, it is perhaps unsurprising that no newspapers exist in the utopian socialist society Morris creates in *News from*

Nowhere. If socialist organs function primarily to provoke revolutionary change, then they are no longer necessary after the change occurs. The society of Nowhere has achieved equilibrium, chugging along effortlessly, progressing in a cyclical, seasonal, seemingly unchanging routine rather than a historical dialectic. Journalism is a moribund genre in a society that has reached the end of history.

The nineteenth-century time traveler who visits Nowhere, William Guest, learns from Old Hammond, his primary informant in the future society, that public debate in Nowhere is customarily verbal rather than textual. When a social dispute or proposed change requires discussion, it is raised at the "meeting of the neighbours, or Mote, as we call it, according to the ancient tongue of the times before bureaucracy" (133–34). Bureaucracy is correlated with a culture of paper, and interpersonal discussion is considered more efficient.[35] If agreement can be reached in that first Mote, "there is an end of discussion, except about details." If there is disagreement, they "put off the formal discussion to the next Mote; and meantime arguments *pro* and *con* are flying about, and some get printed, so that everybody knows what is going on; and when the Mote comes together again there is a regular discussion and at last a vote by show of hands" (134). When dispute occurs in Nowhere's democratic process, the debate might be printed up, "so that everybody knows what is going on," but this happens so rarely that "machine printing is beginning to die out, along with the waning of the plague of book making" (69).

Tellingly, the novel's only allusions to newspapers are in the chapter "How the Change Came," which recounts the revolution that brought Nowhere to its utopian state.[36] Here, Morris reiterates arguments against capitalist print that were forcefully lodged across the radical press. The great harbinger of the 1952 revolution, as Old Hammond tells it, was a mass expropriation of retail provisions, which the press reacted to with more panic than the government. While "the police assist[ed] in keeping order at the sack of the stores, as they would have done at a big fire," the newspapers "determined to force the executive into action" and "threatened the people, the Government, and everybody they could think of unless 'order were at once restored'" (157). According to Hammond's account, the papers are the most reactionary force in the social order; it is only after "a number of the newspaper editors, had a long interview with the heads of the Government" that "the Government proclaimed a state of siege" (157). In Morris's fictional revolution, state brutality and martial law come at the goading of the capitalist press and the Liberal papers are the worst offenders.

A so-called "Liberal" paper . . . which, after a preamble in which it declared its undeviating sympathy with the cause of labour, proceeded to point out that in times of revolutionary disturbance it behoved the Government to be just but firm, and that by far the most merciful way of dealing with the poor madmen who were attacking the very foundations of society . . . was to shoot them at once. (161)

Jürgen Habermas's vision of the fourth estate as a sphere for communicative rationality is utterly unrealized here; instead, Morris presents the press as unavoidably propagandistic, wedded to the institutions on which it reports. Morris's words in his paper's first issue likewise indicate suspicion of Enlightenment ideals of measured disinterest: "*The Commonweal* has one aim—the propagation of Socialism. . . . We shall not, therefore, make any excuses for what may be thought journalistic short-comings, if we can but manage to attract attention to the study of our principles" (February 1885: 1).

Perhaps the most interesting aspect of *News from Nowhere*'s depiction of newspapers is that once the revolution is in full swing, they stop printing altogether: "People did not need to be told that the GENERAL STRIKE had begun" (164). Morris's novel presents newspapers as strictly ideological rather than informational; they can agitate for or against the revolution, but they can never really "cover" it. This is true even of the socialist papers. Hammond says that at the beginning of the revolution, the socialist papers came out "full to the throat [with] well-printed matter" and were "greedily bought by the whole public," but they contained "no word of reference to the great subject." Instead of describing the ongoing revolution, the socialist papers published "educational articles," anything but timely. The papers do not attempt to provide a purportedly objective analysis of current events but instead offer "expositions of the doctrine and practice of Socialism" (165). The radical press, in this fictional novel, exists outside its own present in service of the future.

Just as Morris's ideal society does without newspapers, it also does largely without books. Its inhabitants are literate and the children do learn to read, but according to Dick, "They don't do much reading, except for a few story-books, till they are about fifteen years old; we don't encourage early bookishness." Some children do "take to books very early," but most prefer "genuinely amusing work, like house-building and street-paving, and gardening" (80).[37] Rather than becoming expert readers, the children become expert users of spoken language.

Sometimes even before they can read, they can talk French, which is the nearest language talked on the other side of the water; and they soon get to know German also. . . . These are the principal languages we speak in these islands, along with English or Welsh, or Irish, which is another form of Welsh; and children pick them up very quickly, because their elders all know them; and besides our guests from over sea often bring their children with them, and the little ones get together, and rub their speech into one another. (79)

This multilingualism, providing equal status to indigenous Celtic languages, suits Nowhere's social values better than reading; it facilitates exchange and association between individuals rather than inwardness or privacy.

As in *News from Nowhere*, oral exchange in *A Dream of John Ball* is depicted as a highly effective political medium, much more so than print. *John Ball* is largely made up of dialogue, and a chapter called "The Voice of John Ball" consists almost entirely of a speech by the radical priest John Ball, recently freed from the archbishop's prison by a group of peasants. The chapter begins with an assertion of immediacy: "So now I heard John Ball" (50). Ball begins his address by directly referencing his own bodily presence, the audience in front of him, and the speaking situation: "Ho, all ye good people! I am a priest of God, and in my day's work it cometh that I should tell you what ye should do, and what ye should forbear doing, and to that end I am come hither: yet first, if I myself have wronged any man here, let him say wherein my wrongdoing lieth, that I may ask his pardon and his pity" (50). Instead, he receives a "great hum of good-will." Morris presents this political discourse as interactive in a more immediate way than the written word could ever be.

Morris, himself an active and accomplished speaker on the political stump, often began his own lectures with similarly pointed attention to the moment of the speech, its locale, or its specific audience. This contextual immediacy was a political benefit of oral discourse over print. "Art Under Plutocracy," an early socialist address that would be printed in *To-Day* in 1884, occasioned an uproar when Morris unexpectedly asked his audience at University College, Oxford, to join and fund a socialist organization (Morton 57). The 1883 lecture began: "You may well think I am not here to criticize any special school of art or artist, or to plead for any special style, or to give you any instructions, however general, as to the practice of the arts. Rather I want to take counsel with you as to what hindrances may lie in the way towards making art what it should be, a help and solace to the daily life of all men" (57). Shortly thereafter, he outs himself as a socialist, "For I am 'one of the people called Socialists'" (66), and he declares, "I am representing reconstructive Socialism before you" (83), interfusing his arguments with forceful attention to the speaking situation.

As with verbal address, the oral genre of the song is also an important political medium in *A Dream of John Ball*, where it cements collective solidarity and furthers political activity. In one scene a young man sings a ballad about Robin Hood in hopes that it shall "hasten the coming" of John Ball, for whom the peasants are waiting: "And he fell to singing in a clear voice . . . and to a sweet wild melody, one of those ballads which in an incomplete and degraded form you have read perhaps" (45). Interpolating readers directly with "you," the narrator contends that print ballads of the nineteenth century are less alive and effective than oral ballads of the past, which entail proximity between poet and listener in lieu of the awkwardly imprecise "I" and "you" of textual prose. Many late-century socialists made political use of the ballad form, as I discuss in Chapter 4. Here, the ballad of Robin Hood has the effect of drawing all the men together in solidarity.

My heart rose high as I heard him, for it was concerning the struggle against tyranny for the freedom of life . . . of the taking from the rich to give to the poor; of the life of a man doing his own will and not the will of another man commanding him. . . . The men all listened eagerly, and at whiles took up as a refrain a couplet at the end of a stanza with their strong and rough, but not unmusical voices. (45)

The subtext of the scene—"of a man doing his own will and not the will of another man commanding him"—is an investigation of textual authority. In written texts narrative authority is obscure to the reader, whereas in oral narrative genres narrative authority is transparent, because one can always tell who is speaking. Morris alludes here to the idea that written words are orphaned, fatherless, or cut off from their origins, unlike oral speech; this is a concept with a long history, dating at least as far back as Plato's *Phaedrus* (276). In "Plato's Pharmacy" Jacques Derrida suggests that the idea has contributed to an association of writing with patricide and to the privileging of oral speech above writing in Western culture (*Dissemination* 77–78).

Morris, however, presents oral poetry and verbal forms of discourse as particularly conducive to challenging political authority—in other words, as metaphorically patricidal. In *A Dream of John Ball*, a peasant sings a revolutionary song that encodes seditious messages through symbolic language.[38] Some lines of the song are straightforward— "The Sheriff is made a mighty lord, / Of goodly gold he hath enow, / And many a sergeant girt with sword; / But forth we will and bend the bow" (45)—but others mask a hidden purpose: "And though their company be great / The grey-goose wing shall set us free" (46). Later in the text we learn that "grey-goose wing" refers to a secret weapon: a long bow (about 7 feet high) that shoots yard-long arrows. Here, the intimacy between singer and audience in oral literary forms means that they operate figuratively in a different manner than the anonymous sphere of print.

Written genres can rarely achieve such intimacy, especially in the mass print marketplace, and the scene suggests that they are less conducive to building solidarity. Indeed, *John Ball* presents written language as having fallen from a prelapsarian orality, direct rather than mediated and collectivist rather than authoritarian. When the narrator first awakens in the fourteenth century, he has no trouble understanding the people he meets: "If I were to give you the very words of those who spoke to me you would scarcely understand them," but "at the time I could understand them at once" (37). The narrator, a barely disguised Morris, tells his companions over a meal, "I am in sooth a gatherer of tales, and this that is now at my tongue's end is one of them," and he proceeds to recite an Icelandic saga in verse form: "So such a tale I told them, long familiar to me; but as I told it the words seemed to quicken and grow so that I knew not the sound of my own voice, and they ran almost into rhyme and measure as I told it" (44). That the narrator knows not his own voice suggests that oral literary forms in the time before print possessed an authenticity and directness impossible in the modern age of mediation.

Likewise, in the future society of *News from Nowhere* the literature that persists and thrives has strong links to oral tradition. One night Guest and his friends stay up late telling stories "as if we had belonged to time long passed, when books were scarce and the art of reading somewhat rare" (183). Folk tales, ancient myths, and Grimms' fairy tales have all remained popular in Nowhere, and all are oral narrative forms (145).[39] By valorizing such forms, Morris expresses discontent with contemporary print. In a list of favorite books that he composed for the *Pall Mall Gazette* in 1886, his top picks were epics and folktales that were originally oral: the Hebrew Bible, Homer, Hesiod, the Edda, Beowulf, the Kalevala, the Shahnameh, the Mahabharata, "Collections of folk tales, headed by Grimm and the Norse ones," and "Irish and Welsh traditional poems." These works, he wrote in the margin of the list, "are in no sense the work of individuals, but have grown up from the very hearts of the *people*" (*Collected Letters* 2: 515).

It may seem absurd for Morris to take on print as ill-suited to po-litical discourse in the context of two deeply political novels that were originally printed in a socialist newspaper. The representation of print and textuality in these novels, if not absurd, is at any rate so thoroughly steeped in multidirectional irony that one might reasonably ask to what extent Morris can represent the virtues of oral genres within the pages of a novel. Both *News from Nowhere* and *A Dream of John Ball* exhibit an ironic self-consciousness on this point, because the two novels exemplify in their very existence the insufficiency of oral discourse compared to print. Morris's antiprint sensibility thus operates productively; in their Kelmscott and *Commonweal* contexts and in their break from novelistic realism, the novels generate new print forms out of their dissatisfaction with print. We can see this, for example, in the use of reflexivity in an early chapter of *News*, when Hammond delivers from memory a passage from Homer's *Odyssey*, perhaps the most vital oral narrative in Western culture. Here, the novel interweaves its nostalgia for oral tradition with a deeply textual sensibility. The version of Homer that Hammond recites, which he calls "one of the many translations of the nineteenth century" (105), is Morris's own rendition, reflexively highlighting the novel's textuality and the author's mediating presence in the novel at hand. Elsewhere in the novel Hammond describes how the Nowherians commemorate May Day by having "the prettiest girls . . . sing some of the old revolutionary songs," but the girls do not understand the meaning of the oral forms: "It is a curious and touching sight . . . to hear the terrible words of threatening and lamentation coming from her sweet and beautiful lips, and she unconscious of their real meaning: to hear her, for instance, singing Hood's Song of the Shirt, and to think that . . . she does not understand what it is all about" (113–14). The passage alludes to, and rejects, a longstanding correlation between oral culture and memory; in Plato's *Phaedrus* Socrates worried that writing would "introduce forgetfulness into the soul of those who learn it: they will not practice using their memory because they will put their trust in writing, which is external" (275a). In *News from Nowhere* the song represents a cultural memory of sweatshop labor, encoded in ritual, but not the individual "wisdom" that Socrates associates with memory (275a). In such ironic moments Nowhere's antitextual sensibility actually reinforces the significance of the print medium in which the novel appeared, even as it mourns the loss of oral, communal ritual.

Realism, Flatness, and the Novel

Still, Morris is clearly guilty of what Derrida terms the "debasement" of writing in Western discourse (*Grammatology* 3). As with Plato's *Phaedrus*, Morris is in the dissonant position of using writing to rail against writing. Derrida argues in "Plato's Pharmacy," however, that only "a blind or grossly insensitive reading could . . . have spread the rumor that Plato was *simply* condemning the writer's activity. . . . The *Phaedrus* also, in its own writing, plays at saving writing—which also means causing it to be lost—as the best, the noblest game" (*Dissemination* 67). Morris is also trying to "save" print by "causing it to be lost." His critique of writing and print is aimed at particular developments in literature under capitalism, and considering the moment in which Morris was writing, one is struck most forcibly *not* by orality's primacy above textuality but by a widespread belief in the infinite expandability of mass print. Under such conditions the hegemony of print—the assumption that it is equivalent to social progress—served the financial interests of many.

Addressing this problem in the form of a novel may seem like a self-fulfilling prophecy or a desperate cry for the invention of deconstruction, but as critics such as Patrick Brantlinger ("'News from Nowhere'") and James Buzard have also discussed, *News from Nowhere*'s antiprint sensibility offers an incisive critique of the nineteenth-century novel and can be read as a harbinger of modernist changes in novelistic form. This is apparent in the scene involving the Grumbler, an unpleasant character who claims, "I have read not a few books of the past days, and certainly *they* are much more alive than those which are written now; and good sound unlimited competition was the condition under which they were written" (191). Appalled by his reactionary views, his granddaughter Ellen cries, "Books, books! always books, grandfather! When will you understand that after all it is the world we live in which interests us, the world of which we are a part" (192). Ellen's words reveal the basis of Nowhere's antitextual disposition: Books, print, and texts serve to *mediate*; they rely on a fundamental gap between readers and the world. They may be a palliative for people living in imperfect social conditions—like those of us reading Morris's novel—but according to Ellen, they are no longer necessary. Books "were well enough for times when intelligent people . . . [had to] supplement the sordid miseries of their own lives with imaginations of the lives of other people. But I say flatly that in spite of all their cleverness and vigour, and capacity for story-telling, there is something loathsome about them" (192–93). Anticipating the Brechtian alienation effect, Morris ironically refers to his own artistic form, the book, as loathsome.[40] The scene targets the nineteenth-century novel as a particularly loathsome form, in which "the hero and the heroine liv[e] happily in an island of bliss on other people's troubles . . . after a long series of sham troubles . . . illustrated by dreary, introspective nonsense about their feelings and aspirations, . . . while the rest of the world . . . dug and sewed and baked and built and carpentered round about these useless—animals" (193). As I will discuss in the next chapter, the novel was often singled out in the radical press as a bourgeois and individualist literary genre, hopelessly entangled with consumer capitalism. Recognizing interiority as the purview of the novelistic genre, Morris recoiled from it.

To some extent this critique of the novel is ironically undermined by its own appearance in a novel, but *News from Nowhere* is not particularly concerned with interiority, nor is it a work of realism. *News* could be said to work against the objectionable elements that Ellen attributes to the novel. As John Plotz argues, *News* rejects the Victorian novel's "paradigm of sanctioned identification" and its claim to "convey poignant, peculiar details about any individual's feelings" (*Portable Property* 145–46). Moreover, Morris treats realism—the dominant nineteenth-century novelistic mode—as insidious because it purports a mimetic reproduction of the real but actually creates an unhealthy false reality: "In the nineteenth century, . . . there was a theory that art and imaginative literature ought to deal with contemporary life; but they never did so; for . . . the author always took care . . . to disguise, or exaggerate, or idealize" (146–47). In Morris's view realism is as flawed and disingenuous as the journalistic pursuit of unbiased objectivity.

In the strident antirealism of *News* and *John Ball*, we again see continuities between Morris's socialist novels and the artistic forms of aestheticism.[41] Like Wilde in "The Decay of Lying," these works imply that realism, as an artistic mode, conveys a tacit acceptance of present-day social conditions. *News* and *John Ball* instead work to dissociate readers from their present sense of the way things are. To that end, the flatness of print, the creative medium that Morris turned to after years of working with more porous and three-dimensional fabrics, textiles, and furniture, allowed him to foreground the unreality, the antireality, of the print worlds he created.[42] Utopian fiction is typically distinguished by its characters' flatness, a generic feature harnessed for critique in twentieth-century dystopian fiction. Late Victorian utopian novels are sometimes called paper paradises, underscoring this flatness. Flat characters, flat surfaces, and an emphasis on two-dimensional artificiality function in Morris's socialist print work as rejoinders to the political aims of realist genres.

Caroline Arscott describes a sense of depth in the wallpapers Morris created in the 1870s, before converting to socialism: "A sense of three-dimensionality is given within individual elements by standard illusionistic means, for instance in the elaborate veining and shading of the acanthus leaves" (*William Morris* 35); but Elizabeth Helsinger argues to the contrary that Morris's patterns do not produce the effect of depth so much as "the layering of what are in effect several different flat patterns, such that one appears to lie over the other" (204). With his turn to print production in the 1880s and 1890s, Morris emphasizes aesthetic flatness as opposed to depth, embracing the two-dimensionality of the medium as a means of critiquing the realist mystification that produces seemingly "rounded" characters on the flat surface of an industrially printed page. For example, Plotz argues that the use of initial letters intertwined with botanical growth in the Kelmscott books stresses the two-dimensionality of the foliage by merging it with categorically flat letter text ("Nowhere" 949–50). The *Commonweal*'s wood-engraved title has the same effect. By the time Morris launched the Kelmscott Press, the reproduction of images in print had transitioned from block printing to photomechanical means, but in retaining the use of the woodblock for most of Kelmscott's images, Morris retained the aura of flatness that comes from pressing and stamping a page with a heavy woodblock.

This flatness is a literary as well as a visual effect, because both *News* and *John Ball* depict characters of little psychological depth. Northrop Frye has commented that the future people of *Nowhere* "sometimes seem to be living in a gigantic kindergarten" (313). Robert Blatchford, editor of the *Clarion*, considered *John Ball* one of his favorite books but acknowledged its two-dimensionality: "The characters in *John Ball* are little more than outlines. The faces and the costumes are skilfully done, but the men and women . . . have little personality" (*My Favourite Books* 108–9). Plotz views this lack of roundness as Morris's critique of nineteenth-century modes of novelistic individuation: "Morris proposes that characters be thought of as systematically flat, placed within the novel to fulfill the demands of its plot rather than to represent the excessive human individuality or alterity that makes for poignancy in the realist novel" ("Nowhere" 933). Indeed, given *News*'s internal attack, through Ellen, on the political effects of bourgeois realism, its insistent flatness must be read as a pointed intervention. Morris critiques the realist novel from within a novel that fails to meet the aesthetic requirements of realism.

The flatness and unreality of Morris's novels constitute their revolutionary quality: they suggest that roundness and volume are not for us. Roundness, like art, is the province of the postrevolutionary future. In the utopian future of *News from Nowhere* art, craft, and people are decidedly voluminous, and this fullness is an effect of social health. The glassware they drink from is "somewhat bubbled and hornier in texture than the commercial articles of the nineteenth century." Their furniture is "beautiful in form and highly ornamented," "without the commercial 'finish' . . . of our time" (146). The art of the future is all three-dimensional. Carving has apparently achieved ascendancy over painting; for example, the artist Philippa is shown carving flowers and figures "in low relief" on a new house (215). Printing, as noted earlier, is "beginning to die out, along with the waning of the plague of book making" (69). That the flat arts are apparently dying or dead indicates ever more pointedly the flatness, the unreality, of the utopian story in front of us. The fullness and roundness enjoyed by the characters in the novel are impossible in the present day. Indeed, even the women of the future are curvaceous—they are described as "shapely and wellknit of body, and thoroughly healthy-looking and strong" (64)—whereas the novel's time-traveling protagonist remembers working-class women of his own day as "gaunt figures, lean, flat-breasted, ugly, without a grace of form or face about them" (186). Nineteenth-century women, it seems, are as flat as nineteenth-century art.

The flatness of Morris's socialist print literature resonates with aestheticism's antirealist conception of art as a two-dimensional surface lacking depth. Consider the word *heartless*, which shows up incessantly in Wilde's work. Dorian Gray asks Lord Henry, "I don't think I am heartless. Do you?" (*Dorian Gray* 100). But of course he *is* heartless; he exists only on the flat surface of the page, without interiority or the organs of a three-dimensional body. In Wilde's *Ideal Husband* Lord Haversham tells his son Lord Goring, "You are heartless, sir, very heartless!" (523). He repeats later, "You are heartless, sir, quite heartless," and again, "He is very heartless, very heartless" (556, 571). Lord Goring is a dandy—a character defined by surface sheen and outward style, the opposite of inner depth. Yet later Goring says of his father, "It is very heartless of him, very heartless" (577). All these characters lack depth, Wilde reminds us, whether they are dandies or not. Similarly, in *The Importance of Being Earnest,* Jack says to Algernon, "How can you sit there, calmly eating muffins when we are in this horrible trouble, I can't make out. You seem to me to be perfectly heartless" (403). The word *heartless* also appears in Wilde's play *A Woman of No Importance* and in his short stories "The Canterville Ghost," "A Model Millionaire," and "The Portrait of Mr. W. H." His attachment to the word suggests how central this concept of flatness, the emptying out of Victorian realism's interiority, was to the aestheticist project. George Bernard Shaw, who did not care for *The Importance of Being Earnest,* picked up on this theme; in the *Saturday Review* he derided the play as "inhuman" and "mechanical," and elsewhere he called it "heartless" (Review 194). Yet as I discuss in the next chapter, Shaw's original title for his first published novel, *An Unsocial Socialist,* was *A Heartless Man.* The character referred to in this original title is a flat character, seemingly lacking roundedness and complexity, in a work that is critical of realism and tries to reclaim the bourgeois novel for socialism.[43]

Morris's print aesthetic, in the *Commonweal,* at Kelmscott Press, in *News from Nowhere,* and in *A Dream of John Ball,* attempts to strike a balance between acknowledging artificiality—to avoid the illusory pretense of realism—while simultaneously revolutionizing print in its basic elements. He does not seek to abandon print but to transform it wholesale. Print, Morris suggests, as it exists under capitalism, is a form of mystification not wholly distinct from commodity fetishism; it immerses one in a false reality and alienates readers from an invisible, inaccessible creator. To some extent, this representation of texts hearkens back to Plato's *Republic,* and Morris could be said to share some of Plato's anxieties about false realities.

One might suppose, then, that Morris would have reservations about the visual media beginning to challenge print's supremacy in late Victorian Britain; after all, the false reality created by precinematic devices such as the magic lantern, not to mention heavily illustrated books and periodicals, is less obviously illusory—thus *more* illusory—than print.[44] And yet Morris's novels seem to predict without censure the future dominance of visual media. In his lecture "The Society of the Future," Morris praises "authors who appeal to our eyes . . . who tell their tales to our senses," which he believes will be characteristic of future, post-revolutionary art: "If I may prophesy ever so little, I should say that both art and literature, and especially art, will appeal to the senses directly" (200). We see inklings of this in Morris's novels. At the beginning of *A Dream of John Ball* the narrator describes his dream as resembling an "architectural peep show" (35); this relates the medieval genre of the dream vision to the modern experience of the peep show, one of many new visual entertainments in the nineteenth century. Likewise, *News from Nowhere* focuses on socialists' need to literally *see* the future. Immediately before William Guest is transported to Nowhere, he says, "If I could but see a day of it . . . if I could but see it!" (54). Morris himself often insisted that book designers should conceive of two facing pages together as an artistic unit rather than treating each page in isolation; this highlights his attention to the visual experience of reading, to "reading as a sensuous act," as Skoblow puts it (256).

Morris's emphasis on this kind of visual immersion suggests that what bothered him about print, as it existed in his time, was its echo of the logic of capitalist exchange. *News from Nowhere*, for example, sets up an elaborate parallel between textual and cash economies. The Nowherians consider the archaic system of money to have been a "troublesome and roundabout custom" (60), an unnecessary imposition prohibiting direct human exchange on a person-to-person basis—what Thomas Carlyle referred to as the cash nexus. Books, like money, are viewed as relics of this dehumanized, symbolic culture of capitalism, which replaced human interaction with externalized systems of exchange. Morris wanted to imagine a kind of print literature that would alienate readers from capitalist forms, not reinforce them. In a letter to the socialist poet Fred Henderson, he states that language under capitalism "is utterly degraded in our daily lives," so that "poets have to make a new tongue each for himself" (*Collected Letters* 2: 483–84). He might have added that a socialist printer would also be required to make a new font for himself.

CHAPTER 2   # The Black and White Veil
Shaw, Mass Print Culture, and the Antinovel Turn

Tell me a tale and I'll hear with ears alert—and heart as well!
Yet it must be a tale of life, high life, my thirst to whet,

   . . .

All the din of the Singer machine forgotten by me, its thrall—
Bread and tea and the foreman, and the early morning call.

   . . .

To my story of sorrow and love I turn and weep anew,
Until all things come right in the end, as, at least, in tales they
   do.

—Tom Maguire, "The Novelette Reader"

T HE VICTORIAN NOVEL was the behemoth of nineteenth-
century print culture, whether published serially in
magazines or as triple-decker Goliaths, and the turn
away from novelistic form among many socialists can be read in part as
a turn away from late nineteenth-century mass print in its most expanded mode. That novels were fundamentally bourgeois and individualist,
deleterious in their class politics, was the presumption of many radical
thinkers and writers, as Tom Maguire, a working-class Leeds socialist
and labor organizer, suggests in his poem "The Novelette Reader." The
poem was printed in the *Labour Leader* and was written from the perspective of a young sickly seamstress in the "thrall" of novelistic "high
life."[1] Still, given the dominance of the novel in the cultural scene, it
was perhaps inevitable that socialists would try their hand at the form
even while decrying its limitations. A good many radical writers wrote

novels that stuck more or less closely to the customary forms of the genre at the time: realistic and domestic, interlaying a romance plot with a political-national plot in the classic Dickensian manner. Many were serialized in the radical press, and others were published in volume form by mainstream houses, but few made a significant impact on the radical public of the time or subsequently. As Peter Keating has written, the working-class or socialist novel of the period was "in neither quantity nor quality . . . an impressive response," illustrating "that fictional realism was proving itself incapable of handling many of the formative events of public life" (314).[2] Ian Haywood argues that the realist novel had developed "to express the outlook of the middle classes" and "was deeply biased against reflecting a working-class perspective on society," as is suggested by the "prevalence of plots relying on inheritance and the property stakes of marriage" (*Working-Class Fiction* 3). Working against the constraints of novelistic realism, William Morris's *News from Nowhere* and *A Dream of John Ball* were by far the most successful novels to emerge from late Victorian radical print, but as discussed in Chapter 1, they were fundamentally antinovels, premised on the disruption of novelistic convention.

George Bernard Shaw began his literary career publishing realist novels in the socialist press, and in the course of the 1880s he serialized two in *Our Corner* and two in *To-Day*. Partly because of Shaw's own retrospective account, these novels have been remembered as failures, but they were in fact successful within the limited sphere of the 1880s radical press. Like other radical writers of the era, Shaw was disgruntled with modern mass print and sought innovative means of producing politically and aesthetically vigorous work outside available forms. His novels hew much more closely to realism than Morris's, but they betray a similar frustration with Victorian novelistic form and a similar aspiration to undermine it from within. Critics have read Shaw's dramas, which he began to write in the 1890s and for which he is much better known, as novelistic or print centered in a way that was unprecedented in theater history, but less attention has been paid to the dramatic quality of Shaw's novels, their striving after the dialogic and public features of the theatrical sphere.

In this chapter and in Chapter 3, I will chart a socialist turn *away* from the novel and *toward* the theater in radical literary culture of the era, Shaw being the prime example, and I will connect these turns to broader radical discontent with mass print culture and its seeming incapacity to generate a political counterpublic. If Morris's strategy for resuscitating print's political potency was to reground it in materials and labor, to defamiliarize its mass-produced form, Shaw's strategy was to move radical print from the imagined community of the page to the real, live, visible public of the radical theater. If Shaw marks "a decisive moment in the booking of modern drama," where dramatic performance comes to "reciprocate the rhetoric of print culture" as W. B. Worthen argues (*Print* 13, 9), he also marks a decisive moment for radical print: the transportation of radical print culture to the public space of the theater. Shaw hoped that the radical drama audience would be more politically viable than the radical press audience. At work here is a vision of the theater as synecdoche for the public sphere: "the idea that the audience is more than just a segment of the general public, that it could be seen to represent this diffuse public (or at least to be the politically advanced avant-garde of this public)" (Puchner 47). This sense of the theater audience as the physical realization of an advanced counterpublic—one that was difficult to formulate by means of print—accounts for a radical literary turn from the novel and toward the drama. We begin this chapter with the novel.

Shaw and the Veil of Print

Finding mainstream print to be homogeneous and insipid, Shaw put most of the blame on the capitalist printing industry and its overriding profit motive. In the 1880s and 1890s Shaw wrote prolifically for both the mainstream and the radical press, and he complained in 1891 that "the final degrees of thoroughness have no market value on the Press." Few writers have the luxury to work "without reference to the commercial advantage—or disadvantage" (*Quintessence* 304). Print was big business; it was expected to sell, and to sell the products advertised within it. And the situation was only getting worse: "All the economic conditions of our society tend to throw our journals more and more into the hands of successful moneymakers," resulting in a dismal trend which "can hardly be appreciated by those who only know the world of journalism through its black and white veil" (304). Shaw's image of the black and white veil suggests that the print interface is a medium of obfuscation; readers, accustomed to perceiving print as transparent, fail to see that the business and marketing of print generates (and obscures) its subjects of representation. Shaw, in response, wants to rend the veil, to disturb dominant modes of literary politics and author-audience relations. We can characterize Shaw's early career as an extensive, studied intervention into the black and white veil of literary and print media, especially the novel.

After arriving in London from Dublin in the late 1870s, Shaw wrote five novels in five years, working mainly at the British Library and famously writing his fiction between reading sections of Marx's *Capital* (in Deville's French translation) and Richard Wagner.[3] His mother provided financial support during this time, but Shaw was also engaged in early professional experiences as a ghostwriter (for his mother's companion, George Vandaleur Lee) and as an employee of Edison Telephone Company, for whom he was "to persuade all sorts of people in the East End of London to allow insulators, poles, derricks and other impedimenta of telephoning to bristle about their roofs and gardens" (Holroyd 1: 77). Such experiences would have prompted recognition of the altered status of voice, and especially authorial voice, amid a swiftly changing media sphere. As Leah Price has argued, "ghostwriting," a term that was coined in this era, "disjoined writing from visibility" and "literalized the death of the author" (214). It emerged in tandem with fin de siècle New Journalism, a mode of writing that injected an illusory personal touch into what was, in reality, an ever-more anonymous mass print sphere. Similarly, the telephone, like the phonograph, was a technological mirror of the death of the author, the detachment of voice from body that we also see in ghostwriting. Such developments appeared in the context of a media marketplace that was retooling toward a new mass audience made up of a larger population of readers than ever before. As print and other media were broadening their reach, their tone paradoxically became more individuated.

Shaw was critical of many aspects of mass journalism, but in his preface to *Man and Superman*, he acknowledged New Journalism's influence on his prose style, and in his preface to *Cashel Byron's Profession*, he suggested that New Journalism—characterized by muckraking exploits such as the Maiden Tribute scandal and by an illusory personal tone—was actually a naturalist tonic against the literary idealism he so abhorred: "In 1882 . . . the literary fashion which distinguished the virtuous and serious characters in a novel by a decorous stylishness . . . had not yet been exploded by the 'New Journalism' of 1888" ("Epistle Dedicatory" 6–7).[4] It is significant that Shaw tended to write about New Journalism in his literary prefaces, a genre that he wielded to insert himself into the text, to position his seemingly "personal" voice front and center even in dramatic writing. Shaw's preface for *Plays Unpleasant* is titled "Mainly About Myself," staging a direct address from the ostensibly absent dramatic author. Indeed, in revising his plays for the printed page, Shaw used his prefaces to shift drama from a dialogic to a monologic form, to claim the authorship of the plays for himself or, rather, for the authorial persona he created for himself, for Shaw's prefaces continually remind us of his voice behind the drama, but they also, unlike New Journalism, continually remind us of the artifice of that voice.

Early in his career, Shaw enjoyed exposing the illusory nature of authorial personalism by writing to the press under thinly veiled pseudonyms, such as "G. B. Larking" and "G. B. L.," as well as wholly invented names, such as "Corno di Bassetto," who wrote for the pages of the *Star.* A typically playful letter by Shaw appeared in *Justice*, the Social Democratic Federation paper, on 15 March 1884 under the pseudonym G. B. S. Larking. A correspondent replied in the 22 March issue: "The letter of your correspondent Mr. Larking . . . is one of the most convincing arguments in favour of Socialism which I have seen for some time, though whether or not he intended it to be such, I do not feel quite certain" (7). It was exactly this kind of uncertainty that Shaw's authorial voice effected. Shaw's pseudonymous print personae emerged in the years following his rather traumatic introduction to the anonymity of print subjectivity, when, to his shame, Shaw ghostwrote Lee's column of criticism for the *Hornet.* As Shaw's career advanced, he drew on the lessons of this early embarrassment to produce a print persona for himself as an author that was always overlaid with its own artificiality. Shaw wrought a highly reflexive print voice, and in contrast to the cheap trick of ghostwriting, he let readers in on modern print's performance of personalism.

Very recently the production of a play of mine in New York led to the appearance in the New York papers of a host of brilliant critical and biographical studies of a remarkable person called Bernard Shaw. I am supposed to be that person; but I am not. There is no such person: there never was any such person; there never will or can be any such person. You may take my word for this, because I invented him, floated him, advertised him, impersonated him, and am now sitting here . . . giving this additional touch to his make-up with my typewriter. ("How to Become a Man of Genius" 344–45)

This tactic writ large the illusions of authorial subjectivity for all to see; it showed the constructedness of authorial "personality" by generating an overinflated persona that was self-consistent but evidently synthetic. In a perfect example of this self-exploding persona, Shaw wrote in a preface to the 1905 edition of his novel *The Irrational Knot*:

At present, of course, I am not the author of The Irrational Knot. Physiologists inform us that the substance of our bodies (and consequently of our souls) is shed and renewed at such a rate that no part of us lasts longer than eight years: I am therefore not now in any atom of me the person who wrote The Irrational Knot in 1880. The last of that author perished in 1888; and two of his successors have since joined the majority. Fourth of his line, I cannot be expected to take any very lively interest in the novels of my literary great-grandfather. (vii–viii)

Shaw's attention to the changing status of authorial voice was quite obvious in his early novels, which he would later disown as "five heavy brown paper parcels which were always coming back to me from some publisher" ("Novels of My Nonage" 5). Such efforts to distance himself from his novels were themselves means of destabilizing the idea of a coherent authorial voice, because they separated Shaw writing now from Shaw the 1880s novelist. Of these early experiences in his career as a socialist and as a writer, Shaw would later say:

I was the author of five novels which nobody would publish, and . . . dug them up to make padding for a Socialist magazine called *To-Day*, to which we all had to contribute as best we could. It really had not occurred to me that anyone would read this fifty times rejected stuff of mine: it was offered and accepted solely to bulk out the magazine to saleable size when the supply of articles ran short; but Morris, who read everything that came in his way, and held that nobody could pass a shop window with a picture in it without stopping, had read a chapter of *An Unsocial Socialist*, and been sufficiently entertained to wish to meet the author. (*William Morris* 6–7)

This was the beginning of a beautiful friendship—a friendship that persisted despite political differences—but like many of Shaw's biographical anecdotes, the account is not exactly accurate. Shaw distances himself from the novel and the venue that ran it, but he had actually pushed to have *An Unsocial Socialist*, his first novel to be published, printed in *To-Day* after it was rejected elsewhere, and in that venue many socialists beyond Morris were exposed to it.

After reading Shaw's proposed submission, J. L. Joynes, co-editor of *To-Day* with E. Belfort Bax, wrote to Shaw:

I read your novel with great interest, but then had to consult Bax. I wrote and told him that, as to the question of printing it, I was sure of two things, that we could not get another story so able without having to pay for it whether the magazine succeeds or not, and that in any case we could not get another story so much to the Socialist point, for nobody else would make his hero discourse on surplus value to his lady love with real knowledge of what he was talking about it [*sic*]. I also told him that I thought it was too long and that some passages were slightly tedious (of course, I should not have said this to you,) but that if I could persuade you to make certain excisions, and to condense the first 30 pages into 3 at the outside, I recommended the exploitation of your efforts by the editors of "Today." (27 January 1884, British Library ms, ff. 181–83)

Joynes had to haggle with Bax over the novel's length, but eventually *An Unsocial Socialist* was serialized in the journal. The first chapter appeared in March 1884 along with the second part of Morris's "Art Under Plutocracy." Joynes's letter went on to say that if the novel were printed in *To-Day*, "the Modern Press would like to see you and talk over the idea of publishing it from our type," and indeed the socialist printing house would publish the novel in 1886 from *To-Day*'s type. Thus Shaw had his first volume publication, a 1 shilling paper-covered book.[5]

Despite the tongue-in-cheek tone of Joynes's letter and the general precariousness of *To-Day* and Modern Press as socialist print enterprises, *An Unsocial Socialist* was a hit among the small socialist reading public of the day. David Smith has called it "perhaps the first notable British Socialist novel with any kind of ideological basis" (3), and socialist readers at the time were alert to its astute handling of political economy. *Justice* called the novel a "clever work" in its 30 August 1884 issue (3), and three years later the novel proved popular among readers in an 1887 competition sponsored by Henry Hyde Champion's paper *Common Sense*. (Champion was one of the proprietors of the Modern Press; his use of the reader competition device—a feature of New Journalism—suggests that his relation to the emerging mass-market press was oppositional yet at times imitative.) *Common Sense* asked readers to vote for favorite books in such categories as "best novel by a living author" or "best work for Darwenites [*sic*]" to establish "a list of literature on social questions which can be recommended to persons who are anxious for information" (15 July 1887: 47). In the "best novel by a living author" category, "Mr. G. B. Shaw's 'An Unsocial Socialist' was an easy first, Mr. Walter Besant's 'All Sorts and Conditions of Men,' being next" (15 August 1887: 63). It seems that Shaw's novel had reached as wide a socialist public as was possible in the mid-1880s. Although we do not know how many readers entered the contest, we do know that the prizewinning reader (whose votes most closely mirrored the final tally) was from Leicester and the runner-up was from Carlisle, so the contest was at least national in scope. *An Unsocial Socialist* was published before Morris's *Dream of John Ball* and *News from Nowhere* and before Edward Bellamy's *Looking Backward*, one of which would certainly have won a few years later, but in 1887 Shaw's novel actually was *the* novel of socialism. That it has so long been forgotten is perhaps a testament to the weakness of the field.

Cashel Byron's Profession, Shaw's novel about prizefighting, was also published in *To-Day* (serialized alongside Ibsen's *Ghosts* during some of its 1885–86 run) and in a Modern Press edition in 1886.[6] It would become the most popular and commercially successful of Shaw's early novels from the socialist press, going into several editions. Shaw described the work as "the nearest to a popular novel I had produced," having "crept into print through the back door of a Socialist magazine" (British Library ms 50650, ff. 98–121). Although *Cashel* is not as overtly political as *An Unsocial Socialist*, Morris reviewed it positively in the *Commonweal* (17 July 1886: 126), and *Justice* said it "promises to be the best thing [Shaw] has yet done" (13 June 1885: 5), adding that he "is certainly not excelled in keen humour and clever analysis of character by any novelist now writing" (27 June 1885: 1). Clearly, in the early years of the socialist revival, Shaw was *the* preeminent socialist novelist, at least according to the socialist press.

Shaw's ambivalence about print literature as a medium of political and artistic expression is, however, apparent in his novels and in his early-career abandonment of novel writing, making him a seemingly unusual representative of socialist novel writing. His wholesale rejection of the genre, after five attempts, has usually been read as a reaction against his own failure, a giving up on what he could never achieve. And yet even within the novels themselves, Shaw's impatience with novelistic form is already apparent. It seems he had given up on the socialist novel before he had even written one. Why was this so? Before looking more closely at Shaw's novels, I want to start by examining the broader context of socialist distrust of the novel that his work exemplifies.

The Political Liabilities of the Socialist Novel

Nineteenth-century novels were often published serially in magazines and newspapers before they appeared in book form, and Shaw's novels were no different in this respect, but Shaw presents the novel as politically ham-fisted even when nested in the pages of the radical rather than the mainstream press. Critics such as Linda Hughes and Michael Lund have explicitly linked the serialized novel with the rise of capitalist ideology: The serialized novel mimics capitalism in that it requires investment of time and money over a series of installments, calls for speculation about future outcomes, and squeezes (or diffuses) literary expression into the ready-made procrustean bed of so much space per issue. Moreover, Victorian serialized novels were often sandwiched between dense layers of advertisements and advertising prose, betraying their dependence on and position within the capitalist marketplace (this last point was not always the case for socialist newspapers, as discussed in the Introduction). If print was beginning to be viewed by Shaw and other radical writers as intrinsically tied to capitalist mass production, then novels and periodicals were the ne plus ultra of print capitalism.

In fact, some socialists thought that Shaw's attempt at writing socialist novels was in itself evidence of his essentially bourgeois, anti-revolutionary political sensibilities. Frank Kitz, a working-class anarchist who was a prominent fixture in Morris's Socialist League, wrote angrily to Shaw: "There may be . . . sacrifice made by Middle Class Men of literary tastes when they deign to become Socialists or they may perhaps find it profitable, as in the event of writing sensational Socialistic novels and getting so much per line" (1888, British Library ms 50512, f. 74). He claimed that Shaw's "supercillous [*sic*] style would lead one to infer that he has never known by actual experience what it is to endure the daily life long torture of abject poverty" (f. 74). In fact, Shaw was not paid for the novels that ran in *To-Day*, although Annie Besant did pay him for the novels that ran in *Our Corner*, more as patronage than as payment.[7] But Kitz's accusation reveals a radical suspicion of novel writing—a sense of the genre as capitalistic, individualistic, and middle class. And in truth, Shaw's novels made little effort to expand their point of view beyond that of the bourgeois novel tradition, even when their middle-class protagonists were socialists.[8] Moreover, Shaw's supercilious tone, as Kitz puts it, might have seemed to align his books with a subgenre of 1880s novels that satirized socialism, such as Henry James's *Princess Casamassima* (1886) or Edward Garnett's *Paradox Club* (1888), both of which depict dilettante upper- and middle-class slumming socialists of questionable political astuteness. For example, Miss Ward, the heroine of Garnett's novel, "was always delighted with lectures she did not understand, for she rightly thought they must be exceptionally intellectual" (84).

Certainly, there had been nineteenth-century efforts to expand the class perspective of the novel. As Ian Haywood has argued, in the middle of the century Chartism "produced the first, genuinely working-class fiction by assimilating both popular and polite narrative forms" (*Revolution* 145). Martha Vicinus considers "the rise of fiction as a significant working-class artistic medium" the most important radical literary development of the Chartist era (95). At the end of the nineteenth century, however, the novel had for the most part retained its fundamentally middle-class disposition. In genres such as the "slum novel," some middle-class authors were focusing their fiction on the lower classes and lower-class locales, but such novels were typically written from a middle-class perspective, and as Regenia Gagnier notes, they were "not primarily intended to interpellate working-class readers who were the *subjects* of class conflict but rather readers of the writers' own class, who were to learn thereby the lessons of Christian charity and liberal reform" (*Subjectivities* 114).

Walter Besant's 1882 novel *All Sorts and Conditions of Men* was the best known such novel in the 1880s, and although it is perhaps not naturalist enough to be considered a true slum novel, it does foreground its East End setting. The novel offers little insight into the reality of working-class lives, however, focusing as it does on two upper middle-class characters slumming in Stepney and pretending to be a dressmaker and a carpenter. As noted earlier, the novel garnered second place after Shaw's *Unsocial Socialist* in *Common Sense*'s poll for socialist readers' favorite novel by a living author, but its politics were not radical. When the heroine, the allegorically named Angela Messenger, posturing as a dressmaker, meets a "red-hot" Republican named Dick Coppin, who declares, "I am for root-and-branch Reform, I am," she replies, "But all improvement in Government means improvement of the people, does it not? Else, I see no reason for trying to improve a Government." Dick is dumbfounded, having become so "accustomed to the vague denunciations and cheap rhetoric of his class" that her "small practical point" throws him completely (141). Angela concludes, "You have perhaps turned your attention too much to politics, have you not?" (142). Later, when Angela attends a meeting of the Stepney Advanced Club, of which Dick is a member, she hears speakers who never "made a point, or said a good thing, or went outside the crude theories of untaught, if generous, youth; and their ignorance was such as to make Angela almost weep" (193).

In the radical press it was assumed that even a genuinely socialist novel would reach only middle-class readers. J. Hunter Watts's 1888 review of Grant Allen's *Philistia* considers it "the best Socialist novel we have read" but dryly notes that it "would have done us invaluable service in propaganda among the middle and upper classes, who alone have leisure for novel reading," except that those classes are so unlikely to be swayed (*Justice*, 14 January 1888: 2). The review, published alongside a serialized installment of *The Communist Manifesto*, implies that novels are ineffective socialist propaganda because only the leisured classes read them.

Of course, there were working-class readers of novels, and there were working-class novelists too, especially in the North, who typically wrote for specific localized constituencies. Among socialists the little remembered C. Allen Clarke of Lancashire was probably the most successful working-class novelist of the era, but although Clarke's best-known novel, *The Knobstick*, transcends the middle-class origins of the genre to render working-class experience in realistic detail, the work still betrays the limitations of novelistic form that writers like Morris and Shaw fought against.[9] *The Knobstick* (the title comes from a local term for a strikebreaker) was originally serialized in the *Yorkshire Factory Times* and draws on the Bolton engineering strike of the late 1880s for its subject matter. In some respects the novel attempts a naturalistic representation of workers affected by the strike, à la Émile Zola's *Germinal*, but it offers nothing close to Zola's logistical detail in describing the strike, and it interweaves the strike plot with a sentimental love story and a sensational crime story, which, between the two of them, effectively hijack the novel's course. Harry Belton, the engineer protagonist, falls in love with Lizzie Banks; she is "at that age when a maid reveals herself to a man as America did to Columbus after his weary voyage. To Belton she was an unexplored continent" (36). The overlay of hyperconventional romance attenuates the novel's political force, and eventually the labor plot is laid to rest without explanation and the romance plot takes over along with a related crime plot. In the final pages, nine months have passed, and it is the morning of Lizzie Banks and Harry Belton's wedding: "The strike had long been settled, and the men had been granted their demand" (262). The use of past tense and passive voice here indicate the labor plot's diminished status against the active momentum of the marriage plot.

Clarke himself subtly suggests the novel's enslavement to conventional plotting in a passage from *The Knobstick*, when a character comments on novel and newspaper reading.

I reads t' Bible as oft as I con, an that satisfies me. I used to read newspappers, an novels, an them sort o' things; but not neaw. There's never nowt freish in t' newspappers, nowt only t' same tale o' murders, an divorces, an assaults, an husbands an wives fawin eaut an feightin . . . for God wrote t' Bible Hissel, but they're nobbut only common-made clay what puts t' newspappers together. (50)

Despite the reflexive irony of the passage, which comments on the conventional tracks in which novelistic and journalistic plots tend to run and which links novels and newspapers in their mutual print sensationalism, the potency of the critique (from a radical perspective) is undermined by the character's appeal to biblical authority. Still, like Morris and Shaw, Clarke critiques the novel from within the form of the novel, just as he critiques newspapers from within the pages of a newspaper; this common maneuver among socialist writers indicates an undercurrent of uneasiness about the form even in a conventional novel like Clarke's. Such uneasiness may explain why the socialist revival and the socialist press produced a relatively unimpressive body of novels compared with its other literary output.

A good many late-century radical papers printed serialized novels, but poetry was by far the dominant literary mode of the radical press, and in terms of criticism, radical papers generally paid more attention to theater than to novels. In some respects the radical press was simply too precarious an enterprise to function as a successful forum for the serial novel, which might partly account for its indifference to the genre. Papers started and stopped with depressing regularity. For example, the *Labour Elector* collapsed before completing the serialization of the novel *Connie* by Margaret Harkness (who wrote under the pen name John Law); another radical journal, the *University Magazine and Free Review*, folded before it completed the serialization of Edith Ellis's novel *Seaweed* (1898), as discussed in Chapter 6. Other papers abruptly shifted course. The *Labour Leader*, edited by Keir Hardie, began to serialize a novel called *Mark Main, Miner* by William M'Queen, but in March 1889 the journal provided seven paragraphs as "a summary of the remaining chapters of this story" in lieu of finishing the actual installments. The final sentences of the seven-chapter summary suggest the same kind of romance-over-politics ending that we see in *The Knobstick*: "Mark and Bauldie soon came round, but Bob's eyes were closed forever. Poor wee chap. He was the true hero of the story. Alison and Mark got married and lived happy" (23).

Robert Blatchford, editor of the *Clarion*, was extremely successful as a writer of nonfiction—his *Merrie England*, ostensibly a collection of letters explaining socialism to "John Smith of Oldham, a Hard-Headed Workman, Fond of Facts," sold upwards of 2 million copies in the initial years after its serialization in the *Clarion*—but he never achieved success as a fiction writer, despite several attempts. He took a defensive tone when discussing the matter in the *Clarion*, suggesting that the demands and constraints of novel writing are antithetical to the work of radical journalism. On 4 May 1895, for example, he notes that George Moore is said to have worked on his recent novel, *Celibates*, for two years: "If I could have had two years in which to write 'Merrie England'? But we poor journalists have to 'snatch our books piece-meal'. . . . I had to write 'Merrie England,' 'A Son of the Forge,' and a serial story, a dozen short stories, and some hundred other articles inside of six months, and fill up the gaps by lecturing, answering correspondents, and editing the *Clarion*" (140). In the 9 January 1897 issue of the *Clarion* he again suggests a conflict between novel writing and journalism: "I have the journalist's trick of running in harness—of grinding out copy when copy is due, and never until it is due, and I have the trick of writing things freakishly—of slapping tales or articles together rapidly. . . . Several publishers have asked me to write novels. But I couldn't begin. The two long stories I did were written simply as padding for the *Clarion*" (10). On 6 June 1896 another *Clarion* writer defended these two works of serial fiction, *Tommy Atkins* and *A Son of the Forge*, against the *Manchester City News*'s charge that they have "inartistic" plots. They were, the *Clarion* insisted, "written merely to fill up blank spaces and give variety of contents to the *Clarion*. . . . [Blatchford] has never yet sat down with any serious intention of writing a novel at all" (178).

Margaret Harkness, a.k.a. John Law, was one of the more prolific socialist novelists of the era, yet her relation to the radical press was contentious, and she typically did not publish her novels within its pages (except *Connie*, which was serialized incompletely in *Labour Elector* in 1894). This meant that her books, when appearing with mainstream publishers, could be too expensive for working-class readers, as *Labour Leader* noted in its April 1889 "Book Notes" column. The reviewer gives positive notice to *Captain Lobe* by John Law, praising the writer's sympathetic depiction of the poor, but claims, "Three and sixpence placed it beyond the reach of the workers, and it is a pity that this powerfully written plea for justice . . . should not be read largely by those who are alone able to solve the problem that the book presents" (41–42). This last comment subtly touches on what many socialists thought was a larger problem with Harkness's work and with the novel as a genre: It did not empower or even impart agency to "those who are alone able to solve the problem," namely, the workers. Instead, novels target middle-class readers as the audience and the agents of reform, which opposes a Marxist or revolutionary theory of socialism that looks to the organization of the workers.

The implied middle-class reader is quite evident in Harkness's best-known novel, *A City Girl: A Realistic Story*, which was published in 1887 by Henry Vizetelly (who would be charged with obscenity in 1888 for publishing an English translation of Zola's *La Terre*). In writing the novel, Harkness drew on her experience in the Katherine Buildings tenement, where she lived for a time with her cousin Beatrice Potter (later Beatrice Webb), who was a rent collector there.[10] Despite these "authentic" slum origins, the novel's titular city girl, Nelly Ambrose, is actually the illegitimate daughter of a gentleman, as is the case with so many nineteenth-century novels that purport to focus on a working-class character. Her mother had worked as a lady's maid before her marriage and "could perhaps have told why [Nelly and her brother] were so very different; could have said whence [Nelly] inherited the ways and looks" that set her apart from her East End neighbors (72). In the course of the novel, Nelly, who works as a trousers cutter, is seduced by the married, middle-class Arthur Grant, whom she first encounters when he speaks in a local Radical Club. Grant wonders "how a face like [Nelly's] came to be in Whitechapel," and in a moment of antisocialist satire on Harkness's part, he mistakes her genteel appearance as "confirmation of his Radical opinions, for he believed that with the help of a good tailor, and a little polish, Whitechapel might sit down to dinner in Brook Street" (45). From the novel's perspective, heredity—not equality—accounts for Nelly's superior appearance and manner. (Clementina Black's 1894 socialist novel *An Agitator* similarly focuses on a working-class protagonist who is the secret illegitimate son of a gentleman, which accounts for his superior intelligence and manner; he speaks "with that easy and well modulated voice which is a rather rare endowment in a working-man, and which came to him as his paternal inheritance" [141].)

A City Girl's implied middle-class reader is also apparent in a meta-narrative scene in which Grant takes Nelly to an East End theater. Grant and the narrator disparage the hackneyed drama on the stage, but Nelly and the rest of the audience are moved to tears. The scene presents the working class as more feeling than the middle class but artistically naïve; the working-class response to narrative is one of immersion rather than critical distance. Because Harkness's naturalist mode depends on such distance, the effect of the scene is to suggest that the novel itself is too sophisticated for an East End audience.

A City Girl is perhaps best remembered for a letter that Friedrich Engels wrote to Harkness in April 1888, thanking her "for sending me your 'City Girl'. . . . I have read it with the greatest pleasure and avidity" (Letter 83). Despite this pleasure, Engels offered a critique of the book's politics and its "realism."

In the "City Girl" the working class figures as a passive mass, unable to help itself and not even showing any attempt to help itself. All attempts to drag it out of its torpid misery come from without, from above. Now if this was a correct description about 1800 or 1810, in the days of Saint-Simon and Robert Owen, it cannot appear so in 1887 to a man who for nearly fifty years has had the honour of sharing in most of the fights of the militant proletariat. The rebellious reaction of the working class . . . their attempts . . . at recovering their status as human beings, belong to history and must therefore lay claim to a place in the domain of realism. (83–84)

Interestingly, the letter frames a political critique of Harkness's novel—that it expresses a limited vision of social reform as top-down rather than as emerging from the workers—in terms of the aesthetic problem of realism. Rather than denouncing Harkness's politics, Engels challenges her realism: The book is subtitled "A Realistic Story," but it simply does not ring true with his experience among the proletariat.[11] Fredric Jameson has argued that George Gissing's 1889 slum novel, *The Nether World*, is "best read, not for documentary information on the conditions of Victorian slum life, but as testimony about the narrative paradigms that organize middle-class fantasies about those slums" (*Political Unconscious* 173); a hundred years earlier, Engels made a similar case that Harkness's "realistic" novel portrays a middle-class rather than a working-class "reality."

Engels's letter to Harkness engages with the socialist debate around naturalism, a literary mode that purported to offer an objective, scientific approach to reveal grim social reality in shocking—some said lurid—detail but that seemed to many socialists to convey a hopeless vision of a passive proletariat. As Haywood has argued of the slum novel of the 1880s and 1890s, "There is no mention in this fiction of the important self-help measures that probably did the most to define working-class culture in this period" (*Working-Class Fiction* 13). Contemporary socialist critics such as Engels were alert to this pitfall in ostensibly realistic novels. Indeed, the question of *whose* reality and of *which* reality is being represented in "realism" was a crucial subject of political-aesthetic debate among many late nineteenth-century socialists. Robert Blatchford, writing in the *Clarion*, asked in his 20 March 1897 article "Realism in Literature," "What is a Realist? At first thought one would reply that a Realist is an author who portrays things as they really are. But how *are* they?" (89). Blatchford argues that the "realist" slum novel *A Child of the Jago*, by Arthur Morrison, for example, does not capture the horror of the Shoreditch slums but instead exercises "artistic reticence." "Let anyone who knows the slums consider how the truth is toned down or evaded in 'A Child of the Jago'" (89).[12] Blatchford thinks that this is necessarily the case, that no work of literature can give a truly realistic picture of the slums, but Edward Carpenter's article "Nature and Realism in Art" in the *Progressive Review* argues that in "the ruder facts of life, hitherto somewhat untouched—in wounds and death, in physiological facts, in sex, in the common life of the mass-people, in poverty, in criminality, in ignorance—lie huge stores of associations capable of rousing the most keen and complex emotions. . . . Any artist must see that these associations, these emotions, are there for his use" (September 1897: 503).

The debate about novelistic realism in late nineteenth-century socialism anticipates the debate about realism among twentieth-century Marxist critics. For example, Georg Lukács, in "Realism in the Balance," argues that literary naturalism "take[s] reality exactly as it manifests itself to the writer" and thus "fail[s] to pierce the surface to discover the underlying essence, i.e. the real factors that relate . . . experiences to the hidden social forces that produce them" (36–37). He claims that literature ought "not merely to confine itself to reproducing whatever manifests itself immediately and on the surface" but should strive to represent the totality of social relations: "What matters is that the slice of life shaped and depicted by the artist and re-experienced by the reader should reveal the relations between appearance and essence" (33–34). This absence of a sense of totality is why "the photographically and phonographically exact imitations of life which we find in Naturalism . . . never come alive" (39).

Engels's and Blatchford's views on the limitations of late nineteenth-century literary naturalism anticipate Lukács's critique, as does a review of William E. Tirebuck's novel *Miss Grace of All Souls* in Blatchford's paper, the *Clarion*. The reviewer, R. B. S., credits the perfect accuracy of Tirebuck's realism: "His intimate acquaintance with the inner life of the Lancashire colliers . . . is marvellous in its accuracy of detail. One is almost led to think that Mr. Tirebuck must have had a phonograph concealed in Brookster's Yard, so naturally is the conversation of its inmates reproduced" (26 October 1895: 344). Yet this almost phonographic verisimilitude fails to reveal the political factors that create the circumstances it depicts, just as Lukács would later suggest; the reviewer continues, "It is a great book, but it will not make Socialists." The perspective is too middle-class, too reformist: Tirebuck "seems to think that by appealing to the conscience all will come right in time. But what is the use of trying to awaken that which does not exist? . . . If the workers wait till the moral sense of the capitalists is quickened, they will require a larger stock of patience than Job" (344).

Émile Zola was the premiere naturalist writer of the era, and the Zola novel most admired by socialists was *Germinal*, originally serialized in France from 1884 to 1885. But *Germinal*, for all its shocking exposure of capitalist exploitation in the coal industry, also represents working-class characters as politically ineffectual, an inarticulate mob; it describes a crowd of strikers as a "uniform earth-coloured mass. All that could be seen was their blazing eyes and the black holes of their mouths singing the *Marseillaise*, the verses of which merged into a confused roar" (334). Like other naturalist novels, *Germinal* also entertains a version of Darwinism that chalks social inequities up to irreversible hereditary determinism: "Was Darwin right, then," the protagonist wonders at the end of the novel. "Was this world nothing but a struggle in which the strong devoured the weak?" (496). Shortly after its initial appearance, the novel was noticed in the English radical press: "'Germinal,' by Emile Zola, is in its way as good a propagandist work as can well be found. . . . With few exceptions all the scenes might be found in the Black Country" (*Justice*, 11 April 1885: 2). This is generally positive, but "in its way" and "as can well be found" imply some reservations about the novel, and the reviewer's attempt to relocate the plot in the Black Country suggests a sense that naturalism's version of socialism might not be altogether portable because it depends so much on local context.[13]

The legal harassment of Vizetelly, prosecuted for publishing Zola's *La Terre* in England, shored up socialist support for Zola, but his naturalist method still did not sit well with all British socialists. *Justice* conveyed subtle doubts about Zola, even while defending him.

Zola, the English translation of whose works is now being the subject of a prosecution, has at any rate produced two works which are very significant in their relation to social questions. We mean "Germinal," the book of the proletariat of the mines, and "La Terre" (The Soil), the book of the proletariat of the fields. They are both horrible books, powerfully written. But if the horror exists—? (1 September 1888: 4–5).

In the context of the trial, *Justice* advocates for the political force of free expression, but the phrase "at any rate" and the dash at the end of the last question ("But if the horror exists—?") convey lingering questions about Zola's "scientific" realism.[14]

Harkness's novels attempt a naturalist realism on the order of Zola's but also retain a sentimental appeal that angles for the sympathies of middle-class readers.[15] Her novel *A Manchester Shirtmaker*, originally published by the Authors' Co-operative Publishing Company, depicts a young widow who poisons and kills her baby out of desperate poverty. This was the kind of grisly plot that made Zola's novels so infamous, but the novel does not effect scientific disinterest in Mary, the young widow. Instead, using the pronoun *we*, the narrator invites middle-class readers to sympathize and to imagine themselves in her place: "For nearly a month she had been planning this thing . . . as the only way in which her child could be happy. And now it was done. The baby was dead, dead! We think and we plan, what is going to happen. . . . At last it all becomes a reality. In the icy chill of weird morning we stand up to face

the thing which we have so long been planning. We call on God, then"
(50). The appeal departs from naturalism's tone of objectivity, but if the
novel pushes the affective limits of naturalism, it also suggests the inadequacies of the sentimental tradition. Harkness's novel, like Clarke's,
interweaves a romance plot with social realism, using conventional sentimental machinery such as love at first sight, although Harkness with-
holds a happy ending. The loafer who falls in love with Mary has been a
drunk since he was 6 years old: "No other love [but drink] had entered
his life (although he had been intimate with many women) until the little
widow. . . . But from the day on which he had seen her first, he had been
her lover" (70). Hopelessly incapacitated by alcoholism, he is helpless to
save Mary; she is convicted of killing her child and sent to an asylum
where she commits suicide. The self-inflicted violence of the drunken
loafer who poisons himself with drink and of the suicidal mother who
poisons her own baby indicates how Harkness's lower-class characters
turn their class revolt inward rather than outward. The book ends with
a lecture on social reform by a middle-class socialist doctor; the implication is that he is the novel's one cause for hope, one possible avenue
for change. Engels found such middle-class exceptionalism retrograde.

Harkness was subject to similar criticism in *Justice* after she published
an article under her real name in the 24 March 1888 issue. The piece,
"Salvationists and Socialists," provoked editorial objection for suggesting
that the Salvation Army's East End "feeding place" is "the most communistic place in London at the present time" and that socialists and
Salvationists "ought to work more together than they do at present" (2).
Socialists, including many Christian socialists, tended to be extremely
suspicious of religious charity operations such as the Salvation Army,
which they saw as propagating capitalist inequality by making it endur-
able for the poor and by training them to endure it in peace. (Shaw's 1905
play *Major Barbara* reflects at length on this issue.) A note from *Justice's*
editor, placed at the end of Harkness's article, gives the Salvation Army
"fullest credit" but questions whether it "does not ultimately aggravate
the evils it aims at remedying." Harkness replied to this criticism in the
correspondence column a few weeks later, insisting that hungry men
and women have an immediate need for food, which the Salvationists
provide. The editor objected again, commenting that the provision of

food for the hungry should be a public function and the Salvationists militate against it becoming so (14 April 1888: 6).[16]

The testy relations between Harkness and *Justice* continued a year later, when she wrote another letter to the paper (this time under her pen name, John Law), apologizing for an antisocialist chapter ("Among the Socialists") in her recent novel *Captain Lobe*. The novel was serialized in the popular nonconformist paper *British Weekly* in 1889. "I am sorry to think it gives an untrue account of London Socialists," Law wrote, explaining that its tone emerged from frustrations with the movement rather than genuine antisocialist feeling.

Last Sunday morning I heard Mrs Besant speaking in Manchester on Socialism. She gave a splendid lecture; and I realised as I had never done before, how rapidly things are moving in a Socialistic direction in London. . . . I will frankly own that "Among the Socialists" was written one night when I had suffered a good deal from Socialists. . . . To find oneself without a relation or a friend, because one is by conviction a Socialist, and then to have vials of wrath poured on one's head, by Socialists, makes one inclined to curse. . . . I tried to get that chapter back, but I was too late, it had gone to press, and it is published. It is not true; and I am sorry for it. (*Justice*, 20 April 1889: 3)

It may be that the socialist press's lukewarm reception of Law's novels played a part in this passing attack of antisocialism.

Justice serialized its own original realist novel, *A Working Class Tragedy*, from 1888 to 1889, and this work fell prey to some of the same failings as other socialist-naturalist novels focused on working-class characters. *A Working Class Tragedy* can be said to exemplify such naturalism in the grim progress of its proletarian protagonist, Frank Wilson, an engineer who loses his job, falls into destitution, is falsely accused of murder, and eventually commits suicide; but the novel can also be said to provide analysis of the totality of social relations from a working-class perspective, albeit in an ungainly fashion. Early in the novel, Wilson is described as having "a Radical's contempt for all the pretensions of the Church and the old nobility people, but all a Radical's respect for the self-made man, the capitalist and the money-grabber" (30 June 1888: 2). He is suspicious of socialism but later befriends a socialist, marveling that he "did not wear a heavy beard, nor a slouch hat, and so far as

Frank could see there were neither pistols in his belt nor dynamite in his pockets" (17 November 1888: 3). The author, H. J. Bramsbury, takes the opportunity to explain socialist doctrine to readers through the ensuing exchanges between Wilson and his friend.[17] In the end, however, Wilson falls in love with a wealthy heiress who rejects his advances, and he kills himself after saving her from a fire. As with *A Manchester Shirtmaker*, working-class violence turns inward, in the form of suicide, rather than outward, and ultimately Wilson represents a passive victim of the class system who never really converts to the socialist doctrine the novel promotes.

George Gissing was another novelist whose naturalist tendencies provoked debate in the radical press around the question of realism and lower-class passivity. A characteristic passage from his 1889 novel *The Nether World* describes one working-class family in terms that suggest its utter submission to dismal circumstance.

Stephen took things with much philosophy; his mother would, of course, drink herself to death—what was there astonishing in that? He himself had heart disease, and surely enough would drop down dead one of these days; the one doom was no more to be quarrelled with than the other. Pennyloaf came to see them at very long intervals. . . . She, too, viewed with a certain equanimity the progress of her mother's fate. Vain every kind of interposition. . . . It could only be hoped that the end would come before very long. (253)

Gissing's detached tone, as well as his reliance on the terms *doom* and *fate* to describe the condition of the poor, prompted accusations of political quietism; meanwhile, his emphasis on the acutely sordid prompted accusations of sensationalism. A review of his novel *The Unclassed*, published in the socialist magazine *To-Day* in September 1884, claims that Gissing's narrative specialty is "to cultivate a divine indifference to human affairs, a cruel callousness to human suffering" (304). The reviewer considers *The Unclassed* to be "more human and more humane" than Gissing's other works (304) but nonetheless laments "the unpleasant pieces of sensationalism which the author unfortunately thinks it necessary to intersperse" (305) and the "'blood-thrilling' business, which we might well have been spared" (306). Of its conclusion, the reviewer states, "We must protest against what seems to us the final sacrifice of all [Maud's] aspirations upon the altar, not of the necessity of things, but of the exigencies of the novelistic situation" (308).

To-Day, the journal that serialized two of Shaw's novels, clearly shares Shaw's doubts about the political flexibility of the novelistic form; as we have seen elsewhere, the exigencies of the genre are here identified as the chief barricade to the production of a socialist novel. Importantly, however, what *To-Day*'s reviewer appears to admire most about Gissing's novel is its pointed rejection of aestheticism. From the point of view of the radical press, both aestheticism and naturalism—the poles of fin de siècle literary culture—were politically deficient, as discussed in Chapter 1. But naturalism at least put politics at the front and center of art. The review of *The Unclassed* praises one character's declaration that "perhaps art for art's sake was not the final stage of his development. Art, yes; but combat at the same time. The two things are not so incompatible as some would have us think." *To-day*'s review concludes, "At this excellent sentiment we will take leave of him" (308).

Naturalism left little doubt of literature's engagement with the sociopolitical sphere but threatened to constrain the imagination of what was possible to the grimmest of determinist realities; aestheticism unfettered the imagination to potentially expand the scope of possibility but simultaneously threatened to detach art from political reality altogether. Navigating between these poles was the utopian novel, a genre that was fantastical and political, imaginative and antideterminist, all apparently in service of radical change.[18] The tricky question of realism and perspective—*whose* realism?—that we see with respect to Harkness and Gissing suggests why the novelistic genre that was thought to be most effectively socialistic was not realist at all but utopian. Edward Bellamy's utopian novel *Looking Backward*, although originally published in the United States, was the first major socialist novel of England's socialist revival. Printed serially in the British socialist press in 1889 in J. Bruce Wallace's journal *Brotherhood*, the novel was considered a major step forward in the progress of socialist novel writing (Beaumont, "William Reeves" 100). Morris famously recoiled from the authoritarian, military quality of the socialist vision in *Looking Backward*, but others were inspired by the seeming plausibility of the socialist society it depicts, and even Morris was inspired to write *News from Nowhere*—the most important British novel of the socialist revival—in response to Bellamy.

Justice reviewed *Looking Backward* in March 1889 and said that the novel was remarkable for its author's deep knowledge of socialism, such depth being unusual among socialist novelists.

> Before an author can write a novel from the Social-Democratic standpoint he must, of course, make himself thoroughly acquainted with the economical analysis of the capitalist system of production. . . . If he does not do so—and by far the majority of novel writers on socialistic subjects certainly do not—then his production will not be worth the paper upon which it is written.
>
> Far and away above most other novels of socialistic tendencies stands Mr. Edward Bellamy's work "Looking Backward." Throughout the novel his economics are sound. To that soundness of economics are added a charm of manner. . . . It does not follow by any means that the Social Revolution will take the course which Mr. Bellamy describes. . . . But no fault whatever can be found with the industrial mechanism of the year 2000. . . . No one can assert that the social arrangements of that supposed period are anything but the most possible and probable. (16 March 1889: 3)

Right next to this review, which speaks so disparagingly of existing socialist novels, is an advertisement for Constance Howell's *More Excellent Way*, a realist novel that received a mediocre review from Harry Quelch in the 2 June 1888 issue of *Justice*.[19] On the very next page is an installment of Bramsbury's *Working Class Tragedy*. Even in a context populated by multiple attempts at socialist novel writing, the reviewer speaks of the genre as predominantly antisocialist until Bellamy.

More than a decade later, after many more novels of socialism had been produced, Esther Wood's "Socialism and the Modern Novel," published in the *Social Democrat* in 1901, came to much the same conclusion. Defining the novel as realist and thus not including utopian fiction, Wood charges that most recent novelists who have depicted socialism have little understanding of their subject and use socialist caricatures (15 November 1901: 339). "The great novel of the Social Revolution in England," she concludes, "has yet to be written." This is due to a fundamental feature of the genre: Socialist novelists face the enduring problem of how "the life of the hero or heroine is to be brought into harmony with . . . its true proportion against a larger strife" (341). Shaw's novels, which struggle with this problem of balancing the individual against the social, are not even mentioned. By 1901 he had moved into the dramatic sphere, and his socialist novels were all but forgotten.

Shaw's Unsocial Novelism

Given such widespread socialist suspicion of the novel, why did Shaw choose to write novels in the first place? To be sure, the Victorian novel was itself in a transitional stage during this time of intense socialist impatience with novelistic form. From 1880 to 1914, as Mary Hammond describes, "The shape of the material book changed as the three-decker was allowed to die. The circulating libraries released their long-standing stranglehold on the price and circulation of new fiction. Authors and publishers organized themselves into societies" (8). Still, novels remained the default literary mode. Recalling his 1880 composition of *The Irrational Knot*, Shaw wrote in his preface to the 1905 edition, "Everybody wrote novels then" (vii). He says in his preface to *Plays Unpleasant*, "It is clear that a novel cannot be too bad to be worth publishing" ("Mainly About Myself" 8). This glut of bad novels, this market superfluity, drove Shaw's hopes of publishing one of his own.

Shaw affected this same disdain for novels within his novels themselves. In *The Irrational Knot*, originally serialized in Annie Besant's socialist magazine *Our Corner* from 1885 to 1887, the character Nelly is a young female novelist whose writing ambitions are viewed as a disgrace by her parents. However, her act of writing and publishing a novel is not represented as heroic defiance of bourgeois social convention but rather as one node in a mass marketplace of commercial fiction. In fact, we might read Nelly as a precursor for Vivie Warren of *Mrs. Warren's Profession*, whose choice in the drama's last scene to earn her living independently as an actuary is sometimes read as an act of feminist agency, although the play indicates that her profession is no better than that of her mother, a prostitute; both women are cogs in a broader dehumanizing network of capital exchange. Similarly, *An Irrational Knot* presents Nelly's novel writing not as autonomous feminist expression but as capitalist commercialism masquerading as independent subjectivity. When the colonial edition of Nelly's book *The Waters of Marah* is released, an advertisement reads: "Now Ready, a New and Cheaper Edition." Blurbs from the press promote her novel in terms that suggest its mediocrity as well as her critics'. The *Athenæum* says, "Superior to many of the numerous tales which find a ready sale at the railway bookstall"; the *Examiner* says, "There is nothing to fatigue, and something to gratify, the idle reader"; and the fictional *Middlingtown Mercury* incongruously adds, "Miss McQuinch has fairly established her claim to be considered the greatest novelist of the age" (279). In his 1901 preface to a new edition of *Cashel Byron's Profession*, Shaw claimed to "shudder at the narrowness of my escape from becoming a successful novelist at the age of twenty-six" ("Novels" 5); his fictional account of Nelly's career pinpoints the mercantile mediocrity that he fears.

Elsewhere, in *Love Among the Artists*, also serialized in *Our Corner*, Shaw hints at the political costs of a novel-centered print culture where even newspapers obey the conventions of bourgeois realist fiction, rendering reality in the form of ready-made novelistic narratives. When Marian Lind leaves her husband, Ned, to run away to America with another man, the American papers represent her story through a completely fabricated clichéd seduction plot, as she complains in a letter to her cousin.

One of them actually printed a long account of my going away, with every paragraph headed in large print, "Domestic Unhappiness," "The Serpent in the Laboratory," "The Temptation," "The Flight," "The Pursuit," and so on, all invented, of course. Other papers give the most outrageous anecdotes. . . . The latest version appeared in a Sunday paper. . . . According to it, Ned was in the habit of "devoting me to science" by trying electrical experiments on me. (355)

Like Clarke in *The Knobstick*, Shaw links novels and newspapers as the twin fonts of print mystification. Journalism, like the novel, focuses on the romantic travails of the well born and forces even that trite topic into more conventional chapters than reality, for Marian's husband is an electrical engineer whom her father had forbidden her to marry, whereas the man she runs away with, Sholto, is a gentleman who had been favored by her father in the first place. Benedict Anderson and more recently Matthew Rubery have described the structural and stylistic similarities between the novel and the newspaper in their development as print forms; here, Shaw lodges a critique against their interrelated mutual dependence on stock conventional narratives.

Love Among the Artists originally appeared in *Our Corner,* and the critical discourse around novels in this journal echoes some of the points made by Shaw. The journal tended to take a disparaging, not to say elitist, attitude toward popular culture and mass audiences. An article titled "Popular Judgment in Literature: A Note on Mr. Rider Haggard" in the December 1887 issue argued that "the rapid trend of all things 'toward democracy'" is a good thing that will ultimately make people happier, but in the meantime "the guerdon of success is shifting into [the hands] of a demi-semi-cultivated majority," so that "it is largely by immature judgment, crude tastes, and hasty criticism that rewards are being dealt out." The article, by "Fabian Bland" (the pen name used by Edith Nesbit and Hubert Bland writing together), points to George Newnes's magazine *Tit-Bits* and to the novels of Rider Haggard as examples of the degraded quality of the mass print market. The article concludes, "It seems that however powerful the democracy may be . . . there is one thing which, as yet, it cannot do—decide the claims of authors to greatness. . . . Posterity will, we venture to say, confirm the verdict of the elect" (322–23). The piece, which ran a few months after Shaw's novel concluded its serialization in February 1887, reinforces a class hierarchy in the area of art and culture, if not economics, and it rings with the language of artistic aristocracy: "The democracy may choose its dictator . . . but to weave the laurel crown that means immortality is the eternal heritage of the aristocracy of the mind" (323).

The basic idea at work here is that capitalism has produced a monolithic, impoverished literary and print culture, and that alongside this development a huge swell in the number of readers has emerged. The question is whether the two are necessarily related: Are the newly literate to blame for the state of literature? Conventional wisdom held this to be the case, but many anticapitalist radicals would not accede to this idea or give up the possibility of a democratic audience outside the capitalist market. As we see with William Morris, precapitalist popular culture was one of the few models radicals could draw on to imagine conditions where democratic culture and capitalist mass culture were not coterminous. Other socialists, such as Shaw, "Fabian Bland," and most of *Our*

Corner's critics, struggle to claim a place for anticapitalist print but often end up articulating an elitist dismissal of mass print. For example, in a review of Shaw's novel *Cashel Byron's Profession*, John Robertson argued in *Our Corner* that, although Shaw's novel does rise above "the wilderness of inferior fiction, now being littered knee-deep with the new rubbish of shilling dreadfuls," its "satiric purpose" is nonetheless "cramped by the fiction-form" (May 1886: 302). Shaw's effort to write anticapitalist satire could not, in Robertson's view, be accommodated by the popular novelistic mode.

Cashel Byron's Profession originally appeared in *To-Day*, the most Marxist of the era's socialist journals. *To-Day* ran previously untranslated Marx serially in English and was edited by J. L. Joynes and E. Belfort Bax, the two men who did the most (apart from H. M. Hyndman) to spread Marxist theory among early British socialists. *To-Day* identified itself as a journal of "scientific socialism," based on the foundational principle that social problems can be approached as scientific problems requiring rational examination and solutions based in empirical analysis. Yet despite this scientific focus, *To-Day* was not at all indifferent to art and published a great deal of poetry, fiction, and literary criticism.[20] As the editors wrote in the 14 April 1883 issue, "Fiction is, to our thinking, oftentimes more true than fact" (4).

And yet Shaw's novels published in *To-Day* betray frustration with the alternative print public offered by the radical press, suggesting that such venues are not an adequate response to the problem of capitalist mass print. *Cashel Byron's Profession*, for example, presents the subculture of illegal prizefighting, and its subcultural press, as completely unnoticed and ignored by the public at large. Byron, a prizefighter, is famous at the racetrack and in the sporting press: "You may have seen his name in the paper, sir. The sporting ones are full of him" (147). Yet Lydia Carew, the wealthy bohemian heroine with radical political views, has never heard of him; his profession is a mystery to her for most of their courtship. More surprising, a court of law releases Byron on a charge of illegal prizefighting, although betting on the fight in question "had been recorded in all the sporting papers for weeks beforehand" (260). The public constituted by prizefighting and its press is so self-contained that it operates outside the view of the courts. Shaw's depiction of the sporting press bears on his own minority print venue and subcultural forum, *To-Day*, and the radical press more broadly. Print culture has fractured into a plethora of publics, and although the radical press offers a means of escaping capitalist controls on print content, it also renders its contents invisible to all but enthusiasts.[21]

Shaw's first major work to be published, *An Unsocial Socialist*, was also printed serially in *To-Day* from March to December 1884. Here, Shaw's ambivalence about his print forum resonates in the early pages of the story, which opens with three young women in a boarding school who break school rules by sliding down a banister. Because the school operates on progressive educational principles according to a system of "moral science," pupils are encouraged to write down and reflect on their bad behavior in a book called "The Recording Angel." Everyone is supposed to write in the book and nobody is supposed to read it, but the ringleader of the three girls, Agatha Wylie, a rebellious student with the "instincts of an anarchist" (38), habitually subverts the rules by reading everyone else's entries and writing long sensational entries that entice others to read them: "I always like to have my entries read: it makes me feel like an author" (6–7). The school authorities end up expelling Agatha for her narrative authorship.

An Unsocial Socialist begins, then, with the image of an anarchistic author—Agatha—writing subversive novelistic content in a venue that is not supposed to be read. She deeply wants her scandalous writings to be read, but their existence depends on their remaining obscure. There are obvious parallels here between Shaw and Agatha, two dissident authors in search of an audience, writing in forums that are not widely accessed. Agatha's "arrest" for subversive writing is Shaw's reflexive fantasy of political suppression for writing a socialist novel. (Later, he expresses this desire by writing aggressively censorable plays, as I discuss in Chapter 3.) In the 1880s the radical press no longer has the frisson of illegality that guaranteed its political force in the early years of the century. Radical printers had then been subject to constant threat of suppression and arrest, and Shaw to some extent imagines such suppression as a necessary condition for the radical press's impact, because it generates public interest and sympathy.[22] In the 1880s a magazine like *To-Day* was both free and isolated, a condition that Morris embraced but Shaw did not. This is perhaps one explanation for Shaw's eventual move to the dramatic sphere, which was much more aggressively policed and thus more likely to cause scandal.

Besides Agatha, the other central character in *An Unsocial Socialist* is Sidney Trefusis, the titular unsocial socialist, a wealthy young man who abandons his bride to devote his life to socialist propaganda.[23] Like the protagonists of Walter Besant's *All Sorts and Conditions of Men*, Trefusis poses as a workingman out of political principle, but whereas the joke of Besant's novel is how poorly Angela Messenger and Harry Le Breton hide their "real" identities, Shaw's novel emphasizes instead the flatness and vacuity of Trefusis's "real" self. The novel was originally titled "The Heartless Man," and as we saw in Chapter 1, "heartlessness" was the term used by Oscar Wilde to resist novelistic conventions of psychological interiority. For Wilde, flat, "heartless" characters were an aesthetic revolt against realism; for Morris, such characters were a socialist revolt against the illusory forms of capitalism.[24] That Shaw also wanted to empty his characters of conventional novelistic interiority in service of anticapitalist aims is apparent from his original plan for "The Heartless Man," a novel that would "form the two opening chapters 'of a vast work depicting capitalist society in dissolution with its downfall as the final grand catastrophe'" (Loewenstein 5).

As this original title suggests, Trefusis is indeed a heartless character lacking interiority and complexity.[25] He has two names and two identities, Jeff Smilash and Sidney Trefusis, with two respective class positions, and critics since Richard Dietrich have read him as Shaw's youthful projection of his own fantasies of selfhood into print, suggesting perhaps how unlifelike a character he is. Fittingly for such a "flat" character, Shaw uses Trefusis to exhibit the deficiencies of print, specifically the socialist print that Trefusis imagines waging as a political tool. Although Trefusis articulates an Enlightenment theory of print, hoping to educate the working classes through his socialist print campaign, he admits, "Whether I am really advancing the cause is more than I can say. I use heaps of postage stamps; pay the expenses of many indifferent lecturers; defray the cost of printing reams of pamphlets and hand-bills which hail the labourer flatteringly as the salt of the earth; write and edit a little socialist journal" (62). Words such as "heaps," "indifferent," "reams," and "flatteringly" all imply an abundant supply of radical print, which is ineffectual in the face of a cumbersome, unresponsive mass public.

We hear little more than this about Trefusis's propaganda, but Shaw's novel moves from a critique of radical print to a critique of novelistic form. Six years before *News from Nowhere*, Shaw depicts the novel as a dying medium within the pages of a socialist novel, and he looks forward to a future where the genre is extinct.[26] Trefusis claims that "the only art that interests me is photography" (125), and when asked his thoughts on the future of the arts, he says, "Works of fiction superceded by interesting company and conversation, and made obsolete by the human mind outgrowing the childishness that delights in the tales told by grown-up children such as novelists and their like!" (126). Later, when Agatha tells Trefusis that she is reading a novel, he says, "That is, a lying story of two people who never existed, and who would have acted very differently if they had existed." In pointed allusion to the novel at hand, Trefusis asks if the story will end in a marriage; Agatha replies, "I really dont know. This is one of your clever novels. I wish the characters would not talk so much" (172).

These specific claims against the novel as a genre—its conventional form, its unrealistic realism—exist amid *An Unsocial Socialist*'s larger doubts, echoing Morris, about the possibility of any art at all being produced before a socialist revolution. When one character says that "the sole refiner of human nature is fine art," Trefusis replies, "The sole refiner of art is human nature. Art rises when men rise" (129–30). But this rise will entail the extinction of the novel altogether. As Shaw explains in the novel's epistolary appendix, a "Letter to the Author from Mr. Sidney Trefusis," "Actions described in novels are judged by a romantic system of morals as fictitious as the actions themselves" (199). Trefusis, the protagonist, tells Shaw, the author, "I acknowledge that you have stated the facts, on the whole, with scrupulous fairness," yet "I am sorry you made a novel of my story; for the effect has been almost as if you had misrepresented me from beginning to end" (199). The problem is the medium of the novel, not just its content. A novel can include socialist content, but the form perverts the facts.

Much like Morris in *News from Nowhere*, Shaw claims that the nineteenth-century novel offers fantasies and illusions in the guise of realism: "I grew out of novel-writing, and set to work to find out what the world was really like" ("Novels" 5). This suggests that for Marx-trained socialists such as Morris and Shaw, the realist novel as a genre is guilty of capitalist mystification, preventing the recognition of true social conditions.[27] Driving the point home, Shaw (in Trefusis's voice) concludes his appendix to *An Unsocial Socialist* by directly condemning the novel and modern English literature more broadly as essentially a written record of capitalist oppression, which will die when capitalism does.

> Allow me to express my regret that you can find no better employment for your talent than the writing of novels. The first literary result of the foundation of our industrial system upon the profits of piracy and slave-trading was Shakspere [*sic*]. . . . But the poetry of despair will not outlive despair itself. Your nineteenth century novelists are only the tail of Shakspere. Don't tie yourself to it: it is fast wriggling into oblivion. (203)

By using reflexive narration and flat characterization and by incorporating a critique of the novel into the novel itself, *An Unsocial Socialist* prompts readers' consciousness of the political effects of literary genre and of print itself as a product of mass production.[28]

Moreover, by writing an epistolary appendix in the voice of his character addressing the author, Shaw engages and exploits the shifting role of the author function in the new literary mass marketplace. As suggested earlier in this chapter, developments in the world of publishing such as author photographs, celebrity authorship, and the human interest tone of New Journalism can be viewed as simulations of a personal relationship between author and reader to counteract the reality of an increasingly diffuse mass print market. The experimentation in authorial voice in the appendix to *An Unsocial Socialist* connects with such developments and connects more broadly with what critics such as Gareth Griffith have argued regarding Shaw's loss of faith in and consequent attack on Enlightenment subjectivity.[29] The appendix calls attention to the inauthenticity of Shaw's authorial *I*, which is exposed to be a character on the order of Sidney Trefusis. While developing this artful authorial personality, Shaw likewise discounts the import of authorial intention: "The existence of a discoverable and perfectly definite thesis in a poet's work by no means depends on the completeness of his own intellectual consciousness of it" (*Quintessence* 207). Claims for authorial intention, Shaw suggests, are something like claims for "parental intention": "A book is like a child: it is easier to bring it into the world than to control it when it is launched there" ("Novels" 7). Working as a novelist, Shaw is evidently straining toward the performative space of the stage, where literature is not fixed by the text or constrained by the sense of coherent authorial agency. Contrary to the conclusions of drama critics like W. B. Worthen, who argues that the key point of Shaw's migration to drama was to make plays that "energetically avail themselves of the rhetoric of the book" (*Print* 55) and that transform "the playtext from a dramatic to diegetic form" (72), Shaw was, in fact, moving print toward the theater just as he was moving theater toward print. He turned from the novel to the drama as a more dialogic, potentially more radical literary form. As Katherine E. Kelly concludes, "Shaw the Fabian socialist suspected that sermonizing in dialogue repudiated 'individualism' more readily than sermonizing in long narrative blocks" (28).

Fabian Print and Shavian Socialism

As Kelly suggests, Shaw's turn toward dramatic form is not unrelated to his particular variety of socialism: Fabianism. The Fabian Society was the most middle class of the major socialist groups of the day, politically premised on reform from above rather than on revolution from below. According to the Fabian policy of "permeation," the group would circulate socialist ideas in key cultural, political, and artistic venues so that socialist reforms would be enacted from above and socialist ideas would trickle down to the population at large. Although its middle-class sensibility might suggest that Fabianism would make Shaw more, not less, inclined to write in the middle-class genre of the novel, in fact Fabianism is particularly evident in Shaw's theatrical turn. The theater audience (outside of music halls) was smaller, more select, and more contained than the potential reach of print; such a public was the optimal target of Fabian permeation. As Dennis Kennedy has argued, "The desire to lead London to a promised land of the stage was eminently Fabian, a permeation theory applied to art" (145). Compared to other socialist groups, the Fabians were notably skeptical of print propaganda because the audience for print was more difficult to target. Like other radical groups of the time, the Fabians expressed doubt about the political efficacy of print under the new conditions of mass media, but their response to this situation was to integrate print culture into oral modes of political exchange.[30]

It may seem counterintuitive to suggest that the Fabians were skeptical of print enlightenment, given that they published so many pamphlets with the idea of dispersing socialist facts for use in making the socialist case. But alone among the major socialist organizations of the day, they did not maintain a newspaper or magazine, the centerpiece of political activity for most radical groups. *Fabian News*, a short newsletter for members, was launched in March 1891, but it was specifically intended for a small identifiable set of members, *not* to propagandize: The words "For Members Only" were writ large at the top of the masthead, members received the paper for free, and Edward Pease, founding member and secretary of the Fabian Society, specified that it was "not intended for the general public" (*Labour Annual*, 1895: 39).[31] When the Fabian Society achieved success in print ventures, it seemed to come as a surprise, as Shaw recalled of *Fabian Essays in Socialism*: "When we published *Fabian Essays* at the end of 1889, having ventured with great misgiving on a subscription edition of a thousand, it went off like smoke; and our cheap edition brought up the circulation to about twenty thousand" (*Fabian Society* 19).[32] Pease also marveled that "a six-shilling book, published at a private dwelling-house and not advertised in the press, or taken round by travelers to the trade, sold almost as rapidly as if the authors had been Cabinet Ministers" (88). The group had conceived of the volume not so much as a print intervention but as a record of its oral propaganda. Shaw's preface to the first edition of *Fabian Essays* states, "The essays in this volume were prepared last year as a course of lectures for delivery before mixed audiences. . . . They have been revised for publication, but not recast. The matter is put, not as an author would put it to a student, but as a speaker with only an hour at his disposal has to put it to an audience" (iii).

The Fabian ambivalence about print audiences and print propaganda is evident not only in Shaw's emphasis on the oral origins of *Fabian Essays* but also in the volume's material form, for the first edition of *Fabian Essays* picks up on the Arts and Crafts ideals that so deeply marked Morris's approach to socialist print. Here, the stylistic elements function to target a coterie audience—a known readership, not the anonymous recipients of mass print. That Morris's ideas of handicraft were of interest to the Fabians is apparent in the 1889 Fabian lecture series "A Century of Social Movements," which included "The Revival of Taste: William Morris and the Manual Arts" (Fabian Society Archive, LSE: C 62/1). That same year, Shaw, who edited *Fabian Essays* and oversaw its design, included Morrisian effects in the volume's first edition, such as an artistic binding by May Morris and a cover illustration by Walter Crane (see Figure 16). These aesthetic features register resistance to print

Figure 16. Image for *Fabian Essays in Socialism* (1889).

capitalism and to ideologies of print enlightenment, calling attention to the book at hand as creator—not just transporter—of political meaning. Likewise, Shaw's preface to *Fabian Essays* asks readers to be alert to the volume's mediation and to consider print as a necessary but inadequate substitute for live speech; readers are encouraged to seek out dialogic exchange with the essays' authors in live settings, to get "face to face with the writers, *stripping the veil of print from their personality. . . .* For any Sunday paper which contains a lecture list will shew where some, if not all, of the seven essayists may be heard for nothing" (iii, my emphasis). Again, Shaw figures print as a veil—not a transparent carrier of Enlightenment reason, but itself perceptible, expressive, and distorting.

As with Morris, Shaw's book design for *Fabian Essays* attempts to mount a formal challenge to the logic of print capitalism. If print is itself a metonym for mass production, for high-volume reproducibility, then printing as many cheap editions as possible would latently reinforce the ideology of capitalist production.[33] Of course, printing cheap editions might also diminish the Fabians' social capital, for the Society was known for attracting the cultural elite. This elite quality showed in their aspiration to adopt an artisanal, Morrisian print style for Fabian publications. As Ian Britain notes, the Fabians had "a special 'Committee on Taste' set up in the early 1890s to consider such matters as the lay-out, typography and overall design of the tracts." They were eager to recruit "first-rate book-designers such as Crane, Emery Walker, Arthur Watts and Eric Gill, for the design tasks involved" (167). Shaw was crucial in this choice of house style. He describes how in 1886 the Fabians under his direction

shewed off our pretty prospectus with the design by Crane at the top, our stylish-looking blood-red invitation cards, and the other little smartnesses on which we then prided ourselves. . . . I think it was by no means the least of our merits that we always, as far as our means permitted, tried to make our printed documents as handsome as possible, and did our best to destroy the association between revolutionary literature and slovenly printing on paper that is nasty without being cheap. (*Fabian Society* 11–12)

The Fabians borrowed Morris's style, piggybacking on his cultural cache, but to a different effect, because of what they printed and because of the social makeup of the group.

When pondering the possibility of reaching a wide print audience beyond the social scope of their members, the Fabians supported the same strategy of permeation that they applied to politics more generally; their goal was to penetrate existing institutions with socialist ideas, not to start over with new foundations.[34] For example, the Fabian tracts, which by 1900 numbered around 100, were intended to mete out useful socialist "facts" for targeted political impact, especially on the level of municipal government. *Facts for Socialists* is the prototypical example, and as Edward Pease recalls, it was written with the idea that, although most socialist writers focused on "dissociat[ing] themselves from others" such that "any countenance . . . of the capitalist press was deemed an act of treachery," the Fabians would instead "show that on their opponents' own principles they were logically compelled to be Socialists" (70). This strategy of permeating rather than dissociating from existing institutions was central to the Fabian mission and marked a crucial distinction from the Social Democratic Federation and the Socialist League, both of which were revolutionary organizations advocating a clean sweep of governing institutions and replacement with entirely new establishments.[35] Ultimately, the Fabians thought that state-funded media, leisure, entertainment, and art would diminish the powerful capitalist influence wielded in these commercialized domains, but until that time they advocated permeating print and media outlets from the top.[36]

Shaw was the leading light in formulating these efforts, and his modus operandi is nowhere more obvious than in his rationale for the absence of a regular Fabian newspaper.

The [Social Democratic] Federation runs a newspaper called *Justice*, which has not hitherto been worth a penny to any man whose pence are so scarce as a laborer's. . . . As to a paper, we [Fabians] recognize that a workman expects for his penny a week a newspaper as big and as full of general news as any of the regular Sunday papers. Therefore our policy has been to try to induce some of these regular papers to give a column or two to Socialism. . . . I have no hesitation in saying that the effect of this policy . . . has done more for the cause than all the time and money that has been wasted on *Justice*. . . . Our mission is to Socialize the Press as we hope to Socialize Parliament and the other Estates of the realm, not to run the Press ourselves. (*Fabian Society* 23–24)

Justice was a paper that prided itself on being run by workers and depending on voluntary labor from working-class compositors to survive. But what *Justice* saw as a working-class takeover of the means of print production, Shaw saw as inefficient. Shaw claims to have successfully swayed mainstream papers in the direction of socialist and labor news, but most critics then and now have thought that he exaggerated this influence.[37]

A key difference between the Fabians and other socialist groups, evident in their divergent approaches to print, was that the Fabians were an exclusive organization not actively seeking to recruit. In *The Fabian Society: Its Early History*, Shaw addresses the question of why the Fabians did not originally join forces with the Social Democratic Federation or the Socialist League and attributes the original separation to class rather than political difference.

We were for a year or two just as Anarchistic as the Socialist League and just as insurrectionary as the Federation. It will at once be asked why . . . we did not join them instead of forming a separate society. Well, the apparent reason was that we were then middle-class all through, rank and file as well as leaders, whereas the League and the Federation were quite proletarian in their rank and file. . . . When I myself, on the point of joining the Social Democratic Federation, changed my mind and joined the Fabian instead, I was guided by no discoverable difference in program or principles, but solely by an instinctive feeling that the Fabian and not the Federation would attract the men of my own bias and intellectual habits. (4)

Other middle-class socialists, such as Morris and Carpenter, found a sui generis intellectualism in traditional aspects of working-class life such as pub culture, but Shaw tended to see working-class culture as a culture of privation, which would pass away under a socialist system.[38] Shaw kept up a tireless schedule as a political speaker in the 1880s and 1890s, including countless addresses to working-class audiences on such topics as New Unionism and the eight-hour workday, but he never really sought the literate working-class public that made up the bulk of the new reading audience for print. This audience plays a large part in Shaw and the Fabian Society's rejection of mass print culture.

The Fabian Society was, in fact, set up in such a way so as not to attract such members. In the June 1891 issue of *Fabian News*, the Executive Committee reminded members "of their responsibility for satisfying themselves that any candidates whom they propose or second for admission into the Fabian Society are thoroughly in sympathy with its principles, methods and aims" (14–15). In the 1895 *Labour Annual*, Edward Pease wrote that the Society "does not seek . . . to obtain a large membership" and that every successful candidate for admission must attend two meetings, agree to the Society's principles in writing, "find two members to guarantee the earnestness of his Socialism," and "contribute to the funds" (36). The social connections that were required for Fabian membership, as well as the financial solvency, limited the kind of members who would join the Society. This Fabian exclusivity in print and in membership was exactly what H. G. Wells attacked in his attempt to lead an internal reform of the Society in 1906. In his provocative lecture "Faults of the Fabian," Wells criticized the Society's exclusive sensibility, its failure to advertize, its "self-effacive habits," and its complex process for electing new members; he proposed more fund-raising, more literature, and more propaganda (Pease 165–66). A Fabian committee reviewed his suggestions, proposing that the *Fabian News* might be "enlarged into a weekly review addressed to the public" and that "the Society should cease to treat membership as a privilege" (169–70). But Wells ultimately left the Fabian Society, and most of his efforts were rebuffed.

In part as a result of this exclusivity, the Fabians are often thought of as antidemocratic socialists.[39] As E. P. Thompson has said, in Fabian orthodoxy "the great majority of working people are seen as passive victims," bereft of agency (*English Working Class* 12). The comment recalls Engels's critique of Harkness's novelistic naturalism, suggesting that the socialist suspicion of novels lines up to some extent with a socialist rift between middle-class groups, such as the Fabians, who advocated top-down reform, and groups such as the Social Democratic Federation, who advanced a program of working-class insurgency. Yet although this division might account for Shaw's initial attraction to the middle-class genre of the novel, it does not explain his rejection of it or his broader ambivalence toward radical print. As we have seen, for the

Fabians print retained the association with democratic ideology that it had gained in the battle for the unstamped press, the campaign against the taxes on knowledge, and other free print fights. Coupled with expanding commercial and capital controls over print at the end of the century, these associations account for Shaw's readiness to stretch beyond the era of print.

CHAPTER 3 **Living Language**
Print Drama, Live Drama,
and the Socialist Theatrical Turn

> If he had started a Kelmscott Theatre instead of the Kelmscott
> Press, I am quite confident that in a few months . . . he would
> have produced work that would within ten years have affected
> every theatre on earth.
>
> —Shaw, "William Morris as Actor and Dramatist"

A S WE SAW IN CHAPTER 2, George Bernard Shaw was a
literary socialist seeking to move beyond the radical idiom of print liberalism and beyond liberalism's
emblematic literary form—the novel. To many socialists, liberalism,
like the novel, was grounded in the idea of the independent rational
subject, who would read and absorb print alone in a state of coherent
subjectivity, whereas the theater appeared to offer an oral, live, mutual
experience, less mass-oriented but more communal than print. Socialist
Holbrook Jackson argued in a 1904 lecture to the Leeds Art Club that
the novel "could go no further, because the individualization of life had
reached its peak. The novel was dead; as life reverted to a more public
and communal state, other forms of literary expression like the drama
would predominate" (Steele 81). If the novel's unsuitability for socialism
was partly due to its roots in a middle-class creed of individual advance-
ment, the theater promised to create the kind of communal feeling that
might form the basis for a socialist public. The 12 December 1891 issue
of the *Workers' Herald: A Socialist Weekly* included an account of a lecture
by Rev. J. H. Crawford titled "A Theatre for the People"; in it Crawford

argued that "the theatre was the only place where all were swayed alike by the movements of the play—where all were touched at the same moment by the same impulse." The theater was, in short, "an institution capable of being enlisted among the social forces" (10).[1]

Martin Puchner has described the long-standing idea that theater has "a more direct relation to the social and the public spheres" than other art forms: "Anecdotes and histories about uprisings and revolutions caused by theater performances occupy a prominent place in the imagination of theater enthusiasts. And indeed, the communal gathering of a public in the theater has been used as a recurring model for the public at large" (10). Yet theater also developed within the socialist revival as a mode of containment against the outsize anonymous public being newly formed by mass print. The theater was circumscribed; it created a public but drew a wall around that public; it called forth a crowd, with all the revolutionary implications of that action, but it also contained that crowd. This dynamic was especially apparent with the emergence of the late Victorian private theatrical sphere, which provided a means for "advanced" drama to circumvent the censor but also created a semiprivate radical public. Until the Workers' Theatre Movement took hold in the 1920s—a movement that, according to Raphael Samuel, "opened up a whole new epoch . . . in the relationship of socialist movements to their theatrical auxiliaries" (Samuel et al. xix)—the socialist theater in Britain had been characterized by antipopular exclusivity.[2] In this chapter I focus on the early years of the socialist theatrical turn and the work of three key dramatists for 1880s and 1890s socialists: George Bernard Shaw, Henrik Ibsen, and Percy Bysshe Shelley. Although their work strongly influenced the development of socialist theatricality for years to come and although the radical theatergoing public that formed around their plays did sow the seeds of twentieth-century proletarian drama, the imagined audience operating in fin de siècle socialist drama was not working-class but "upper-middle class Bohemians" (Samuel et al. 50).[3]

After the death of William Morris in 1896, Shaw, in "William Morris as Actor and Dramatist," considered what might have happened if Morris "had started a Kelmscott Theatre instead of the Kelmscott Press" (215). Could Morris have pioneered a socialist reimagining of theater as he did print? His only play, *The Tables Turned; Or, Nupkins Awakened* was a hit within the small socialist community of the Socialist League, but otherwise Morris generally ignored the theater, which Shaw took as a reflection on the quality of current drama: "You would never dream of asking why Morris did not read penny novelettes, or hang his room with Christmas-number chromolithographs. We have no theatre for men like Morris" (213–14). In his 1897 piece "Not Worth Reading," Shaw compared the 1890s theatrical revival with Morris's revival of print. Both, he says, required a wholesale remaking of the conventions of the form: "When William Morris founded the Kelmscott Press, and recovered for the world the lost art of making beautiful books, he had to make his printers do exactly the opposite of what they had been taught to regard as the perfection of tasty workmanship" (114). This, Shaw says, must likewise be done with stage conventions.

Shaw was clearly inspired by the prospect of doing to the theater what Morris had done to print. Similarly, when Annie Horniman founded the Gaiety Theatre in Manchester in 1908—the first repertory theater in England, which staged copious productions of Shaw and Ibsen—she emulated Kelmscott Press in all the print documents associated with the theater. Her prospectus for the Gaiety (see Figure 17) was produced with Morrisian paper, ink colors, and effects and stressed the company's collectivist ethos: "working as they do for the art, collectively, and not individually" (*Miss Horniman's Company* 4–5).[4] W. B. Yeats's drama was also deeply influenced by Morris. Yeats had participated in Socialist League events at Morris's home in Hammersmith and had attended and admired a 17 June 1888 performance of *Tables Turned* (Wiens 21). We can see the influence of Morris's theory of print in Yeats's desire, described in his 1903 lecture "Poetry and the Living Voice," to return to the kind of oral community that existed "before printing disseminated news so far and wide, and inculcated a drab uniformity of thought and belief from which many of us now seek to escape" (qtd. in Steele 126–27).[5]

Disenchanted with the political potency of print literature in the age of mass publishing, many in the late nineteenth-century radical public turned toward theater as a potentially more effective medium. But ultimately Shaw and his fellow theatrical socialists drew an elite, exclusive public in the theatrical sphere, just as the Kelmscott Press had done in the print sphere. At the same time, the radical turn toward theater ended

Miss Horniman's Company : : :

Under the direction of Mr. B. Iden Payne

HE work of Miss Horniman's Company, under the direction of Mr. B. Iden Payne, seeks not only to afford regular playgoers an opportunity of witnessing the finest dramatic works, but also aims at drawing back to regular theatre-going all those who have lost this habit.

Its main features are :—

(*a*)   A Repertoire Theatre with regular change of programme, not wedded to any one school of dramatists, but quite catholic, embracing eventually the finest writings, both tragedy and comedy, by the best authors of all ages, with a specially widely-open door to present day writers.

(*b*)   A permanent Company of carefully chosen actors and actresses added to from time to time by special people for particular parts.

(*c*)   Intelligent and careful productions.

These are the lines on which this Company, under the Direction of Mr. B. Iden Payne, commenced their successful career at the Midland Theatre, in Manchester, and immediately won for themselves the cordial appreciation of the local Press, and the hearty support of the playgoing public.

I

Figure 17. Annie Horniman's prospectus for the Gaiety Theatre, Manchester. John Rylands Library, University of Manchester.

up following the track of early nineteenth-century print radicalism in adopting the anticensorship, free-expression credo (foundationally liberal in principle) as its primary political strategy. Indeed, despite Shaw's evident desire to transition socialism away from the liberal Enlightenment idiom, in migrating from the page to the stage, Shaw became increasingly absorbed in the late nineteenth-century version of the battle for the unstamped press; he called in 1895 for "a stage free as the Press is free and as speech is free" ("Late Censor" 54–55). The war for free print transmogrified into the war for a free stage, which borrowed its liberatory rhetoric from early nineteenth-century print radicalism but sought distinct cultural effects. If a large-scale working-class readership was at stake for early nineteenth-century print radicals, a small-scale "advanced" public was the focus of the free stage fight.

Although long dead, Percy Bysshe Shelley, bard of early nineteenth-century radicalism, also played a role in this story; the radical independent theater movement that emerged in the 1890s initially coalesced around the 1886 effort to privately stage Shelley's play *The Cenci*, which had never been staged because it could not pass the censors. In the debate surrounding this landmark production, *Cenci* advocates borrowed from a long tradition of radical arguments for free print—arguments that had been so powerful in Shelley's own day—but reoriented them toward a smaller middle-class theatrical audience of forward-thinking cultural elites. Thus the *Cenci* production and the socialist theatrical turn more broadly point to shifting ideas about literary-political influence within the radical sphere. We see the continuing influence of the old radical argument for free expression with a new focus on artistic freedom for a relatively elite group in lieu of efforts to connect with a wide cross-class audience.

Shaw, the Private Theatrical Sphere, and the Print Drama

Jonathan Rose claims that Shaw, like other "modernist" writers, sought to use literature "to maintain social distinctions in an increasingly democratic and educated society" (393). This perhaps overstates the case, but Shaw clearly thought that the mass market of newly literate readers had in many ways hurt rather than helped the political potency of print. In creating a new market of print buyers, mass literacy raised the commercial stakes in the printing industry and strengthened the commercial grip on it; Shaw believed that the liberal idea of the print sphere as an arena for free exchange was utterly corrupted by the commercial pressures within that sphere. But even apart from the question of commercial contamination, Shaw was never entirely sold on the idea of print enlightenment. His ambivalence came not only from a perception of capital's control over the free print marketplace but also from an underlying doubt that the public sphere could function as a space for what Jürgen Habermas would call communicative rationality (*Structural Transformation*). In his 1896 essay "The Illusions of Socialism," Shaw maintains that the intellect "can only be roused by an appeal to [one's] feelings and imagination" (410) and that socialism is "founded on sentimental dogma," like "all modern democratic political systems" (412). Shaw often expressed skepticism about the foundational truths of the liberal tradition; in his 1888 essay "Freedom and the State," he wrote, "So much for the theory of 'liberty.' Like other abstract superficialities it has done good service in its day. At present it is a cast off garment of eighteenth century sociology" (39).

The desire to generate a real living public was at stake in Shaw's shift from the novel to the stage, but some thought that the theatrical public that formed around his plays was too private to be a real public at all. *The Link*, a women's socialist paper published by the Twentieth Century Press (not to be confused with Annie Besant's 1880s paper *The Link*), reviewed *Fanny's First Play* in September 1911 and concluded, "It is all very, very amusing, extremely well-acted, and a clever smack at some critics. But would the author please to remember that half-a-crown as the lowest price of admission is quite a lot for some people, and . . . the public, the real public, not the Shaw public, cannot and will not see it?" (9–10). Likewise, in an otherwise positive review of *Candida*, the *Clarion* noted that the price of admission "to all parts of the house" was 1 guinea, a fee that did not dispose the audience to "the display of much enthusiasm" (6 April 1895: 107). A review of *Arms and the Man* in the *Labour Leader*, meanwhile, gushed over the socialist celebrity of the audience: "Stepniak beamed on the house from one of the stage boxes, and Mr. and Mrs. Webb were in a box on the grand tier. Graham Wallas, Olivier, Stewart Headlam, Hubert Bland, and Mrs. Sparling, were in various parts of the theatre" (28 April 1894: 3). Shaw targeted his work at an advanced guard of literary and political reformers, and as this review suggests, writing for the theater allowed him to reach that audience.

Shaw articulates his vision for just this effect in *The Quintessence of Ibsenism*, published in 1891, his first major piece of criticism and a work that served as the hinge between his careers as a novelist and as a playwright. Acclaiming Henrik Ibsen's dramas, Shaw charts a progressive theory of cultural transformation that envisions incremental advancements over time: "It has often been said that political parties progress serpent-wise, the tail being to-day where the head was formerly, yet never overtaking the head. The same figure may be applied to grades of playgoers, with the reminder that this sort of serpent grows at the head and drops off joints of his tail as he glides along" (298–99). A play need not target a wide public—*The Link's* "real public"—to have wide effect, only the public's "head." This was crucial theoretical grounding in Shaw's turn to the theater.

Of course, Shaw's turn from print to the theater was really not so much a turn as an amalgamation, a bringing together of the two media. As discussed in Chapter 2, his print literature attempts to inculcate the dialogic, performative qualities of the stage, whereas in developing the drama as a print genre for reading, Shaw used his frustration with print to generate a new form of print, to unite the theatrical and print spheres. *Quintessence* was Shaw's first major attempt to merge print, theater, and live voice in one format. It was a work about the theater as a place of significant political debate, originally spoken in live voice to the "private public" of the Fabian Society and later published to the world in print—the first book on Ibsen published in English.[6] *Quintessence* originated in the 1890 Fabian Society lecture series "Socialism in Contemporary Literature" (a flyer advertising the series is pictured in Figure 18). That Shaw chose to speak on Ibsen and not on the socialist novel, a subject tackled by Hubert Bland, is itself suggestive. In his preface to *Quintessence*, Shaw explains that Bland "undertook to read all the Socialist novels of the day," which was "a desperate failure" (207). Shaw gave his Ibsen paper two weeks after Bland's lecture, which positioned Shaw's advocacy of Ibsen as a remedy for the failures of the socialist novel.

Shaw's Ibsen lecture caused a socialist sensation. The minutes from the meeting record that "the effect on the packed audience was overwhelming" (Pease 94–95). Afterward, the lecture prompted lively debate in *Seed Time*, the journal for the Fellowship of the New Life, a middle-class socialist group that shared origins and members with the Fabian Society. In the October 1890 issue, "Individualism as Masquerade," by "A Fabian," appeared; the author expressed outrage at Shaw's lecture:

𝔉𝔞𝔟𝔦𝔞𝔫 𝔖𝔬𝔠𝔦𝔢𝔱𝔶.

A Course of Seven Lectures

on

SOCIALISM in CONTEMPORARY LITERATURE

will be given in

The French Chamber, St. James' Restaurant, W.

On *FRIDAY EVENINGS*, at 8 o'clock.

1890.

April 18	Emile Zola	SYDNEY OLIVIER
May 2	William Morris	ERNEST RADFORD
May 16	Bax, Kirkup, Gronlund and Bellamy	A. R. DRYHURST
June 6	Tolstoi, Tchernychewsky and the Russian School ...	EDWARD R. PEASE
June 20	Edward Carpenter and Karl Pearson	WILLIAM BOULTING
July 4	Recent English Socialistic Novels	HUBERT BLAND
July 18	Henrik Ibsen	G. BERNARD SHAW

(*Admission Free.--Entrance from Piccadilly.*)

These lectures are intended to illustrate certain Socialistic tendencies in recent literature. Some of them will deal with the writings of avowed Socialists, who have embodied in books their ideas of an amended social system, either as deliberately planned Utopias, or as criticisms of one aspect or another of the existing state of Society and of the struggle for a better; others with writers who, in novel or drama, have depicted the anomalies and injustice of things as they are, indicating, more or less, the direction in which they look for amendment.

For all information relating to the Fabian Society, apply to the Secretary, E. R. PEASE,

2, Hyde Park Mansions, W.

Figure 18. Flyer for the Fabian Society lecture series "Socialism in Contemporary Literature." Fabian Society Archive, Library of the London School of Economics and Political Science.

"Mr. Shaw's position, as I understand it, is one of pure, unadulterated individualism; and that he should be taken by himself and others for a leader in the Socialist movement is the most ironical feature of the present singular and bewildering situation" (11–12). In the January 1891 issue Henry Salt defended Shaw against this attack: "Mr. Shaw is *not* an individualist . . . but an avowed and particularly out-spoken socialist."

"A Fabian" had confused "the lower commercial individualism" with "the higher intellectual individualism—the claim for free development of distinctive character—which socialists . . . admit to be of the utmost importance" (12–13). The debate previewed many Shavian controversies to come, but it also positioned radical drama as a new space for meaningful political-literary intervention.

In analyzing Ibsen's controversial dramas, Shaw saw his own future in the collective space of the theater rather than the liberal space of print. Shaw's socialist critique of the novel, articulated in his own novels, encourages us to view his abandonment of novel writing for playwriting as an attempt to move beyond a politically unfruitful mode of print literature. Plays offered a new opportunity through a new configuration in the dramatic world that resembled the slow print dynamic of the radical press: the private theatrical society. Through groups such as the Independent Theatre, the Stage Society, or the Pioneer Players, Shaw's plays would reach advanced audiences even if they could not obtain a license from the censor. Even more significantly, they could reach these audiences despite the soft censorship imposed by capitalism and the need to make a profit in a commercial theatrical run.[7] But if the private theatrical society offered refuge from state censorship and the culture industry, it also functioned as what Puchner calls "a deliberate retreat from a mass public into an intimate and private space" (19–20). The private stage offered a public that Shaw could see, know, grasp, and contain within the space of the theater, in contradistinction to the increasingly anonymous author-reader relations in the mass print marketplace. For Shaw the new forum of the private theatrical society was necessary for the rise of intellectual drama as a challenge to the literary form of the novel: "It is now so well understood that only plays of the commonest idealist type can be sure of a license in London, that the novel and not the drama is the form adopted as a matter of course" (*Quintessence* 301). Stage licensing was the key hindrance to the development of a radical drama, but the private theatrical society circumvented this necessity.

Just as Shaw's early novels ran in socialist magazines, his early plays would debut in private stagings—the theatrical counterpart to journals such as *To-Day*. Shaw's early plays indeed appear to be directed toward a public created by the radical press. His first play, *Widowers' Houses*, was staged by J. T. Grein's Independent Theatre, a key early stage society that relied on unpaid professional actors, a membership that never surpassed 175 people, and an income of only £400 a year (Kennedy 134). According to Grein's preface to the first printed edition of *Widowers' Houses*, which he also edited, audiences likened the play to "a socialist pamphlet in three-act form" (vi). In the same volume Shaw insists the play is not "a pamphlet in dialogue" (xix) but a "bluebook play" and that "the dramatized or novelized bluebook or Fabian Essay (so to speak) has ten times as much chance of success as the mere romance" (113). This dramatized blue book, Shaw says in his preface to the volume, is "intended to induce people to vote on the Progressive side at the next County Council in London" (xix). The comparison to a blue book and the baldly electoral aims claimed for the play indicate that Shaw imagined it as a theatrical remediation of the matter of the radical press.

That government-produced blue books might potentially serve as a neutral substitute for the capitalist press was the hope of some in the radical sphere. The 1896 *Labour Annual* offered an index of blue books, "Official and Parliamentary Publications," to make them "better known by social reformers" and to alleviate "their dullness and heaviness" (150). "Blue Books, &c., for Public Libraries," which appeared in the 1901 *Reformers' Year Book*, called for a parliamentary measure requiring "the automatic supply of Government publications to Public Libraries" because the "electorate needs more trustworthy sources of political information than the Press" (129). Clearly, for some, blue books held the promise of Enlightenment transparency on the part of the state, but they were not depicted as such in *Widowers' Houses*. When Sartorius, the slumlord, learns of the accusations made against him in a government housing report, he says, "I dont care that for my name being in bluebooks. My friends dont read them; and I'm neither a Cabinet Minister nor a candidate for Parliament" (82). In fact, as Oz Frankel has argued, there was at this time a growing "perception that government was manufacturing reams of purposeless, or worse, self-indulgent printed matter" (42), "subvert[ing] the demand for transparency by complying with it excessively. The state is supposedly telling us everything it can in order to deceive us not by lying but by divulging the truth in its unreadable entirety" (69). That blue books had to be purchased—and were not supplied free to public libraries—was a further detriment to their usability. In the 1830s radical press tremendous faith had been placed in the idea that abundant information has a cleansing effect, that it can wipe out and prevent corruption (Hollis 286). By the end of the century Fabian leaders Beatrice and Sidney Webb regarded print "transparency" on the part of the state "first and foremost as a political tool" (Frankel 139). Keeping in mind this Fabian critique of print statism and the play's critique of blue books as irrelevant to men like Sartorius, Shaw's designation of *Widowers' Houses* as a "bluebook play" suggests that he saw the radical drama taking over where print enlightenment had failed. His play achieves "transparency" not by claiming disinterest where it does not exist but by proudly declaring its manipulative ends: "to induce people to vote on the Progressive side at the next County Council in London" (xix).

A crucial point at stake here, however, is that the play's meaning actually *depends* on such parallels with print culture. It depends on audience familiarity with blue books, pamphlets, and other print documentation of "the housing question." Moreover, debate about *Widowers' Houses* extended into radical print culture by way of the radical press and Grein's edition, which was the first in a planned print series of radical dramas. *Justice* reviewed this print edition on 20 May 1893, in a review titled "Stage Socialism," and although the review was negative—the reviewer thought that Shaw "dealt too lightly with the evils he aims at exposing"—it presented another opportunity to reflect in print on the political power of the stage: "The utility of the stage as a means of exposing the intrinsic rottenness of modern society, and of propagating the truths of Socialism, cannot well be over-estimated" (6). In turning from the novel to the theater, Shaw was not so much abandoning print as merging print and dramatic media to create a new political-literary forum with the capacity for a fresh impact. In this sense antiprint sentiment was actually productive of new print forms: the print drama.

Grein produced his print edition of *Widowers' Houses* in 1893, envisioning it as the first in the Independent Theatre Series of Plays, which would print radical dramas after their appearance at the Independent Theatre. In the end only three such plays were published, but Grein's preface to the series was a mini-manifesto for the merging of radical theater and radical print: "The works produced by the Independent Theatre are not

merely plays to be seen: they are plays to be read. They belong to Literature as well as to Drama; and I should consider the work of the Independent Theatre only half done if it did not succeed in making its repertory
known throughout the country to those who are out of reach of its performances" (v–vi). This was a point that Shaw made too; the reproducibility of print was the problem with print, because it aligned print with
capitalist mass production, but it also represented print's advantage over
drama: "For the sake of the unhappy prisoners of the home," Shaw wrote,
"let my plays be printed as well as acted" ("Mainly About Myself" 19).

Shaw's second play, *The Philanderer*, was also written for the Independent Theatre (although Grein opted not to run the sexually controversial
play, thereby denting Shaw's optimism about the autonomy of the private
theatrical sphere). Like *Widowers' Houses*, *The Philanderer* makes a point
of its coterie status and its intimate knowledge of its own audience. Much
of the play's action takes place at the "Ibsen Club," a club for those with
"advanced" views and a subtle reminder that Grein founded the Independent Theatre in 1891 by staging a private performance of Ibsen's *Ghosts*,
a play that would not pass the censor until 1914. Outside the radical
public the *Ghosts* performance had sparked a magnificent outcry: "Never
has English criticism gone through such a month as March, 1891. The
press became fairly hysterical and screamed aloud in its rage. The most
staid papers lost all sense of decorum and . . . joined in the contagious
orgy of abuse" (Franc 37). In a pointed reference to this foundational
performance, the plot of *The Philanderer* turns on an imaginary afflic-
tion called Paramore's disease, a pun on paramour's disease, referencing
the venereal disease in *Ghosts* that was a major factor in its censorship.
As these inside jokes suggest, *The Philanderer* is almost literally a play
for those in the Ibsen Club—which is to say, the Independent Theatre.

Candida, another early Shaw play, also appeals to a delimited counterpublic constituted by radical print and radical theater. It initially appeared in a one-off performance by the Independent Theatre in 1897, but
the newly founded Stage Society mounted a more extensive production
in 1900. The Stage Society was launched in 1899 at the London home
of Frederick Whelen, a member of the Fabian Executive Committee.
Whelen, with fellow Fabians Walter Crane and Charles Charrington,
invited "a select group of people known to be interested" to participate.

The Stage Society "was never an official part of the Fabian Society" but was "in effect, an affiliate organization . . . depending for much of its support, in its early days at least, on a 'Fabian public'" (Britain 173–74). Stage Society members paid a yearly subscription of 2 guineas to attend what were called meetings rather than performances. The maximum membership was raised from 300 to 500 in the summer of 1900; by 1907 it would reach 1,200 (Kennedy 135). Actors received only nominal pay, and no scenery was used on stage (Holroyd 2: 92).

Befitting this purposefully exclusive, anticommercial setting, *Candida* interpellates its audience as a subcultural public characterized by a shared socialist canon. Books feature prominently in the play's mise-en-scène, and Shaw's stage directions highlight the print library of Reverend Morell, a socialist clergyman: "a yellow backed *Progress and Poverty* [Henry George's study of land nationalization], *Fabian Essays*, *A Dream of John Ball*, Marx's *Capital*, and half a dozen other literary landmarks in Socialism" (94). Specific titles would be difficult to see in a stage production; the details appeal primarily to those who would be reading the play in print. A few pages into this first scene, Morell's secretary rattles off the reverend's speaking schedule for the week, including such venues as the Tower Hamlets Radical Club, the English Land Restoration League, the Greenwich branch of the Independent Labour Party, and the Mile End branch of the Social Democratic Federation (96)—the oral counterparts to the books on Morell's bookcase. Then we return to print: Morell opens the new issue of the *Church Reformer* "and glances through Mr Stewart Headlam's leader and the Guild of St. Matthew news" (97). (The Guild of St. Matthew was the major outlet of Christian Socialism, led by Stewart Headlam.) *Candida* sits within a real-life, existing socialist subculture constituted by overlapping oral and print discourse; Shaw's play, appearing in print and on stage, was itself part of this discourse.

Candida is a play for insiders, for those already well versed in socialist countercultural discourse, but it also focuses on an overabundance of language without effect, suggesting Shaw's continuing strikes against the media culture of overprint at stake in his early novels. The character Marchbanks decries Reverend Morell's long-winded pontification: "Everlasting preaching! preaching! words! words! words!" (128). Morell himself tires of a constant barrage of speaking invitations, likening himself to one of the era's new audio technologies: "They think I am a talking machine to be turned on for their pleasure" (138). Prossy, his secretary, complains that she is being asked to type too fast: "Much too fast. You know I cant do more than ninety words a minute" (151). *Candida* emphasizes a surfeit of words in modern mass media culture, stripping language of its power and effectiveness. Both Morell and Prossy (like Eliza Doolittle a few years later) complain of instrumentalization, of being reduced to word machines rather than speaking subjects, an obvious parallel with Marx's critique of dehumanizing labor under industrial capitalism. Shaw connects Marx's critique of alienation and industrial labor to the media ecology of the fin de siècle, the fast-paced world of mechanized modern media: typewriters, phonographs, and "words! words! words!"

You Never Can Tell, another early Shaw play, debuted in 1899 as the Stage Society's inaugural production and makes a similar critique of the culture of overprint. At the play's outset the twins Phil and Dolly—themselves a figure for overproductive reproducibility—explain that their mother is "the celebrated Mrs Lanfrey Clandon, an authoress of great repute." In Madeira, where they live, "no household is complete without her works. We came to England to get away from them." The works are the "Twentieth Century Treatises" and focus on such topics as "Twentieth Century Cooking," "Twentieth Century Clothing," and "Twentieth Century Conduct." The series encapsulates Shaw's disparaging view of mass-market print; topics are apparently chosen according to their alliterative value rather than the author's expertise, and the author herself, Mrs. Clandon, exemplifies how modern celebrity authorship actually obscures the person whom it purports to make more familiar. Well loved by her readers, Mrs. Clandon is not nearly so up-to-date as her book titles indicate. She fancies herself a radical woman but still thinks that married women's property, Darwin, Mill, and Huxley constitute revolutionary opinions. Her ex-husband tells her, "There is only one place in all England where your opinions would still pass as advanced . . . the theatre" (241). Having formulated a critique of mass print culture, Shaw takes the opportunity to make a metatheatrical crack at the mainstream theatergoing public, from which viewers of this play might thereby distinguish themselves.

Page and Stage

As these examples suggest, Shaw found the advanced, live, contained public constituted by private theatrical societies to be fertile ground for extending his critique of capitalist print and the culture of overprint exemplified by the novel. However, his transition from page to stage did not signify a thoroughgoing abandonment of print but an effort to move radical print culture into the live venue of theater and to draw on the tangible audience of the theater to constitute a new reading public. Shortly after his move into drama, Shaw attempted to reinvigorate print as a political medium by invigorating drama as a genre for the reading public. Shaw was not the first person to have the idea of publishing radical drama in print form—Ibsen's plays were being read in Britain at this time, as I discuss later in this chapter—but except for acting editions, plays written for the stage were not usually printed. This mode of publication had its disadvantages. As Shaw explained, "The presentation of plays through the literary medium has not yet become an art; and the result is that it is very difficult to induce the English public to buy and read plays" ("Mainly About Myself" 23). But the printed drama also offered an opportunity in its unfamiliarity as a literary mode and in its connection to the audiences of the private theatrical societies. The veil of print in this case offered nothing less than "the institution of a new art" (24).

Shaw would apply the Morrisian aesthetic that he brought to bear on *Fabian Essays in Socialism*, discussed in Chapter 2, to the print publication of his early plays. His volumes *Plays Pleasant* and *Plays Unpleasant*—which included *Arms and the Man, Candida, You Never Can Tell,* and *The Man of Destiny* in *Plays Pleasant* and *Widowers' Houses, The Philanderer,* and *Mrs Warren's Profession* in *Plays Unpleasant*—use print form to disavow the logic of mass production that Shaw read between the lines of the cheaply printed page. By the time these volumes were published together in 1898, Shaw had been deeply influenced by the print principles that Morris had put into practice at Kelmscott Press, and *Plays Pleasant* and *Plays Unpleasant* were published with Morris-style layout, margins, and bindings (see Figure 19). Shaw, like Morris, sought out the blackest ink he could find; he "encouraged tightly knit spacing within a word, and even spacing between words" (Kelly 42), following Morris, who had expressed horror at the "ugly rivers" of white space that rich man's fancy and get the benefit of his money by marrying him? — as if a marriage ceremony could make any difference in the right or wrong of the thing! Oh, the hypocrisy of the world makes me sick! Liz and I had to work and save and calculate just like other people; elseways we should be as poor as any good-for-nothing, drunken waster of a woman that thinks her luck will last for ever. [*With great energy*] I despise such people : theyve no character; and if theres a thing I hate in a woman, it's want of character.

VIVIE. Come now, mother : frankly! Isnt it part of what you call character in a woman that she should greatly dislike such a way of making money?

MRS WARREN. Why, of course. Everybody dislikes having to work and make money; but they have to do it all the same. I'm sure Ive often pitied a poor girl, tired out and in low spirits, having to try to please some man that she doesnt care two straws for — some half-drunken fool that thinks he's making himself agreeable when he's teasing and worrying and disgusting a woman so that hardly any money could pay her for putting up with it. But she has to bear with disagreeables and take the rough with the smooth, just like a nurse in a hospital or anyone else. It's not work that any woman would do for pleasure, goodness knows; though to hear the pious people talk you would suppose it was a bed of roses.

VIVIE. Still you consider it worth while. It pays.

MRS WARREN. Of course it's worth while to a poor girl, if she can resist temptation and is good-looking and well conducted and sensible. It's far better than any other employment open to her. I always thought that oughtnt to be. It cant be right, Vivie, that there shouldnt be better opportunities for women. I stick to that : it's wrong. But it's so, right or wrong; and a girl must make the best of it. But of course it's not worth while for a lady. If you took to it youd be a fool; but I should have been a fool if I'd taken to anything else.

Figure 19. From George Bernard Shaw's *Plays Unpleasant* (1898).

ran through a poorly typeset block of text (Morris, "Note" 77). Still, Shaw's printed plays depart from Morrisian principle in key respects, such as the use of monotype (Holroyd 1: 402–3) and cheaper, though not cheap, paper (Kelly 41). Moreover, Shaw's original idea for publishing the plays, although it proved impracticable, would have been as much a critique of Morris as an homage: Shaw had wanted to publish *Plays Pleasant* and *Plays Unpleasant* in one volume, "printing the 'Unpleasant' on light brown paper with an ugly print face and the 'Pleasant' ones on white paper in the best Kelmscott style" (Holroyd 1: 404). He was not able to publish this bifurcated volume, but its conception suggests both the influence of Morris, in the use of print form to make meaning, and a discomfort with Morrisian aestheticism. Shaw claimed that his own "attempts at Art for Art's sake" were "like hammering tenpenny nails into sheets of notepaper" ("Who I Am" 448). He wanted his volumes to aesthetically resist mass-produced form, like Morris's, but he did not want aesthetics to become their final end.

One means by which Shaw distinguished his print work from mass print culture without veering too far into aestheticism was his distinctive system of orthography. The *Pleasant* and *Unpleasant* volumes call attention to their form and question linguistic practice by using, for example, the obsolete "shew" for "show" and by eliminating the apostrophe in contractions, as in "I dont want to be worthless. I shouldnt enjoy trotting about the park . . . or being bored at the opera to shew off a shopwindowful of diamonds" (*Mrs Warren* 158). This was a technique that Shaw made more liberal use of in his printed plays than in his novels; although some of his serialized novels use eccentric orthography (such as the use of "dont" in *The Irrational Knot*, originally serialized in *Our Corner*), others do not (*An Unsocial Socialist*, as it appears in *To-Day*, uses regular apostrophes in contractions), and none are as conspicuous about this as the plays.

W. B. Worthen argues that Shaw's attentions to orthography and page design "inevitably represent the identity of drama in the age of print: they frame the mise-en-page as a site of performance," positioning drama squarely within the larger set of print culture (*Print* 11). But in his preface to *Plays Unpleasant*, Shaw suggests that part of his challenge in printing the plays is inherent in written language, because it is impossible to convey within print the distinctive power of live language on the stage: "The art of letters . . . is still in its infancy as a technical speech notation: for example, there are fifty ways of saying Yes, and five hundred of saying No, but only one way of writing them down" ("Mainly About Myself" 25). In commingling oral and print forms by constructing a drama for the page, Shaw sought to improve the efficacy of the written word by bending the rules of orthography—putting extra spaces between the letters of emphasized words, for example—and by advocating phonetic spelling. Thus, whereas Worthen sees the late nineteenth-century rise of printed drama as symptomatic of "print's final achievement" at the zenith of print culture (*Print* 9), it is equally symptomatic of cracks in the ideology of print.

G. K. Chesterton called Shaw's interest in spelling reform a "mad imp of modernity" (64). In fact, a small radical community had formed over the issue, and impractical as it may now seem, spelling reform was at heart a progressive, cosmopolitan movement. The goal was to ease literacy and educational schemes by making the English language simpler to master. *Home Links*, a communistic journal, was a strong advocate of spelling reform, font reform, and the development of a universal language. Its 20 April 1899 issue notes that a new feature of the magazine will be "specimen articles of an international, uniform, easy system of spelling for the English, French and German Languages . . . together with the elementary grammatical outlines and scientific structures of . . . a proposed universal language" (184). The 1 December 1899 issue includes a feature on "International Language," promising futures samples of Esperanto (225), and a feature on an "International, Uniform, Easy, Phonetic System of Spelling," as well as "a new system of 𝕽oman-𝕲othic 𝕷etters" "calculated to supersede not only those of our letter-press in general use, but those also that have been designed by the late William Morris" (226–27). In 1896 the *Labour Annual* listed in its annual directory of reform societies the "Orthografic Union," whose mission was "to secure the simplification of English orthografy" (27). In 1902 the *Reformers' Year Book* printed an article titled "Spelling Reform," "Ritn in simplified spelling," that began: "The anomalis and inconsistencis of English spelling constitute such a hevy handicap to our children in their studis and to our nation in its forein comunications that the regularizing of our orthografy is wel werthy the efforts of every tru reformer" (27).

The radical rage for new print forms was obviously not confined to Morris and Shaw. Although Shaw did not go so far as the Orthografic Union in his own orthographic radicalism, his moves in this direction, especially evident in *Plays Pleasant* and *Plays Unpleasant*, defamiliarize the print experience for readers. Such defamiliarization served as a baseline condition for socialist efforts to reinvigorate print as a political medium: Morris disrupted the transparency of print with Kelmscott craftsmanship, and Shaw did it by tweaking orthographic convention. Reviewers of *Plays Pleasant* and *Plays Unpleasant* did not always understand the stakes of this experimentation, but Shaw took care to publicly advocate the rationale for his philosophy of orthography and to connect it to Morris's principles of print. In an April 1898 letter to the *Glasgow Herald*, Shaw replied to a skeptical reviewer: "Literary men never seem to think of the immense difference these details make in the appearance of a block of letterpress, in spite of the lessons of that great author and printer, William Morris, who thought nothing of rewriting a line solely to make it 'justify' prettily in print" (*Agitations* 42). Following Morris, Shaw asserts a system of value—in this case, aesthetic value—that trumps the institutional practices of capitalist print, and he rejects a utilitarian notion of print wherein content is all and form is immaterial.[8] In Shaw's plays formal experimentation on the level of the printed page met experimentation on the level of genre: the merging of print and dramatic form.

In some ways Shaw's merging of radical theater and print is most evident in *Man and Superman*, which Shaw published himself in 1903. The play is typically viewed (along with *Back to Methuselah*) as the most print oriented, as opposed to performance oriented, of all his plays, but it was staged for the first time in 1905 by the Stage Society and has been successfully staged many times since. The drama appears on paper almost as a dare to directors who might try to mount a production. It includes tremendously long stage directions and a long third act known as "Don Juan in Hell," made up almost entirely of oral debate. The play, itself dauntingly long, is accompanied by a manifesto, *The Revolutionist's Handbook*, ostensibly written by the play's protagonist, and an "epistle dedicatory," which situates the drama from the outset in the world of written exchange. Altogether, with dedicatory epistle, four acts, *The*

Revolutionist's Handbook, and the "Maxims for Revolutionists" appended to the *Handbook*, the entire text is about three times as long as Shaw's other plays. It appears to be a creature of print rather than the stage.

Yet *Man and Superman* also suggests the limitations of print, demonstrating how Shaw used antiprint sentiment to generate the new print form of the drama for reading. John Tanner, the play's central character, is a political agitator and propagandist. His *Revolutionist's Handbook*, included as a supplement to the printed version of the play, reveals the print manifesto to be an exhausted and ineffective political mechanism. In a culture of mass print, with an overabundance of commercial publications to compete against, radical print cannot attract an audience. Shaw says as much in his epistolary preface, after a few requisite pages on the vital role of the critic in a democratic society: "But I hear you asking me in alarm whether I have actually put all this tub thumping into a Don Juan comedy. I have not. I have only made my Don Juan a political pamphleteer, and given you his pamphlet in full by way of appendix. You will find it at the end of the book" (18). Print dissent is reduced to an appendix, and Shaw is reduced to slipping the medicine of politics in with the sugar of romantic comedy. Just as Tanner, who calls for the abolition of marriage, will ultimately succumb to Ann Whitefield and agree to marry her, so will Shaw—his authorial counterpart—submit to the marriage plot at the end of the play. As one character says, "You must cower before the wedding ring like the rest of us" (68).

Conventional ending notwithstanding, *Man and Superman* includes a great deal of political reflection, but it also implies that radical print is a dead medium for such reflection. *The Revolutionist's Handbook*, an appendix that would not be performed in a staged version of the play, expresses Shaw's sense of print's political futility. The pamphlet begins by establishing that "revolutions have never lightened the burden of tyranny: they have only shifted it to another shoulder" (178). Lest this antirevolutionary language be confused for Fabian gradualism, the pamphlet is equally skeptical of progressive reform, and Tanner accuses the Fabian Society of "eliminating the element of intimidation from the Socialist agitation," thus "sav[ing] the existing order from the only method of attack it really fears" (198). If Tanner is a figure for the ineffectual radical press, then Ann, the predator who has him in her sights, is a figure for the indifferent mass public that the radical writer cannot reach: "She has the law on her side; she has popular sentiment on her side; she has plenty of money and no conscience" (38). Ramsden, the paternal authority figure of the play, likewise represents this public, despite his protests against being treated "as if I were a mere member of the British public. I detest its prejudices; I scorn its narrowness; I demand the right to think for myself" (41), but this last declaration is exactly what he cannot do. Freedom, says the Devil in Act III, is a false consciousness, an illusion created by the press and the government: "Englishmen never will be slaves: they are free to do whatever the Government and public opinion allow them to do" (115).

In *Man and Superman*, as in his 1890s plays that would make up *Plays Pleasant* and *Plays Unpleasant*, Shaw uses diverse inventive means of merging print and theatrical form to create a hybrid literary drama with a sharp political edge. *Man* is not essentially print based or performance based but is premised on the crossing of the two domains. After serializing four novels in the radical press, Shaw turned away from the print culture of novels and radical newspapers and took to revising the drama on the page and the stage as a new avenue for literary-political intervention. Implicit in this was a turn toward the dialogic, performative ethos of the drama, but at the same time, evident in this choice is Shaw's desire for a more contained counterpublic audience than late nineteenth-century print could offer.

Perfect Ibsenites

Although Shaw did not seek a wide working-class audience for his plays, it was not the case that no socialists thought such an audience would appreciate and benefit from the new radical drama of the 1890s. In the 23 May 1891 issue of *Workers' Cry*, J. Runciman in "Art for the Workers" urged readers to see Ibsen's *Hedda Gabler*, a play that Runciman considers "as much an expression of the longing for fuller, nobler, freer life as is the demand for an Eight Hours' Bill" (13). *Workers' Cry* was a socialist paper aimed at a working-class audience, and Runciman was a journalist of humble origins who possessed, according to W. T. Stead, "the materials out of which an English Zola might have been made," had he not died before age 40 (xxi). Runciman says he used to think that the stage drama had been ruined by commercialism, its authors having "become mere bread earning machines competing in the open market," but he changed his mind after Shaw's famous lecture on Ibsen (the lecture that became the *Quintessence*). With *Hedda Gabler*, Runciman's antitheatrical prejudice is "blown to pieces," and he declares, "Every worker should pay his shilling and see it" (13). Runciman connects the dots between *Hedda Gabler* and the Eight Hours Bill, but many readers were skeptical of this vision of Ibsen as the cornerstone of a new democratic art. A week later, in the 30 May issue, Runciman reports having "been told that it is not much use talking about Ibsen in a paper read by 'workers'" (9).

Ibsen was a hot topic in the socialist press even before Shaw presented his landmark 1890 Fabian lecture, the lecture that sparked Runciman's dramatic conversion. Five years earlier, in 1885, the socialist journal *To-Day* had serialized the first English translation of Ibsen's provocative drama *Ghosts*, translated by Henrietta Lord. This printing of the scandalous, previously unavailable play, which would be denied a license for performance in 1891, was perhaps the first major instance of the radical press venturing into the territory of radical drama. Before 1885 Ibsen had already drawn a few socialist fans in England; Henrietta Lord published a translation of *A Doll's House* under the title *Nora* in 1882, and it was this translation that created the first sparks of socialist Ibsenism in England. Edmund Gosse may have been the first to translate Ibsen into English, but Lord translated him for radicals, depicting him in the preface to her 1882 volume as a visionary who sees "the friendly dawning promise for all our retarded human development . . . the daylight side of the future" (28). The first English staging of *A Doll's House* was far less in tune with radical audiences than Lord's print version, however. *Breaking a Butterfly*, a bowdlerized version, had a short, ignominious run in London in 1884. Edward Aveling printed an excoriating review in *To-Day*, outraged that the adapters "carefully conventionalized the startling original, placed the setting in England, and supplied a radiantly happy ending" (June 1884: 474). The play "was said to be founded on Ibsen's 'Nora.' A better description would have been 'foundered on Ibsen's Nora'" (473).

Many late Victorian socialists first encountered Ibsen—the unexpurgated Ibsen—in print rather than on stage, but his earliest adopters formed a small socialist circle who shared Ibsen through private at-home readings before his work was widely known or available.[9] As Tracy Davis notes, "Social contacts were important in spreading the message about Ibsen. One important Ibsenite clique, consisting of Eleanor Marx Aveling . . . , Edward Aveling, and Olive Schreiner, inspired a later member, Havelock Ellis, to edit a volume of plays" (27). Ellis's volume—including *An Enemy of the People*, *The Pillars of Society*, and *Ghosts*, translated respectively by Eleanor Marx, William Archer, and Lord—was published in 1888, three years after *To-Day's* serialization of *Ghosts*. In his preface to the volume, Ellis presents Ibsen as "the most revolutionary of modern writers" who "can never be genuinely popular," but he assures readers that "the ideas and instincts . . . which inspire his art, are of the kind that penetrate men's minds slowly. Yet they penetrate surely, and are proclaimed at length in the market-place" (xxix–xxx). All of this took place before the first public staging of *A Doll's House* in June 1889, an event that has sometimes been taken as the origin point for socialist Ibsenism.[10]

This group of socialists took Ibsen's plays seriously as harbingers of a new literary and political age. Following Lord's 1882 publication of *Nora*, Eleanor Marx was so enthusiastic that she learned Norwegian to translate Ibsen's plays (Ellis, Preface xxx), and she organized a private reading of *A Doll's House* in January 1886, which proved definitive in its influence. Shaw took part in the reading, which set him on the path toward writing *The Quintessence of Ibsenism*, although he would later claim in his 1905 preface to *The Irrational Knot* that his novels had actually done Ibsen before Ibsen.

When Miss Lord's translation of A Doll's House appeared in the eighteen-eighties, and so excited some of my Socialist friends that they got up a private reading of it in which I was cast for the part of Krogstad, its novelty as a morally original study of a marriage did not stagger me as it staggered Europe. I had made a morally original study of a marriage myself [*The Irrational Knot*]. . . . I chattered and ate caramels in the back drawing-room (our green-room) whilst Eleanor Marx, as Nora, brought Helmer to book at the other side of the folding doors. (19)

Shaw claims to have been unruffled by "the door slam heard 'round the world," but as Sally Ledger has argued, "This private performance of *A Doll's House* proved to be an auspicious occasion for what emerged in the 1880s and 1890s as 'Ibsenism', a political and cultural formation consisting of Marxists, socialists, Fabians, and feminists, who jointly hailed Ibsen as spokesman for their various causes" ("Ibsen" 80).

Readers of the radical press, even those who never took part in at-home readings among the socialist elite, would certainly have heard about Ibsen through dramatic and literary reviews. For example, the *Radical Leader*, a London paper that aimed at an audience of Radical (not socialist) workers, reviewed the 1888 Ibsen edition edited by Ellis in its "Book Chat" column. The enthusiastic reviewer presumes the volume will be of interest to the paper's working-class readers: "These dramas deal with social problems of the highest moment in a spirit at once scientific and poetic" (8 September 1888: 5). Three years earlier, just after *Ghosts* had completed its serial run in *To-Day*, the 7 March 1885 issue of *Justice* was less convinced. Its review of the serialized drama is skeptical of the play's overall value but emphasizes the potentially stimulating political effects of its shock factor.

'Ghosts' . . . is a ghastly drama, and to us the action of the hero or the victim seem physiologically and psychologically incorrect. But there is no denying the power of the play. . . . Ibsen has rather hinted at possibilities in this direction than worked out successfully a great idea. . . . Still, in these days of timidity and mediocrity we welcome any attempt at revolt against the mere boudoir school of drama or melodrama. (3)

The reviewer praises *Ghosts*' assault on convention but is dissatisfied with its handling of the determinism of social conditions; this connects back to the central critical problem at stake in the socialist novel.

The 1896 *Labour Annual* included Ibsen in its annual biography of social reformers, and, like *Justice*, it suggests that the political power of Ibsen's plays is in their shock value: "More controversy has arisen over his dramas than has attended any other dramatist of our era, and that alone may be taken as evidence of his originality and power" (204). This tendency on the part of the radical press to emphasize the tonic political effects of Ibsen's shocking content and to privilege censorable literary material suggests how the logic of free print and the radical Enlightenment argument for free expression continued to direct much radical thought about literary-political relations. Ibsen himself was not a declared socialist, but he was claimed by the socialists, a difficulty that the *Labour Annual* evaded by calling him "one of the leaders of the new thought, which is tinged so deeply with Socialism," and by assuring readers that, "according to Havelock Ellis, Ibsen, in private conversation, describes himself as a Socialist, though he has not identified himself with any definite school of Socialism." (The citation, though not acknowledged, is from Ellis's preface to his 1888 volume [xii]). Ibsen, the *Labour Annual* concludes, "has securely won his place amongst thinking playgoers" (203–4).

That Ibsen required, perhaps, more than just "thinking" but a specific kind of thinking that came from practice and training in literary response was a matter of concern to H. H. Sparling in his review of two plays, George Moore's *Strike at Arlingford* and Ibsen's *Master Builder*, for the *Workman's Times* on 4 March 1893. *Workman's Times* was a socialist newspaper associated with the Independent Labour Party, edited by Joseph Burgess, and aimed at trade unionists. Sparling's review finds Moore's play too conventional (the characters "might have walked straight out of a *Family Herald* supplement") and fears that Ibsen's play, although appreciated, strays too far in the other direction: It "is symbolic to the ninth degree, and will take some watching as it goes along to pluck the heart out of its mystery" (3). Sparling, previously the subeditor of the *Commonweal*, appears hesitant to wholeheartedly endorse such an esoteric drama in the context of a working-class-oriented socialist newspaper.

The *Clarion*, the most mass-oriented socialist paper of the day, went further than Sparling in distancing itself from Ibsenism. The paper ran a regular theater column but was more conservative in its tastes than most socialist papers, a mark of its populist objectives.[11] Virtually alone among socialist papers, it did not take Ibsen seriously as a socialist thinker. A review of Ibsen's *Master Builder* mocks the audience—"Very stolid, earnest playgoers these Ibsenites, undue levity or ill-timed flippancy . . . being frown-checked at once"—and complains of "the monotony of the never-ending duologues" and the "endless talkee-talkee" (25 February 1893: 3). These were familiar criticisms lodged against Shaw as well as Ibsen but not typically in the radical press. The next week's column continued in this vein: "All that I have to say personally about the Scandinavian Sick-ologist is that his morbid introspective studies are confoundedly prolix and dull" (4 March 1893: 3). A review of *An Enemy of the People*, staged by the Manchester branch of the Independent Theatre, was slightly more positive but no less sarcastic: "As the great Scandinavian's mighty dramatic grasp is in this play to be seen without bewildering laterality of symbolism or poetry, the solid British intellect has, upon this occasion, been able to understand, and even, in some degree, to appreciate" (3 February 1894: 3). A few years later, Robert Blatchford, the paper's editor, joked, "I used to like Ibsen very much until Shaw began to explain him; but if Ibsen means what Shaw says he means Ibsen is not the man I took him for" (30 January 1897: 37).[12]

Aside from the *Clarion*, however, most socialist papers claimed Ibsen as their own, as did anarchist and other radical papers. The *Revolutionary Review*, a short-lived anarchist monthly edited by Henry Seymour, kept readers up-to-date on the groundbreaking Ibsen performances of the summer of 1889, emphasizing Ibsen's capacity to generate political conflict and—of special interest to anarchists—to expose the inherently suppressive character of the government and the capitalist press. Seymour, who had survived a blasphemy prosecution in 1882, was a veteran editor of radical print; he was responsible for the *Anarchist* and the *Free Exchange* and would take over editing the *Adult* after George Bedborough's 1898 arrest, as I discuss in Chapter 6. In the July 1889 issue of the *Revolutionary Review*, Seymour discusses the landmark June staging of *A Doll's House*, the first significant public performance of Ibsen in England: "Henrik Ibsen's 'Doll's House' at the Novelty Theatre, has been indeed a novelty to London playgoers, being pervaded with free-love and revolutionary sentiments. Of course the prostitutes of the press, the 'critics', raised an indignant howl" (98). Next month, Seymour wrote of a one-night benefit performance: "A second play by Henrik Ibsen has been given in English . . . drawing (much to the surprise and disgust of the conventional critics) a large and sympathetic audience. 'The Pillars of Society' is a play which too thoroughly exposes the corruption of modern society to please the hireling apologists of the newspapers" (August 1889: 114). To Seymour, Ibsen's plays present an invaluable opportunity for capitalist newspapers to reveal themselves as the "prostitutes" they are, and the stage is the new site for revolutionary literary-political action: "The fact that a revolutionary play can be performed on the London stage speaks volumes" (114). A month later, however, he reinterpreted these events in light of divisions within the British left instead of broader political conflicts: "London has been treated lately to a couple of Henrik Ibsen's famous plays, which the state socialist element, not less the anarchists, found considerable delight in. Are the state socialists aware that Ibsen is the bitterest foe of their constructive policy, and that he is responsible for the following anarchistic sentiment? 'The state is the curse of the individual'" (September 1889: 132).[13]

By 1897 the Independent Theatre had produced a series of Ibsen's more controversial plays, including *Ghosts, A Doll's House,* and *The Wild Duck.* As with Shaw's plays, many of the earliest Ibsen stage performances in England occurred by way of private theatrical societies. The private nature of such societies allowed refuge from the Lord Chamberlain's office but likewise delimited audience reach. The productions sought to reach the public's "head" if not its "tail," in Shaw's terms, and to model an anticommercial theater that could eventually serve as the prototype for a national theater in the public interest. As Langdon Everard wrote in "Socialism and the Theatre," published in the Independent Labour Party paper *Labour Leader:* "The influence of the modern theatre is greater than that of the pulpit," but "commercialism in the English theatre is slowly strangling the drama." The cure "lies in the removal of the incubus of capitalism from the theatre" through "socialisation" (30 October 1908: 689).

The simultaneously statist and antistatist urges at work in the private theatrical sphere—the desire for a state-funded theater, yet to be free of state censorship—suggest the confidence that some state socialists, especially Fabians, had in the idea of reforming corrupt state institutions for the good. For example, Harley Granville Barker, a leading actor in the Stage Society and a member of the Fabian Executive Committee, was a great advocate for the foundation of a national theater to ameliorate commercial control of the stage. He wrote that the drama was "the art most ripe for public organization" because "drama can only exist with an elaborate organization, and in buildings over which public authorities already exercise control in the interests of physical safety" (qtd. in Britain 262).[14] The quotation speaks to the elitist fantasies at work in some Fabian ideas of the theater: Barker senses an inherent advantage in being able to control one's audience, to physically contain them in a way that was not possible with print. This idea of a "private" public, in the sense of being limited and controlled, circulated alongside a socialist ideal of the theater as a more communal activity than solitary reading. Thus the Fabian conceptions of theater and print operate both with and against Benedict Anderson's notion of an imaginary public created through reading; in this case, ambivalence about a large, invisible reading public was an animating factor in the socialist turn to the theater.

Shelley Among the Socialists

Many in the radical public were disenchanted with the political potency of print literature in the age of mass publishing and turned toward theater as a potentially more effective medium, and Percy Bysshe Shelley, though long deceased, played a key role in this development. The radical independent theater movement that emerged in the 1890s coalesced around the 1886 private staging of *The Cenci*, and the socialist reception of Shelley's work had already provoked conflict around the issue of class and audience, evident in the *Cenci* controversy. Anticipating J. T. Grein's controversial staging of Ibsen's *Ghosts* in 1891, the event that inaugurated the Independent Theatre, the 1886 performance of *The Cenci* showed that there was a way to get around the censor and make radical theater available to an emerging theatrical counterpublic, but it also imagined this counterpublic as the bourgeois cultural elite who would change society through top-down reform. In the debate and discourse surrounding this landmark production, *Cenci* advocates borrowed from a long tradition of radical arguments for free print—arguments that had been so effective in the past—but reoriented them toward a smaller theatrical audience of forward-thinking cultural elites.

The 1886 *Cenci* production thus points to shifting ideas about literary-political influence within the radical sphere; the old radical argument for free expression is called on but with a new focus on artistic freedom for a relatively elite group. Thinking back to Shaw's and Yeats's arguments about the exhaustion of print as a radical medium and the way their advocacy of theater necessarily entailed a restricted audience, we can see how the *Cenci* performance fed into existing currents of elitism in the arena of literary politics. Morris, who steadfastly maintained that revolutionary change must emerge from below, did love Shelley, but he called the effort to stage *The Cenci* "a great mistake" (*Collected Letters* 2B: 507).[15] This suggests how the figure of Shelley had come to represent a socialist drift away from notions of democratic cultural change championed by Morris and toward notions of a cultural avant-garde who would lead the way in aesthetic as well as political change, championed by Shaw.[16]

Despite internal squabbling in the late Victorian radical sphere, Shelley was a figure around whom all could seemingly unite. His work appeared in a wide range of leftist forums, from anarchist papers such as *Freedom* and the *Torch* to moderate parliamentarian socialist journals such as *Our Corner* and *Labour Leader*, and to claim Shelley as an entry point for youthful radicalization was practically ritualized speech among British socialists. Walter Crane describes how, as a young man, reading "Mill, Darwin, and Herbert Spencer, and above all the poems of Shelley, I soon decided for Free Thought" (*Artist's Reminiscences* 80). Bruce Glasier, the working-class Scottish leader, derived his socialism from "the poetry of Burns and Shelley, and the great stream of social idealism that has come down the ages" (*J. Bruce Glasier* 16). As a youth, Shaw read Shelley "'prose and verse, from beginning to end,'" making him "a momentary anarchist and a lifetime vegetarian" (Holroyd 1: 39).

Anarchists, theosophists, Nietzschean protomodernists, and all sorts and conditions of socialists loved Shelley. Charlotte Despard, theosophist and socialist suffragette, attributed to Shelley "everything from her passion for social justice and her feminism to her vegetarianism and her belief in reincarnation" (Dixon 185). A July 1896 article in the anarchist journal *Freedom*, titled "The Poet of Freedom," claims that "no man in the whole range of English literature had a higher conception of the deep and profound necessity for Freedom in the evolution of social life than Shelley" (91). *Justice*, the Social Democratic Federation paper, ran two long articles on Shelley in its first few years and printed sections from *The Revolt of Islam*, *Queen Mab*, "The Mask of Anarchy," "Declaration of Rights," and "A New National Anthem." E. Belfort Bax's short-lived 1883 paper *Liberty* used Shelley as the epigraph on its masthead: "Kings, Priests and Statesmen blast the human flower." The *Adult* reprinted part of "Epipsychidion" in July 1898 under the title "Shelley on Free Love" (184). Meanwhile, Edward Carpenter and George Barnefield found in

Shelley the prototype for an evolved homosexual identity, as Carpenter writes in their book *The Psychology of the Poet Shelley*: His "nature was really intermediate (or double) in character—*intermediate* as between the masculine and feminine or *double* as having that twofold outlook upon the world" (45). Shelley, it seems, had something for everyone. Among the era's diverse interconnected radicalisms, Shelley emerges as a rare common denominator, an axis around which such an eclectic group might possibly move in sync. Shelley signified for all these groups an indigenous British strain of individualist socialism, which could be usefully opposed to Marxism and other Continental schools of thought and which provided a historical logic of inheritance for the British left.

The story of the 1886 private *Cenci* performance demonstrates how Shelley's continuing presence in the radical sphere structured thinking about literary radicalism, print, and the radical public. Shelley was, after all, a martyr for the cause of free print—from his Oxford expulsion for printing *The Necessity of Atheism* to the surreptitiously circulated *Queen Mab*—and every Shelley reference in late Victorian socialism was at some level a reiteration of the conceptual model of print enlightenment, a model that was increasingly inadequate at the end of the century but that radical writers found it difficult to move beyond. In Shelley's lifetime a working-class readership had famously expropriated *Queen Mab* years after its initial private printing. Later, in the 1840s, *Queen Mab* was dubbed "the Chartist Bible" and was "by far the most quoted literary work in the reformist radical press" (St. Clair 336), yet the poem continued to be censored.[17] Members of the Brighton Workingmen's Institute, for example, agitated for its inclusion in the institute's library, which the director forbade, resulting in a "thorough reorganization of the institute, in the course of which the atheistically inclined seem to have been purged" (Altick 197). Under such conditions the political force of the free print ideal seemed indisputable, but at the end of the century Shelley's writings were subject to no such custody, at least in print. A passage on English oppression in the preface to *Hellas*, long suppressed, was restored in 1892 (Kearney 62), and although *The Cenci* was banned from the stage, it circulated freely in print.

The figure of Shelley thus reflects the uneasiness of free print rhetoric at the end of the century. His persistent presence in radical discourse was a way to keep such rhetoric alive amid seemingly incongruous conditions, but he also signified the theoretical abstraction and literary abstruseness that plagued many socialist efforts to reach a working-class audience. The difficulty and density of some of his work meant that to read Shelley backward and forward, as Shaw claimed to have done, required a degree of literacy beyond the capacity of most readers. As the anarchist paper *Freedom* admitted, "Portions of his poetry will always remain beyond the understanding of a few" (July 1896: 92). In his lifetime most of Shelley's work had reached a small audience. An 1898 article in the radical paper *University Magazine and Free Review* hoped "Shelley's generous message, which more than seventy years ago fell on deaf ears" would fare differently "on the threshold of a new era" (January 1898: 338). This authorial legacy—the prophet whose words met deaf ears in his own time—was consistent with many radical writers' new orientation toward a smaller audience of forward-thinking cultural elites.

Henry Salt, perhaps Shelley's greatest champion on the late Victorian literary left, wrote and edited more than a dozen books, pamphlets, and articles on Shelley, claiming he was "misunderstood by his own and by later generations" because "he delivered [his] message through a medium which the majority cannot comprehend . . . that is to say, he thought as a revolutionist and wrote as a poet" (*Shelley as a Pioneer* 4). For example, *Prometheus Unbound* was a hopeless challenge for many working-class readers, yet in the conventional wisdom of the day it was his best and most revolutionary work.[18] Shelley had a long history of popularity among the trade unions and radical working classes, but some texts were obviously more accessible than others; both "Men of England" and the refrain from "The Mask of Anarchy" were set to music and had a long afterlife in socialist songbooks.[19] Works such as *The Cenci* did not speak to as wide an audience. As William Sharp says in his 1887 biography of Shelley, "Shelley is still reverenced and loved by thousands who would never think of reading the 'Prometheus' or the 'Cenci,' or who would not care for it if they did" (112–13).

These two Shelleyan referents—the martyr to the cause of free print, whose work showed the snags of print enlightenment rhetoric—came to a head in the 1886 movement to privately stage *The Cenci*, which had been denied a license for public exhibition. Focusing as it does on the rape of Beatrice Cenci by her father, the play had never been staged, and the Shelley Society determined to redress this injustice. When the Society successfully staged *The Cenci* on 7 May 1886 to an audience of 2,400 people, the *Morning Post* said that the "brilliant audience . . . included many persons of high literary celebrity," such as Robert Browning, George Meredith, James Russell Lowell, and Sir Percy and Lady Shelley (rpt. in Preston 12). John Todhunter of the Shelley Society presented a poetic prologue, congratulating the audience on its intelligent, nonprurient—read "middle class"—theatrical gaze:[20]

Can your eyes
Delight their sense with tawdry properties,
The pomp of theatres, the glittering shows

. . .

Nay, who sit here
Quicken to rarer influence, from that sphere
Supernal, of the pure unbodied mind. (qtd. in Shelley, *Cenci* [1886] xii)

Shelley had become the darling of the left wing of the literary elite through the offices of the Shelley Society. The Society was not an explicitly political organization, but its membership was rooted in various schools of leftist politics. Paul Foot's 1980 study, *Red Shelley,* a book that reclaims Shelley for twentieth-century socialists, blames the Shelley Society and other Shelley fans of the era for "castrating" Shelley and claims "an orgy of cultured Shelley-worship, which reached its climax in the 1880s and 1890s" "laid the basis for the disguising of Shelley which has lasted for nearly 100 years" (241, 244). This claim grossly caricatures the politics of the Shelley Society, however. Foot claims that William Michael Rossetti, who chaired the Shelley Society from 1886 to 1895, "really got [the orgy] under way," but Rossetti's politics were actually quite radical. According to his anarchist daughter, he had inherited these politics from Shelley: "For all his placid demeanor and domestic virtues, William Michael Rossetti was a daring and revolutionary thinker"; "Shelley . . . played a great part in forming religious and kindred matters" (Agresti 28). For example, Rossetti wrote in a 22 January 1908 letter, "My opinions . . . as to marriage, quasi-marriage, etc etc, are essentially much the same as Shelley's. I think that a man and woman are justified in uniting when they like, and again justified in separating when the one or the other ceases to value the union" (John Rylands Library, GB 133 Eng MS 1277).

Of course, not all the Society's members were as "daring and revolutionary" as Rossetti, and even Rossetti, a civil servant in the Inland Revenue Office, was not in a position to act on all his political principles.[21] Most of the Society's members declined to sign a petition for clemency of the Chicago anarchists sentenced to death in the Haymarket affair; Shaw, Edward Aveling, and Rossetti were the only ones to sign.[22] Some objected to Aveling because he was not legally married to his partner, Eleanor Marx, and Rossetti was so appalled by their hypocrisy on this point that he withdrew from the Society until Aveling was admitted. Aveling's rejection, he wrote, "appears to me to make a Shelley Society a travestie upon itself . . . on the same grounds the Shelley Society would have turned out Shelley himself" (British Library ms Ashley 1448, 1449). The decision was reversed, and Aveling and Marx would soon present to the Society their cowritten paper, "Shelley's Socialism," reprinted in the socialist magazine *To-Day* in 1888 and then again as a cheap pamphlet that went into multiple editions. The essay's point was to "claim [Shelley] as a Socialist" and, more specifically, as a proto-Marxist socialist: "More than anything else that makes us claim Shelley as a Socialist is his singular understanding of the facts that to-day tyranny resolves itself into the tyranny of the possessing class over the producing, and that to this tyranny in the ultimate analysis is traceable almost all evil and misery" (Aveling and Aveling xx).

Despite the climate of aestheticism in the literary culture of the day, the Shelley Society emphasized the interrelation of Shelley's poetry and politics.[23] Frederick Furnivall, founder of the Shelley Society, was an inveterate creator of literary societies and one of the architects of the *Oxford English Dictionary*; he was passionate about creating good scholarly literary editions for a wide audience of readers, but he was also an agnostic with a long history of involvement in Christian Socialism and social work in the slums who taught for many years at the London Working Men's College and who would join the Fabian Society in 1891.[24] At the Shelley Society's inaugural meeting in March 1886, socialist leader Reverend Stoppard Brooke gave the opening address to a crowd of 500 people and stated the Society's objects in utopian, socialist, almost millenarian terms: "Many are content to take the world as it is, but those who, like Shelley, are not content, who find in him their prophetic singer of the advancing kingdom of faith and hope and love, are not to be blamed for loving him well" (*Notebook of the Shelley Society,* 1886: 6). He stressed Shelley's "desire for a more rapid advance of the welfare of mankind": "Few have done more to overthrow false conceptions of God, and to shake the foundations of superstition, caste, tyranny, and slavery of mind and body" (3–4). Brooke's address offers one version of the opening meeting, and Shaw provides another. As Shaw tells it, at this meeting "I made my then famous (among 100 people) declaration, 'I am a Socialist, an Atheist and a Vegetarian' (ergo, a true Shelleyan), whereupon two ladies who had been palpitating with enthusiasm for Shelley under the impression that he was a devout Anglican, resigned on the spot" (*Collected Letters* 2: 760). The truth of this anecdote has long been subject to debate—Shaw liked to cast himself in the role of the shocking revolutionary—but the story has played a key role in the Society's historical depoliticization.

Like the Fabian Society or the Leeds Art Club, the Shelley Society was an organization that was socialist but almost exclusively middle class, and it had an uneasy relation to Shelley's special status for the radical working classes. Its version of socialist politics reflects a broader artistic and informational crisis of the era, which emerged amid new conditions of mass media and mass print. The Society celebrated an author remembered for his association with free print, just as free print was becoming beside the point in class politics. It was responsible for printing and reissuing a great many of Shelley's works—so many, in fact, that it went bankrupt from printing bills—but these were scholarly editions rather than cheap accessible ones. As Rossetti put it, they were aimed at "serious and well grounded students of Shelley's life and writings—persons of the class in whose interest the Shelley Society is founded, and who may be expected to abound in its ranks" (*Memoir* i). Foot claims the Society's members wanted to mass market Shelley, but this is actually the opposite of what they wanted to do; they wanted to claim Shelley for anticapitalism, but in doing so, they also claimed Shelley for an elite readership.

Of course, Shelley's special status for the radical working classes did fit many of the group's ideals and was promoted as such. Members of the Society, including Furnivall and Shaw, co-led the Shelley Centenary celebration in August 1892 at the Hall of Science, a venue that was "the heart of artisan / small shopkeeper radicalism" where "Bradlaugh celebrated his greatest triumphs and Secularism became most notorious" (Royle 46).[25] The setting paid homage to the radical working classes in the free thought movement. The Society's periodical publication, *Notebook of the Shelley Society*, likewise honored Shelley as a poet loved by the workers, who "find in him their poet, perhaps their priest" (1886: 7). Still, no poem of Shelley's had more working-class readers than *Queen Mab*, and at the second meeting of the Society, on 14 April 1886, H. Buxton Forman gave an address on "The Vicissitudes of Queen Mab," later reprinted in the *Notebook of the Shelley Society* and in the *Athenæum*, which disparaged these readers. Forman thought that the poem's popularity had lowered Shelley's literary reputation.

The "furiousness" of its style *as well as the largeness of its circulation* tended to set the more cultivated of Englishmen against the author. Had Shelley failed in 1813 to find a printer, the growth of his better opinions would undoubtedly have been more rapid. To this day, he is far more widely known as the author of "Queen Mab" than as the author of "Prometheus Unbound." . . . [We] desire to see all that changed. (29, my emphasis)

The talk sparked passionate dispute. Afterward, Shaw declared *Queen Mab* to be "far superior to 'The Cenci'" and "a perfectly original poem on a great subject" (31). The poet Philip Bourke Marston wrote later: "A man called Bernard Shaw, who frankly declared himself at the start an atheist and a socialist, a man who I know slightly and much hate, an Irishman who speaks with a strong accent, arose in his glory and said that he regarded *Queen Mab* as a much greater work than the *Cenci*. I wanted to get up and murder him" (qtd. in Thirlwell 203).

Despite such disagreements, the politics of the Shelley Society were clearly far more radical than critics such as Paul Foot and Stuart Curran have suggested.[26] The Society must be differentiated from another group of Victorian commentators who mounted, as Anthony Kearney puts it, "a determined critical effort . . . to save Shelley's poetry from his ideas" (63). These critics romanticized him as a misunderstood martyr, thanks to what Salt, writing in *Justice*, called "the 'poor, poor Shelley' theory," the "ludicrous supposition" that "if he had only had a better education, religious and moral . . . this erring lamb would have developed into one of the most orderly and respectable sheep in the fold of Orthodoxy" (31 October 1885: 2). Matthew Arnold famously called Shelley "a beautiful *and ineffectual* angel, beating in the void his luminous wings in vain" (327); and G. K. Chesterton claimed that "Shelley was only the earthly name for a spirit . . . with whom we can no more agree or disagree than we can measure a cloud with a yard measure" (qtd. in Salt, *Shelley's Principles* 3). Such posthumous, ethereal respectability was hugely irritating to the Shelley Society, especially Shaw, who spilled much ink attempting to refang Shelley. In his 1892 article "Shaming the Devil About Shelley," originally printed in the short-lived monthly review *The Albemarle*, Shaw protested the absurdity of Horsham, a district distinguished by its "gloriously solid Conservative vote," founding a Shelley Library and Museum ("Shaming the Devil" 315). The speech given at its opening, Shaw said, presented Shelley as "so fragile, so irresponsible, so ethereally tender, so passionate a creature that the wonder was that he was not a much greater rascal" (319).

Shaw was press officer for the Shelley Society's *Cenci* production, and he devoted himself to keeping the flame of Shelleyan scandal alive. He took the opportunity in "Shaming the Devil About Shelley" to remind readers of Shelley's opinion that brother-sister incest "is no crime," which to Shaw's mind represented the most extreme length of Shelley's brave propensity to smash ideals and look beyond established moral codes for a higher truth: "The freedom to curse a tyrannical father is not more sacred that the freedom to love an amiable sister. In a word, if filial duty is no duty, then incest is no crime" (316–17).[27] It was this quality of Shelley's thinking, Shaw claimed in *The Quintessence of Ibsenism*, that made him an emblematic "first pioneer" of cultural progress, "the man who declares that it is right to do something hitherto regarded as infamous," which to Shaw was braver and better than declaring "that it is wrong to do something that no one has hitherto seen any harm in" (*Quintessence* 209). Shaw attributed Shelley's view of incest to his heroic readiness to question the most unquestionable orthodoxy, the most ingrained and seemingly instinctual of social ideals. As Shaw wrote in 1905, incest is the best illustration of "the force of custom": "There is no other case in which a pure convention masquerades so effectually as a human instinct" (*Collected Letters* 2: 577). For Shaw, Shelley was a true radical because he would always remain beyond public understanding and approval; he was not the poet of democracy but the poet of the avant-garde. This was the version of Shelley that would triumph with the Shelley Society's private staging of *The Cenci*.[28]

Unspeakable Incest Dramas: The Cenci *and* Mrs Warren's Profession

The Cenci was censored because it depicted incest—a distinction it shared with Ibsen's *Ghosts* and Shaw's *Mrs Warren's Profession*. Count Cenci, the villain of the drama, personifies the interrelated patriarchal authority of father, church, and state. The pope, aware of Cenci's cruelty to his family, refuses to intervene because "He holds it of most dangerous example / In aught to weaken the paternal power, / Being, as 'twere, the shadow of his own" (II.ii.54–56).[29] Beatrice Cenci's decision to commit patricide after being raped by her father thus has an unmistakably revolutionary cast in the context of the play. In the end the pope refuses to commute Beatrice's death sentence because he fears that "Authority, and power, and hoary hair / Are grown crimes capital" (V.iv.23–24).

The 1886 staging of *The Cenci* drew together various political threads of the radical moment: the push for independent theater, freedom of sexual expression, anti-authoritarianism, and, importantly, feminism. The play was after all the story of an abused daughter's revolt against patriarchal sexual domination, and its staging converged with existing 1880s debates around women's access to the public sphere. Alma Murray, the actress who played Beatrice Cenci, won rave reviews for her performance, but reviewers remained unconvinced that the play was suitable for female viewers. A review in the *Echo* stated that *The Cenci* "is wanting in every quality that would make it acceptable to a mixed audience" (Preston 18). The *Daily Telegraph* was more resigned: "The ladies, many of them young, who went to Islington yesterday, presumably knew, or ought to have known, the kind of subject that Shelley had selected for his tragedy, and it was their fault, or that of their husbands, fathers, and brothers, if they were shocked at the atrocious and bloodthirsty utterances of Count Cenci." Women might after all read the play: "The text of *The Cenci* is not kept under lock and key in any library, and if women like to see the play performed it is their look out" (Preston 10).

In many ways the entire production turned on the question of what it meant to see a play, as opposed to reading it. Shelley had written the play to be staged, not as a closet drama like *Prometheus Unbound,* but because of its subject it had never been performed.[30] The 1886 staging was billed as an experiment to find out whether *The Cenci* would work on the stage as it did in print and as an experiment to see whether censored plays could be staged in private performances. The Shelley Society wanted "to test the question whether the greatest lyric poet is not also a great dramatic one" (*Notebook of the Shelley Society,* 1886: 8). As to the first experiment, the production was thought by most reviewers to be a failure: "After witnessing the experiment, and seeing strong men writhe in anguish as they listened to the fearful speeches put into the mouth of the aged monster, Count Cenci," *Lloyd's Weekly* concluded, "*The Cenci* is a drama too full of unnatural horrors to admit of public representation" (Preston 30). But as to the second experiment, the staging was thought to be a success, proving the viability of private performance outside the censor's jurisdiction: "The experiment resembled the first attempts to introduce the performance of stage plays under Puritan rule," said the *Athenæum* (Preston 22).

These responses to the staging implied print's insufficiency. Far from being a dangerous tool of subversion, print cannot fully express the horror and violence of a Count Cenci and thus is less in need of regulation than a live medium like the stage. Yet print copies of the Society's edition of the play were supplied to every audience member, suggesting that the production was also on some level an effort to revitalize radical literature in an age of debased print. (The model anticipates Grein's planned print endeavor, the Independent Theatre Series.) In the discourse surrounding the production, attention to the differences between speech and writing and a tendency to depict the written word as supplemental to the spoken word perfectly suited the theme of *The Cenci.* Much of the play is a meditation on the unspeakability of Count Cenci's crime and the impossibility of objecting to that which cannot be spoken aloud; it is a play about the political value of free expression, which explains why it kindled socialist investment in a radical idiom of free print. In his preface Shelley makes an Enlightenment argument for the power of open speech, introducing the play "as a light to make apparent some of the most dark and secret caverns of the human heart" (*Cenci* [1977] 239). In the play, after Beatrice Cenci is raped by her father, she is thrust into a crisis of language and finds there is no way to articulate what she has suffered.

> What are the words which you would have me speak?
> I, who can feign no image in my mind
> Of that which has transformed me. I, whose thought
> Is like a ghost shrouded and folded up
> In its own formless horror. Of all words,
> That minister to mortal intercourse,
> Which wouldst thou hear? For there is none to tell
> My misery. (III.i.107–113)

Trapped without words, Beatrice decides to act instead—"If I try to speak / I shall go mad. Aye, something must be done" (III.i.85–86)—and she hires assassins to kill the father who has raped her. But Beatrice is ultimately sentenced to execution, after a trial scene that emphasizes the futility of speech: "That which thou hast called my father's death / Which is or is not what men call a crime, / Which either I have done, or have not done; / Say what ye will. I shall deny no more" (V.iii.83–86). She determines to be silent: "No other pains shall force another word" (V.iii.89).

Fittingly enough, given the drama's emphasis on the unspeakability of incest and the interrelation of restrictions on language and more overt forms of oppression, many reviewers of the *Cenci* performance claimed that they could not properly assess the play because they could not bring themselves to discuss its subject. The *Globe* evasively stated: "Into the question whether it is expedient that the repulsive and unhallowed crimes which form the subject of *The Cenci* should be set before youths and maidens, it is inexpedient in a public newspaper to enter" (Preston 17). Shelley's contemporary reviewers had struck a similarly dissonant note of noticing the play while refusing to describe it. The *Literary Gazette* said in 1820, "We have much doubted whether we ought to notice [*The Cenci*]; but, as watchmen place a light over the common sewer which has been opened in a way dangerous to passengers, so have we concluded it to be our duty to set up a beacon on this noisome and noxious publication" (rpt. in Reiman 517).

And yet in 1880s reviewers' responses to *The Cenci* we see an emerging sense that moral objection alone is not enough to condemn the play, which marks a key shift in literary-critical perspective. In Shelley's day, despite the play's anonymous publication, critical response to *The Cenci* mainly consisted of attempts to determine which of the author's many personal vices were to blame for the drama. The *New Monthly Magazine* wondered "at the strange perversity of taste" behind the play (rpt. in Reiman 734), and Baldwin's *London Magazine* referenced the suspected author's sexual reputation: "One of this stamp will propose lending his wife to his friend, and expect praises for an enlarged and liberal style of thinking" (rpt. in Reiman 566). Six decades later, reviewers of the *Cenci* production felt compelled to support their moral objections to the play with a judgment of its aesthetic failings. How reliable or untainted such aesthetic judgments were is another matter, but reviewers felt obliged to supply them. The *Times* deemed the play boring, despite its shocking subject matter: "It is blood-curdling, horrible, revolting even, but it is uniform, and . . . weariness is apt at the end of the first hour or two to take the place of the shudders of disgust" (Preston 9). The *Daily Telegraph* also complained of tedium: "Four long hours of a lovely May afternoon were yesterday occupied by the Shelley Society in laboriously proving the worthlessness of *The Cenci* for all practical stage purposes" (Preston 10).

This change in critical discourse was a sign of the times—this was, after all, the age of aestheticism—but to members of the Shelley Society the reviewers' aesthetic judgments revealed nothing so much as entrenched moral objections. The preface to the Society's *Notes on the First Performance of Shelley's Cenci* claims, "The treatment that the subject has received from the critics is exactly that which was naturally to be expected. The discussion of the work from a literary point of view does not fall within the dramatic critic's province, although some have attempted it" (Preston 6). Shaw himself, ever the contrarian, spoke out in the radical press against the play's quality, but he also adjusted the terms of the debate from the artistic quality of *The Cenci* to the political import of its censorship. In *Our Corner* Shaw wrote that Shelley had "certainly got hold of the wrong vehicle when he chose the five-act tragedy in blank verse" for *The Cenci*, and thus the performance was "a failure in the sense in which we call an experiment with a negative result a failure" (June 1886: 371–72). Shaw wanted to argue against the play's censorship regardless of its dramatic quality, but his criticism also belies the major influence that the *Cenci* staging would have over Shaw and his post-1886 turn to the drama from the novel.

As noted earlier, Shaw was the press officer for *The Cenci* staging, and its influence on his own dramatic career—not yet begun in 1886—is especially apparent in the treatment of incest and paternal authority in *Mrs Warren's Profession*. While working on *Mrs Warren* in 1893, Shaw wrote to William Archer, "I have finished the first act of my new play, in which I have skillfully blended the plot of The Second Mrs Tanqueray with that of The Cenci. It will be just the thing for the I[ndependent] T[heater]" (*Collected Letters* 1: 403). Many critics have thought that the incest theme does not sit well in *Mrs Warren's Profession*, but it serves to reference *The Cenci* as well as Henrik Ibsen's *Ghosts* (and to a lesser degree *The Second Mrs. Tanqueray*, in which an unwitting daughter almost marries her stepmother's former lover). *Ghosts*, of course, had been serialized in *To-Day* in 1885, and in 1891 it debuted on the English stage with Grein's Independent Theatre, having been denied a license for performance. The private staging attracted a torrent of critical outrage on the order of that caused by the private staging of *The Cenci*. Clearly, for socialists the anticensorship cause still had significant radical charge, although the main barriers to radical expression in this era were commercial rather than legal.

On the heels of *The Cenci* and *Ghosts*, incest had become a figure for the unspeakable and for the censorship debate, and Shaw took up this theme in *Mrs Warren's Profession* to communicate a coherent stance on the politics of print and literary culture. Like all late Victorian radicals, Shaw had inherited a familiar political language concerning the liberatory potential of free expression and unimpeded print, even though he questioned the Enlightenment basis of such language. At the end of the century, faced with a relatively libertarian print sphere and a public that remained politically intransigent, he railed against public taste and the commercialization of culture but continued to rehearse the old arguments in his attacks on stage censorship: "What is wanted is the entire abolition of the censorship and the establishment of Free Art in the sense in which we speak of Free Trade" (*Quintessence* 301). Of course, the abolition of state censorship of the theater would not release the stage from the commercial control exercised under conditions of free trade, but Shaw was speaking in the idiom of early nineteenth-century campaigners for free print. Incest, as a theme, signifies the continuing relevance of this idiom at the end of the century, but it also suggests how these old lines of thought were redirected amid new cultural conditions toward new fronts for political-aesthetic activism, especially concerning freedom of sexual expression over and above class-oriented radicalism.

Although not the focus of the drama, incest haunts *Mrs Warren's Profession* like a Shelleyan or Ibsenian ghost. The play toys with possible futures in which Vivie Warren marries a man who might be her father, or another man who might be her half-brother. Shaw ratchets up the ick factor of these scenes by depicting in both cases a confusing mélange of familial and romantic attraction. Crofts, the man who might be Vivie's father, says he is unsure whether he is attracted to Vivie because she might be his daughter or because he wants to marry her. Vivie's relations with Frank, possible brother and possible suitor, unnervingly mingle flirtation, baby talk, and childish play: "Mustnt go live with her," Frank says "babyishly," "Spoil o u r little group. . . . The babes in the wood: Vivie and little Frank. . . . Lets go and get covered up with leaves" (134). The play is best known for its frank treatment of prostitution, but there is little doubt that these incestuous threads played a role in the play's censorship. As far as dramatic censorship goes, Shaw noted, there are "three great taboos on the question of sex: 1) You must never mention an illegal obstetric operation. 2) You must never mention incest. 3) You must never mention venereal disease" (*Agitations* 96). Ibsen included two of these three in *Ghosts* and in some ways went further than Shelley or Shaw by implying that incest was a common occurrence; in *Ghosts* Mrs. Alving says to her clergyman, "Don't you think there are plenty of married couples out here in the country, just as closely related as [half-siblings]?" Pastor Manders replies, "Unfortunately, family life isn't always as pure as it ought to be" (238).

Clearly, Shaw had a pretty good sense of what would happen when he raised the ghost of incest in *Mrs Warren*. The play was an open attack on stage censorship and restricted speech. In publicly defending it, however, Shaw took the line that incest appears in the play as an argument against sexual nonmonogamy, because it is "one of the inevitable dilemmas produced by 'group marriage'" (*Agitations* 99).[31] This suggests that in writing about incest, Shaw and by extension Ibsen and Shelley were acting as guardians of sexual morality rather than advocates of freer sexual discourse in the public sphere (ironically, given that public aversion to Shelley stemmed partly from his reputation for unorthodox sexual behavior). Shaw, who took inordinate delight in reversing commonly held assumptions, must have found it amusing to pitch Shelley's play along with his own as propaganda for sexual purity: "If the stage is the proper place for the exhibition and discussion of seduction, adultery, promiscuity and prostitution, it must be thrown open to all the consequences of these things, or it will demoralize the nation" (100). But this rationale for the incest in *Mrs Warren* (to illustrate the social perils of promiscuity in consanguinity) registers as political expedience, because elsewhere Shaw promoted the evolutionary good of diverse births from nonmonogamous reproduction, as in a 1905 letter: "In the long run it will be seen that the arch-incest is the sexual intercourse of husband and wife, and that the intercourse from which the race will be bred will be an intercourse between people who do not know one another" (*Collected Letters* 2: 579).

Incest functions in *Mrs Warren's Profession*, as it does in *The Cenci*, as the ultimate example of how silenced speech preserves corruption.[32] As Vivie Warren says of her mother's profession: "There is nothing I despise more than the wicked convention that protects these things by forbidding a woman to mention them." Like Beatrice Cenci, she must articulate the experience of not being able to speak: "The two infamous words that describe what my mother is are ringing in my ears and struggling on my tongue; but I cant utter them: the shame of them is too horrible for me" (150–51). Unable to say the words aloud, Vivie instead writes them down, but Shaw never makes the audience privy to what Vivie writes. The scene suggests the absurdity of a situation where words can be written but not spoken, or, rather, where words can refer to an existing reality but cannot be uttered on stage. It is Shaw's ironic, metadramatic comment on the condition of his own play, which can be read but cannot be spoken aloud in public, like Vivie's two words and like *The Cenci*.[33] The overwhelming effect of the scene is a sense of incomplete information and understanding, a sense that a printed play cannot substitute for a performed one.

Shelley made a similar move in *The Cenci*. Drawing on Plato's conception of the written word as orphaned, fatherless, cut off from its origins—and thus associated with patricide, as Jacques Derrida has claimed—Shelley compares Beatrice's silenced, inarticulate state in the aftermath of her rape with her contemplation of the idea of fatherlessness. Beatrice's stepmother, Lucretia, says, "Her spirit apprehends the sense of pain, / But not its cause; suffering has dried away / The source from which it sprung," to which Beatrice responds, "Like Parricide . . . / Misery has killed its father: yet its father / Never like mine [. . .] I have no father" (III.i.34–36, 38–40, first ellipsis in original). Here, Beatrice's inability to articulate her pain is compared to the experience of fatherlessness, of detachment from origins, which ironically registers the play's own suppression as a voiced drama on stage. Later, a character says of the word *parricide*, "The bare word / Is hollow mockery" (III.i.342–43); the sign is detached from the horror of that which it signifies, yet even the sign cannot be said.

In *Mrs Warren* Shaw draws on Shelley's use of incest to describe authoritarian controls over speech, thereby making an overt argument against censorship and an implied argument about print. In the eyes of the Lord Chamberlain's office, print is a safe zone for the expression of unspeakable ideas; there is a special threat in having shocking words or ideas enacted, spoken, or realized on stage, in contrast to print mediation, which distances words and ideas to make them harmless for expression. Both *The Cenci* and *Mrs Warren* were legally circulating in print for many years before they were licensed for the stage. For Shaw the situation was both an indication of print's limits and a reason to return to print; the entire situation implied that print was less "real" than dramatic production, but recognizing that he could publish *Mrs Warren* before it could be staged was central to his decision to rework his dramas for a reading audience as opposed to a theatrical one.[34] William Morris found political breathing room in print's apparent detachment from the present-day conditions, but for Shaw such detachment was a benefit primarily insofar as it created a space outside the censor's gaze.

Although written in 1893, *Mrs Warren's Profession* was not licensed for performance in England until 1925; *The Cenci* was licensed a few years earlier, in 1922.[35] In the thirty-odd years it took for the censors to pass *Mrs Warren*, internal debate in the censorship office rehashed points raised in the dispute over *The Cenci*. In 1916 G. S. Street wrote, "No doubt the theme is important and can be rightly discussed in the press. But the theatre is not the place, except before an audience well knowing what it is to expect, and of a special kind, as is the Stage Society" (British Library ms L.C.P. Corr. 1924/5632). As with *The Cenci*, we see here a willingness for the play to exist freely in print but not to be performed except for the "special" audience of private theater societies. This is a throwback to long-standing arguments against theater based on the premise that only the literate can handle politically subversive material. But by 1916 England had had universal public education for almost fifty years—conditions had drastically changed since the movement for free print escalated in the early part of the century and its rhetoric had become awkward. Ultimately, the Shelley Society's effort to stage *The Cenci* exemplifies the persistent class divisions that attended all turn-of-the-century efforts to sever art from the market. *The Cenci*, like *Ghosts* and *Mrs Warren's Profession*, represents a key shift in literary radicalism away from democratic Enlightenment and toward newer, more exclusive fronts for political-aesthetic activism.

CHAPTER 4

Measured Revolution
Poetry and the Late Victorian Radical Press

'Tis the ordered anger of England and her hope for the good of
the Earth

. . .

Sick unto death was my hope, and I turned and looked on my
dear,
And beheld her frightened wonder, and her grief without a tear.
And knew how her thought was mine—when, hark! o'er the
hubbub and noise,
Faint and a long way off, the music's measured voice.
And the crowd was swaying and swaying, and somehow, I knew
not why,
A dream came into my heart of deliverance drawing anigh.

—William Morris, "Sending to the War"
(*The Pilgrims of Hope*, pt. 3)

WILLIAM MORRIS'S *Pilgrims of Hope*, a "proletarian epic"
set during the 1871 Paris Commune, is perhaps the
most famous poem—little known though it is—to
emerge from the late Victorian radical press.[1] The thirteen-poem epic
was serialized in Morris's socialist newspaper the *Commonweal* from
March 1885 to July 1886, and in the passage quoted in the epigraph,
Morris describes London socialists preparing to travel to Paris to defend
the Commune. His emphasis on the socialists' "ordered anger," "music's
measured voice," and a crowd swaying in unison exemplifies a broader
tendency of radical press poetry in this era: to depict revolutionary po-

litical aims in "measured" terms, to situate radical ideals within the familiar forms and rhythms of the past, and to claim poetic tradition as a precapitalist formation.[2] Poetry of the radical press did not privilege the political value of formal innovation; rather, the political value of the poetry was in its capacity to draw together readers of the radical press into an alternative culture made familiar by appeals to the past and brought to life by oral poetic forms. Radical press poems, which include many songs, traverse the print-performance divide by using regular meter and rhyme, which is easily transferable into oral, spoken expression. Literature of the radical press sought in all instances to create a new culture and a new public, a literary tradition for a new day. Print remained the most obvious means of interpellating a public, but poetry and song held the promise of rendering the communion of print into the realm of live voice and live action.

The late Victorian radical press operated from the premise that it was possible to create an alternative public sphere independent of the capitalist press, but Raymond Williams, discussing the 1960s profusion of radical print and its reaction against a seemingly monolithic commercialism in the communications sphere, has warned that such oppositional networks can be an inadequate political response to capitalist media conglomeration: "Called, rather hopefully, an alternative culture . . . it can very easily become a marginal culture" (186–87). Can a print counterculture be autonomous without being irrelevant? In its oppositionality, does it risk marginality? These questions are of special concern in poetry of the late Victorian radical press, because more than other genres published in such journals—fiction, drama, journalism—radical press poetry explores its relationship to cultural tradition and its status as an alternative tradition. Owing in part to the formal and allusive qualities of poetry as a genre, radical press poetry tends to establish continuities rather than divisions; it seeks to co-opt dominant poetic traditions or to assert a prior claim on these traditions rather than simply to reject them. Radical press poets could have chosen to be more experimental or innovative in their approach to poetic form, and certainly the politics of form were debated in the journals' critical discourse. But for the most part, even in the midst of wholesale political critique, radical press poets worked within the forms, sounds, and in some cases melodies of the past, relying especially on traditional verse forms with familiar aural features. In their rendering of poetic tradition and form, poems of the radical press theorize a particular vision of cultural change: that one can engage and transform dominant culture from within the forms of that culture.

A wide survey of late Victorian radical periodicals reveals that nearly all included verse. Whether monthly journals or weekly papers, whether targeting an audience of workers or intellectuals, most ran at least one poem per issue. This was not a unique aspect of radical print; in fact, all kinds of Victorian magazines and newspapers featured poetry, and recent critics have become more attentive to the life of poetry within such quotidian settings. Natalie Houston notes that poetry was included not only in literary periodicals such as *Cornhill* but also in everyday newspapers such as the *Times.* Much of this newspaper poetry was light and topical and has been ignored by critics despite what it tells us about Victorian reading practices. An analysis of poetry from the *Times* leads Houston to conclude, for example, that "poetry functioned as one of several interpreting frameworks for public events" (241). Victorian readers, including readers of the radical press, were accustomed to imbibing poetry as news and poetry with news; their visual sense of a newspaper page would have included "the aura of unmarked space" marking off "the presence of a poem on a densely printed page" (Robson 260).

Verse in the radical press dealt with the same topics as the other writing surrounding it; the poems stress communist or collectivist principles, advocate social change, or attack capitalist ideology. Still, these poems constitute a distinctive textual form within this context in that their approach to poetic tradition does not always accord with the political values of radical journals. Tradition, revolution, and form intersect and struggle in this domain. Poets writing for revolutionary journals are wedged between literary history and print context; they tend to adhere to past literary traditions yet express metapoetically the contradictions between their form and setting. Most of the periodicals I discuss in this chapter advocated thoroughgoing revolution—imagined as a wholesale break from the political and economic traditions of the past—but their use of poetry forged a more transformative relationship to tradition. The politics of form appear in this setting as accrued and malleable rather than innate.

I do not seek to measure these poems against a formally innovative modernist aesthetic that was yet to fully emerge; part of what I do seek to demonstrate, however, is the long history of the sudden rupture associated with literary modernism. In her recent study *Modernism and Cultural Conflict, 1880–1922*, Ann Ardis calls for "a much more detailed and nuanced topographical mapping of the period than modernism's classic 'narrative[s] of rupture' have ever produced," arguing that the "competition among emergent aesthetic and political traditions in turn-of-the-century Britain" was fierce and that critical histories have failed to account for "the voracious borrowing of ideas" among rival traditions (10). The prevailing view of fin de siècle poetry, as Joseph Bristow and Jerusha McCormack have shown, has stressed attenuated tradition rather than rupture, "a doom-laden affair that hurtled the Victorian age toward its terminal point" (Bristow 39).[3] However, poetry of the radical press is thoroughly taken up with the notion of historical rupture, typically by means of the figure of revolution; it formulates a poetics of political rupture that precedes modernism's aesthetic rupture. Poets of the radical press seek to create a new culture for the life to come but imply that new forms of thought and new structures of desire can emerge by way of familiar forms. Through their aural appeal these poems and songs suggest the possibility of a live, collective public drawn together by radical print; their reliance on traditional aural rhythms implies a broader sense that, to be politically effectual, a print public must find means of transmuting into a live, voiced public.

With a few exceptions this poetry is a forgotten body of work. Some songs published in the radical press have had afterlives in British working-class movements and radical songbooks, and Morris's *Pilgrims of Hope* has drawn critical interest.[4] But most poems published in these journals were obscure when they were published and are yet more obscure today. I am not interested in establishing a place for them in the poetic canon or in arguing for their aesthetic value—not because I think they lack quality, for I think many are very good. Instead, I want to develop an aggregate notion of how these poems operate in the radical press to express revolutionary ideas in traditional forms. By examining poems and the discussion of poetry in the radical press, we can see that poets of the radical press developed their own theory of cultural rupture through modest adaptations of genre and form.

Form and Reform: Some Examples

Poems of the radical press can be divided into five main types: (1) new work by contemporary radical poets of some renown, such as William Morris or Edith Nesbit; (2) new work by obscure radical poets or by readers of the radical press (some of whom are working class); (3) older poems situated as part of a radical canon, including poems by Percy Bysshe Shelley, the Chartist poets, and continental writers such as Ferdinand Freiligrath; (4) reprints from other radical periodicals; and (5) songs meant to be sung together to build community at socialist events. All these poems work to establish a radical poetic tradition based on traditional poetic form; they assert a prior claim on poetic culture as a precapitalist and preprint formation.

Even anarchist journals took pains to show that culture in its familiar forms would persist under anarchy, but writers in this domain faced elements of poetic tradition seemingly incompatible with the journals' political vision. Anarchist and socialist politics conflict with traditional aspects of English poetry, such as the nationalist ideal in the epic tradition or the primacy of individualist perspective in the lyric tradition, but some poets draw on these elements to craft hybrid forms that can at times ring oddly against their ostensible message. For example, "Dirge for a Despot," a poem that ran on the front page of the June 1885 issue of the London *Anarchist*, commemorates the 1881 assassination of the Russian czar (Figure 20). It was composed by Henry Glasse, a prominent anarchist known for translating Peter Kropotkin into English, and was in some ways a brave poem for Glasse and the *Anarchist* to print. Johan Most, a German anarchist living in London, had been sentenced to sixteen months in prison in 1881 for publishing an article approving of the czar's assassination in his paper *Freiheit*.[5] Despite its transgressive aim, the poem wavers between following and flouting elegiac convention. It offers "All honor to the martyrs / Of Russian liberty," initially appearing to honor unnamed collective agents and a political conspiracy that failed to achieve its objective, challenging traditional notions of heroism: "Success may be the idol / Of cowards and of slaves, / But honor to their failures." Ultimately, however, it celebrates the one successful assassin, indicating that it has not outgrown the habits it associates with cowards and slaves: "The hand at last that triumphed /

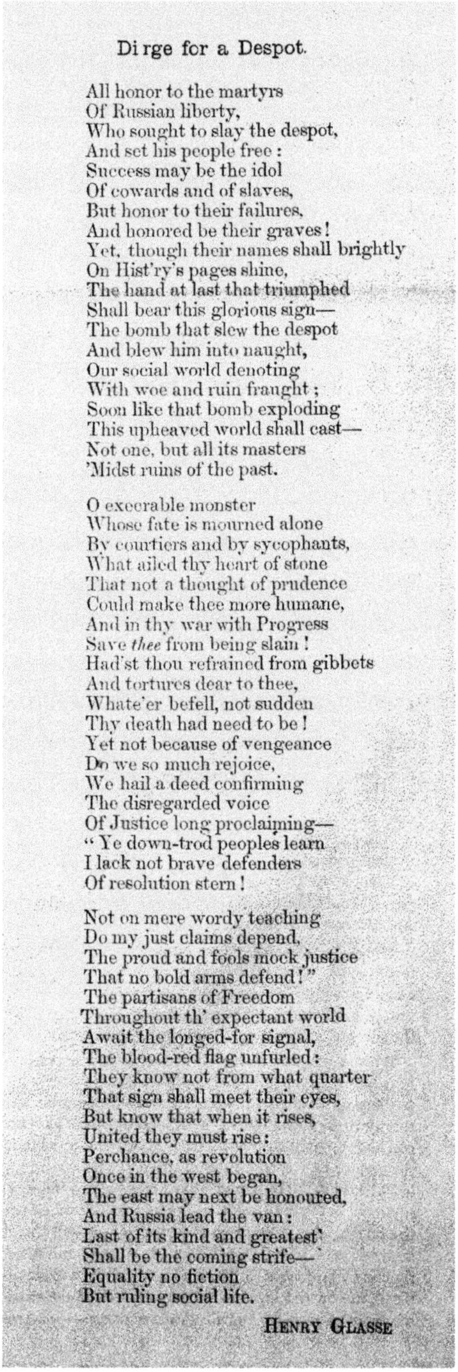

Dirge for a Despot.

All honor to the martyrs
Of Russian liberty,
Who sought to slay the despot,
And set his people free :
Success may be the idol
Of cowards and of slaves,
But honor to their failures,
And honored be their graves !
Yet, though their names shall brightly
On Hist'ry's pages shine,
The hand at last that triumphed
Shall bear this glorious sign—
The bomb that slew the despot
And blew him into naught,
Our social world denoting
With woe and ruin fraught ;
Soon like that bomb exploding
This upheaved world shall cast—
Not one, but all its masters
'Midst ruins of the past.

O execrable monster
Whose fate is mourned alone
By courtiers and by sycophants,
What ailed thy heart of stone
That not a thought of prudence
Could make thee more humane,
And in thy war with Progress
Save *thee* from being slain !
Had'st thou refrained from gibbets
And tortures dear to thee,
Whate'er befell, not sudden
Thy death had need to be !
Yet not because of vengeance
Do we so much rejoice,
We hail a deed confirming
The disregarded voice
Of Justice long proclaiming—
" Ye down-trod peoples learn
I lack not brave defenders
Of resolution stern !

Not on mere wordy teaching
Do my just claims depend,
The proud and fools mock justice
That no bold arms defend !"
The partisans of Freedom
Throughout th' expectant world
Await the longed-for signal,
The blood-red flag unfurled :
They know not from what quarter
That sign shall meet their eyes,
But know that when it rises,
United they must rise :
Perchance, as revolution
Once in the west began,
The east may next be honoured,
And Russia lead the van :
Last of its kind and greatest'
Shall be the coming strife—
Equality no fiction
But ruling social life.

HENRY GLASSE

Figure 20. "Dirge for a Despot" in the *Anarchist* (June 1885). Labadie Collection, University of Michigan.

Shall bear this glorious sign." Its politics are all about revolutionary rupture—"Soon like that bomb exploding / This upheaved world shall cast— / Not one, but all its masters / 'Midst ruins of the past"—but its form is reformist.

"Dirge for a Despot" ran near an article called "What Is the Right Word?" which argued that anarchists must find new words to describe their desired mode of social organization, because existing words are too burdened with connotation. The piece pinpoints a key problem for the radical poet: how to overcome political traditions embedded in linguistic forms. In his utopian novel *News from Nowhere*, Morris imagines that in the socialist future certain words are altogether lost to the English language, understood only by antiquarian hobbyists— *politics, government, lower classes, boycotting.* Poets of the radical press, however, generally seek to revise linguistic form rather than reinvent it, and many are more imaginative revisionists than Glasse in "Dirge for a Despot."

"The Roll Call of the Ages" is an example of such revisionist work. The poem was published almost simultaneously in the August 1884 issue of the socialist journal *To-Day* (154–55) and in the 2 August 1884 issue of *Justice* (5), the newspaper of the Social Democratic Federation (the *Justice* version attributes the poem to *To-Day*). Both journals were Marxist, and *To-Day* was the most theoretical and intellectual socialist organ of the era. Its editors, James Leigh Joynes and Ernest Belfort Bax, wrote at the commencement of the 1884 series: "'TO-DAY' will be the exponent of scientific Socialism. . . . We maintain that Socialism is the inevitable out-growth of the ages." The journal serialized sections of Karl Marx's *Capital* in 1883, three years before the first English translation was published in book form, and included rigorous articles by erudite Marxists, such as Edward Aveling. "The Roll Call of the Ages" was printed with the pseudonymous byline "J. Hope" ("I hope") in *To-Day* but with the name of the author, J. L. Joynes, in *Justice*.[6] In *To-Day* the poem's stanzas were arranged with six eight-beat lines, but in *Justice* they appear as twelve four-beat lines, presumably because of the constraints on line length in a newspaper column versus a magazine (Figures 21 and 22).

The Roll Call of the Ages.

Hark the voice of every nation mid its toil and tribulation
Working out its own salvation, pressing onward to the goal;
Bidding no man turn or tarry, bidding each his burden carry,
Till the bride her bridegroom marry, till earth's wounded hearts be whole;
Till the world-wide Revolution in its triumph of ablution
Sweep each outworn institution down the flood Time's waters roll.

Come then, lest we be benighted ere the world-old wrong be righted,
Let our promise here be plighted that we will not shun the strife;
Though our host should be a stranger, or our hiding-place a manger,
Though our path be dark with danger of the noose or of the knife,
We in spite of foes will never stay or slacken our endeavour,
Till the shears of fate shall sever our thin-woven threads of life.

Hark to those who went before us, hero hearts whose death-pangs bore us,
Us they call to swell their chorus though they know not of our name.
Let us follow where they lead us, caring nought who hate or heed us,
For the sake of them that need us recking lightly of the shame.
Our's the faith that wins believers, our's it is to scorn deceivers,
Our's to know the world's great weavers of the storied weft of fame.

Ah, but how our foes would jeer us, knowing nought of need to fear us,
If they did but overhear us making music of our wrong;
Hark how one saith to his neighbour, " Put away the pipe and tabor;
"What hath mirth to do with labour? what hath toil to do with song?
" Yea if yet ye must be singing and your silly rhymelets ringing,
" Better were it ye were stringing words in praises of the strong.

Figure 21. "The Roll Call of the Ages" in *To-Day* (August 1884).

THE ROLL CALL OF THE AGES.

(From the August number of *To-Day*).

———

Hark the voice of every nation
Mid its toil and tribulation
Working out its own salvation,
      Pressing onward to the goal ;
Bidding no man turn or tarry,
Bidding each his burden carry,
Till the bride her bridegroom marry,
      Till earth's wounded hearts be whole ;
Till the world-wide Revolution,
In its triumph of ablution,
Sweep each outworn institution
      Down the flood ·Time's waters roll.

Come then, lest we be benighted
Ere the world-old wrong be righted,
Let our promise here be plighted
      That we will not shun the strife ;
Though our host should be a stranger,
Or our hiding-place a manger,
Though our path be dark with danger
      Of the noose or of the knife,
We, in spite of foes, will never
Stay or slacken our endeavour,
Till the shears of fate shall sever
      Our thin-woven threads of life.

Figure 22. "Roll Call of the Ages" in *Justice* (2 August 1884).

The poem advocates a Marxist theory of history through form, but it also offers a subtle reading of Marxist revolution as a continuation rather than a break. Its first stanza presents revolution as the unavoidable telos toward which all nations are moving.

Hark the voice of every nation mid its toil and tribulation
Working out its own salvation, pressing onward to the goal;
Bidding no man turn or tarry, bidding each his burden carry,
Till the bride her bridegroom marry, till earth's wounded hearts be whole;
Till the world-wide Revolution in its triumph of ablution
Sweep each outworn institution down the flood Time's waters roll.

The stanza pits the notion of revolution as a *break* from the outworn institutions of the past against a Marxist conception of revolution as the inevitable unwinding of history. Revolution in this poem is a metaphorical consummation (the bride marrying the bridegroom) and a healing (earth's wounded heart made whole); it is not so much a break as a coming together. The form of the poem supports this theme. The regularity of rhyme and rhythm makes the endpoint of each line seem foreseeable, inevitable. Moreover, the consistency of the line breaks, which in most cases are marked by punctuation, naturalizes the necessity of the "break" in poetic form as in history. The poem's fifth line, which introduces the term "Revolution" into the text, is a rare instance of enjambment in the poem, expressing all the more clearly that revolution does not occasion a fracture or break so much as a spilling over. All but two of the poem's line endings are clearly demarcated by punctuation, but this line flows from "ablution" to "sweep"—words stressing fluidity and cleanliness—without stop. The image of flooding here, and the emphasis on the simultaneously destructive and regenerative power of "Time's waters," underscores the point that a revolutionary break is actually an uninterrupted historical progression, not a traumatic rupture.

The discourse around poetry in *To-Day* and *Justice* indicates that many of Joynes's readers would have paid close attention to the significance of form in his poem. For example, H. M. Hyndman reviewed Joynes's *Songs of a Revolutionary Epoch* in the 7 April 1888 issue of *Justice*, and although the review was generally positive, Hyndman took issue with minute formal details in some of the poems. *Songs of a Revolutionary Epoch* translated the German poets of 1848—Ferdinand Freiligrath, Georg Herwegh, Georg Weerth, and Heinrich Heine—into English, and in discussing Joynes's translation of Herwegh's "A Midnight Walk," Hyndman objects to the loss of a caesura in one of the lines and discusses the effect this has on the poem's meaning (3). In *Justice* the political effect of a caesura or a line break was not overlooked.

The steady regularity of "Roll Call of the Ages" theorizes socialism and revolution as inherently ordered—even measured—phenomena, and like other poems of the radical press, the poem could be said to redefine social order rather than disrupt it. A poem by J. Bruce Glasier, "The Ballade of 'Law and Order,'" makes much the same move. The poem, which ran in the April 1886 issue of the *Commonweal* (Figure 23), features an ironic jingoistic speaker but balances its antagonism toward nationalism with the

BAD TIMES.

The present condition of England's workers could surely not have been imagined by the slipshod economists who taught that the people would become better off as their country grew richer and greater. So long as England was "expanding," the condition of the working-class was little heeded. When the present depression in trade began a few Socialists were insisting that the people were as badly off as ever they had been in spite of the nation's enormous trade. Of course such "ridiculous assertions" were easily refuted. Figures galore were cited to show the vast strides that had been made in the comfort and general prosperity of the people. Bright gave us glowing pictures of the results of fifty years' progress, Bradlaugh thundered against those who would dare infringe the sacred rights of property. Brassey showed from the memoirs of his enterprising father, how the British working-man could hold his own against the world. Giffen and Levi floundered about in a chaos of figures which were drawn from suspicious sources and gave conclusions entirely opposed to all practical experience of everyday life. Socialists industriously argued away these elaborate sophisms but got very little thanks for their trouble, as well-to-do people didn't want to be convinced and badly-off people didn't need to be. Now the glaring facts are sufficient to convince all that England's commercial prosperity does not mean that her people are happy. What now of Mr. Bright's statement that the country is "better worth living in and more worthy of our affections"? Would the great reformer repeat this now in Trafalgar Square? What now of Brassey's irresistible British working-man? What of the statistician's 200 per cent, improvement?

The workers have been very apathetic of late, and deserve a good deal of blame for their indifference to the future of their own class. But now that they feel the pinch more keenly they will become more intelligent. As their wages fall their manliness will rise. And once the people do take this matter in hand there need be no doubt of their settling it in a satisfactory way.

The first thing to make itself plain is that our trusted economists are unable to deal with the situation. They are now at their wits' end to account for the great paradox of modern economic conditions—universal famine and superabundance of wealth appearing as twin evils. Men wont starve in a rich country, and Mansion House Funds, be they ever so well stimulated by street riots, will not ward off the evil.

It is every day becoming more plain that the capitalists are unable to handle our great industries without plunging the mass of the people into misery which is quite unnecessary in a land so wealthy as this. In the first place, the capitalists are only anxious for their own enrichment and are regardless of the welfare of the community. In the second place, the system of competition will not allow them to be otherwise. Competition among capitalists makes it above all imperative that goods should be produced cheap. Cheap goods can only be had by cheap labour. We have learnt the important lesson that profits can be increased by lessening wages. (The capitalists knew this before any one told them, and all of them are fully conscious of it to-day without the aid of any political economist.) Cheap labour may be got in two ways: first, by paying small wages to each workman, and second, by introducing labour-saving—that is wages-saving—machinery. By the aid of this machinery the capitalist can raise wages and get his labour cheaper at the same time: he employs fewer hands to do the same amount of work. By this means the artisans have been gulled into thinking they are improving their condition, and even Robert Giffen has been bewildered—or pretends to have been—into stating that the working class are getting a larger share of the national wealth than formerly, whereas in reality they are getting a smaller share of what they produce than ever. That this should be so is inevitable under the present capitalist system, which can only sustain itself by the most rigid cutting down of the labourer's share of wealth. So long as English capitalists have the monopoly of the world's markets, and so long as trade goes on increasing, the workers might never become miserable enough to make revolution a necessity. But our trade is now declining. English commercial supremacy is decaying—and more power to the destructive force! More than a century ago Adam Smith said—what we can now see the truth of—that when a society begins to decline, the first and cruelest suffering must fall on the labouring class. As our markets are being wrested from us, the capitalist is compelled to reduce wages that he may sell his goods cheaper; and thus hastens the destruction of the system by trying to save himself. For when wages are low property is not secure, as M'Culloch naively assures us. Even Giffen now admits that wages must be considerably reduced, and appeals to the workers to accept the reduction in order to save our commerce, upon which our greatness as a nation rests. When patriotism means a reduction of wages, we may look out for the speedy collapse of jingoism. But this patriotism by smaller pay will be made compulsory, and the free Briton brought nearer to starvation that the integrity of the empire (i.e., the unbridled licence of the enterprising trader) may be maintained.

The only way out of these evils is for the working men to take the industries of the country under their own direction and produce goods to supply the wants of the population. The time is ripening very fast. Already the results of the reign of enterprising individualism are being seen in the armies of unemployed, which are steadily growing larger in all our big manufacturing towns. What to do with these men is a question which neither economists, capitalists, nor politicians can settle. But settled it must be, for if the capitalists cannot settle the unemployed, the unemployed will settle the capitalists. No doubt some makeshifts for toning down the present distress can be found, but it is certain that all, from the fund started at the Mansion House, to the Relief Works proposed by the Social Democrats, will prove of very little use. Society has come to a miserable state and civilisation is a sham when men have to starve because their toil has been too productive. Out of the evil there is but one way, and that is for the workmen—and especially the trades' unionists—to be in readiness, so that when a crisis comes they will be able to seize upon the factories, mines, railways, stores, and other means of making and distributing wealth. How this can be done is what they must now consider. If the different craftsmen would discuss among themselves how they could "sack" their employers and manage the workshops, etc., in the interests of the community instead, the matter would soon become easy of settlement. But this at all events we must make up our minds to—the time is not far off when there will be but two courses open to us. Either to stand by quietly, and allow "law and order" to assert itself by butchering the hungry and turbulent masses, or make a determined effort to seize hold of the machinery of industry and manage it for the common good of all.

J. L. Mahon.

The Ballade of "Law and Order."

A Song I sing to celebrate
    Our nation's chiefest glory;
Oh, that I had the language bold
    Of ancient allegory!
What tho' upon hyperbole
    My words might sometimes border?
Know that the stalwart theme is mine
    Of British "Law and Order"!

Our battles won on land and sea,
    Have bards enough to sing them;
New anthems greet our victories,
    As fast as heroes bring them:
And must our nation's nobler fame
    In verse have no recorder?
Shall not a loyal song be sung
    In praise of "Law and Order"?

Our venerable church and state—
    These are its glorious trophies!
It keeps the monarch on her throne,
    The minister in office.
From prince and peer and prelate
    down
To poor parochial boarder,
There's not a British heart but feels
    The power of "Law and Order."

It binds the social fabric firm
    From knavish twists and twitches;
Protects the poor man's poverty,
    And guards the rich man's riches.
It wraps its might round Freedom
    fair,
From Treason's knife to ward her;
Rebellion hides its hideous head
    When stand forth "Law and Order."

'Tis true some trifling blots are seen
    Upon its bright escutcheon,
But these, no loyal subject would
    Now think of dwelling much on.
What tho' a few facts here and there
    A little untoward are—
Spots can be seen upon the sun—
    Thy emblem, "Law and Order"!

Alas! how oft the people have
    Proved purblind and ungrateful!
(What care we how our fellows fare
    When we have got our plate full?)—
And so, in past times deeds were done
    Greatly to be deplored, ere
The mob was tutored in the love
    And fear of "Law and Order."

King Edward, partial to the Scots,
    True "Law and Order" gave them,
Somehow they barbarously thought
    He meant it to enslave them;
So him, and his philanthropists
    They drove right o'er the border,
And said, "Tir king, we do not want
    You, or your "Law and Order"!

King Charles "Law and Order" made
    A mighty state appliance,
Indeed it may be said that he
    Reduced it to a science.—
When to the block they led him forth,
    He spake thus to his warder:
"Alas! I die a martyr in
    The cause of 'Law and Order.'"

King James on pious things intent,
    A church reform projected;
He "Law and Order" wisely thought
    The best means to effect it.—
He crossed the channel in a smack,
    And when he went aboard her,
A bright star left the firmament
    Of British "Law and Order."

Now all our institutions are
    In danger at this moment,
From notions which those Radicals
    There utmost do to foment.
Against all their vile principles,
    Which truly most abhorr'd are,
Let every patriot invoke
    The power of "Law and Order."

When factions bawl about the wrongs
    To which they are subjected,
From press and platform shriek the
    cry:
"The Law must be respected!"
And if we firmly would maintain
    The power of king and lord, or
Privileged class, we must proclaim
    Loudly for "Law and Order."

Some talk of "Right," "Equality,"
    And other such like phrases;
To hear them speak, why really me
    It perfectly amazes!
Do good forsooth! I tell you what,
    They apples of discord are!
Ah, nothing like the good old plan
    Of thorough "Law and Order"!

Some people may have different views
    How best to enforce it,—
Now Buckingham's opinion was—
    And firmly I endorse it:
"Of all the methods I have tried,
    The hangman and the sword are
The stoutest means to propagate
    Respect for 'Law and Order.'"

Now let the clergy inculcate
    In all their prayers and sermons,
How blest peculiarly are we
    Above the French and Germans;
And let their admonition be:—
    "These blessings the reward are
Of our unbounded loyalty
    And love of 'Law and Order.'"

In every nursery and school,
    And barrack room and prison,
Let sheets be stuck upon the walls
    Conspicuous to the vision;
On which, in ornamental text,
    With neat appropriate border,
Set forth the words, "Sedition shun,
    And reverence 'Law and Order.'"

And let us sing, "God save the
    Queen,"
We could not do without her,
And all the peers and gentlefolks
    She likes to keep about her:
And while our voices and our heart
    In glorious accord are,
Acclaim the peerless apothegm
    Of "Long live 'Law and Order'

J. Bruce Glasier.

By means of government and statute law the idle few are licensed to plunder the industrious many.—*Alarm*.

ballad form. Glasier was a close comrade of Morris's—Morris, editor of the *Commonweal*, told him, "I think your 'Ballade' is good; brisk & spirited" (*Collected Letters* 2B: 526)—and was known as an active Scottish socialist. As "the chief apostle of Socialism in Scotland" (Whitely 7), Glasier's authorship inevitably evokes the populist folk resonance of the Scottish ballad, and Glasier himself, according to J. W. Wallace, was prone to reminiscing about ballads sung by his maternal relatives, a family of Highland crofters.

The ballad was the poetic structure "most obviously linked to an account of culture which relied on narrative coherence and the passing on of tradition" (Janowitz 33). Francis James Child and other nineteenth-century collectors and publishers of Scottish ballads had linked this form to oral folk tradition and to cultural continuity rather than innovation. This understanding was in some ways misguided. As David Vincent has claimed, the "'oral tradition' is now regarded more as a by-product of European intellectual history than a substantive category of cultural analysis" (91), and as Ivan Kreilkamp has more recently argued, the "voice of 'primary orality' . . . never existed except within the very culture that is said to have destroyed it" (178).[7] But Glasier and his readers did not know this; in fact, the 25 October 1890 issue of the *Commonweal* printed an ostensibly traditional ballad (in dialect) with the following question to readers: "Does any one know whether any old songs of this kind are still current among the people in remote parts of the country? If any one can send us some we shall be glad to publish them" (343). For the *Commonweal* audience, embedded in the ballad form was an imperative to preserve collective tradition from the assaults of capitalist modernity. But even though some nineteenth-century radicals, such as W. C. Bennett, argued for straightforward preservation of traditional oral ballads as a political measure, Glasier's poem achieves a balance between ironic opposition to modern forms of "order" and formal conjuring of collective tradition by way of the ballad.[8] The poem asserts a prior claim over traditional poetic order and aligns it with a revolutionary critique of the modern British state.

The ballad is an ordered poetic form, relying on repetition, refrain, and regular meter and rhyme that make it easy to learn and remember. Using irony, Glasier's poem sabotages the predictability of the formula, undermining the supposedly inexorable rule of law and order. Even the title, "The Ballade of 'Law and Order,'" incorporates scare quotes to signal its ironic relation to "law and order." The poem's ironic speaker slavishly honors "law and order" as sacrosanct entities: "A Song I sing to celebrate / Our nation's chiefest glory." This glory is "British 'Law and Order,'" an undercelebrated theme according to stanza 2.

Our battles won on land and sea,
Have bards enough to sing them;
New anthems greet our victories,
As fast as heroes bring them:
And must our nation's nobler fame
In verse have no recorder?
Shall not a loyal song be sung
In praise of "Law and Order"?

Glasier uses the regular rhythm and rhyme of the ballad to mock the speaker's unvarying allegiance to formula, which eventually yields awkward and inept phrasings.

When factions bawl about the wrongs
To which they are subjected,
From press and platform shriek the cry:
"The Law must be respected!"
For if we firmly would maintain
The power of king and lord, or
Privileged class, we must proclaim
Loudly for "Law and Order."

The awkward ring produced by the caesura at the end of the sixth line ("lord, or") disrupts the stanza's uniformity, but the speaker doggedly sticks to balladic law; alternating between iambic tetrameter and trimeter, he resorts to an embarrassing rhyme between "lord, or" and "order." Two lines down, Glasier uses a trochaic rather than iambic foot at the beginning of a line ("Loudly for 'Law and Order'"), implying that the order the speaker celebrates is not so orderly after all. No doubt some readers would see these lines merely as examples of flawed form, but I attribute these particular poetic defects to the speaker rather than the author; in a verse that is all about the suppression of dissident political voices, Glasier humorously suggests that dissonance and discord may be superior to a forced or strained harmony.[9] Just as the clumsy rhyme between "lord, or" and "order" disrupts the poem in the name of preserving its rhythmic law (a law it will violate two lines later), so British "law and order" fails to produce a well-ordered society.

The Politics of Formal Innovation

As these examples suggest, traditional poetic forms served as culture-building media in the radical press. During this period, Chris Waters has argued, "the socialist movement attempted to develop a politics of everyday life—and a politics of popular culture" (*British Socialists* 13–14). Poetry was a crucial part of everyday Victorian life and popular culture, as critics such as Houston and Robson have established, but it also represented an elite literary tradition that seemingly hovered above the mass market, independent of popular life. In his 1891 essay "The Soul of Man Under Socialism," for example, Oscar Wilde rails against popular tastes: "The arts that have escaped best are the arts in which the public take no interest. Poetry is an instance of what I mean. We have been able to have fine poetry in England because the public do not read it, and consequently do not influence it" (1185). Wilde is obviously ignoring the vast amount of poetry published in everyday reading materials such as newspapers, not to mention socialist journals, but his comment suggests how poetry as a genre was both low and high culture at the same time. The radical press seized on both aspects of poetry; in the actual poems they printed, editors used traditional poetic forms with aural appeal to develop an appealing socialist popular culture, but the critical discourse around poetry also emphasized the need to create a literary canon suited for the postrevolutionary future society.

To some extent this dual role made for a conflicting sense of what radical poetry should be. Should it be, to adapt Matthew Arnold, "the best that has been thought and said" in radical discourse? Or is this presumption of an elite caste of thinkers itself bourgeois or anticommunitarian? Should a radical poetry instead be communal and democratic in conception? Both ideas are represented in the radical press. In the *Clarion*, a paper that targeted working-class readers, Percy Dearmer argued that to be a "true poet" is to "feel intensely what most men feel but vaguely, to see clearly what they see confusedly, to speak with subtle frankness when they are dumb" (18 May 1895: 160).[10] Sidney E. Dark made similar claims in the *Workman's Times*, another paper aimed at working-class readers. In his article "Poetry for the People," Dark acknowledges how difficult it is for such readers to develop an appreciation for poetry: "Literature and art are almost as much class monopolies as rent and interest. . . . Writing in a paper read by busy hard-working men with little leisure and less spare cash, it is useless to talk about a very extensive or exhaustive study of poetry or anything else" (25 March 1893: 2). He suggests nonetheless that for working-class readers, "an acquaintance with the writings say of Byron, Shelley, Morris, Edward Carpenter, and Walt Whitman cannot but make a man a better Democrat and a more earnest Social Reformer" (2). In his view good socialist poetry is the recorded visions of a few great men: "For our ideals we must go to the poets, to the men who see farther than the rest of us" (2).

In contrast to this Romantic view of poetry—written by "men who see farther than the rest of us"—Alfred Orage argued in a 1904 lecture on the "Idea of Poetry" for the Leeds Art Club (a middle-class, mostly socialist group) that "the basis of poetry was 'rhythmic utterance' . . . the key to it lay in the primitive communal nature of man of which the most distinguishing elements were dance and cooperative labour. Out of this communion of joy and toil arose rhythmic and measured expression" (Steele 80). Orage would go on to edit *New Age*, a socialist journal that became a crucible of modernist cultural debate about literary form, but here he argues for a democratic rather than an elect vision of the poet. As noted in Chapter 3, Orage's co-editor, Holbrook Jackson, predicted in this 1904 lecture that the "novel was dead; as life reverted to a more public and communal state, other forms of literary expression like the drama would predominate" (81). Poetry, which hearkened back to the "primitive communal nature of man"—a preprint state—was, like drama, better suited for the new socialist society.

In communal fashion, readers of the radical press contributed their poems, and many journals reported being inundated with submissions. Response to such submissions again reflects conflicting ideas of what a radical poetry should be. The idea of poetry as collective implied that poems might potentially be contributed by anyone, but this went against the prevailing idea that poetry requires the imprimatur of individual genius. Henry Hyde Champion's *Common Sense* ran poems but actively dissuaded readers from sending them: "Poets . . . are cordially invited to mark their contributions in the left-hand bottom corner with the initials W. P. B. [waste paper basket]" (May 1887: 8). The *Clarion* also complained of inundation: "Voluntary offerings in the shape of contributions received by us during the past two weeks, have been so numerous that we might easily have filled THE CLARION for half-a-dozen issues with gratuitous poems. . . . All these favours . . . we have been compelled to decline." The paper actually appealed to capitalist competition to justify its lack of inclusion: "It is *not* comforting to know that the raw poem of two columns . . . is the anxious work of some poor clerk or governess, struggling to keep a brave young head above water. . . . But an Editor must be brutally just, or he is a failure. . . . It is one of the grand results of competition" (26 December 1891: 4).[11]

The flood of poems received by radical papers suggests that readers yearned for a more interactive literary medium, and eventually the *Clarion* learned to appeal to this yearning with a trick from New Journalism's playbook. On 5 March 1892 the paper held a "Competition for Budding Poets," pitched as a defense mechanism against a torrent of unsolicited poetry.

The alarming prevalence of Poetry in the North of England, manifested unto us by recklessly prodigal contributions to our official waste-paper basket, calls imperatively for retributive measures. We have therefore decided to discourage THE POETICAL FRENZY . . . by offering a prize of one guinea for the most remarkable nursery rhyme of five lines on any political subject of the day. (4)

Weeks later the paper claimed to be wading in 335 submissions to the contest (16 April 1892: 3). The *Clarion Cyclist's Journal*, a spin-off publication for members of the Clarion Cycling Club, likewise offered in its August 1896 inaugural issue a "Prize Competition" for "the best poetry having reference to country life." The prizes offered were "good, useful lamps" (1).

The archive for the Socialist League, which produced the *Commonweal*, is full of letters from hopeful readers sending poetry. Some made it in, but most did not. Reginald Beckett wrote to Morris, editor of the paper, on 8 May 1885, introducing himself and asking, "May I so far trespass upon your kindness as to ask you to read the enclosed lines? . . . I fear you will not find them well done: but I can vouch for their being written in my best heart's blood" (Socialist League Archive, f. 825). Beckett, who was 20 years old at the time, went on to publish thirteen poems in the *Commonweal* and more poems elsewhere, eventually earning biographical notice in the 1898 *Labour Annual*.

Reginald Arthur Beckett: b. Hull 1865. . . . Poorly educated owing to family misfortunes. From age 14 earned living as insurance clerk. . . . Contributed frequently to *Commonweal*, under editorship of Morris; also to *Justice, Christian Socialist, To-Day,* &c. . . . Took charge of *Labour Prophet* [as editor] at a few days' notice, without previous experience, Sept., 1896, and has edited it continuously since. Published "Post-mortem and Other Poems," 1895. (193)

Post-Mortem and Other Poems received a positive review in the *Clarion*: "The poems are graceful, metrically perfect, and very musical" (25 January 1896: 26).

Other readers were not so fortunate, but their letters suggest a general belief that poetry in a socialist paper should be broadly democratic, not the preserve of acknowledged geniuses. An undated letter to Morris, editor of the *Commonweal*, from Sydney Jephcott pleaded: "Of all men in the world at present I most disire [*sic*] your opinion on the the [*sic*] poems herein. And because we sail in the same social boat I make bold to ask it" (Socialist League Archive, f. 1833). Louise V. Boyd offered several poems to the *Commonweal*, writing to Morris on 24 March 1886: "I here offer you some verses, which if they can be available to you in any way will give me pleasure. . . . If you do not find any use for these why no matter—I will not be hurt. You need not even take the trouble to notify me of the fact" (Socialist League Archive, f. 915). Her poems, which persist today in the League archive along with other rejected verse, never appeared in the paper.

One of the operating ideologies in the radical press's appeal to reader-poets was a notion of what we might call the well-versed amateur, which related to late-century ideas of craft and the democratic idea that anyone can develop artistic skill. An emerging concept of craft as a revised version of art was crucial to late nineteenth-century leftist aesthetics, and the figure of the "enlightened amateur," Glenn Adamson notes, was idealized in the Arts and Crafts movement (139–41). In general, radical papers were less interested in positing the native, undiscovered genius of unknown poets than in emphasizing that anyone might develop skill in oration, propaganda, or poetry—quite unlike modernism, which, Adamson notes, only received the work of outsider artists by effacing their amateurism "through an insistence on their native genius" (139). The notion of artistic creation as a kind of craft lessened the distinction between laborers and artists. In a *Clarion* review of Richard Le Gallienne's poetry, for example, Percy Dearmer considered "literary craftsmanship" an "outcome of the workmanlike spirit" (18 May 1895: 160). Veneration of the craftsman-laborer, working outside institutional frameworks that grant "genius" status, dates back at least to John Ruskin but reached a pitch with the late-century Arts and Crafts movement.

To some extent this debate over poetry that we see in the radical press—as a communal craft or as a work of genius exhibiting the excellence of socialist culture—mapped onto divergent approaches to poetic form. Edward Carpenter's *Towards Democracy* is perhaps the most important example of formally innovative late nineteenth-century socialist poetry; it was first published as a volume in 1883, not in the radical press, but it was frequently discussed in radical forums, where its innovation was seen as socialistically and artistically significant.[12] Still, its poetic mode—abstract free verse, first-person voice, imitative of Walt Whitman—did not take root in the radical press. Carpenter uses free verse to evoke new freedoms outside the bonds of conventional forms, whereas radical press poetry typically relies on the familiarity of traditional verse forms. Poems of the radical press likewise do not tend to use first-person-singular speakers, whereas *Towards Democracy* is disarmingly direct in the appeal of its "I" to the reader: "These things I, seizing you by the shoulders, will shake you till you understand them! But my words whether you understand or not is nothing to me—I sort rather with those who do not read them" (1). The speaking voice of the poem is not a fixed "I"—"I am a seeing unseen atom travelling with others through space" (71)—but nevertheless is first-person and is often, apparently, Carpenter: "Lovers of all handicrafts of labour in the open air, confessed passionate lovers of your own sex, Arise!" (33). The "I" of the poem serves to develop what Leela Gandhi has called "a cogent ethics of radical intersubjectivity" (139), but such poetry was unusual in the radical press, and we can see in the reception of Carpenter's volume a socialist debate about the politics of form.

Excerpts from *Towards Democracy* did not often appear in the radical press, and even Whitman, whose name was often evoked as a great poet of democracy, was reprinted somewhat infrequently; this kind of poetry simply did not fit, materially (its lines were too irregular for the newspaper column) or stylistically.[13] Readers were more often exhorted to read Whitman than presented with the words of Whitman. In *Workers' Cry*, a London paper aimed at working-class readers, J. F. Runerman proclaimed in "Art for the Workers," "Reader, don't be an ass! Be a reasoning, feeling man when you look into 'Leaves of Grass,' and a reasoning, feeling man will look out and warmly welcome you" (13 June 1891: 13). An appreciation of Whitman as a person appeared in *Home Links*, which barely mentioned his poetry (15 January 1899: 149–50). The 23 January 1892 *Clarion* says that Whitman "preached the politics of democracy and the doctrines of universal brotherhood" but that he "is not yet very widely known in England" and "has failed as yet to reach the class for whom he wrote" because of form: "One of the chief causes of his failure to catch the general ear lies in the form he has chosen for the expression of his thoughts. . . . He has abandoned both rhyme and rhythm." Remarkably, the article prints not a single line from Whitman. Ultimately, it suggests that the problem is not so much Whitman as the reader: "The 'general reader'—spoiled by daily contact with journalism . . . is not used to searching below the surface" (6). This implies that the periodical medium in the age of mass print is simply not suited for poetry like Whitman's and Carpenter's.

Prefiguring modernism, the aim of Carpenter's poetry was decidedly not broad, immediate comprehension, much less comfortable familiarity, as the quoted lines suggest: "My words whether you understand or not is nothing to me" (*Towards Democracy* 1). Radical press reviewers recognized the esoteric quality of *Towards Democracy* but thought it might be better understood by future generations: Henry Salt, writing in *Labour Leader*, says that "the message of the poem" is "perhaps beyond the full understanding of the present, but destined to be remembered and realised in some future revolutionary epoch" (19 June 1897: 207).

This was also the line taken by Charles Sixsmith, a friend of Carpenter's who often lectured on *Towards Democracy* in radical venues. Sixsmith's notes for a lecture titled "Edward Carpenter, Poet and Reformer," given at the Bolton Labour Church in the 1898–99 session, claim that Carpenter "stands today as [the preeminent] Democratic Poet of England" but that there is a truer democratic ideal apart from what "the demos" actually care to read: "By Democratic poet I don't mean the poet who is read and accepted and cheered by the populace. They don't as yet know much about either Democracy or Poetry. . . . Carpenter has voiced more truly the democratic Spirit" (Sixsmith Collection, 1171/3/2/1). Sixsmith describes Carpenter shaking off metrical form in terms that evoke his celebrated (or notorious) abandonment of boots for sandals: "The form is not that of the ordinary, rhyming verse. That is too cramped and formed for his thought and feeling. He requires and adopts a looser freer style which shall be vital to his purpose" (Sixsmith Collection, 1171/3/2/2). Yopie Prins notes that the idea of form and prosody as a "regulation of thought" appealed to Carpenter's contemporary Alice Meynell, who thought, "All true poets love the bonds of prosody . . . because all true poets have something of the wild at heart that looks for bonds" (268, 264). By contrast, Carpenter's abandonment of poetic bonds signaled freedom from social and political bonds.[14]

Within the radical press Carpenter himself was a voice for formal innovation and protomodernist aesthetics. His article "Wagner, Millet and Whitman: In Relation to Art and Democracy," published in the *Progressive Review* in October 1896, states:

Whitman, as he constantly tells us, accepted most heartily the foregoing literature and literary forms. Then why did he not *use* the old literary forms? But the question is, Why should he use them? Anyone who reads such a poem as Shelley's "Adonais" intelligently, must see that the high-water-mark of expression in rhyme and metre of this kind has already been reached. Nothing *more* perfect in that line can possibly be done. . . . No work can be done in the same form which shall at the same time *enlarge the boundary* of human expression. (67)

Carpenter's essay equates poetic value with innovation and aesthetic rupture and presumes that the task of a poet is to reach a high-water mark over and above what others have achieved. This notion of the poet hearkens forward to modernism but bears little relation to the kind of poetry that was printed in the radical press.

Indeed, a review of Carpenter's *Towards Democracy* in the *Clarion* suggests the unsuitability of his poem for the radical press. Although the review is exceedingly positive, the author, Nunquam (Robert Blatchford), suggests that the poem cannot really be captured in the medium of the *Clarion*: "I cannot properly review this book; it is too big . . . the book is very wide and deep, and we are packed very close for room in the *Clarion*, and I am pressed for time" (16 April 1892: 2). The limits of the periodical medium do not allow for the kind of allusive abstraction that is Carpenter's métier, so Blatchford provides a synopsis: "The book is a panegyric of freedom, nature, and love. It teaches democracy, brotherhood, and the realisation of the human being—the body as well as the soul. It demands the emancipation of mankind, the shaking off of all the shackles. . . . It demands free thought, free speech, free action, and free life" (2). Alfred Orage also reviewed *Towards Democracy* in the 6 June 1896 supplement of the *Labour Leader*. Although Orage would later, as editor of the *New Age*, disparage Carpenter, in 1896 he admired Carpenter's innovation: "Until the appearance of Whitman and Carpenter, and the beginning of a new poetic revolution, the very heart of poetry seems inseparably bound up with regular measure." But "things have suffered a sea-change. . . . In science, in art, in politics, in religion, as in poetry, Democracy has itself to justify. And this justification in poetry cannot be made in the old forms." Orage goes on to associate Carpenter with the primitive, rhythmic, communal conception of poetry that he also developed in his "Idea of Poetry" lecture: "Rhythm in poetry is primarily an imitation of vibration in nature. . . . The conception of nature as One, whose every atom pulsated in sympathy with the very heart of a world, itself a beat in the life of a universe." This is "the highest conception of the form of poetry under democracy . . . to express the universal in terms of humanity—this is the function of the poet of Democracy. . . . *Poetry is the expression in words of the universal in man*" (97). Carpenter's poetry, Orage suggests, may be in first-person voice, but it is nonetheless universal, communal, and collective.

These reviews of *Towards Democracy* in the radical press make the case for the political value of innovative poetic form, yet the poems published alongside the reviews do not innovate in Carpenter's manner. They reach for the same effects that Orage believes Carpenter achieved through formal rupture—universality, collectivity, communal rhythm—but they produce these effects by way of familiar poetic forms. A key difference between these two means of achieving universality—formal innovation versus appeal to familiar forms—is that the traditional poetic forms used in the radical press rely on regular sound and aural effect, whereas Carpenter's poetry does not. Lines from *Towards Democracy*— "Of that which exists in the Soul, political freedom and institutions of equality, etc., are but the shadows (necessarily thrown); and Democracy in States or Constitutions but the shadow of that which first expresses itself in the glance of the eye or the appearance of the skin" (12)—do not exactly have a ring to them. Poetry of the radical press implies the possibility of live, communal voice emerging from print, while Carpenter's verse is squarely print based. Tom Maguire, reviewing *Towards Democracy* under the pen name Gurth, praised the poem's "absolute disregard of everything 'properly' conventional," "in the matter of form, the old halt and lame measures of so many feet to a line and so many lines to a verse" (*Workman's Times*, 19 November 1892: 1). But he maintains that "rhyme and metre will always be the one charming vehicle of song and ballad, and lyrical poetry generally," and Maguire's own poetry leans heavily toward ballad and song. The charm and appeal of traditional poetic rhythms and meters clearly had its own political value within the radical press.

Irony and the Politics of Tennyson Parody

If poetry of the radical press depends on the forms and rhythms of the past, in service of collective appeal and in hopes of stimulating a live voiced public, then how does it define itself as a separate, radical poetic culture? As suggested by Glasier's "Ballade of 'Law and Order,'" irony was for many writers a valuable technique in merging poetic tradition with revolutionary themes because it allowed for critical distance from familiar forms while reaping the benefits, such as audience engagement, of those same forms. Many radical press poems use parody to simultaneously engage and critique established poetic tradition. Again, these poems work both high and low cultural ends; some parodies take the form of light, humorous verse interweaving radical ideas with popular culture (e.g., the *Commonweal* published five Gilbert and Sullivan parodies, reworking the songs with radical themes), whereas others make pointed attacks on the literary elite.[15] Among the latter sort, Alfred Tennyson was the favorite target. For example, the poem "Discharge of the Dark Brigade," by P. E. Tanner, parodied "Charge of the Light Brigade" in the Glasgow newspaper *Anarchist* (distinct from the London *Anarchist*) (22 November 1912: 6). Tanner transforms Tennyson's call to "honor the charge they made"—that is, to honor dutiful nationalism—into a call for the abolition of nation states.

When can their glory fade?	Down with the 'Dark Brigade'!
O the wild charge they made!	Governments of every shade;
All the world wondered.	Too long on us they've preyed,
Honor the charge they made!	And we've been plundered!
Honor the Light Brigade,	Let us raise flaming hell!
Noble six hundred!	Engulf the lot pell mell!
(Tennyson, final sestet)	Already they know full well
	Their days are numbered!
	(Tanner, final octet)

Like Tanner's poem, Tennyson's poem was published in a newspaper, the *Examiner*, appearing "as natural addendum to war news in the 9 December [1854] issue" (Ledbetter 126). Tanner's parody recognizes the poem's appealing mode of popular interpellation, mimicking Tennyson's enthusiastic use of exclamation points. He changes the structure and rhyme scheme from tercets of AAB AAB to quatrains of AAAB CCCB, perhaps indicating that he is adding a line, an addendum, to Tennyson's poem; no doubt the shift also reflects Tanner's inferior rhythmic skill.

As poet laureate for forty-two years, a term that ended only with his death in 1892, Tennyson was the official poetic voice of the nation, and as Kathryn Ledbetter notes, his laureate poems "appear on the newspaper page as inseparable partners with royal celebrity and promote [his] reputation as a privileged insider" (148). The radical press reviled his conservatism and his coziness with the royal family. The poem "A Hindu Poet to Alfred Tennyson," printed in *Our Corner* (January 1883: 36–38), refers to the "prostitution" of Tennyson's mind, evincing his laureate position as proof of his compromised integrity. A similar point is made in the 9 January 1896 issue of *New Age*, in an article titled "The Laureateship."

We have no sympathy with those who have been protesting against the appointment of Mr Alfred Austin to the Laureateship. It seems to us that Mr Austin is just the man for a job of this sort. . . . It is well known that Mr William Morris might have been Poet Laureate if he liked. But Mr Morris is a true man as well as a true poet, and therefore would scorn to write odes to Battenberg babies or to discharge court functions of that kind. But Mr Austin likes to discredit the Muse in this way. He has always proved himself to be a very loyal supporter of the Tory party, of whose achievements he has bragged in verse. . . . We think it a pity that the Laureateship should have been revived. (225–26)

The laureateship was vacant for four years after Tennyson's death but was ultimately filled by Austin, an "immensely prolific Tory nationalist" (Bristow 5) who was "an appalling, if respectable, verse maker" (McCormack 56).

Fred Henderson's 1887 poem "At the Queen's Jubilee," from the *Commonweal*, derides Tennyson's poetic "discharge" of "court functions" by parodying his "Carmen Saeculare: An Ode in Honour of the Jubilee of Queen Victoria," originally published in the April 1887 issue of *Macmillan's Magazine*. Tennyson's occasional poem sententiously ordered the empire to celebrate the Queen's Golden Jubilee.

You then joyfully, all of you,

. . .

Deck your houses, illuminate
All your towns for a festival,
And in each let a multitude
Loyal, each, to the heart of it,
One full voice of allegiance,
Hail the fair Ceremonial. (*Poems* 3: 160)

Henderson, a young socialist activist who later became a Labour alderman and lord mayor of Norwich, imagines a rather different scenario.

The great crowd stretches silently;
No sound of cheering rose from them
While all the pomp and pride swept by,

But mutterings from clenched teeth,

And angry murmurs rose and fell,

And as she passed, the men-at-arms

Had no light task to guard her well. (*Commonweal*, 9 April 1887: 115)

A gloss following the poem (see Figure 24) takes Tennyson to task for writing jingoistic jingles: "The above verses . . . it is to be hoped will voice the sentiments of the workers far more faithfully than the fulsome Jubilee jingle of Baron Tennyson." The gloss is not credited but may have been written by Morris, the journal's editor.

During Queen Victoria's Golden Jubilee in 1887 and her Diamond Jubilee in 1897, antijubilee sentiment ran high in the radical press, and parodying Tennyson's jubilee poem was a source of widespread amusement.[16] John Plunkett has argued that "the imperial extravaganzas" of the jubilees are often "taken to exemplify Victoria's apotheosis as an imperial and national figurehead," "the populist invention of the British monarchy" (17). The radical press, responding to jubilee-mania, is alert to these political stakes. Like Henderson's poem, Henry Salt's "Workmen's Jubilee Ode" from the 16 April 1887 issue of *Justice* imagines a radical response to the celebrations.[17] Mimicking the ceremonial formality of Tennyson's language, Salt depicts revolutionary fires rather than fireworks as the proper means of observing the jubilee: "Yea, by the kindling fire of Revolution, / Great Empress Queen, we bid thee hail, all hail!" (3). The poem appeared at a moment of state anxiety that the jubilee celebrations would be interrupted by violent political protest. Some radicals hoped this would be the case. Charlotte Wilson, anarchist editor of *Freedom*, allowed that she "hoped the Queen would only get well shaken and not killed" (qtd. in MacKenzie and MacKenzie 86). Salt's poem offers an explanation for such hostility: "Lo! all the lands thou holdest in possession / Send thee for triumph-song the self-same tale; / Falsehood, corruption, selfishness, oppression— / These are the satellites that bid thee hail!" (3). Salt had declared a few years earlier, when Tennyson accepted a seat in the House of Lords, that "it is perhaps better that we should now have in Lord Tennyson a professed opponent rather than a lukewarm friend" (*To-Day*, February 1884: 137).

Salt was not alone in seeing Tennyson as "a professed opponent." Morris included a character named Tennyson in his play *The Tables*

AT THE QUEEN'S JUBILEE

FULL fifty years o'er these fair isles
　Plump lady Vic had held the sway,
And all the courtly lords had met
　To celebrate the crowning day.
"For sure," said they, "it is but right
　That loyal subjects every one
Should praise our queen for all the deeds
　Her gracious royal hands have done."

So on a glorious day in June
　A glittering pageant moved along,
And knights in gay attire were there,
　And men in armour stout and strong ;
And banners in the sunlight waved,
　And trumpets filled the air with sound
While in the midst Victoria rode,
　Her head with gaudy jewels crowned.

And far away to right and left
　The great crowd stretches silently ;
No sound of cheering rose from them
　While all the pomp and pride swept by,
But mutterings from clenched teeth,
　And angry murmurs rose and fell,
And as she passed, the men-at-arms
　Had no light task to guard her well.

The good archbishop all the while
　Thought of his goodly golden store,
And pondered deeply in his mind
　How to increase it more and more ;
And all the bishop friends of Christ
　Thought of the very self-same thing ;
While at the ropes in many a tower
　Stout arms made all the church bells
　　ring.

Far on the outskirts of the crowd
　A tattered beggar viewed the pride,
And scorned and jostled by the throng,
　Hugged his rags closer to his side,
And muttered underneath his breath,
　While down the street the banners
　　passed,
"How long shall earth go rolling on
　Ere idle pride shall breathe its last ?

How long before yon sun on high
　Shall look upon the earth and see
Freedom's red banner borne aloft
　By brave men struggling to be free ?
Go on thy way, oh queen, awhile ;
　Enjoy thy little day of pride,
But all around thy pomp and show
　Riseth red revolution's tide.

Go on thy way, the robes thou hast
　Are woven out of sighs and tears,
And every hope thy proud heart knows
　Is built upon the people's fears.
Hide from thine eyes the sight of those
　Whose lives, as mine, are full of woe,
Live out thy little day in peace
　Till comes the day when thou shalt
　　know—

That underneath thee all this while
　Surges and boils a rising fire ;
Whose flame of discontent each day
　Grows ever fiercer, ever higher ;
It undermines thy throne. E'en now
　Methinks I see thy jewelled crown
And all thy pomp and rotten pride
　Into the wild flame falling down.

The people waken. All too long
　Their ignorance hath kept thee up,
But knowledge spreads with misery,
　And while they drink deep sorrow's
　　cup,
Fierce curses in their hearts arise
　At thee and all thine idle show,
Thou puppet on a gilded throne
　The time shall come when thou must
　　go !

Defender of a useless faith
　That tricks the people into prayer,
They find that all the gods are deaf,
　And they are crying to the air.
Unconscious heaven will give us naught
　Lo, we must up and act as men ;
Vampires, who draw our blood to-day,
　How we shall sweep you from us
　　then !

I envy not thy pampered ease
　Though with keen hunger I may cry,
My rags may flutter in the wind
　And life may drag on wearily ;
A little longer I can wait,
　Nor shall the time be overlong,
Till thou and all thy lordly state
　Learn how despair can make men
　　strong !

Ours is the power to destroy
　What by our toiling is upheld,
And out of ruin once again
　A bright new world of hope to weld.
But thou and all thy crew must go,
　Earth has no place for such as thou ;
When men shall rise and strike the
　　blow,
　Would they were ripe for striking
　　now !"

FRED HENDERSON.

[The above verses which it is to be hoped will voice the sentiments of the
workers far more faithfully than the fulsome Jubilee jingle of Baron Tennyson,
acquire additional interest from the fact that the writer is now unjustly imprisoned in Norwich Castle for directing attention to the injustice of present society.]

Figure 24. "At the Queen's Jubilee" in the *Commonweal* (9 April 1887). Labadie Collection, University of Michigan.

Turned, and here the poet laureate utters lines such as "I don't want to understand Socialism" (61). After Tennyson's death, Morris wrote to Shaw, "I consider that I have a piece of luck in not being a professional journalist any longer. Just think if I were still Editor of Commonweal I should have *had* to write something about Tennyson. As it is I needn't and flatly, as you have guessed, I *won't*" (7 October 1892, *Collected Letters* 3: 453). An article on Tennyson in the *Democrat*, a radical journal that promoted land nationalization and adult suffrage, noted: "As a politician we esteem him capable of talking nonsense more eloquently than any other man now extant. The new Democracy is hateful to him" (1 January 1887: 101–2). Six months later, in the 1 June 1887 issue, the journal included a satirical verse on the jubilee, repurposing lines from Tennyson's jubilee poem to make an opposite political argument. The anarchist journal *Freedom* also repurposed Tennyson lines for antijubilee effect; under the headline "The Jubilee" on the front page of the June–July 1897 issue, the editors printed an excerpt from Tennyson's "Locksley Hall Sixty Years After," beginning with "It is [*sic*] well that while we range with science glorying in the time, / City children soak and blacken soul and sense in city slime. / There among the gloomy alleys, progress halts on palsied feet. / Crime and hunger cast our maidens by the thousand on the street," and ending with, "And the crowded couch of incest in the warrens of the poor." *Freedom* credits the lines to Tennyson but does not indicate their source; printing them on the occasion of the Diamond Jubilee, under the headline "The Jubilee," implies that they are a fitting summation of the Queen's reign. The lines were also reprinted in Henry Hyde Champion's Aberdeen paper *Fiery Cross*, to the same effect (29 June 1892: 2).

A subtler reworking of Tennyson was printed in the journal *To-Day* in June 1883 (126–30). Here, the long anonymous poem "Ulysses" offers a far different portrait of its subject than Tennyson's 1842 "Ulysses" and exemplifies why it was so useful for radical poets to draw on and engage with enemy poets. Tennyson's poem depicts an older Ulysses who longs to leave home and return to the sea, but *To-Day*'s Ulysses is lost at sea and longing to return home: "So was I driven about of wind and wave— / And, though methought I sailed a shoreless sea, / And though it seemed all hope of life was gone, / Still, with faint hope, unto the mast

I clave." This is a Ulysses in the midst of struggle, appropriate for a socialist audience "with faint hope." The poem is an allegory of utopianism, revolution, and reformism. Ulysses lands on an island populated only by a beautiful girl, utterly adrift from the rest of the world: "Until this morn / Save hers, no foot the ocean isle had prest, / Which free from every human care and sound / Had ever been." The virgin island is a figure of Utopia—the wholesale break from "our empirical present," as Fredric Jameson puts it (*Archaeologies* 147)—but the poem implies that no such break is possible because of the unstated parallel with Tennyson's poem and because of human desire and memory. Ulysses is happy on the island, "Yet oft across my maddest hours would dart / A memory of times that were no more." He determines to leave.

Why should I tarry here, while far away
The noisy world was toiling evermore?
Oh! I could not eternally forego
All thoughts of home . . .
          . . . ever backwards they would flow
To days long past . . .

At the end of the poem, "from that lonely place, / We steered towards the haunts of living men." The backward flow of the speaker's thoughts mirrors the backward flow of the poem itself, which draws on an ancient story, recently retold by a famed poet. Ultimately the poem comes down on the side of "living men" and the "noisy world" rather than Utopia. It is a poem of engagement, and in the context of the revolutionary socialist magazine in which it was published, it suggests that the revolution can emerge in the forms of the past. Even Tennyson will endure, revised, after the rupture.

The Poetry of the Commonweal

Following these examples of how traditional poetic form and appeals to poetic tradition operate in a radical print context, I want to offer two more focused case studies: an account of the poetry of the *Commonweal* (the revolutionary socialist paper edited by William Morris) and an account of the career of Tom Maguire, a working-class Leeds socialist poet who published in a variety of radical journals, often under the name Bardolph. Because poetry of the radical press is a largely uncharted literary field, my object in these sections is to offer a more detailed picture of how one journal and one author used traditional poetic forms to make an argument about socialist change.

From a literary point of view, the *Commonweal* was the most significant socialist paper of the era, but its use of poetry was typical of the radical press. The paper is best known for Morris's contributions. It included his weekly column "Notes on News" and originated several of his key literary texts, including *News from Nowhere*, *A Dream of John Ball*, and *The Pilgrims of Hope*, and important essays such as "How We Live and How We Might Live" and "The Worker's Share of Art." But these relatively well-known works by Morris only scratch the surface of the journal's literary content. From 1885 to 1894 the journal published 309 poems, 86 percent of which were published between 1885 and 1890, while Morris was editor.[18] Morris left the paper when the Socialist League's anarchist contingent took over in 1890, after which the paper's poetic output declined with the paper more generally; as detailed in the notes to this chapter, the paper went from a weekly to a monthly format and often printed poems anonymously, whereas under Morris it had nearly always named poems' authors.[19]

The *Commonweal* advocated international socialism and included news from around the world in every issue, and its poetry was also cosmopolitan: 53 of its poems (17 percent) were translations. J. L. Joynes alone, editor of the socialist journal *To-Day*, published thirty translations of radical German poets in the *Commonweal*'s pages from 1885 to 1887; these were later published in his 1888 volume *Songs of a Revolutionary Epoch*. (Joynes also published a long serial poem of his own composition, *The Lord Burleigh*, in the *Commonweal*.) Likewise, Laura Lafargue, daughter of Karl Marx, translated eight works by radical French poets. Developing an international canon of radical poetry was key to the *Commonweal*'s literary mission, but many of these poems dated from much earlier in the century, so there was a temporal lag in this kind of transmission.

Similarly, sixty of the *Commonweal*'s poems (19 percent) were identified as reprints from other sources; this kind of reprinting—sometimes called scissors-and-paste journalism—was as common in the radical press as in mainstream newspapers.[20] Often, the sources for these poems were Chartist newspapers of the 1840s, indicating that the *Commonweal* saw itself as carrying on the work of those papers, although it advocated a revolutionary rather than an electoral political program. The journal used poetry to trace a direct line from Chartism to revolutionary socialism, and perhaps to claim a working-class identity for the paper, for although Chartism was a genuinely working-class movement, late Victorian socialism was not. The *Commonweal* had struggled to reach a working-class audience, and, as E. P. Thompson describes, it "never seemed to reconcile the twin tasks of a theoretical journal and a popular propaganda weekly" (*William Morris* 391). The editors seem to have viewed Chartist poetry in particular as a means of bringing a populist sensibility into the paper. The 17 July 1886 issue included "Songs for the People. I. the Selfish Tyrannical Whig," attributed to the *Chartist Circular* (123); there was no need to identify the poem as a "song for the people" when it appeared in the 22 February 1840 issue of the *Chartist Circular*, but it was labeled as such in the *Commonweal*. On 22 June 1889 the *Commonweal* printed another poem from the *Chartist Circular*, "The Strength of Tyranny," attributed to "Charles Cole, A London Mechanic" (195).[21] The *Commonweal* did not typically name the profession of the poets whose work it published, but in the case of working-class poets, it sometimes did. In addition to these and other poems from the Chartist press, the *Commonweal* also published work by established Chartist poets: Ernest Jones most often, but also John Bedford Leno and J. Bronterre O'Brien.

The *Commonweal* used not just Chartist poetry but all poetry as its dominant medium of popular appeal, which accounts for its emphasis on familiar verse forms. It was sorely in need of such appeal, according to the many readers who complained about the dullness of the journal's prose. A letter from Matthew Brown, a London reader, said that the *Commonweal* "seems too high—too magazine-essayical, and its economics too abstruse, for quick *popular* comprehension" (5 April 1886, Socialist League Archive, f. 961). An undated letter from Leonard Hall makes the same complaint: "However splendidly our journal may be fulfilling its ostensible purpose as educator amongst those . . . who are sufficiently informed to understand thoughtful composition, yet to those of us and not of us who toil and spin so much that there is no room in their existences to learn or know, the *Weal* is Grecian Classics and undecipherable hieroglyphics" (Socialist League Archive, f. 1637). Hall had himself submitted poems to the *Commonweal*, although they were not printed, indicating that poetry suited his idea of what a working-class *Commonweal* would look like. Fred Henderson, the young socialist poet from Norwich, also wrote to the editors to complain about the paper's inaccessibility and also sent poetry (7 September 1887, Socialist League Archive, f. 1692). His own volume of poems, *By the Sea and Other Poems*, was positively reviewed in the 2 May 1891 issue of *Workers' Cry* precisely on the strength of its potential for broad appeal: "The work is not only popular in tone, but popular in price, and should create a large demand amongst workers" (10).[22]

The *Commonweal*'s strategy of creating an everyday, popular socialist culture by way of poetry is especially obvious in its songs. Forty-seven of the poems published in the *Commonweal* (which is 24 percent of the journal's poetry, not including translations and reprints) are identified as songs, and of those, about half (26 of 47) list a well-known tune meant to accompany the words. As with other radical groups, singing was an important part of Socialist League efforts to build an alternative culture. According to agendas in the League archive, meetings began with a song, and another song was sung later during the collection (f. 632). Clearly, the ghost of religious ritual is operating in this structure, but singing extended to many aspects of League life. Figures 5 and 10, flyers from Socialist League concerts and entertainments, exemplify the prominent role of song at League events. The 16 March 1889 issue of the *Commonweal* printed the lyrics to four songs (including "La Carmagnole" in French) to be sung at an upcoming League celebration (85). The 11 October 1890 issue printed the words to three songs and even included sheet music for "La Carmagnole" (with English lyrics this time). The inclusion of these songs promised to translate the print public of the socialist paper into a live-voice community. As with Shaw's transition from the novel to the drama, the move here is not so much a rejection of print media in favor of oral media but an attempt to merge print and orality, to create a path from print to live public.

As with the ballad, nostalgia for an ostensibly more communal culture of orality was key to the socialist attraction to the song form. Yeats's 1906 lecture "Poetry and the Living Voice," originally presented to the

Leeds Art Club, pleaded "for the revival of the old organic community between the poet and the folk" that predated print (Steele 126–27). Many voices joining into one was obviously an impressive metaphor for collective action, and singing was also a way to weave revolutionary principles into everyday life; the words of a catchy tune could stay in one's head long after the meeting ended. Morris's "Socialists at Play," one of the first poems printed in the *Commonweal*, originally recited at a League social event, declared: "Let the cause cling / About the book we read, the song we sing" (July 1885: 56). Socialists might create the future, the idea was, by creating its poetry and song. In Walter Crane's "To the Hammersmith Choir," from the 12 January 1889 issue, listening to a socialist choir helps the speaker imagine this future: "My heart took hope and courage good / In thought of days to be, in time untold" (12).

Because they were often set to existing music, songs printed in the *Commonweal* underscore the complicated relationship between form and content in radical press poetry. By providing new words for old melodies, these texts refill the casks of the past with the proverbial new wine. Chris Waters, in an analysis of socialist songbooks, notes that there were complaints about the use of ill-fitting tunes for socialist songs. For example, many critics "felt that the attempt to fit the 'Hymn of the Proletariat' by the Austrian anarchist Johann Most to the tune of the 'British Grenadiers' was an exercise in futility" (Waters, *British Socialists* 117). Yet surely there was an element of irony in such choices that parodied the patriotic sentiments of songs like "British Grenadiers." The 2 August 1890 issue of the *Commonweal* printed D. J. Nicoll's "The British Grenadiers: An Anti-Patriotic Song," which called on British soldiers to abandon the state and align with the people when the revolution comes.

Now all you gallant soldiers
Think of your comrades all;
Remember, too, your tyrants,
And when on you they call
To shoot the starving people down,
Away with coward fears.
Throw every rifle to the ground
Ye British Grenadiers! (238).

This was clearly not a desperate grasp for familiar forms of any sort but a pointed repurposing of retrograde forms.

Radical writers were intensely alert to the kind of ideological power that such popular nationalistic songs could wield, and they sought, in repurposing them, to undermine that power. The revolutionary song "When Labour First in Strength Awoke," from the 26 September 1891 issue of the *Commonweal*, was sung to the tune of "Rule Britannia," a song that was the butt of endless jokes in the radical press (120). In the *Clarion's* satirical poem "A Song Before Sunrise," for example, an ironic, jingoistic speaker declares, "I say Britannia rules the waves, / Her standard shields the weak; / And Britons never have been slaves, / Nor shall be—so to speak" (29 February 1896: 65). *Common Sense* printed a collection of blue book extracts on the oppression of shop workers under the ironic headline "Britons Never, Never, Never Will Be Slaves" (May 1887: 14). And a cartoon in *Labour Leader* juxtaposed a starving girl against the backdrop of government ministers toasting champagne, under the heading "Rule Britannia Britons Never Never Shall Be Slaves" (25 August 1894; see Figure 25). Similarly appealing to irony to undermine the song's jingoistic pull, C. Allen Clarke's novel *The Knobstick*, discussed in Chapter 2, describes a crowd's reception of a detachment of soldiers arrived to quell the miners' strike: "A huge crowd met them on the Manchester road. . . . But there was no antagonistic demonstration. Strange to say the assembled people greeted the redcoats with cheers, and—oh, bitter sarcasm and unconscious irony on themselves!—commenced to sing—Rule, Britannia, Britannia rules the waves, Britons never, never, never shall be slaves!" (205).

In a review of Glasier's collection *Socialist Songs*, James Leatham took Glasier to task for assuming that socialist songs should *not* be sung to the tunes of nationalist or otherwise offensive songs such as "Rule Britannia": "I venture to dissent from his conclusion that it would be unwise to wed 'songs breathing the spirit of a new social life to airs of the past many of which are instinct with feeling or reminiscences of an anti-socialist character.' As a matter of fact, several of the best songs in the book are already sung to tunes of an anti-socialist character" (*Labour Leader*, June 1893: 14). Leatham suggests that the socialist lyrics will, over time, supplant the earlier versions: "Burns' songs were almost all set

Figure 25. Cartoon from the *Labour Leader* (25 August 1894) parodying "Rule Britannia."

to old airs; but his songs were so much better than those whose tunes he borrowed that they have taken the place of the older songs. Why should not the same thing happen with our new words to old music?" (14). The incremental, palimpsestic theory of cultural change that we see here exemplifies the broader approach to poetry in the radical press: Old forms are rewritten or redeployed rather than discarded.[23]

In addition to songs, recitation was another means by which the *Commonweal*'s poetry traversed the print-oral divide, gesturing toward a live public emerging from a print public. Poetry recitation was a common practice of the day and a staple of Socialist League activity. A program for one League event has Edward Aveling reciting Morris's "Message of the March Wind," which originally appeared in the *Commonweal* as the first installment of *The Pilgrims of Hope*, and David Nicoll reciting Morris's "March of the Workers," which originally ran in the first issue of the *Commonweal* (Socialist League Archive, f. 3448). The performance of poems that had already been printed in the paper enacted the kind of literary communion that all of the poems and songs in the journal promised, through their reliance on verse with familiar aural features.

While drawing primarily on established poetic forms, the *Commonweal* did make significant political adaptations in its rendering of received traditions into a socialist poetics. Consider its relation to Romanticism. On the one hand, the *Commonweal* claims for socialist tradition the Romantic turn toward a representation of "low and rustic life" and "incidents and situations from common life" (Wordsworth, Preface to *Lyrical Ballads* 596–97). Reprinting William Blake's poem "The Little Vagabond" in the 5 February 1887 issue, Morris added a headnote: "William Blake was almost the first, if not the first, of those poets who drew English poetry from the slough of conventional twaddle in which the 18th century had sunk it; and visionary as he was, he was able to look at realities, and to make his words mean something" (43). Blake's "Little Vagabond" dwells on such unpleasant "realities": "Dear mother, dear mother, the Church is cold, / But the Ale-house is healthy and pleasant and warm." Radical press poetry shares this interest in depicting low and common life; not including translations and reprints, 28 percent of the *Commonweal*'s poetry (54 poems) depict the suffering poor, and 16 percent (32 poems) describe common forms of labor.

The *Commonweal*'s approach to representing such topics, however, diverges sharply from Romanticism. Instead of using the lyrical "I" to express the voice of the suffering individual, the *Commonweal* poets tend to write from a third-person or first-person-plural point of view. Apart from translations and reprints, 22 percent of the journal's poems (44) are spoken from a "we" perspective, and 44 percent (86) are from a third-person perspective. (Of those in third-person, many are addressed to a plural "you": socialists, workers, readers of the magazine.) Only 28 percent (55) are spoken from the first-person "I" perspective, and a third of those are from Morris's and Joynes's long serial poems *The Pilgrims of Hope* and *The Lord of Burleigh*, which are in many ways uncharacteristic of the journal's poetry (my calculations count each serial installment as a separate poem).[24] If we discount those two works from our calculations, only 19 percent (37) of the journal's poems are in first-person voice, and many of these feature an ironic first-person speaker, as in Glasier's "Ballade of 'Law and Order.'" This tendency indicates that the *Commonweal* poets are less interested in drumming up sympathy for suffering individuals—who theoretically could be aided by individual acts of philanthropy—than in calling for wholesale systemic change. In seizing on the Romantic glorification of common man, the journal rejects Romanticism's inclination toward what Jonas Barish describes as "inwardness, solitude, and . . . a pure expressiveness that knows nothing of the presence of others" (326). Just as radical writers were drawn to the collective space of the theater over the individualized space of the novel, so too were they drawn to a collective rather than individual poetic voice.

Another key innovation of the *Commonweal*'s poetry is its thematic emphasis on the anticipatory and on revolutionary historical rupture. Not including translations and reprints, 15 percent of its poems (29) depict the future, and 16 percent (32) make direct references to a future revolution; many more refer indirectly to revolution or the postrevolutionary future. As with "Roll Call of the Ages," published in *To-Day* and *Justice*, revolution in the *Commonweal*'s poetry is ordered by poetic form. Imagery emphasizing revolution as part of a natural order occurs again and again. Marching imagery suggests steady progress, and images of the dawn, the seasons, seeds, and the wind are also common, depicting revolutionary change as part of a natural cycle. Such imagery was not, of course, invented by the *Commonweal*—one thinks of the wind in Shelley's "Ode to the West Wind" (1820), the dawn in Swinburne's *Songs Before Sunrise* (1871), or seeds and seasons in Émile Zola's *Germinal* (1885)—but here the imagery expresses a nuanced version of the *Commonweal*'s political agenda. As discussed in Chapter 1, Morris and the Socialist Leaguers were anti-Parliamentarian socialists who were against participating in electoral politics and who dissuaded readers from voting or participating in reform activities aimed at incremental change. Their position was that only wholesale revolution could eradicate capitalism and usher in socialism, and their political mission was to prepare workers for this eventuality. However, many of the journal's poems present revolutionary rupture as akin to a steady march of progress or a seasonal evolution rather than a break. C. W. Beckett's poem "For Fellowship" is one example: "You may sneer, if you will, at our numbers; / The pathway of progress is steep; / . . . Yet we march, and our footstep is steady, / . . . For we live in the future already" (*Commonweal*, 3 March 1888: 67).

The steady march formulation is particularly surprising in light of the division between reformist socialist groups, such as the Fabian Society, and revolutionary socialist groups, such as the Socialist League and the Social Democratic Federation—a division that was a key hurdle in the development of a unified socialist movement. Even among revolutionary socialist groups, debates about how much to engage in electoral politics and trade unionism and whether and how to back efforts at reform were intensely fraught. Still, a significant portion of the *Commonweal*'s poetry envisioned how the future revolution would occur, and these poems often re-form the revolutionary rupture that the journal advocated into a march of progress poetic. A sonnet by Reginald Beckett, titled "Evolution," begins, "All life is progress," and it ends with the sestet

Fight then beneath this banner, and be bold,
Knowing that Fate, though silent, never sleeps
Though gazing long into the mists of old,
And far into the future's mystic deeps,
For vigil-vision thou mayst but behold
One of its slow gigantic spiral sweeps. (*Commonweal*, 7 January 1888: 5)

In some ways the poem could be read as straightforwardly Marxist: Readers should not be afraid to fight and be bold because history has a form ("gigantic spiral sweeps") moving inevitably toward revolution. But the poem's title is an indirect rebuttal to revolutionary socialism, because "Evolution, not revolution" was a rallying cry for those who wanted to attain socialism by way of incremental reform rather than violent revolution. (The phrase is especially associated with the Fabians.) The poem uses the tightly ordered form of the Petrarchan sonnet, exemplifying how the bonds of traditional poetic form work to transform the *Commonweal*'s revolutionary sentiments into a more "measured" argument.[25]

The point I seek to make here is not that poetic form is somehow antirevolutionary but that the *Commonweal*'s use of it was an attempt to naturalize the idea of revolution for a broad reading audience. The journal used poetry as a popularizing strategy and a form of engagement, suggesting that revolution was not a force of anarchic destruction but an inevitable outgrowth of an older order. Thus the *Commonweal* published poems in traditional forms with aural appeal that gestured toward a new cultural tradition for the future. Its commitment to poetry was part of a socialist project of transforming language, culture, and tradition by drawing on the familiar forms through which people understand and experience their lives; this project attempted to create a wholesale rift from mass print culture and its attendant capitalist ideals, but not from familiar cultural and aesthetic forms.

The Poetry of Tom Maguire

Earlier in this chapter, I described the role of well-versed amateurs in producing radical press poetry. One such amateur who regularly published in the *Commonweal* was Tom Maguire, a working-class Leeds socialist and labor organizer (see Figure 26). Maguire died on 9 March 1895 at the age of 29, but in his short life he contributed significantly to the rise of socialism in both literary and organizational ways. While still in his early 20s, he was a leader in instigating the tide of New Unionism—the effort to broaden the scope of organized labor to include unskilled and semiskilled workers—that swept Leeds in a number of important strikes in 1889–1890, including dyers, gas workers, tailoresses, builders' laborers, and bricklayers. From 1885 to 1895 Maguire also published a great

Figure 26. Photograph of Tom Maguire, from *Tom Maguire, A Remembrance* (1895).

deal of poetry, songs, fiction, and journalism in radical papers such as the *Commonweal*, the *Labour Leader*, and the *Yorkshire Factory Times* as well as in his own short-lived paper, *Labour Champion*. But aside from *Machine-Room Chants* (a posthumous volume of poetry published by the *Labour Leader* in 1895) and *Tom Maguire, A Remembrance* (another posthumous volume published by the Manchester Labour Press in 1895), Maguire's poems exist almost exclusively in the archives of the radical press; even these two posthumous volumes reprint verse that originally appeared in socialist newspapers.[26] In publishing their work, working-class poets were especially likely to be limited to periodical venues, and it is only in looking to the context of the radical press that we can bring poets like Maguire to light.[27]

In 1880s Britain most of the major early socialist organizations were based in London but were eager to make footholds in the industrial North, which was everywhere recognized as fertile ground for socialist agitation because of labor conditions and because of its radical legacy, abiding in local movements such as cooperativism. Maguire was born in a working-class Irish Catholic family from what his friend Edward Carpenter called "the dingy wilds of East Leeds" ("Memoir" ix), a neighborhood that Tom Steele describes as a "densely populated slum . . . hous[ing] an enormous immigrant Irish population, possibly 20,000 strong. . . . The crowded courts and alleys where disease and pollution were widespread, were the breeding ground for socialists like Tom Maguire" (26). According to Carpenter, Maguire, who was responsible for his mother after his father's death, "earned what living he could" as "errand-boy, then as photographer's assistant, and photographer" ("Memoir" ix). At age 18 he was drawn to socialism after coming across a copy of the *Christian Socialist* at the Secular Hall bookstall (the apparent inconsistency of the venue and the magazine perfectly illustrates the unfussy bedfellowism of 1880s socialism). A year later, in 1884, Maguire helped set up a Leeds branch of the Social Democratic Federation, and in 1885, following Morris and others who left the Federation, he launched a Leeds branch of the Socialist League. Later, after the collapse of the League in the early 1890s, Maguire helped form the Leeds base of the Independent Labour Party. Unlike the Federation or the League, the Independent Labour Party was not a revolutionary organization but was focused on winning socialist parliamentary representation, and its roots were in the North rather than in London. To E. P. Thompson, "If we must have one man who played an outstanding role in opening the way for the I.L.P., that man was a semi-employed Leeds-Irish photographer in his late twenties—Tom Maguire" ("Homage" 279).[28]

Thompson observes of Maguire, "Provincial leaders are commonly denied full historical citizenship" ("Homage" 277). Maguire was a key provincial leader in early British socialism, but he was one of its key early writers as well. A general bias against the provincial in literary and historical studies has contributed to his eclipse, as has the general lack of attention to periodical poetry. Leeds was not London or Manchester, but it was an important base for late Victorian socialist literary activity. As I discuss in Chapter 5, at the turn of the twentieth century the Leeds Art Club, an "advanced" group formed in 1903 by Alfred Orage and Holbrook Jackson, "became one of the most interesting sites of radical thought and experimental art outside of London. It popularized the introduction of Nietzschean thought, cradled the early formation of Guild Socialism, [and] exhibited impressionist and post-impressionist painting" (Steele 1). The group was able to take root in Leeds because of this provincial city's "heightened political consciousness," which was the result of the "sudden blossoming of political societies in the 1880s and 1890s, in local branches of the Social Democratic Federation, the Socialist League, the Fabian Society . . . and ultimately the Independent Labour Party" (13). Thus in a sense Orage and Jackson, the "youthful guerilla culturists" of British modernism, emerged from a cultural and political infrastructure that had been built by the young working-class Tom Maguire (16).

As we have seen, most literary socialists were middle or upper class, but many hoped that in the wake of the 1870 Forster Education Act talented writers of working-class origins would emerge as literary leaders in the movement. As Peter Keating remarks, "In an age of self-conscious democracy, emergent Socialism, and Board School education, there were frequent claims that within the working class there was a large, dormant literary talent that universal literacy would awaken" to "give expression to experiences which had been neglected for centuries" (313). Even Oscar Wilde, the apostle of aesthetic autonomy, was thrilled by the poems *and* life story of Joseph Skipsey, the coal miner poet whose work he reviewed in "Miner and Minor Poets" for the *Pall Mall Gazette.*

The conditions that precede artistic production are so constantly treated as qualities of the work of art itself that one sometimes is tempted to wish that all art were anonymous. Yet there are certain forms of art so individual in their utterance, so purely personal in their expression, that for a full appreciation of their style and manner some knowledge of the artist's life is necessary. To this class belongs Mr. Skipsey's *Carols from the Coal Fields,* a volume of intense human interest and high literary merit . . . the life and the literature are too indissolubly wedded ever really to be separated. (1 February 1887: 123)

Skipsey worked in the mines for forty years, having begun at age 7, and his poetry, which Wilde compares to Blake and Burns in its literary qualities, reflects such experiences. To Wilde, Skipsey exemplified the new literary horizons that working-class poets seemed to promise.[29]

Among socialists, Tom Maguire held the same kind of promise, and he received much encouragement from the socialist literati. H. H. Sparling, managing editor of the *Commonweal*, actively sought out Maguire's poetry. In an 1887 letter to another socialist comrade, he wrote, "Ask Maguire if his poetry engine won't turn out something more of the 'Be Content' kind?" (Socialist League Archive, f. 2844). ("Be Content," which ran in the 18 December 1886 issue of the *Commonweal*, is discussed in Chapter 1.) Some of the earliest poems turned out by Maguire's "poetry engine" were printed in the *Commonweal*, published under the direction of Sparling and Morris. "Science for the People. I. Oxygen" appeared in the 14 August 1886 issue when Maguire was 20 years old (Figure 27). Although its title, "Science for the People," alludes to working-class educational schemes along the lines of rational recreation and autodidacticism,

SCIENCE FOR THE PEOPLE.
I.—OXYGEN.

WERE it not for oxygen
You and I and other men
Could not live ; bethink ye, then,
    And praise the gods for oxygen.
Animals : the birds and kine,
The fish that swim, the grunting swine,
All live, but scientists opine—
    They could not live sans oxygen.

Since oxygen sustaineth men
Of light and lore and mystic pen,
My blessings over and again,
    My blessings upon oxygen.
Since singing birds and milchen kine,
And fish that swim, and grunting swine,
Are all of use to me and mine,
    I do not grudge them oxygen.

But there are those that cumber earth,
Producing nought, and nothing worth,
Who feast without the fear of dearth,
    And spoil the sweetest oxygen.
I say 'twere better they should die,
And so I'd limit their supply,
And this should be the reason why :—
    They were not worth their oxygen.

T. MAGUIRE.

Figure 27. "Science for the People" by Tom Maguire, published in the *Commonweal* (14 August 1886). Labadie Collection, University of Michigan.

the poem humorously suggests that violent revolution is a more useful lesson for the people than the human respiration system. It begins, "Were it not for oxygen / You and I and other men / Could not live; bethink ye, then, / And praise the gods for oxygen" (155). Two stanzas later:

But there are those that cumber earth,
Producing nought, and nothing worth,
Who feast without the fear of dearth,
And spoil the sweetest oxygen.
I say 'twere better they should die,
And so I'd limit their supply,
And this should be the reason why:—
They were not worth their oxygen.

The poem parodies the self-culture tradition so crucial to Chartist literary ideology forty years earlier. Maguire suggests that a socialist movement must go beyond the autodidactic, self-cultural terms of the Chartist era to promote collective action, not individual improvement.

In terms of politics Maguire was more pragmatic and less of a purist than many in the Socialist League, and his writings for the *Commonweal* reflect this. For example, the League's official position on trade unionism was that it was a palliative preventing comprehensive economic change, but Maguire recognized that the New Unionism, which extended trade unions from the so-called "aristocracy of labour" to the unskilled trades, had the potential not only to make major improvements in the lives of workers but also to radicalize them, paving the way for greater advancements down the road. Perhaps because of his own working-class origins, Maguire's prose writing for the *Commonweal* also shows an awareness of and attention to the question of how to appeal to a working-class audience, unlike many other writers in the paper. Maguire wrote to the editors on 7 June 1885 to suggest "that an effort should be made to simplify and popularize somewhat more the language and style of many of the articles appearing in the *C.* Latin sentences, peculiarity of style (clever and amusing but not adapted to the end in view . . .), scientific phraseology . . . all this palls upon the plain stomach of the worker" (Socialist League Archive, f. 2130).[30] By contrast, Maguire's article "The Yorkshire Miners and Their Masters," in the November 1885 issue, uses the techniques of New Journalism to interest a national audience of socialist readers in the lives and trials of Northern miners. Written as a first-person narrative, the report takes readers along on a journey to visit the miners.

Desirous, during the dispute, of knowing and seeing somewhat of the facts of the situation, I, in company with a few comrades paid a visit to Middleton, a neighbouring mining district some three miles away from Leeds, where the men were holding out against the exactions of their masters. . . . Imagine us in the back parlour of a wayside inn, surrounded by a score of committee men—the executive of the strikers—who are met to dole out the scanty supply of bread and pennies collected during the day from the sympathizing public. (98)

In contrast to the dull, impersonal strike reports that so often filled the pages of the radical press, Maguire uses here classic features of New Journalism as it was emerging in the 1880s: He puts himself into the story, effects a "human interest" tone, and constructs the piece in terms of a narrative arc, inviting readers to imagine the "back parlour of a wayside inn." W. T. Stead had shown earlier that same year, in his "Maiden Tribute of Modern Babylon" series in the July 1885 *Pall Mall Gazette*, just how powerful a form of activist literature the New Journalism could be. The series provoked a firestorm of reaction when Stead demonstrated that for £5, a wealthy man could buy a 13-year-old girl for the purpose of sexual exploitation. Maguire's piece reminds us that the activist quality of New Journalism that Stead tapped into was a legacy of its origins in the working-class popular press. Maguire realized that using some stylistic features of the popular press could make a powerful appeal to working-class readers, and he brought this realization to his own weekly paper, the *Labour Champion*.

The *Labour Champion* was short-lived even by the standards of socialist newspapers. It lasted only five issues from October to November 1893. Printed at the Leeds and County Co-Operative Newspaper Society, the paper was edited by Maguire and crystallizes features of his authorship evident across his literary work. The paper's title design depicts a jester sitting cross-legged, a worker fighting a dragon, and a poor woman holding a baby (Figure 28). The tagline "semper eadem"—everything the same—suggests the condition of economic and political stasis that

Figure 28. Masthead for the *Labour Champion* (11 November 1893).

the paper militates against. The mother and child, the fighting worker, and the medieval dragon were utterly standard in socialist iconography of the era, but the jester is unusual and points to Maguire's use of humor, sarcasm, and irony as political tools. For example, an article titled "The Municipal Show," by "His Nibs" (presumably Maguire), effects the voice of a sideshow barker: "Walk up! Walk up! Ladies and gentlemen. The municipal candidates are about to perform. . . . Be in time, gents, and see the two recently captured Liberal Labour Chameleons—positively their last appearance in public. A prize of one penny is offered to anyone who can tell their true colours" (21 October 1893: 2). The implication is that British politics have become so absurd they can only be discussed in the language of fools, clowns, and circuses.

In many ways the style of the *Labour Champion* can be compared to the *Clarion*, Robert Blatchford's socialist newspaper launched in Manchester in 1891. The *Clarion* achieved a much wider readership than other socialist papers by using elements of popular mass press journalism to present socialist material.[31] The *Clarion* tended toward New Journalism, playing up the personalities of the paper's staff and running lots of human interest stories; it also ran advertisements and sporting news and emulated the language of the sporting press; moreover, Blatchford tended increasingly over the years to strike a nationalistic tone in an attempt to appeal to workers' sense of race.[32] Maguire's paper has the same features, but his political commentary was sharper and more aggressive than the *Clarion*'s. The *Labour Champion* made an effort to use the stylistic features of the popular press to garner a wide audience, but it also wanted to push that audience into political action in a far more confrontational manner than the *Clarion*.

Maguire published a great deal of poetry in the *Labour Champion*, and it was here that he initially developed the poet persona Bardolph, who would go on to publish some fifty poems in the pages of the Independent Labour Party newspaper *Labour Leader* from 1894 to 1895.[33] Bardolph's poetry, typical of Victorian newspaper poetry, tended to be light and topical, commenting on unpleasant news in familiar and pleasing linguistic forms. "An After-Song for Electors," in the 4 November 1893 issue of *Labour Champion*, bemoans the results of the 1 November election by playing on the old Guy Fawkes Day nursery rhyme: "Remember, remember! . . . Municipal treason, / And all round un-reason / Should ne'er be, by workers, forgot" (1). Another Bardolph poem, "A New Nursery Rhyme," draws on popular verse to make an argument against aristocratic privilege: "Isn't it a dainty dish / To lay before the Queen?" (11 November 1893: 1). "The Animal Man," also by Bardolph, targets the base materialism of the capitalist class.

The animal man is a wonderful chap,

He has settled how things should be;

You'd never believe he was suckled on pap,

Or bounced on a feminine knee;

You'd think he was dropt, in a thunder-cloud wrapt,

And let out like a lightning streak,

Full-grown, full-blown, with a will of his own,

And a liberal allowance of cheek. (21 October 1893: 1)

The poem retains the simple ballad meter and rhyme typical of Bardolph's bouncy verse, but the interplay of animal/material and divine/ideal in the poem appeals to both a Marxist materialist critique of capitalist dehumanization ("His heart is a kind of mechanical trick") and an ethical socialist critique of capitalism as immoral and anti-Christian ("His soul is a matter of doubt"). Maguire was a secularist, interested in science and political economy, but he saw poetry and song as a means of generating socialist feeling. As he wrote in a letter to a friend, "People call themselves Socialists, but . . . they haven't got it inside of them" (qtd. in Carpenter, "Memoir" vi).

Maguire's poem "A Victim (Whose Name Is Legion)," from the 30 June 1887 issue of the *Commonweal*, is perhaps his first piece written in the voice of a female speaker, which became a common device of his later poetry for the *Labour Leader*. The first-person perspective was not standard for radical press poetry, but in Maguire's poems the gender difference between speaker and author serves to deindividualize or universalize the lyric voice. "A Victim" depicts a factory girl led to contemplate prostitution and suicide.

O! I am tired of factory toil

   . . .

The factory air is choking close,

   . . .

It is not so in the streets without,
Where all are free to go gaily about

   . . .

'Tis but a step from the factory door
To the streets—to laughter and song and wine,
To the sullen river but one step more,
And there is an end to this life of mine. (245)

The poem is somewhat unremarkable in its sympathetic articulation of the ugly alternatives that drive young women into prostitution, but it does cast light on the particular situation of the female factory worker, who must endure "the factory bully, that comes and goes, / Has never a word—save a curse—to greet." In his later poems written from the perspective of working-class women, Maguire is not always as sympathetic as he is here, but these later poems also reflect his years of experience organizing women workers, some of whom were averse to being organized.

Nearly every poem in Maguire's *Machine-Room Chants* deals with the lives and labors of working-class women, and many are in the voice of factory girls. Maguire himself put together the collection from poems originally printed in the *Labour Leader*, although it was not published until after his death. "Unspoken Confidences (Not Known of the Lady-Visitor)," which originally appeared in the 9 February 1895 issue of the *Labour Leader*, is a rewriting of the earlier poem "A Victim (Whose

Name Is Legion)" from the *Commonweal*, but here the working-class female speaker is married and searching for an escape from her home as well as the factory. The poem voices her private thoughts, unshared with the ladies who call on her out of charity.

Oh! I am tired of factory life,
Tired, tired, as you would be—
I fain would be a rich man's wife,
Or any man's wife but a poor man's wife,
For I am sick of the worry and strife,
As you would be if you were me. (*Machine-Room Chants* 16)

Maguire promoted women's equality within the socialist movement and strongly backed efforts to organize women workers, but many of his poems express frustration with women workers who saw marriage, not unionization, as their sole avenue to a better quality of life. In "Unspoken Confidences" the street offers freedom from the factory prison but also offers release from the prison of marriage.

Drear is the lot of the poor man's spouse,
Drear, drear and dull, ladye,
A prison-cell is the poor man's house,
And what of the rights the law allows?
There is no rest for the poor man's spouse,
There are not rights for such as she. (*Machine-Room Chants* 16)

Marriage, the poem suggests, is not the solution to the problems of factory women but in fact produces additional constraints; systematic reform of women's labor is the only solution—a collective rather than individual solution. Marriage cannot save the speaker from the contemplation of prostitution and suicide that also concluded "A Victim": "'Tis but a step to the streets, and the roar / Of life," she considers, "and but one step more / To the sullen river—when all is o'er— / And there is an end to my shadow and me" (*Machine-Room Chants* 17).

Maguire's poem "An Under-Paid Agitator" best encapsulates the kind of response from women workers that he writes against in "Unspoken Confidences." "An Under-Paid Agitator" appeared in the 29 December 1894 issue of the *Labour Leader* but draws on Maguire's experience in organizing the Leeds tailoresses' strike of October 1889. Maguire, with Clementina Black and Isabella Ford, led 1,000 seamstresses to unionize and strike at Arthur & Co. tailoring works, and they were so successful that "the strike fund had been receiving nearly £100 a day from public donations as a result of the campaign for fair play led by Maguire" (Battle 9). Regrettably, the strike collapsed after six weeks, with the women returning to work under unchanged conditions, but a few months later Arthur & Co. granted some of their demands.[34] "An Under-Paid Agitator" is written from the perspective of a factory girl in favor of unionization, although her co-workers are resistant.

> It's cruel to cut things so fine—
> It's strange that the girls will not learn
> To fall into line, and boldly combine
> To keep up the wages they earn.
>
>   . . .
>
> And first when I entered the work-girls' union,
> I put it to Sarah Anne Lee;
> But she laughed in my face and called me a 'luny 'un,'
> "No union but marriage for me!" Says she. (*Machine-Room Chants* 29)

Again, the marriage "union" is the agitator's main impediment to unionizing women workers. The next stanza addresses some of the particular indignities that had driven the seamstresses at Arthur & Co. to strike.

> It's shameful to put us on "piece,"
> And fine us at times if we're late,
> When the work in the shop has come to a stop,
> And there's nothing to do but to wait.
>
>   . . .
>
> And I put it to Sarah Anne Lee, that the union
> Said fines such as them shouldn't be;
> But she snapped and declared I was always a "moony 'un,"
> "The tight marriage union for me!" (*Machine-Room Chants* 29)

Sarah Anne Lee goes on to marry, but as in "Unspoken Confidences," she must continue working in the factory because of her husband's low wages. Eventually, her husband abandons her, and she and her baby die in childbirth. The final stanza puts the lesson to readers directly: "The work-girl wife still toils for dear life, / And attends to her home-work as well"—which feminists now call the second shift— "We bend to our slavish lot, / And pile up the wrong, till our prince comes along, / When we go, arm in arm, straight to pot." The poem goes on to make a direct attack on recalcitrant women workers: "You proud women-snobs, who sneer at the union, / What fools in your hearts are ye! / Vain self-loving slaves! you are bidding for graves / Like that which holds Sarah Anne Lee—Rent free." Blunt accusation was part of Maguire's confrontational literary style, whether speaking to women or men; here, he seeks to disabuse women readers of the *Labour Leader* of the idea that marriage is an escape from the oppressive conditions of factory labor.

Maguire's poetry could be harsh and accusatory toward readers, but the dominant note running through these poems is outrage at the exploitation of women workers. Again reflecting the influence of New Journalism that we see in his prose, Maguire's poem "The Minotaur," from the 15 December 1894 issue of the *Labour Leader,* presents women's factory labor in the garment trades as a form of abuse akin to what W. T. Stead uncovered in the "Maiden Tribute of Modern Babylon" for the *Pall Mall Gazette.* Stead's series used the mythological figure of the minotaur to depict the buying and selling of girls as a primeval human sacrifice of virgins in the modern metropolis. As Judith Walkowitz notes, one of Stead's villains was "a retired doctor, called the London Minotaur, 'who devotes his fortune to the 'ruin' of three maids a night'" (99). Echoing Stead, Maguire's "Minotaur" depicts female factory workers in the clothing trade as "tribute" for the "factory Minotaur": "Clothes are cheap in the world to-day— / Cheaper the women are, / And mournfully they their tribute pay / To the factory Minotaur" (*Machine-Room Chants* 19).

Stead's series produced a thunderclap of shock across the nation, but Maguire's poem suggests that readers should be equally shocked by the *legal* exploitation of women. "The Minotaur" graphically illustrates the unsanitary conditions of garment production, presenting the Leeds factories as cesspits for the dregs and contaminants of Continental castoffs.

Cholera rags, diphtherical tags,
Are bundled to England in bales and bags,

Worn-out stockings, and socks, and pants,

Shirts and bodices, blouses from France,

Cast-off singlets and derelict rugs—

The whole lot seething with alien bugs;

In short, all wear that has reached its last level,

Is forwarded Yorkshire—*via* Leeds—to the "devil."

The rags are cast in the "devil's" wide maw,

He tears them to tatters with steel tooth and claw:

From tatters he rends them asunder to shreds,

Till nothing remains but manure and fine threads;

    . . .

And thus are the sheddings of every poor body

Reclaimed from the gutter and made into Shoddy. (*Machine-Room Chants* 18)

Focusing on the use of clothing rags as material in Yorkshire textile manufacturing, the poem stresses the health threats to young women workers surrounded by "alien bugs." In references to French underwear, we see the appeal to nationalism (complicated by his Irish heritage) that at times manifests in Maguire's literary work. But the emphasis is on the cheapness, shoddiness, and repulsiveness of the manufactured products: the "fine threads" interwoven with "manure" and "the sheddings of every poor body." Textile manufacturing in Leeds entails the human sacrifice of young women for the production of fabric that is putrid and poor.

Not all of Maguire's work is this denunciatory; to counterbalance such poems as "The Minotaur," Maguire, a lover of music, also published a great deal of songs—songs that celebrate the joy of group expression and work to prompt collective spirit rather than collective outrage. Alf Mattison, a Leeds socialist, recalled the influence of Maguire's songs among the workers he organized: When Maguire spent several months "organising a strike of the Jewish workers in Leeds—some 3000 in number . . . a great feature of the strike was a song written by Maguire, entitled 'The Song of the Sweater's Victim'—the singing of which by several hundred Jews in their broken English may be better imagined than described" (xvii). Because of Maguire's work organizing Jewish garment workers, historians such as E. P. Thompson and Sheila Rowbotham have considered him an "internationalist" socialist, despite the appeal to nationalism evident at times in his writing.[35] "The Song of the Sweater's Victim" indeed expresses an internationalist vision.

We hope with best of all good men
Better days yet to see,
When hand in hand all over the land
United we all shall be.
Every worker in every trade,
In Britain and everywhere,
Whether he labour by needle or spade
Shall gather in his rightful share. (rpt. in Kershen 67–68)

Edward Carpenter printed two songs by Maguire, "Hey for the Day" and "March, March Comrades All," in his influential song collection *Chants of Labour*.[36] Carpenter compiled the collection to sustain an early socialist movement eager for collective song and an alternative musical canon. "Hey for the Day," which took pride of place as the first song in Carpenter's collection, used the familiar socialist trope of the dawn as symbol of the change to come.

Darkest is night,
We do not fear;
Dawning is near—
Soon we shall see
Morning all bright
Burst into sight:

         . . .

Then hey for the day! (Carpenter, *Chants* 1)

"March, March Comrades All," like "Song of the Sweater's Victim," makes an internationalist appeal to workers of the world.

Lo! we gather a valiant throng
Over the world of nations.
We shall triumph o'er wealth and wrong,
Ranks and creeds and stations.
March, march, comrades all,
Onward ever boldly. (Carpenter, *Chants* 15)

In *Chants of Labour* Carpenter had intended to showcase literary and musical creation by working-class socialists. The songs, he says in the volume's preface, "are for the use of the people, and they are mainly the product of the people." Many have "the merit of being genuinely accepted and in use among Socialist bodies of workmen—some too composed by hearty and active members thereof. Thus the book is in no sense . . . a merely 'literary' production—but emanates rather from the heart of the people. May it help to give voice to those who have so long been dumb!" (vi). Carpenter published the occupations of the writers alongside their names in the table of contents, listing Maguire as a "photographer."[37]

After such an active and prolific youth, Maguire died alone in a state of depression and alcoholism. As Thompson describes, "Not yet 30, he was to be found more and more often drinking in the Leeds Central I.L.P. Club" ("Homage" 314). Impoverished and sick, he contracted pneumonia and was found in his home without food or fuel; he died shortly after. Socialist activism and socialist poetry, it turns out, were not exactly lucrative endeavors, as Maguire wryly acknowledged in the "Advertisement" for his planned book of poetry: "Hi, hi, hi! come and buy, come and buy, / You surely wouldn't stand to see a fellow peak and die, / For a poet's sometimes hungry, and he's often rather dry, / And you're earnestly invited up to buy, buy, buy" (*Tom Maguire* 18).

Maguire's funeral offered one more chance for him to unite a vast crowd together in song. More than 1,000 mourners joined the procession, singing together (Barnard 91). It was, in J. Bruce Glasier's memory, "an imposing procession of his comrades in Leeds and neighbouring Yorkshire towns." They "followed his body, borne shoulder high, to the grave" (Maguire, *Machine-Room Chants* 9). Afterward, Maguire's name continued to appear in the radical press, often with an appeal that it not be forgotten. Years after his death, a tribute poem by J. Connell ran in the *Labour Leader*: "Make his sacrifice known, keep his memory green, / Hold the model to all who succeed him; / Such lives and such deaths, oft unsung and unseen, / Are the price that we pay for our freedom" ("Tom Maguire," 7 May 1898: 155). The poem defines another crucial purpose for poetry of the radical press: to preserve memories of the "unsung" for postrevolutionary generations.

Conclusion

Reading Maguire's poetry in the context of the radical press where his work originally appeared illuminates a literary and political moment when working-class writers represented the hope of a literature, and society, to come. Opportunities for young working-class poets such as Maguire to publish in the radical press went hand in hand with a broader tendency in such journals to imagine poetry as collective and communal art, not just the province of Romantic genius. In service of this vision, radical press poetry had many distinguishing features: conventional verse forms; lots of parody, ballads, and songs; regular rhythm and rhyme; pleasing aural qualities; a tendency against first-person-singular speakers. Formal innovation was not one of these distinguishing features, and yet the formal qualities of radical press poetry nonetheless suggest a theory and politics of poetic form on the part of radical writers and editors. Poetry had the virtue of clothing new, radical, and untraditional ideas in familiar and appealing linguistic forms. It could undermine the pernicious ideologies of familiar nationalist tunes and popular poetic forms. Most of all, it could unite the power of live voice within the radical print sphere, promising to translate a print public into a living political alliance.

CHAPTER 5   **Enlightenment Beyond Reason**
Theosophical Socialism and Radical Print Culture

IN THE PREVIOUS CHAPTERS I have sketched out a growing skepticism among late nineteenth-century radical writers toward the ideology of print enlightenment. The ideal of print as a transparent medium for the conveyance of rational debate, only requiring freedom from governmental restriction to circulate enlightened thought among a literate populace, no longer seemed a realistic goal as it had in decades past. Within this larger turn against print enlightenment, we can also see among radical thinkers a movement toward antirational systems of thought, such as theosophy and spiritualism. As Terry Eagleton has said of the fin de siècle, "The period's impatience with discursive rationality leads it . . . to various mysticisms and occultisms . . . to so-called cosmic consciousness and spurious fascination with the Orient" (18). In this chapter I want to consider two prominent socialist writers and editors of the era—Annie Besant and Alfred R. Orage—who were deeply involved in theosophy. This involvement had important consequences for their rendering of authorial voice and subjectivity in their literary and print work for socialism. Their versions of what we might call theosophical socialism were quite distinct, but both writers represent a broader radical turn against print enlightenment ideals under the influence of antirationalist mysticism.

Theosophy is an esoteric, mystical philosophy heavily influenced by Eastern religion—part of a broad spectrum of late nineteenth-century occultist movements, although it was far more articulated than most such movements. Theosophists believe in a universal divine consciousness, the unity of all being, reincarnation, and astral projection; they advocate the study of comparative religions and argue that "the occult side of Nature has never been approached by the science of modern civilization" (Blavatsky 9). The movement grew from the writings of Helena Petrovna Blavatsky, who founded it in 1875 with Henry Steel Olcott. Blavatsky was responsible for Annie Besant's conversion. After Blavatsky's death in 1891, Besant took over as leader of the Theosophical Society in Europe and India, and Olcott led the Society in the United States. Theosophy was not a socialist movement, in the sense of demanding or requiring socialist principles among followers, yet in England many socialists were attracted to theosophy and found an affinity between theosophical and socialist ideals. As William Jameson put it in the *Labour Annual* for 1898, "One of the aims of Theosophy is practical brotherhood—the recognition . . . of the *family ties* that connect every single member of the human race. . . . It follows from this that all social problems whatsoever are closely related to Theosophy" (109).

Besant is the most prominent example of the overlap between socialism and theosophy at this time, but Alfred Orage, W. B. Yeats, Herbert Burrows, and many other late nineteenth-century radicals were likewise drawn to theosophy. Many activists were also drawn to spiritualism, Christian Socialism, the Labour Church, and other religious and anti-rationalist sections of the movement. Even the Fabian Society, noted for its empiricism, originated partly through social links formed by way of spiritualism. Edward Pease, a founding member and secretary of the Fabian Society, recalls attending one of the first meetings of the group that became the Fabian Society "on the invitation of Frank Podmore," with whom he had "become friends through a common interest first in Spiritualism and subsequently in Psychical Research." It was "whilst vainly watching for a ghost in a haunted house at Notting Hill" that Podmore told Pease of "the teachings of Henry George in 'Progress and Poverty,' and we found a common interest in social as well as psychical progress" (28).

Besant and Orage will be the focus of this chapter, not only because of the challenge they pose to Enlightenment notions of print and subjectivity but also because of their prominence as editors and contributors within the radical literary sphere. As a militant secularist in the 1870s, Annie Besant had co-edited the important journal *National Reformer* with Charles Bradlaugh before converting to Fabian socialism in the

1880s. During the 1880s she launched and edited two socialist journals, *Our Corner* and *The Link*, before converting to theosophy after reviewing Blavatsky's *Secret Doctrine* for the *Pall Mall Gazette* in 1889.[1] After her conversion she edited a number of theosophical and other counter-cultural publications, including the Indian nationalist paper *Commonweal: A Journal of National Reform*, titled after William Morris's socialist paper *Commonweal: The Official Journal of the Socialist League*.[2] Inspired in part by Besant, Alfred Orage joined the Theosophical Society in 1896, by which time he had already begun to earn a reputation as a formidable critical voice in the socialist press through his regular literary column for the *Labour Leader*, "A Bookish Causerie," which he wrote from 1895 to 1897. In 1903 Orage and Holbrook Jackson would found the Leeds Art Club, a key bastion of Northern middle-class radicalism, but Orage is most famous for his work as editor of the prominent socialist literary journal the *New Age*, which he took over with Jackson in 1907. Orage and Jackson purchased the *New Age* with the financial backing of George Bernard Shaw, whom they knew from the Fabian Society, and Lewis Wallace, whom they knew from the Theosophical Society (Martin 24). The *New Age* was originally conceived as an independent socialist journal that would be loosely Fabian in perspective, but instead it came to reject parliamentary socialism altogether and became an important seedbed for modern literary movements such as imagism.

The link between the *New Age*, theosophy, and modernism speaks to a parallel strategy of purposeful linguistic difficulty, not to say incomprehensibility, among these discursive domains. Even Besant, in her favorable review of *The Secret Doctrine* for the *Pall Mall Gazette*, admitted that "to ninety-nine out of every hundred readers—perhaps to nine hundred and ninety-nine among every thousand—the study of the book will begin in bewilderment and end in despair" (25 April 1889: 3). Modernist literature, as it emerged in the early twentieth century in journals such as the *New Age*, could be viewed as similarly "hostil[e] toward the common reader," as Jonathan Rose put it (393). Thomas Strychacz, historicizing this propensity, argues that the "perceived value of esoteric writing strategies and the communities of competence they create" was heightened with the rise of mass culture in this era (29). Anticipating the modernist emphasis on obscure prose, Edward Carpenter's *Towards*

Democracy, originally published in 1883, was beloved by countless socialists but was a determinedly difficult, ambiguous, and abstract poetic
work. Carpenter was interested in theosophy, occultism, and Eastern
philosophy, and his poem, as discussed in Chapter 4, challenged the
conventional idea of authorial subjectivity and the author function as
it had emerged in Western culture: "Not of myself—I have no power
of myself— / But out of you who read these words / Do I write them"
(158). His work provides one example of how the obscurities of esoteric
philosophy were absorbed into late nineteenth-century radical literary
discourse in ways that could be said to anticipate modernist poetry.

The esoteric qualities of theosophy—a system of belief that demanded
perpetual study and the pursuit of wide knowledge—fit in with a broader
tendency among some socialist writers, such as Carpenter, to purposefully obfuscate their prose so as to defamiliarize the print interface, to
break away from the easily digested pap of mass print. However, cryptic
theosophical allusions could also function in an elitist way to delimit an
audience apart from the expansive public of mass print, in the manner of
the private radical theater societies discussed in Chapter 3. Defamiliariz-
ing the print interface and delimiting the audience were common radical
strategies of the moment, but they were opposed to the print strategy of
the *Clarion*, for example, or Tom Maguire, who sought to draw on techniques of the popular press. Indeed, despite the popularity of theosophy
among socialists, many socialist journals joked about the impenetrability and incomprehensibility of theosophical doctrine. "Dangle" declared
in the 3 June 1893 issue of the *Clarion*, "Theosophy is simple enough.
Here is a slab of it:— 'The turn of a four dimensional world is near, but
the puzzle of science will ever continue until their concepts reach the
natural dimensions of visible and invisible space.' That so" (5). Maguire, the socialist poet discussed in Chapter 4, likewise published a comic
poem titled "The Lay of a Loose Essence" in the 4 February 1893 issue
of the *Workman's Times*; spoken from the perspective of "Atma-Buddhi,"
a spirit from the East, the poem parodies the fanaticism for theosophy
and Eastern religion within the socialist movement (4).[3]

In this chapter I position the emergence of theosophical socialism
in the context of a changing media and print sphere at the turn of the
twentieth century. In discussing the emergence of mass print and mass

media at this time, Kevin McLaughlin notes the "fundamental inadequacy of a traditional perspective on subjectivity to the workings of the mass media" and "the challenge posed by the mass media to subjectivity" (5). Likewise, Terry Eagleton describes this historical moment as one of "a veritable transformation of subjectivity, as the high-rationalist subject of Mill or *Middlemarch* gradually imploded into Madame Blavatsky and Dorian Gray" (11). Situating theosophical socialism within this moment, I want to suggest that the revised notion of subjectivity offered by theosophy and other esoteric and spiritual movements, especially evident in the work of Besant and Orage, spoke to a need for new models of authorship and readership at a moment when the ideology of print enlightenment was breaking down in the face of an unrestrained mass-oriented capitalist print marketplace. In the context of the radical press the shift in subjectivity that McLaughlin and Eagleton describe is evident in the construction of audience and authorial voice by such theosophical socialists as Besant and Orage.

Mediating Materiality:
Annie Besant, Theosophy, and Print Subjectivity

Annie Besant's *Autobiography* begins with the typical apologetic tone of Victorian autobiographers, who felt the need to justify from the outset prolonged exercises in self-assertion: "It is a difficult thing to tell the story of a life. . . . The telling has a savour of vanity, and the only excuse . . . is that the life, being an average one, reflects many others, and . . . may give the experience of many rather than of one. And so the autobiographer does his work because he thinks that, at the cost of some unpleasantness to himself, he may . . . stretch out a helping hand" (5). Even in the context of this conventional opening, Besant's unconventional idea of selfhood shines through. She imagines stretching out a hand through the medium of the text, as though the text itself facilitates physical oneness among many, and she insists on a universal shared human experience "of many rather than of one," a baseline equivalency among all human beings: "All of us have the same anxieties, the same griefs, the same yearning hopes, the same passionate desire for knowledge" (6). Besant's autobiographical voice in this opening section reflects her theosophical notion of self, where the ego is essentially an illusion that prevents us from recognizing the unity of all life. Alongside these gestures toward communion with readers is a chart of the astrological conditions of Besant's birth, implying that her seemingly individual self is in mystical connection not only with her readership but also with the wider universe: "Keeping in view the way in which sun, moon, and planets influence the physical condition of the earth, there is nothing incongruous with the orderly course of nature in the view that they also influence the physical bodies of men, these being part of the physical earth, and largely moulded by its conditions" (11). Her autobiography ends with a final gesture of communion, a blessing: "PEACE TO ALL BEINGS" (364).

Besant wrote *An Autobiography*, published in 1893, after her conversion to theosophy; earlier, when she still ascribed to a scientific, socialist, secularist materialism, she had written another autobiography titled *Autobiographical Sketches*, which was serialized in her monthly radical journal *Our Corner* from January 1884 to June 1885. The two texts indicate how Besant's sense of self changed amid her conversion and how her representation of print subjectivity transformed accordingly. *An Autobiography*'s opening and closing passages position Besant's text as a means of traversing space and time, of reaching out in a semimystical way to those of us on the other end of the page. In contrast, the first installment of *Sketches* presents Besant's life story as an assemblage of discrete evidence, documentation, and facts for evaluation: "I have resolved to pen a few brief autobiographical sketches, which may avail to satisfy friendly questioners, and to serve, in some measure, as defence against unfair attack" (*Our Corner*, January 1884: 1).[4] This is the classic liberal model of the subject: an autonomous self accounted by way of rational exposition. By 1893, however, Besant's new autobiographical subjectivity cannot be detached from either her readers or the astrological cosmos.

The disparity between these two autobiographical perspectives recalls what many of Besant's biographers have noted about her: She is a woman who seems almost to have lived multiple lives. She began adult life as a devout young Christian who married a stern clergyman before losing her faith. Her refusal to take communion at church precipitated legal separation from her husband, and thereafter she became a freethinker, then an atheist and a scientific materialist, and eventually England's most prominent female advocate for secularism and free speech. For years she co-edited with Charles Bradlaugh the controversial secularist journal *National Reformer,* but in the 1880s she dismayed Bradlaugh by taking up socialism, countering his belief in individualist self-reliance. She joined forces with the Fabian socialists—middle-class advocates of parliamentary socialism through incremental reform—and from January 1883 to December 1888 edited her own journal, *Our Corner,* which became a key socialist publication of the era.[5] Besant distinguished herself nationally by leading the London match girls' strike in the summer of 1888, one of the most important events in the groundswell of labor agitation known as New Unionism (the movement to extend labor unions into the unskilled trades). She won election to the London school board after, as Shaw put it, "such election meetings as, thanks to her eloquence, are unique and luminous in the squalid record of London electioneering" ("Annie" 8). And she attempted to bring unity to the disparate socialist movement in the wake of the 1887 Bloody Sunday outrage in Trafalgar Square by cofounding, with William Stead, the Law and Liberty Defense League and its journal, *The Link.*[6] In 1889, however, Besant suddenly decided that humanity's soul was in most dire need of liberation. Soon she was stumping for theosophy and editing a theosophical journal, and in 1891 she took over as leader of the Theosophical Society. Her connection with the socialist movement continued but to a lesser degree. As the *Labour Annual* said in 1898, "Mrs. Besant's life has been such a human kaleidoscope that it is difficult to decide whether to-day she is a Socialist, but she has undoubtedly done great service to the people's cause" (194). In 1898 Besant emigrated to India, where she embraced the cause of Indian nationalism and became a prominent anticolonial activist and the first woman president of India's National Congress.[7]

Besant's biographers, speculating on her multifaceted life, have long attempted to find unity in her seemingly fractured political experience, but Besant's own account, *An Autobiography,* uses the author's life in print—or rather, lives in print—to articulate a version of selfhood and authorship opposed to the unified, Enlightenment, rational subjectivity associated with Victorian life writing.[8] Although *An Autobiography,* unlike *Autobiographical Sketches,* was not originally published in the radical press, the volume retrospectively recasts the late Victorian radical print sphere in terms of a significantly revised author function, one inflected by theosophical notions of self, voice, and print mediation. Besant's *Auto-biography* can be read as an effort to formulate a composite disunified authorial voice by reprinting writings from radical periodicals and pamphlets of the 1870s and 1880s; she quotes extensively from earlier writings, creatively molding a synthetic self that is divided into multiple voices.

Besant's *Autobiography*, written once she had fully transitioned from scientific to theosophical socialism, draws on various conversions and deconversions throughout her life to create the sense of a fluctuating self and an ephemeral authorial voice; her "writing self" does not emerge as the crowning development of all her earlier selves but as one more self in a long succession, befitting her new theosophical beliefs in reincarnation and astral projection.[9] By contrast, in *Autobiographical Sketches* the climactic and principal narrative event is Besant and Bradlaugh's trial for publishing the *Fruits of Philosophy*, a birth control pamphlet by Charles Knowlton, which they published out of free print principle.[10] The event gives a shape and unity to *Sketches* that is lacking in the 1893 autobiography, because Besant's entire life journey into free thought and secularism could be said to lead her to the Knowlton trial—the culmination of *Sketches*—whereas her later autobiography goes on to narrate the intellectual about-face of her conversion to theosophy, which occasioned a reversal of her positions on atheism, birth control, and many other issues. *Sketches*, the earlier autobiography, also follows an Enlightenment vision of print rationality; in raising the subject of the Knowlton trial, Besant avers, "It is because accusations have been widely made that I here place on permanent record the facts of the case, for thus, at least, some honest opponents will learn the truth and will cease to circulate the slanders" (*Our Corner*, 1 February 1885: 82). In her 1893 autobiography print is not simply a "record" but a mystical medium that allows for the bending and buckling of space, time, and subjectivity.

Biographers such as Arthur Nethercot and Anne Taylor have taken Besant's volatile autobiographical subjectivity as evidence of charming unpredictability or erratic whimsy, but I see her emphasis on a multiplicity of selves in the context of a particular crisis in print and authorship at the end of the nineteenth century. As Gauri Viswanathan has argued, when it comes to critical work on Besant, "the biographical fallacy has succeeded in thwarting any attempt to place Besant's intellectual shifts and religious conversion in a context larger than her own personal travails" (181); critics have failed to consider how her "individual conversions" might serve as "an index of cultural change" (185). In fact, Besant's authorial conversions reveal a great deal about cultural changes in the area of media and print. At this epistemological moment writing had occupied a binary position in relation to embodied speech at least since Plato, but new technologies such as photography and recorded speech, not to mention the marketing of authorial personality in mass print culture, were disrupting the speech-writing binary in terms of embodiment and absence. These shifts inform Besant's representation of print as facilitating a spiritual and material union with an audience she cannot see; they provide an explanatory logic for her quasi-metaphysical depiction of print and authorial voice as well as her construction of a fluctuating authorial subjectivity. Besant's autobiography thus negotiates a broader crisis in authorship and print culture by means of a theosophical doctrine that allowed for mystical dissolution of the bounds between author and reader, present and past.

Consider, for example, the photograph Besant reproduced as the frontispiece to her 1893 autobiography and the piercing fixity of her locked gaze (Figure 29). The photograph insists on the author's embodiment; it implies that the speaking voice of the volume has emanated, or always "is" emanating (in grammatical convention), from this individual body. Yet these words are not embodied. The multiple photographs of Besant interspersed throughout her autobiography keep her body always present before the reader, as a constant reminder of the origin from which the words are detached. Besant uses photography—increasingly reproducible in texts as the century wore on—to draw attention to her words' origins in *and* separation from her body; the ghostly words on the page bear the trace of the body they have transcended, disrupting the Platonic notion of writing as that which is wholly cut off from a speaker's body. In the early 1890s the use of author photographs was becoming ever more common as part of the broader development of a culture of authorial celebrity. With such photographs the ontology of writing and print was being transformed in relation to embodiment and absence. In the context of Besant's autobiography—her mystical musings on theosophy, her multiplicity of perspectives, her habit of quoting earlier writings with which she no longer agrees—the use of photography highlights a

Figure 29. Frontispiece photograph from *An Autobiography* by Annie Besant (1893).

quasi-supernatural element to the sense of authenticity, the illusion of author-reader intimacy, that author photographs evoke.

Besant's discussion of pseudonyms and names has a similar effect. Names, like photographs, pin down individual identity in distinctive ways, yet as her autobiography describes, when Bradlaugh initially hired Besant for the *National Reformer,* she felt compelled to use a pseudonym: "My first contribution appeared in the number for August 30, 1874, over the signature of 'Ajax'. . . . I wrote at first under a *nom de guerre*, because the work I was doing for Mr. Scott would have been prejudiced had my name appeared in . . . the terrible *National Reformer*, and until this work—commenced and paid for—was concluded I did not feel at liberty to use my own name" (*Autobiography* 180).[11] Such authorial masquerading did not sit well with Besant, however, and she notes with relief how in January 1875 she finally "threw off my pseudonym, and rode into the field of battle with uplifted visor" (190). Besant regrets her use of the pseudonymous mask, but in the mid-1870s era being described, authorial anonymity was actually the default position in periodical discourse, as Leah Price discusses.

In 1877, the newly founded *Nineteenth Century* still provoked outrage by putting authors' names on the cover; by 1907 even the conservative *Quarterly* had begun to attribute its articles. Between those two dates, the collapse of the circulating libraries . . . spurred publishers to invent new marketing gimmicks . . . autographed photographs, illustrated interviews, . . . even directories listing home addresses of pseudonymous writers. (214)

Radical publishing was a unique print context, and its writers had distinct reasons for signing articles or remaining anonymous, but anonymity and attribution posed the same thorny questions in the radical press as elsewhere regarding authenticity and objectivity.[12]

Writing in the *Fortnightly Review*, one of the first journals to do away with authorial anonymity, John Morley argued in 1867 that signed articles would produce a new degree of authenticity and earnestness in the periodical press: "If controversy is to become more sincere, more earnest, more direct, and if, therefore, is to be more hard hitting, it is indispensable that those who take a part in it should give the strongest possible guarantee that they mean exactly what they profess to mean, neither more nor less, and that they are ready to stand by it" (313). The decline of default anonymity in Victorian periodicals, however, did not in fact portend a new degree of authorial authenticity within the culture of mass publishing; rather, it signaled a new commitment (often pseudonymous) to the premise of authentic authorship. Besant's pen name, Ajax, is obviously pseudonymous and therefore effectively anonymous, but she describes how she chose the name after a statue at the Crystal Palace, site of the Great Exhibition and a monument to mass production and markets. She does not remark on the irony of this choice, but it reminds us that authors' names and the premise of authentic authorship are as much a part of the new conditions of mass-market publishing as author photographs and other "personalizing" techniques of fin de siècle print.

Laurel Brake describes anonymity policies in nineteenth-century periodicals as a means of asserting a "corporate identity" that "mitigates the differences of . . . individual contributors" (*Print* 4). In this sense Besant's decision to sign her contributions to the radical press and to maintain a policy of attribution in the journals she edits signifies an opposing effort to maintain individualism within a collective body, anticipating her theosophical belief that "each individual is a single consciousness, a unit of consciousness" even as "all consciousnesses are fragments, parts, of the one all-pervading consciousness" (*Communication* 4). Indeed, the idea that writings not only signify individual selfhood but also actually bear it characterizes Besant's treatment of her print career throughout *An Autobiography*. She describes her decision to join the National Secular Society by reviewing her first copy of its newspaper: "I sent my name in as an active member, and find it is recorded in the *National Reformer* of August 9th" (135). Here, Besant's self exists as an entity precisely by means of textual realization. The ego may be an illusion, but it is a text-created illusion. Likewise, in composing her autobiography, Besant borrows extensively from the journals she has edited and the countless pamphlets and articles she has written, quoting freely as a means of recreating her "self" at various moments in the past.

In fact, *An Autobiography* often resembles a collection of Besant's contributions to the late Victorian radical press, woven together with an account of the conditions under which they were composed.[13] This was not a particularly unusual technique in nineteenth-century author autobiographies, but because of Besant's varying allegiances, she no longer advocated many of the positions she quotes herself espousing, which has the effect of highlighting the contradictions and unevenness of her life rather than presenting it as a unified document. *Autobiographical Sketches*, by contrast, uses far fewer quotations from Besant's earlier writings, excerpting only a few *National Reformer* pieces focused on the Knowlton trial.[14] In these few instances Besant's present authorial voice is still in accord with the perspective of her earlier writings; thus the limited use of past writings does not introduce a competing authorial self into the *Sketches*, as it does in the later *Autobiography*.[15] Indeed, although critics such as Nancy Paxton conclude that *An Autobiography* "is framed in retrospect" (341) by Besant's conversion to theosophy, her frequent recourse to past work with which she no longer agrees serves to break the frame of her contemporary worldview, in deference to the ideological multiplicity of her life. The effect is to transform in retrospect the nature of her radical print authorship.

In Besant's use of past writings, print, not voice, becomes the organizing principle of subjectivity. Her frequent recourse to past publications serves not merely to provide a record of experience but to bring the past into the living moment of the present, disrupting chronological succession in an almost magical way. Print emerges as a radically immanent medium: not the dead letter but the living word. One might suspect that this autobiographical mode would pose difficulties when Besant describes sentiments or positions she no longer upholds, but she embraces the possibility of intermingling multiple autobiographical selves by intermingling multiple print sources: "In order that I may not colour my past thinkings by my present thought, I take my statements from pamphlets written when I adopted the Atheistic philosophy. . . . No charge can then be made that I have softened my old opinions for the sake of reconciling them with those now held" (*Autobiography* 140). Far from attempting to deflate prior positions, she reprints them alongside new ones, producing a dialectical autobiography rather than a strictly progressive one.[16] *An Autobiography* excerpts and comments on, for example, Besant's 1876 pamphlet *Gospel of Atheism*, written in the first throes of liberating doubt.

"The ideal humanity of the Christian is the humanity of the slave, poor, meek, broken-spirited, humble, submissive to authority, however oppressive and unjust; the ideal humanity of the Atheist is the humanity of the free man who knows no lord, who brooks no tyranny, who relies on his own strength. . . ." A one-sided view? Yes. But a very natural outcome of a sunny nature, for years held down by unhappiness and the harshness of an outgrown creed. It was the rebound of such a nature suddenly set free, rejoicing in its liberty and self-conscious strength, and it carried with it a great power of rousing the sympathetic enthusiasm of men and women, deeply conscious of their own restrictions and their own longings. (158)

As a theosophist, Besant no longer holds the same heroic view of atheism, yet she places her earlier self from the pamphlet in dialogue with her present authorial self: "A one-sided view? Yes. But a very natural outcome." Her rekindling of this past self suggests that the former self still exists, not so much within Besant as within the pamphlet itself. Rather than suppressing the multiplicity of her past in favor of a fully unified subject position, Besant gives her former selves equal time in the memoir through the transcendent medium of print.

In some cases Besant's past print selves overrule her writing self. Describing the bitter attacks to which she has been subjected, she mentions one critic who said she was "at the mercy of her last male acquaintance for her views on economics."[17] Besant, who prided herself on her tenacity in mastering difficult subjects such as physics and political economy, comments, "I was foolish enough to break a lance in self-defence with this assailant. . . . I certainly should not now take the trouble to write such a paragraph as the following: 'The moment a man uses a woman's sex to discredit her arguments, the thoughtful reader knows that he is unable to answer the arguments themselves'" (*Autobiography* 315). The irony, of course, is that Besant retaliates in the voice of her past self while her writing self remains above the fray.

Besant's reconjuring of former selves is especially evident when she discusses her long legal struggle to print the Knowlton pamphlet, *Fruits of Philosophy*, the struggle that led to the loss of her daughter's custody when she was convicted of obscenity. She acknowledges in *An Autobiography* that she no longer agrees with her former advocacy of preventive checks on reproduction: "I gave up Neo-Malthusianism in April, 1891, its renunciation being part of the outcome of two years' instruction from Mdme. H. P. Blavatsky, who showed me that however justifiable Neo-Malthusianism might be while man was regarded only as the most perfect outcome of physical evolution, it was wholly incompatible with the view of man as a spiritual being" (237). Now, she believes, "By none other road than that of self-control and self-denial can men and women now set going the causes which will build for them brains and bodies of a higher type for their future return to earth-life" (242).[18] Despite her shift to a philosophy of what we might call reincarnational abstinence—substituting spiritual and corporal reincarnation for sexual reproduction—Besant's *Autobiography* offers a convincing argument for birth control as a social measure. It describes the "passionate gratitude evidenced by letters from thousands of poor married women . . . thanking and blessing me for showing them how to escape from the veritable hell in which they lived" (223–24). The chapter "The Knowlton Pamphlet" gives ample voice to the former self who published the illegal manual: "I had seen the misery of the poor, of my sister-women with children crying for bread; the wages of the workmen were often sufficient for four, but eight or ten they could not maintain. . . . Did it matter that my reputation should be ruined, if its ruin helped to bring remedy to this otherwise hopeless wretchedness of thousands?" (208). To voice this position in the rhetorical form of the question repositions Besant's dilemma in the present tense, bringing her past self into the present and posing an unresolved problem for readers. The ghostly presence of an earlier self asserts itself alongside the theosophical Besant who is holding the pen.

According to grammatical convention, texts are often discussed in the present tense; they take on a permanently active tense and are always restating what they say. Besant harnesses this ghostly feature of textuality, using the enduring presence of her past writings to provide a forum for her past selves. As Richard Menke has pointed out, Victorian conceptions of print literature "tended to align storage with materiality, transmission with immateriality, so that writing—with its dual capacity for storage and transmission—occupied a shifting and ambiguous ground between the two" (11). A radical writer such as Morris emphasized print materiality out of Marxist and Ruskinian principle, but in contrast to Morris's use of print—which Jerome McGann argues "is the opposite of transcendental because we are not borne away with [Kelmscott's] pages, we are borne down by them" (*Black Riders* 75)—Besant uses print as a mystical, atemporal, even reincarnational medium. Of course, for Besant thoughts and ideas are themselves material and persist in material forms beyond the written or printed word, which calls into question the very distinction between "material" and "immaterial."

[Man] is ever creating round him thought-forms, moulding subtlest matter into shape by these energies, forms which persist as tangible realities when the body of the thinker has long gone back to earth and air and water. When the time for rebirth into this earth-life comes for the soul these thought-forms, its own progeny, help to form the tenuous model into which the molecules of physical matter are builded for the making of the body. . . . So does each man create for himself in verity the form wherein he functions, and what he is in his present is the inevitable outcome of his own creative energies in his past. (*Autobiography* 241)

Print thus emerges in Besant's autobiography as a material manifestation of the "thought-forms" that constitute the everlasting self, with a special capacity to transmit this eternal self to others.[19]

Doubtless, there is a supernatural element to the idea that one's self can somehow achieve continual reincarnation or permanent presentness by means of print, but Besant, a believer in astral projection and reincarnation, does not accept that materiality and physicality necessarily entail spatial and temporal limitations. Her view of texts follows the odd combination of materialism and mystical occultism also at work in theosophy and spiritualism. For example, in *An Autobiography* Besant excerpts an article that she wrote on theosophy and materialism.

All the Theosophists aver is that each phase of matter has living things suited to it, and that all the universe is pulsing with life. . . . "Spirit" is a misleading word, for, historically, it connotes immateriality and a supernatural kind of existence, and the Theosophist believes neither in the one nor the other. With him all living things act in and through a material basis, and "matter" and "spirit" are not found dissociated. But he alleges that matter exists in states other than those at present known to science. (356–57)

The theosophical idea of a transcendent materiality that exceeds scientific understanding inflects the handling of print and textuality in Besant's work; the text is a living manifestation of an author's fleeting embodied perspective, metaphysically capable of conjuring that presence in ways that violate the dictates of space and time. For Besant the material text becomes a manifestation of its author's spirit, a kind of self-projection impervious to temporal change. As Joy Dixon argues, theosophy challenges the "liberal vision of the body as marking the outer limits of an autonomous and independent self" in favor of a more fluid notion of selfhood (123). Print, in Besant's autobiography, both contains the author's self and brings it into union with others. In this way Besant depicts writing as a medium fully imbued with its author, not orphaned, fatherless, or cut off from its origins as alleged in Plato's *Phaedrus*. Recalling her career on the stump and her career in print, Besant, unlike Plato, puts writing and speech on equal footing: "The written and the spoken word start forces none may measure, set working brain after brain, influence numbers unknown to the forthgiver of the word, work for good or for evil all down the stream of time" (*Autobiography* 189).

Besant was a legendary speaker on the socialist stump. Shaw says that at the time of her conversion to socialism, she was "the greatest orator in England, perhaps the greatest in Europe. . . . I have never heard her excelled; and she was then unapproached" ("Annie" 4). Some parts of Besant's autobiography do privilege the spoken word as an almost erotic form of intercourse between speaker and audience: "What joy there is in the full rush of language that moves and sways; to feel a crowd respond to the lightest touch" (*Autobiography* 117). And yet Besant's first powerfully intoxicating experience as an orator, as a young woman alone in her husband's church, involved no live audience at all.

A queer whim took me that I would like to know how "it felt" to preach. . . . The longing to find outlet in words came upon me, and I felt as though I had something to say and was able to say it. So locked alone in the great, silent church . . . I ascended the pulpit steps and delivered my first lecture on the Inspiration of the Bible. I shall never forget the feeling of power and delight—but especially of power—that came upon me as I sent my voice ringing down the aisles. (115–16)

This famous scene of Besant claiming her voice has an obvious feminist resonance, yet critics have not been alert to the full significance of its absent audience. The scene relies on a new sensibility related to aural media, in particular, the invention and proliferation of the phonograph in the 1870s and 1880s. Here, the power of speech is no longer indexed to the physical proximity of speaker and audience; this discounting of bodily presence accords with Besant's mystical approach to print and authorship throughout the autobiography.[20] Besant's *Our Corner* had occasionally discussed advances in phonographic technology, as in the January 1888 "Science Corner" column: "It is now reported . . . that it will be possible for the phonograph to be used as an ordinary means of communication" (54). The sermon scene in her autobiography also resonates with a scene in Edward Bellamy's widely read socialist novel, *Looking Backward* (1888), in which a live sermon is broadcast to an audience that is absent in body but listens from afar by means of a telephonic device. The subject of Besant's sermon is another instance of powerful words emanating from an invisible speaker: the "Inspiration of the Bible." The point here is not that writing is in danger of being displaced by speech with the development of modern media but that speech and writing are no longer defined by their proximity to originary bodies. Viewed in this context, Besant's mystical vision of textuality emerges not merely as theosophical claptrap; theosophical claptrap itself reflects the changing status of self and voice within a new media sphere.

Besant's autobiography thus draws on periodical journalism and oral speech—two seemingly ephemeral media—to highlight a newly indistinct line between speech and writing. In this way *An Autobiography* makes a subtle connection between a new, modern, transitory sense of self and a new, modern, transitory form of print. In the era of mass print, as print is losing its claims to permanent authority, so too is the self becoming a more variable and transitory entity. The new transitory sense of self, voice, and print at work in Besant's text captures a cultural moment marked by an unprecedented explosion of print media and manifold new aural and visual technologies. All these shifts affected the way that author, narrator, and voice functioned in print discourse. Suddenly, more voices and perspectives were making their way into print and finding a wider audience than ever before, and at the same time new visual and aural technologies were altering the role of the subject in conveying information. These ghostly new mass media transformed written and spoken language's relation to originary bodies and speaking selves; in line with such changes, Besant offers a radical revision of the liberal Enlightenment version of authorial subjectivity.

This new vision of authorial subjectivity perfectly suited Besant's theosophical worldview. When describing her conversion to theosophy, which occurred after she read Blavatsky's two-volume *Secret Doctrine*, Besant describes the work as having both an aural and a textual metaphysical power. She claims to have heard its voice weeks before holding the text in her hands: "Sitting alone in deep thought . . . I heard a Voice that was later to become to me the holiest sound on earth, bidding me take courage for the light was near. A fortnight passed, and then Mr. Stead gave into my hands two large volumes. 'Can you review these?'" (*Autobiography* 340). Theosophy in general and *The Secret Doctrine* in particular brought Besant to a new, mystical understanding of textuality, and *An Autobiography* was written in the wake of this revelation. But despite her account of reading *The Secret Doctrine*, Besant's metaphysical conception of print does not spring wholly formed from her encounter with Blavatsky. Her new vision of print also fits the media conditions of her moment, and we can see signs of a shifting perspective before her theosophical conversion. In the pages of *Our Corner*, in the years leading up to *An Autobiography*, Besant's authorial voice slowly transforms from the rationalist Enlightenment voice of secularist free thought to the mystical voice of theosophical socialism.

In its early years *Our Corner* typically advocated a highly rationalist approach to social problems and the old radical line on print enlightenment and free print. The inaugural issue of the journal, the first publication Besant edited entirely on her own, included the first installment of a series called "Real Heroes," and the real hero that Besant chose to launch her publication with was radical pamphleteer Thomas Paine. Paine had special resonance for secularist agitators, who saw themselves following in his free print footsteps; but for Besant the allegiance to Paine was part of a lingering secularist ideology rather than a burgeoning theosophical-socialist one.[21] Also representative of such secularist rationalism was J. H. Levy's November 1885 article "The Method of Unreason," which argued that if "reasoning may be considered our special occupation, unreason is that which we should especially endeavor to eschew. It is the great barrier to the progress of mankind" (260). Likewise, in her "Publishers' Corner" column in November 1887, Besant mocked the irrational lunacy of the theosophists, although she herself would join this seemingly absurd movement a few years later: "Very strange are some of the publications of this last quarter of the nineteenth century. What is to be said of such a magazine as *Lucifer*, 'a theosophical monthly'? . . . The contents are mere ravings; it may suffice to say that during the perusal of one story the reader is requested to accept 'the theory of the reincarnation of souls as a living fact'" (313). Besant herself would become editor of *Lucifer* a few years down the road.

Alongside such appeals to secular reason, however, the journal also described new intellectual challenges to Western rationalism. It did not ignore the flood of influence from the wider world that was to some extent undermining the hegemony of the Western intellectual tradition. Eastern philosophy and religion were common topics of discussion throughout the journal's run, and such discussions are one place where we can track Besant's mental conversion from scientific rationalism to theosophical socialism.[22] In the January 1886 issue of *Our Corner* J. M. Wheeler argued in "The Hindu 'Song Celestial'":

> As India is receiving Western Science, she is paying us back with her own speculation. The curious modern movement calling itself theosophy admittedly looks to the East for guidance in spiritual dynamics. . . . The influence of a study of oriental faiths in breaking down the exclusive pretensions of Christian dogma and in showing the historic course of religious thought is already a strong one, and is likely to have a yet more prominent place in future. (11)

Published in Besant's journal several years before her own conversion, the article positions theosophical thought as part of a new challenge to the dominance of "Western Science."

Our Corner was likewise one of the few radical journals, as noted in Chapter 4, to publish an excerpt from Edward Carpenter's long mystical poem *Towards Democracy*, and the section that it ran expressed a critique of Western scientific rationalism: "Science empties itself out of the books; all that the books have said only falls like the faintest gauze before the reality—hardly concealing a single blade of grass, or damaging the light of the tiniest star" (1 October 1888: 208–9). Elsewhere the journal published a series of articles by Herbert Courtney on "Hylo-Idealism or Positive Agnosticism," which again challenged the rationalist bases of Western thought. Hylo-idealism was a late nineteenth-century philosophical fad according to which one "logically infers the existence of *one* absolute, which however he recognises as being in itself (even phænomenally) unknowable, inasmuch as the ego, living on a purely relative plane, cannot transcend itself or reach the absolute beyond self" (1 September 1887: 152). The line of thought is contrary to theosophy in its antitranscendental solipsism, yet like theosophy, it emphasizes the limits of human reason. Courtney's series is yet another instance where we see Besant, in her capacity as editor, including articles that call into question the rationalist basis of print enlightenment and secularist free thought.

Besant's development toward theosophical socialism is also evident in her tendency to view society as a collective organism rather than as a whole made up of separate parts; this mode of thought emerged from her intellectual commitment to evolutionary theory but ironically led her to make pronouncements on the nature of being that verge, through science, on mystical theosophical discourse. In her series of articles "The Evolution of Society," which ran in *Our Corner* in 1885, Besant communicates a relationship between individual part and social whole that reaches a conclusion similar to that of theosophy by way of evolutionary theory. She suggests that society be "regarded as an organism instead of as a bag of marbles" and that "it be conceded that the health of the whole depends upon the healthy functioning of every part, *in correlation not in independence*" (July 1885: 8, my emphasis). Human society has evolved to require "association for the common weal" and "the submission of the individual to restraints for the general good." The emphasis on individual submission to collective good was also Fabian orthodoxy and represents a common thread in Besant's evolutionary, Fabian, and theosophical interests. Likewise, in her September 1886 apology, "Why I Am a Socialist," Besant's first rationale for her socialism is, *"I am a Socialist because I am a believer in Evolution.* The great truths that organisms are not isolated creations, but that they are all linked together as parts of one great tree of life" (158). In such writings for *Our Corner* we can trace Besant's anti-individualist, associative strain of thought from evolutionary theory to Fabian socialism to theosophical mysticism.

Besant's doubts about democratic Enlightenment—an inclination of mind that drew her to the Fabian Society as opposed to the more democratic socialist groups, as well as to esoteric theosophy—is another place where we can identify a continuity from her earlier thought to her theosophical socialism. Despite many years of labor for the cause of the working classes, Besant did not subscribe to a revolutionary political ideology and her views on art and culture tended to be elitist, like other members of the Fabian Society. In a two-part article titled "How London Amuses Itself," published in *Our Corner* in 1886, Besant compares West End and East End entertainments, concluding:

If we sum up East End amusements, and the amusements open to the poor all over London, we must sorrowfully confess that the gates of art are closed and barred against them. Amusements there are, but art there is not, and from the nobler and higher enjoyments they are shut out. The music-hall is better, far better than nothing; but where are the music, the painting, the drama, that delight, that elevate, that refine? . . . Throw open all treasures of art to the workers; educate the children, train their capacities, polish their tastes. Let art, the great humaniser, bring them under its gracious sway, softening manners, purifying thought, and gladdening life. (August 1886: 116)

William Morris also wanted to expand working-class access to art, but Besant's tone—"softening manners, purifying thought"—reveals a far less revolutionary vision of art, according to which existing middle-class art forms need only be disseminated, not themselves transformed as Morris argued. The article likewise suggests an unwillingness to recognize value in existing working-class cultural and artistic forms or to consider reaching the working classes on their own cultural terms. Such feelings were typical of Fabian socialists, as Ian Britain argues: "It must be admitted straightaway that none of the Fabians—though more indebted to Morris than is generally recognized . . . ever came close to working out a comparable blueprint for popular culture in a socialist society" (232). He describes a few Fabians, including Besant, as being guilty of "a singular failure to depict the art of the future and the nature of its popularity throughout society as anything more than an extension and redistribution of the most refined artistic enjoyments currently available to their own and higher classes" (232).

The typical Fabian position on art and the masses was also articulated in *Our Corner* by Shaw, who for a time wrote the journal's "Art Corner" column: "The safe and usual course in theatres is to present the public with nothing above the mental capacity of children. . . . The result of this is that serious people, as a class, do not go to the theatre. When the manager declares that 'the public' will not have this, that, or the other, he means that frivolous people will not have them" (January 1886: 59). Regardless of the accuracy of his assessment, the elitism of Shaw's tone—"serious people, as a class"—is telling. Shaw once said that it was through Besant's experiences as a socialist agitator that she "lost her illusions, if she had any, as to the impudent idolatry of the voter which we call democracy" ("Annie" 8). Besant's esoteric theosophy can be viewed as another version of the antidemocratic response to mass print and mass culture that we also see in Shaw and other Fabians. Theosophical speculation entailed a body of knowledge that was purposefully difficult to read and master, and Besant's immersion in it was not unrelated to her proclivity toward middle-class socialism. Unsurprisingly, it was generally middle-class, not working-class, socialists who went in for theosophy.

Thus Besant's changing authorial perspective reflects both her conversion to theosophy and her engagement in broader shifts of the day around media, print, and culture. Although we can identify continuities in her work from *Our Corner* to *An Autobiography*, there is an obvious distinction between Besant's pre- and post-theosophical rendering of selfhood and voice by means of print. *Autobiographical Sketches* presents a unified, developing subjectivity, which culminates in the Knowlton trial; in the later *Autobiography*, when Besant does attempt to identify a unifying theme across her life, she focuses on self-immolation: "Looking back to-day over my life, I see that its keynote—through all the blunders, and the blind mistakes, and clumsy follies—has been this longing for sacrifice to something felt as greater than the self. It has been so strong and so persistent that I recognize it now as a tendency brought over from a previous life and dominating the present one" (57). It is only the transcendence of self—"sacrifice to something felt as greater than the self"— that Besant can present as her overarching selfness. This complicates the separation between self and other, suggesting that these categories do not constitute binaries but aspects of a moral universe that is in the end undivided. Theosophy was essentially a monist philosophy, and Besant's autobiography reflects this in its refusal to clearly delineate the authorial voice as a unified, coherent entity apart from the rest of the universe.

Alfred Orage, Northern Socialism, and a New Age of Print

When Alfred Orage joined the Theosophical Society in 1896, he was, as Tom Steele argues, "inspired by Annie Besant's transcendentalism and Edward Carpenter's mysticism" (2), but he was also expressing a regional inclination.[23] Theosophy, like the Independent Labour Party, was endemic among Leeds and Bradford area socialists, and in general Northern socialism tended to be more religious and less scientific in sensibility than the London movement: "The Socialism that grew up in the North," Stanley Pierson writes, "particularly in Lancashire and the West

Riding of Yorkshire, was a peculiar, indigenous species" ("John Trevor" 464). Carpenter's back-to-the-land mysticism and skepticism toward Enlightenment rationalism had had a great impact in the area, and residual evangelicalism likewise manifested in movements such as the Labour Church, founded in 1891 by Unitarian minister John Trevor. Logie Barrow notes that the "geographical pattern" of interaction between spiritualism and the labor movement "remained predominantly northern and Pennine until the 1900s" and "corresponded very closely to that of Keir Hardie's Independent Labour Party (founded 1893) and with the Labour Churches which, during the 1890s, were virtually the ILP at prayer" (43). Socialism was at its most fervent in this part of the country, and it was a form of socialism particularly disinclined toward scientific rationalism and inclined toward spiritual feeling.

The Labour Church was a key manifestation of this tendency. As founder John Trevor explained in the organization's paper, the *Labour Prophet*, the Labour Church was not religious in theology so much as in sentiment; the idea was "not to bring Christianity into the Labour Movement, but to insist on the fact that the Labour Movement is itself a religious movement, and does not need to have any particular type of religion imparted into it" (May 1892: 40). Although the *Labour Prophet*'s audience was much more plebeian than that of Annie Besant or Alfred Orage, Trevor had many of the same discursive tendencies as these writers in his handling of authorial perspective and the nature of print.[24] For example, in an enthusiastic May 1894 article about Carpenter's *Towards Democracy*, Trevor envisions a metaphysical print medium along the lines imagined in Besant's *Autobiography*.

Quite a long time ago . . . I wanted to write some sort of a book which should address itself very personally and closely to any one who cared to read it—establish so to speak an intimate personal relation between myself and the reader, and during successive years I made several attempts. . . . I began to think the quest was an unreasonable one. . . . While it might not be difficult for any one with a pliant and sympathetic disposition to touch certain chords in any given individual that he met, it seemed impossible to hope that a *book*—which cannot in any way adapt itself to the idiosyncrasies of the reader—could find the key of the personalities into whose hands it might come. For this it would be necessary to suppose, and to find, an absolutely common ground to all individuals. (49)

At last in 1881, Trevor recalls, he seemed to have found this common ground. He became "conscious of the disclosure within me of a region transcending in some sense the ordinary bounds of personality, in the light of which region my own idiosyncrasies of character . . . appeared of no importance whatever. . . . I also immediately saw, or rather *felt*, that this region of self existing in me existed equally (though not always equally *consciously*) in others" (*Labour Prophet*, May 1894: 49). Like Besant in the opening pages of her autobiography, Trevor seeks to touch a common, universal chord among readers, but it is not until he reads *Towards Democracy* that he finds this common chord given utterance in print: "All I can say is that there seems to be a vision possible to man as from some more universal stand-point . . . a sense that one *is* those objects and things and persons that one perceives (and the whole universe)" (*Labour Prophet*, May 1894: 50). Carpenter's poem suggests to Trevor a breakdown of the author-reader binary, a collapse of being between the perceiver and that which he perceives; this is akin to what Leela Gandhi calls "the self-endangering pleasures of radical inclusiveness" characteristic of fin de siècle spiritual movements (141). Trevor goes on to speculate about the nature of the authorial "I."

What or Who in the main is the "I" spoken of? . . . The "I" is myself—as well as I could find words to express myself: but what that Self is, and what its limits may be; and therefore what the self of any other person is and what *its* limits may be—I cannot tell. . . . It seems to me more and more clear that the word "I" has a practically infinite range of meaning—that the *ego* covers far more ground than we usually suppose. . . . Are we really separate individuals, or is individuality an illusion, or again is it only a part of the *ego* or soul that is individual, and not the whole? . . . Or lastly is it perhaps not possible to express the truth by any direct use of these or other terms of ordinary language? (*Labour Prophet*, May 1894: 50–51)

Here, Trevor questions whether the conventions of language and authorship are capable of expressing a new, wider sense of universal consciousness that transcends the individual ego.

Trevor was speculating on these questions in 1892, three years before Orage began his career as a columnist for the Independent Labour Party paper *Labour Leader*, but Orage's work reflects the same regional socialist outlook evident in Trevor's work for the *Labour Prophet*. As

Tom Steele notes, Orage joined and participated in many, if not all, the key socialist outlets in the Leeds area: the Clarion Club and the central Independent Labour Party Club in Briggate, which "brought working-class militants, both men and women, into contact with social-ist middle-class intellectuals like the Ford sisters and Edward Carpen-ter," as well as the local Fabian Societies, which were more exclusively middle class (257). Orage's most important sphere of socialist activ-ity, however, was "the lodges of the Theosophical Society," where the "mode of discussion of contemporary events and issues in the light of the 'higher' knowledge" became the model for the Leeds Art Club, an important socialist cultural organization that Orage would form with Holbrook Jackson in 1903.[25]

Theosophy operated in a discursive register that was far less acces-sible than that of the Clarion Clubs or the Independent Labour Party, and indeed, in Orage's theosophy, his zeal for Nietzsche, and his member-ship in the Fabian Society, we can identify a tendency toward demand-ing socialist vocabularies and exclusive socialist networks from early in his career. Orage's literary column for the *Labour Leader*, "A Bookish Causerie," was likewise exclusionary in its attitude toward literature, print, and the mass reading public. In his 28 December 1895 column, Orage complained of being snowed in by a deluge of books released for the Christmas season.

Air! Air! What I want is air. . . . Every November they add a stratum to the geol-ogy of literature and upset all the geography. . . . Literature has fallen grievously into bondage of the publishers. . . . The amount is everything, the matter nothing. . . . There is no time for thought, only for writing; and the print comes wet from the toweled head. Our mountains of matter bring forth only a mouse of thought, and the beginning of books is the end of ideas. (1)

This is a typical socialist attack on the culture of overprint, but as the column continues, it crosses the line from critique of the speed- and scale-oriented model of the capitalist publishing industry to a critique of print's democratic accessibility.

If only language were a sort of laborious hieroglyphic affair, and printing an art for "old experience," we should have fewer publications. . . . But as it is when everybody with two ideas and a pen can find a publisher . . . when printing is

done at the devil's speed, and writing is done on the while-you-wait principle . . .
what wonder that as of old there is no open vision . . . and that our young men no
longer dream dreams, but only nightmare for copy. (1)

As with Morris and other radical writers of the era, it is the speed of
industrialized print—"done on the while-you-wait principle" at "the
devil's speed"—that Orage blames for the state of mass-market literature. But he also refers to the democratization of print—"everybody
with two ideas and a pen can find a publisher"—and expresses a wish
that language could be a "laborious hieroglyphic affair," as though wide
literacy is part of the problem.

Theosophy could fairly be called the discursive equivalent of "laborious hieroglyphics," given its widely acknowledged impenetrability, so
its appeal for Orage is little mystery. As we saw with Besant, theosophical socialism offered a means by which the movement could absorb and
express the antidemocratic anxieties of middle-class socialists. And yet
one way in which Orage's theosophical socialism is quite distinct from
Besant's is in his attraction to individualism and individualist thought.
Whereas Besant always emphasized associative principles, the illusion
of the ego, and the underlying unity of all being, Orage and Holbrook
Jackson were both absolutely enamored with Nietzsche, and like Shaw,
whom they also adored, they had cobbled together an idiosyncratic
philosophical foundation of Nietzschean individualism meets socialist
collectivism. Orage's version of individualism was distinctively theosophical, however, in that it was premised on the instability of the ego
and individual personality. For example, in a discussion of Ibsen in
the 16 January 1897 "Bookish Causerie" column in the *Labour Leader,*
Orage quotes Ibsen as saying, "I will sacrifice my feelings to the claims
of no organised mass, be it Party, Society, or State. . . . The expression
of our individuality is our first duty, not its subordination to the interests of the community" (18). Orage concludes from the quotation that
Ibsen "is evidently an individualist anarchist," but Orage goes on to
question this categorization: "Ibsen . . . is all things to all men; in one
mood an anarchist, in another a tory, in another a jingo, in another a
vegetarian, and inconsistency is the mark of his genius." Orage then
denounces fixity of personality as a deplorable failure of imagination;
citing the example of an exchange between Grant Allen and a critic

from the *Daily Chronicle*, Orage wishes that the reviewer had "boldly declar[ed]—as the infinity of nature would have allowed him to declare with at least equal truth—the opposite of what he had previously said" (18). Orage's celebration of personal inconsistency and reversal of opinion complicates his version of individualism, because he clearly does not imagine the individual as a coherent, unified, or fixed entity. The "infinity of nature" allows for endless change, endless shifting in the expression of individual selfhood.

Orage was a more wide-ranging thinker than Besant, never quite so thoroughgoing in his commitment to theosophy, and did not go as far as her in his rejection of scientific socialism. He argued in his 20 February 1897 "Bookish Causerie" column, "It is important that alongside of idealism . . . there should be science. . . . Carpenter without Karl Marx is useless. Each is necessary to explain the other" (58). He advocated on this basis for the production of a new shilling edition of *Capital*'s first nine chapters, "which contain the gist of Marx's theory," even though he admitted that most socialists "do not understand Marx." Marx, like Blavatsky, could create his own kind of sublime obscurity for many late Victorian socialists, although the mystification was scientific rather than spiritual. Even William Morris admitted that *Capital* caused him "agonies of confusion of the brain over reading the pure economics of that great work" ("How I Became a Socialist" 242). For Orage, advocating a cheap edition of Marx was not in this sense all that different from advocating theosophy, Nietzsche, or Carpenter's poetry; all posed great difficulty for less literate socialist readers. Robert Blatchford's *Merrie England*, on the other hand, was a popular, user-friendly, widely available explication of British Marx-Morris-style socialism, but it did not meet Orage's approval: "'Merrie England,' which in spite of its many failings has made more Socialists than any book published, has too little of the ground work and basis of economics. It is largely coloured by Socialist prejudices" (*Labour Leader*, 20 February 1897: 58). Recognizing the book's influence, Orage seeks its correction through a shilling edition of Marx.

Orage's column was widely admired among socialists for the quality of its literary criticism, but "A Bookish Causerie" put forth a particular version of socialist literary culture, one that called on radical literature to separate itself from the popular literary marketplace—not to emulate its attractive features, as Blatchford did—and to privilege intellectual rigor and aesthetic ambiguity above accessibility. This was preliminary to an idiom of literary modernism that "depends on an esoteric discourse distinguishable from mass-produced writings" (Strychacz 31), the idiom that Orage would later promote in the *New Age*. After giving up his column in the *Labour Leader* in 1897, Orage would continue to give shape and organization to socialist literary culture in this direction, first in the Leeds area where he began and later in London. In 1903 he formed with Holbrook Jackson the Leeds Art Club, "with the object of 'reducing Leeds to Nietzscheism'" (Steele 1–2). The club sponsored lectures, exhibitions, and discussions of modern art's relation to philosophy and social reform. As discussed in Chapter 4, it grew out of and expanded on the bedrock of socialist community infrastructure that had been built up in the Leeds area through the work of people like Tom Maguire and groups like the Independent Labour Party, but its steep membership dues ensured an exclusively middle-class orientation.

Later, Holbrook and Orage took the model of the Leeds Art Club on the road to London, launching the Fabian Arts Group in 1907. The object of this group, according to its description in the *Reformers' Year Book* for 1908, was "the interpretation of the relationship of Art and Philosophy to Socialism" (208).[26] It was formed with the blessing of the Fabian "Old Gang" (the Webbs, Shaw, Pease, etc.) but soon became a rival faction within the Fabian Society, as Orage and Holbrook tried to effect through the Fabian Arts Group major changes in Fabian socialism. As Ian Britain has noted, "Criticisms of the Fabian Society's traditional approach to the arts—or lack of approach—were more than implicit" in Jackson and Orage's initial proposal to launch the group (169); the Old Gang accepted this, but they did not anticipate how the Arts Group would challenge more fundamental aspects of Fabian socialism. Orage and Jackson hoped to push the Fabian Society, by way of the Arts Group, toward a more decentralized vision of social organization and toward a less empirical, less scientific approach to socialism.[27] The effort was unsuccessful, and as the Arts Group's lectures and activities became more and more "abstrusely philosophical" (173), it would soon collapse, but not before Orage and Jackson received Fabian funds and Fabian endorsements to help launch their next socialist literary effort: the *New Age*.

As noted earlier, the *New Age* was funded equally by theosophical and Fabian money: George Bernard Shaw, the Fabian, and Lewis Wallace, the theosophist, each contributed £500 toward Orage and Holbrook's purchase of the paper.[28] The *New Age* was on the market because of financial insolvency, but it had existed in various incarnations since 1894, having had a good run for a radical periodical of the era. Under the editorship of A. E. Fletcher in the 1890s, it was a moderate ethical-socialist journal that printed poetry, fiction, and literary criticism and expressed admiration for William Morris and Robert Blatchford. Later, the editorship was taken over by Joseph Edwards and F. W. Pethick Lawrence, and the subtitle became "A Democratic Review of Politics, Religion, and Literature." At this time the paper advocated "Economic Reform . . . Public Ownership of Public Services. . . . Foreign Policy Reform: International Relations governed by the Commandment—'That ye love one another'" (*Reformers' Year Book*, 1904: 188).

When Orage and Jackson took over the *New Age*, their first issue included endorsements in the form of letters from several prominent Fabians, including Sidney Webb, Edward Pease, Hubert Bland, Edith Nesbit, and H. G. Wells. With the exception of Wells, who had his own difficulties in accommodating his politics (and personality) to the Fabian Society, these were all members of the Old Gang, seemingly aligning the *New Age* with Fabian orthodoxy. Pease's letter to the editors articulates expectations in this direction: "We wanted a paper to express continuously the typical Fabian view of affairs, and yet the difficulties of an official organ, controlled by the Society, seemed to be insuperable. Official Fabianism welcomes independent criticism more cordially than the invariable approval which their own organ would have to express. *Our members, I am confident, will help you to make the new venture a success*" (2 May 1907: 3, my emphasis). Pease presumes that the journal, although written from an independent perspective, will function as a de facto Fabian publication. However, Wells's letter portends that the paper will not necessarily toe the Fabian line: "Socialism in England has long stood in need of what you propose to give it—a Review which, without being official, shall be representative, and which shall direct itself primarily not to propaganda nor to politics, but to the development of Socialist thought." He looked forward especially to its "handling of contemporary literature and art . . . from a definitely Socialist position" (2 May 1907: 3). Orage and Jackson took over the paper together, but Jackson left by the end of the year, leaving Orage to edit the paper on his own for most of its tenure.

The *New Age*'s statement of purpose, in a piece titled "To Our Readers," was typical of slow print in this era in that it defined the publication by way of opposition to mass print: "From the great dim multitudes engaged in the laborious pursuit of banal information through the pages of the popular weeklies we can expect nothing." Less typically, the statement also defines the journal specifically against mass print's appeal to a plebeian audience. Indeed, whereas many socialist papers were effectively written for a middle-class audience, the *New Age* wrote for a *declared* middle-class audience: "THE NEW AGE, we are aware, is not, and cannot become for a long while, the paper of the 'people.' But with the co-operation of our readers it may, and we hope it will, become the established organ of high practical intelligence and the representative of the best imagination of English social reformers" (24 October 1907: 408). Adjectives such as "high" and "best" claim the paper as directed toward the aristocrats, intellectual or otherwise, of the socialist movement, not "the people."

Despite the paper's apparent start as a Fabian-tinged journal—half-funded by Shaw and launched with the imprint of Fabian endorsements, with a characteristically Fabian appeal to the upper reaches of the movement—it quickly ran afoul of its Fabian origins through its growing emphasis on guild socialism.[29] But the theosophical influence on the paper remained constant. Wallace Martin has argued that until 1919 Orage was "careful not to let [his theosophy] impinge upon his activities as an editor" (286), but even when the subject of theosophy is not directly engaged in the paper, the influence of theosophical socialism and its consequences for authorship and print are evident, such as in the contributions of Florence Farr, whom Orage had engaged as a regular columnist for the paper in its early years.[30] Farr had become known in the London radical sphere as an actress appearing in Shaw and Ibsen dramas; she played the lead, for example, in the groundbreaking 1892 staging of *Widowers' Houses* with the Independent Theatre. Farr was also a close friend of W. B. Yeats, who in 1890 had brought her into the

Hermetic Order of the Golden Dawn, an occultist secret society (Johnson 72).[31] In June 1902 Farr expanded her spiritualist connections by joining the Theosophical Society in London (92).

Orage and Farr's shared interest in theosophy is unmistakable in Farr's contributions to the *New Age*, many of which were adapted from material that Farr had composed for a diary begun in November 1904 to document her spiritual and philosophical speculations (Johnson 94). Farr's piece "The Sword of Laughter," from the 18 July 1907 issue of the *New Age*, calls into question the Enlightenment subjectivity on which earlier radical versions of print, authorship, and politics were based. As with Orage's columns for the *Labour Leader*, Farr's notion of subjectivity emphasizes inconsistency and contradiction.

> It is through our inconsistencies that we alone can learn the reality that lies behind human delusions. It is because we have not the courage to face our own complexities that we are still almost entirely ignorant of the real nature of the human mind. . . . We pose as persons, individuals with unchanging convictions, but we do not realise that our convictions are subtly changing all the time. (182)

Like Orage and other theosophists, Farr imagines the individual self as unfixed yet alienated from its own variability: "Very few of us can examine . . . our own natural instability" (183).

In 1907, the same year that the *New Age* published this piece by Farr, Orage published his own study of consciousness, *Consciousness: Animal, Human, and Superhuman*, which addresses many of the same points. The book originated in the Northern radical lecture circuit, having its basis in "the substance of some lectures which were delivered under the auspices of the Theosophical Lodges of Manchester and Leeds" (preface), and it resonates with the metaphysical speculations about subjectivity, authorship, and readership that we see in the writings of Farr, Trevor, and Besant. Orage begins by discussing the problematic nature of the word I, a difficulty that had also troubled Besant and Trevor: "Strictly speaking, we can no more speak of ourselves than we can stand on our own shoulders. For in every self-communion and introspection there is the self which speaks and the self which is spoken of; and they are never the same" (9). Conscious alienation from the reality of selfhood and poor understanding of the nature of the self are major emphases of the book.

Orage sets out in *Consciousness* to challenge the Western Enlightenment ideal of the rational, coherent self. In contrast to John Locke's tabula rasa, Orage declares that human minds "have been scrawled upon by the experiences of millions of years" and "are too sophisticated cosmically" to be conceived of as a blank slate that is filled by merely individual experience (12). Like Besant, Orage discounts the usefulness of reason in confronting questions of selfhood and consciousness: "It is not a rational quest, but an imaginative quest we are on; and unless our normal reason is put to sleep . . . there is little chance of our imagination coming into play" (30). Ultimately, *Consciousness* argues for the existence of a "Transcendental Self" beyond the ego, "the larger consciousness in which human consciousness develops" (56). Orage posits a universal consciousness, which he refers to as "superman" consciousness, amalgamating Nietzsche and theosophy.

Consciousness was not originally published in the *New Age*, but Farr reviewed it in the 6 June 1907 issue, summarizing the book's main points. The review was quite positive (perhaps not surprisingly, since the book was written by the journal's editor), and Farr took the opportunity to link Orage's ideas about self and consciousness to his learning in Eastern philosophy, gained through theosophy.

Mr. Orage's mind is equipped by nature and subtle Eastern practices to give us a far clearer idea of Superhuman or Aristocratic Consciousness than we gather from the songs of Nietzsche or from Shaw's great classic, "Man and Superman." . . . Mr. Orage is more intimately in touch with Greek and Brahmic traditions than Mr. Shaw; he has the knack of entering into such phrases of existence and holding them up to our view, warm and throbbing with their own ecstasies. (92)

The phrase "Aristocratic Consciousness" is telling, because it again suggests how theosophical socialism could be said to substitute a class system based on intellectual, cultural, or spiritual capital for a class system based on economic capital.

Farr expands in this review from Orage's ideas in *Consciousness* to her own philosophy of what we might call theosophical feminism, similar to that of Besant. To Orage's discussion of "transcendental consciousness," she adds, "Curiously enough, in many systems of mysticism this state of consciousness . . . is mystically feminine" (*New Age*, 6 June 1907: 92). As with many spiritualist and occultist movements, female leaders such as Besant and Blavatsky dominated theosophy, and Farr herself had attained "the exalted position of Praemonstratrix" in the Hermetic Order of the Golden Dawn (Johnson 58).[32] Farr's writings for the *New Age* connect her theosophical socialism to a kind of occultist feminism, which, unlike Besant's version of theosophical feminism, was also sexually radical. In her *New Age* article "Marie Corelli and the Modern Girl," for example, Farr exposes female chastity as mere convenience for a patrilineal property system: "That chastity should be encouraged under patriarchal conditions is economically necessary because chastity is a most valuable asset, and marriage is a profession in which the amateur commands a higher price than the skilled artist" (1 August 1907: 214).

Farr took her mystical, feminist, theosophical sex radicalism even further in "The Rites of Astaroth," which appeared in the 5 September 1907 issue of the *New Age*, arguing that prostitutes might be exalted in Western culture as priestesses rather than criminals and that prostitution might be reimagined as a sacred office.

From time immemorial, Jewish priests, ancient Egyptians, ancient Hindus, agreed that the vagaries of nature must be obeyed; and certain women, trained as dancers, were dedicated to the gods and their worshippers. In their temples prostitution is and was a sacred institution, but in the West sacred institutions are not popular and men have seen fit to drag the veil of the flesh away from the temples and leave it in the gutter to fare as well as it can. . . . In the East, as I have said, the religious-minded can make a ritual both of marriage and prostitution. (294)

The article generated protest from readers in the next issue. A letter from P. R. Bennett argued, "If your excellent translators . . . would devote their attention to Miss Farr and turn her interesting article on 'The Rites of Astaroth' into plain English they would, I think, give a wholesome shock to some of the less clear-headed of your readers" (12 September 1907: 318–19). Deriding the numinous obscurity of Farr's theosophical prose style, Bennett implies that Farr's work for the paper, no matter how outré, can have little effect on readers' ideas because few can understand her.

In the editorial practices of Orage, the effect of the *New Age*'s esoteric qualities—its difficult prose, its forum for peculiarly outré ideas—was to distance the journal from the working-class side of the socialist movement.

The journal had a good circulation, achieving "its all-time high water mark at 22,000 in 1908" (Ardis, "Dialogics" 417), but its perspective was socially elite. Jonathan Rose's *Intellectual Life of the British Working Classes* discusses the memoir of Edwin Muir, a poorly paid Glasgow clerk who graduated from reading the *Clarion* and participating in the Clarion Scouts to the "sour irony" and "Nietzschean elitism" of the *New Age*. The effect, in Muir's recollection, was poisonous: "Reading [the *New Age*] gave me a feeling of superiority which was certainly not good for me. . . . The tone of the paper was crushingly superior and exclusive. . . . On the strength of this I acquired a taste for condemnation" (qtd. in Rose 427–28). The *New Age* signified within the movement a broader correspondence between theosophy and those schools of socialism that called for or even required a certain form of intellectual elitism.

Perhaps unsurprisingly the *New Age* is best remembered today "for its contribution to the cultural ferment that produced modernism," as Carey Snyder puts it in an article that barely has cause to mention the journal's socialism (126), and Orage has come down as "a significant broker of modern literary prestige" who had a legendary nose for sniffing out new talent (125). Snyder argues that through the use of parody, Orage's journal launched what would come to be a familiar modernist line of attack on Victorian-style realism, personified by authors like Arnold Bennett. And yet if we read the *New Age* in the context of antecedents such as the *Commonweal*, we can see how this attack on realism grew out of the antirealism of earlier socialist writers, such as William Morris and George Bernard Shaw. Moreover, recognizing the *New Age*'s roots in theosophical socialism gives us a fuller understanding of the paper's rejection of a brand of realism that was associated with empiricism, science, and rationalism. Indeed, the *New Age*'s deep roots in radical literary culture are indisputable; as Ardis remarks, the journal initially "had far more in common both graphically and thematically with late-Victorian socialist weeklies like the *Clarion, Justice,* and the *Labour Leader*" than with what came to be known as modernist little magazines ("Staging the Public Sphere" 35).

In the literary and editorial work of Besant and Orage, we see the trace of a distinct socialist subculture that drew together strands of theosophy, Fabian socialism, feminism, and the fad for spiritualist and occultist movements influenced by Eastern religion. This assemblage of discourses formed what we might call theosophical socialism—a school of socialism that was antagonistic to the print mass market and tended to be elitist and esoteric but that also expressed broader shifts in the media and information culture of the moment, particularly in its revision of traditional radical accounts of subjectivity. Theosophical socialism registered a challenge to Enlightenment notions of selfhood, print, and the author function as they had emerged in the eighteenth and nineteenth centuries. We can connect Besant and Orage's work in this direction to parallel trends in antirational socialism among lower-class strata of the movement, such as the Labour Church and John Trevor's *Labour Prophet*. But we can also connect their work to the exclusive modernist literary discourse that would foment in the pages of the *New Age*. As with fin de siècle sex radicalism, which I discuss in the next chapter, we can identify in theosophical socialism a line of connection from turn-of-the-century radical literature to the emergence of literary modernism—two literary fields that have often been viewed as antithetical.

CHAPTER 6 Free Love, Free Print
Sex Radicalism, Censorship, and the Biopolitical Turn

I N THE INAUGURAL ISSUE of the *Revolutionary Review*, an anarchist monthly edited by Henry Seymour, an article by
"Verax" declared "Free love" to be "the natural law of
the sexes" (January 1889: 6). In this formulation free love is not really
free but is governed by natural law and thus does not require state or
social intervention. This was also the position of Grant Allen, author of
The Woman Who Did (1895), the era's most notorious free love novel—a
novel that called on the enlightened to "embrace and follow every instinct of pure love that nature, our mother, has imparted within you"
(112).[1] It was also the position that Havelock Ellis attributed to Thomas
Hardy's *Jude the Obscure* (1895) in a prominent 1896 review; the novel,
Ellis said, "recognizes a moral order in Nature," not in "laws framed
merely as social expedients" (rpt. in Cox 310). Indeed, in Hardy's novel
Sue says to Jude of her marriage to Phillotson, "It is none of the natural
tragedies of love that's love's usual tragedy in civilized life, but a tragedy artificially manufactured for people who in a natural state would
find relief in parting!" (226).

That regulatory social and legal institutions unhealthily distorted
"natural" sexuality and therefore should be abolished was the position of
many late nineteenth-century sex radicals, and the topic was debated not
only on the fringes of radical culture but also in widely discussed novels of
the day. Many other radical thinkers, however, believed that a completely
neutral social forum for the expression of uninhibited natural sexuality,
even if it were desirable, would be impossible under present conditions.
Did not commercial forces, in addition to legal and social forces, shape

sexuality? And if so, what was the point in reforming marriage laws or revising sexual mores before an economic revolution? In the very next issue of *Revolutionary Review*, Lothrop Withington argued, contra Verax, that it would be useless to "patch up the ragged remnants of commercialism" by trying to improve marriage laws, because free love cannot exist under "present economic arrangements" (February 1889: 19–20). Thus the debate around free love at the fin de siècle resonated with the debate around capitalism, free market principle, and free print. A libertarian ideal of a healthy, free informational order that would emerge in the absence of state intervention—something like Jürgen Habermas's ideal of communicative rationality (*Structural Transformation*)—no longer seemed possible in the commercialized domain of late Victorian print. Was it equally impossible for sex? Was it true that free love, like free print, could not exist until after the revolution?

As these examples suggest, sex radicalism and the biopolitical became key areas of debate in the late nineteenth-century radical sphere, intersecting with tensions around liberalism, censorship, governmental control of print, and anarchist ideals of natural life. A dynamic at work in radical literature, which I outline and explore in this chapter, is the migration of free print and print enlightenment rhetoric—a residual discourse left over from early nineteenth-century radicalism—to specifically sexual radicalism in the final decades of the century. As Andrew King and John Plunkett describe in their recent account of Victorian print culture, "Our overall narrative . . . entails a transformation from regulation tied in with government of the social and political body to that concerned with the individual sexualized body." In other words, "whereas in the 1830s Henry Hetherington went to gaol for printing his criticisms of the government and demanding the vote . . . the publisher Henry Vizetelly was imprisoned in 1889 for publishing 'obscene' translations of Zola's naturalist novels" (81). Along with this shift in regulation was a shift in radical accounts of free print: Sexual radicalism became the cornerstone of the waning, yet enduring radical cause of free print.

A connection between sex radicalism and free print long predated the fin de siècle. As Lynn Hunt notes, the conceptual category of pornography (if not the term itself, which was first used in 1842 according to the *Oxford English Dictionary*) emerged in the late eighteenth and early

nineteenth centuries "in response to the perceived menace of the democratization of culture" (13). This era saw a great deal of overlap between
the printing of class-oriented radical material and the printing of obscene
material, as exemplified by the career of William Dugdale, who "adapted
the language of the Enlightenment . . . to argue for a new sexual order"
(Sigel 16). By the middle of the nineteenth century, "rising prices, new
distribution patterns, and, most important, a new relationship between
privilege and pornography" had severed this tie between radical and
erotic print (55). At the fin de siècle, however, sexually explicit material
would become the predominant target for overt governmental censorship, and secular and politically radical print became subject to far less
regulation; this development meant that the radical argument for free
print could function coherently only with respect to sex radicalism. Thus
many writers in the radical press, operating in a forum wholly separate
from print pornography, were newly drawn to sex radicalism and the
cause of open sexual discussion in the public sphere.

The movement of the free print argument into the domain of the
sexual had a number of significant effects. First, it politicized the domains of the body and sexuality in a new way by making them major
players in a familiar tradition of radical activism around free print. It also
staged a site of conflict between socialist and liberal principle, because
forums for sexual radicalism overlapped considerably with the socialist
press. Finally, it became a major source of class tension within radical
groups, because according to conventional wisdom in the movement,
working-class radicals were more conservative on sex questions than
middle-class socialists. As sex radicalism became the new bastion for the
old free print argument, the late Victorian radical sphere was taking a
turn toward body-centric politics; vegetarianism, sexual liberation, dress
reform, and back-to-the-land movements came increasingly to the fore
in radical print. Attention to this dynamic reveals a path of connection
from the literary socialists of the 1880s and 1890s to the inward turn of
twentieth-century modernism. We have seen that late Victorian radical
literature was in many respects, such as literary form, not an obvious
influence on the emergence of modernism, despite the many overlapping
characters in the radical and modernist casts. In the domain of the biopolitical, however, the political legacy of fin de siècle radicalism is quite

evident in modernist literature. For modernist writers who challenged print censorship, sexuality was their central sphere of radical activity, and the class arguments that had once dominated the free print credo fell away. I wish to show that the development of this discursive dynamic was marked and partly determined by earlier political contests around the question of free print.

In this chapter I describe how the biopolitical became the new ground for free print agitation. Biopolitics addresses the regulation of living populations: techniques for governing en masse birth, death, health, and sexuality, all of which are flashpoints in debates about liberalism and the role of the state. In 1979 Michel Foucault began a course of lectures meant to address the topic of biopolitics with a long analysis of the emergence of Western liberalism: "Only when we know what this governmental regime called liberalism was, will we be able to grasp what biopolitics is" (*Birth* 22). Liberal governmentality, he claimed, requires constant recalibration of the optimum level of governmental intervention to best preserve the state: "This art of the least possible government, this art of governing between a maximum and a minimum . . . should be seen as a sort of intensification or internal refinement of [reason of state]; it is a principle for maintaining it, developing it more fully, and perfecting it" (28). In a liberal state such as Victorian Britain, the exercise of biopower must also preserve the sense of a populace made up of "natural" bodies left alone to live and die and reproduce organically outside state regulation. Yet for late Victorian radicals, there was scarce agreement on what a class-conscious biopolitics would look like. Their positions ranged from Fabians who advocated active state involvement in reproduction, to anarchist proponents of free love, to working-class socialist forums such as the *Clarion*, which tended to be sexually conservative yet provided a forum for birth control advocacy.

Sexuality had replaced labor politics and blasphemy as ground zero for the censorship debates, and this development was not unrelated to escalating radical interest in biopolitical activism. In England governmental restrictions and controls on print had been a galvanizing cause for political radicals from Thomas Paine to William Cobbett to the Chartists, all of whom saw minimal state restriction of the print sphere as the basis for democratic political enlightenment and saw governmental checks on popular print as a violation of liberal principle. Beginning in the eighteenth century, free print became a basic premise and a rallying cry for English political radicals who sought to transform the class order, and the principle of free print became an end in and of itself. But, as we have seen, by the end of the nineteenth century advocates of radical economic and political change had lost faith in the narrative of print enlightenment, because the achievement of a mostly unfettered print sphere and the emergence of hundreds of cheap radical papers had failed to counter the hegemony of commercial mass print. Clearly, in a mass-oriented market society the right to print and circulate without governmental obstruction was not enough to generate radical political change. In the specific realm of sexual radicalism, however, the state continued to retain tight control over information that could circulate by means of print. Thus, in the face of governmental censorship, campaigners for sexual liberation took up the mantle of free print, the old liberal underpinning of English radical thought, and socialists of many stripes rallied to their support.

Free Love in Print

Consider, for example, a group of writings published by the University Press at Watford, an operation unconnected to any university, run by the mysterious printer Roland de Villiers, who had a long record of aliases and arrests across Europe. The University Press is now best remembered for publishing Havelock Ellis's important early study of homosexuality, *Sexual Inversion*, which was censored and suppressed upon publication in 1897 when its seller was convicted of obscenity. The seller, George Bedborough, was editor of a free love journal titled *The Adult* (Figure 30), which was also published by the University Press and also seized in the 1897 raid.[2] Besides being the author of *Sexual Inversion*, Ellis was a socialist and a member of the Fellowship of the New Life, and he wrote poetry for socialist journals such as *To-Day*. Yet in the preface to the University Press edition of *Sexual Inversion*, Ellis suggests that sexual radicalism was, by 1897, more imperative than class-oriented activism: "Now . . . that the problem of labour has at least been placed on a practical foundation, the question of sex—with the racial questions that rest on it—stands before the coming generations as the chief problem for solution" (x).

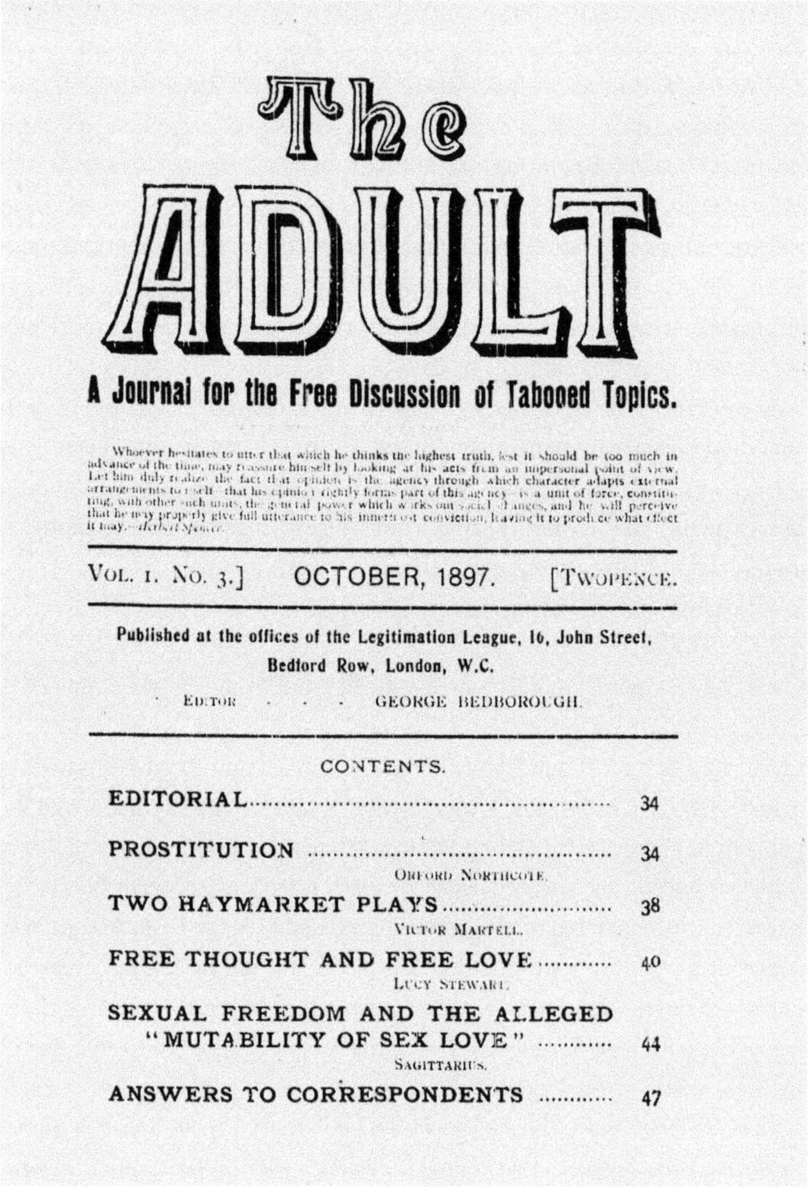

The

ADULT

A Journal for the Free Discussion of Tabooed Topics.

Whoever hesitates to utter that which he thinks the highest truth, lest it should be too much in advance of the time, may reassure himself by looking at his acts from an impersonal point of view. Let him duly realize the fact that opinion is the agency through which character adapts external arrangements to itself—that his opinion rightly forms part of this agency—is a unit of force, constituting, with other such units, the general power which works out social changes, and he will perceive that he may properly give full utterance to his innermost conviction, leaving it to produce what effect it may.—*Herbert Spencer.*

VOL. I. NO. 3.]   OCTOBER, 1897.   [TWOPENCE.

Published at the offices of the Legitimation League, 16, John Street,
Bedford Row, London, W.C.

EDITOR ․ ․ ․ GEORGE BEDBOROUGH.

CONTENTS.

Figure 30. Masthead and table of contents, the *Adult* (October 1897).

This passage reads as Foucault 101, exemplifying the rise of a scientific discourse "regulating sex through useful and public discourses" (*History* 25), as Foucault puts it. Indeed, throughout his preface Ellis uses the language of print enlightenment to justify his foray into the illicit topic of sexual inversion; he claims his "life-work" is "to make clear the problems of sex," but he will be "content if I do little more than state them. For even that . . . is much; it is at least the half of knowledge" (*Sexual Inversion* v–vi). Simply "stating" the problems of sex, articulating them in print, is halfway to making them "clear." Similarly, an article printed in the *Adult* titled "Wanted: A New Dictionary" called for a new "terminology of the art and science of sexual life" to "enable ordinary people to discuss in set, clear-cut, and clean phrases, the sexual thoughts, doubts, and desires which arise in the minds of almost every human being" (November 1897: 57–58). Both Ellis and the *Adult* suggest that print transparency can tidy up the messy and indelicate subject of sex, both rely on the conventional tropes and language of Enlightenment, and both were actually banned by the state, reminding us that the appeal to transparency had a radical charge in the context of the moment. This was the residual effect of the radical Enlightenment.

Ellis's volume and the journal *Adult* establish sex as the next great frontier of social reform in works that were prominently banned by the state, suggesting an ongoing attachment in the radical sphere to the political value of prohibited speech, an attachment with roots in the long history of British radicalism. After Bedborough's arrest, Henry Seymour, the *Adult*'s interim editor, printed the leading column "To the Breach, Freemen!": "An attack upon the freedom of the Press has been made. . . . The book in question deals with sexual inversion and discusses the causes of sexual abnormality from the most disinterested and lofty standpoint. More than this need not be said. Mr. Bedborough has an unquestionable moral right to sell such a book" (July 1898: 159). The Free Press Defence Committee was quickly formed, including prominent socialists from the Fabian Society (Grant Allen, Walter Crane, George Bernard Shaw, and Henry Salt) and the Social Democratic Federation (H. M. Hyndman and Harry Quelch), and stalwarts of sex radicalism such as Edward Carpenter. Some of the committee's members, such as the Marxist E. Belfort Bax, were hardly advocates of gender and sex reform.[3] Yet the ideology of free print—unmistakable in the name Free Press Defence Committee—shaped a response in which the expression of the unprintable was in itself a political act of vast radical implication.[4] In the radical press *Justice* sought to represent the case "as a matter of free speech rather than an issue in its own right" (K. Hunt 108). Likewise, the socialist journal *Home Links* was not wholly in agreement with the *Adult*'s position on free love but declared, "That is not the point. The question at issue is: is the Press in Great Britain really FREE, or is it to become as in Germany or Russia?" (1 July 1898: 88). Amy Morant's "Liberty of the Press," in the same issue of *Home Links*, argued: "The attack upon public liberties is a serious one, and all earnest-minded persons should rally to the defence . . . of this freedom of tongue and pen in relation to sex-matters" (86–87).[5] Sheila Rowbotham's recent biography of Edward Carpenter refers to the Free Press Defence Committee as an "inadvertent" result of Bedborough's trial, "shifting the question of sexual inversion onto the terrain of civil liberties" (202), but a close look at the University Press's publications, including the *Adult*, suggests that this appeal to civil liberties predated the trial and was anything but inadvertent.

The *Adult* as a journal sought to make the case for free love, for "the disestablishment of love so far as the State is concerned" (qtd. in Humpherys 65). In its first issue Bedborough stated the journal's mission in terms of civil liberties: "The name of our paper, THE ADULT, signifies that we recognise the paramount right of the individual to self-realisation in all non-invasive directions. THE ADULT advocates the absolute freedom of two individuals of full age, to enter into and conclude at will, any mutual relationship whatever" (June 1897: 1). The non-gender-specific language of this mission statement and the fact that its editor was arrested for selling *Sexual Inversion* suggest that we can understand the *Adult* partly in terms of the 1890s emergence of a new discourse around homosexuality. The journal often touched on this topic, favorably reviewing work by Havelock Ellis and Edward Carpenter as well as Oscar Wilde's "Ballad of Reading Gaol."[6] R. A. Gordon discussed Ellis's *Sexual Inversion* in the March 1898 issue, claiming, "That the sexual invert is not a criminal, and that we commit a terrible wrong in treating him as such, has been recognised by scientific men all over the world" (40). The journal's focus on heterosexual free love, however, is evident in the personal advertisements for heterosexual free unions on the inside back cover. For example, in the October 1897 issue we find the ads "A Middle aged gentleman wishes to correspond with a lady aged 25 to 30 with a view to a permanent union on Ruedebusch's principles. Please write in confidence with photo" and "A Lady, tall, dark, strongly built, wishes to meet a gentleman going to Socialist colony, with a view to union" (48).[7]

The term *free love* dates back to the eighteenth century but came into general usage at the end of the Victorian era, when the catch phrase "free love"—infamous in the wake of Grant Allen's *The Woman Who Did* and Thomas Hardy's *Jude the Obscure*—coupled easily with the phrase "free print" and appealed to the same vision of natural, uninhibited expression. The *Adult* originated with a group called the Legitimation League, which formed in Leeds in 1893. At the League's inaugural meeting one speaker declared, "We are for Free Love in the same way . . . that we are for Free Trade and a Free Post and a Free Press" (qtd. in Humphreys 65), suggesting how long-standing tenets of Enlightenment liberalism were deployed to normalize the outré doctrine of sex deregulation. As the *Adult* put it, "Truth, as *Milton* long ago pointed out, has all to gain by being brought to the test of free discussion" (November 1897: 49). The journal described "The Free Printing Press" as the "[obstetrician] of Europe in its parturition from the embryonic era of mediævalism" (January 1898: 164). In the Editor's column of February 1898, six of nine items dealt with free print or censorship, and one item described censorship of the journal itself, which was at the mercy of its printers because it did not control its own means of print production: "For purely local reasons we employed a Leeds firm to print the New Year's number. . . . Messrs. *Suddick* declined to print the report of Mr. Dawson's recent lecture, which will consequently appear as a separate pamphlet" (2).

Tensions arose in the *Adult* regarding the use of free print rhetoric in a radical moment characterized by socialist challenges to the premises of British liberalism. A September 1897 article, "Sexual Freedom in Relation to Women and Economics," tracks the movement of free print agitation from earlier radicalisms, class- and religion-oriented, to sexuality: "The breakdown of authority, making way for the advent of rationalism, has made it possible to ventilate *ideas* with such (relative) freedom that heterodoxy of *any* sort can hardly excite the same degree of horror as in the days when mere opinion, if rationalistic, was combatted with the prison, the rack, or the stake." Still, this "comparative immunity for rationalistic propaganda is enjoyed less by the advocates of sexual freedom" because "it is newer . . . and the marriage laws and customs are the last citadel and bulwark of authority" (26). The writer goes on to make an ideological connection between economic and sexual oppression.

There are two barriers to sexual freedom—public opinion and the economic enslavement of five-sixths of the people under our wage system. While there is economic dependence there cannot be complete sexual (or any other) freedom. . . . We are confined, therefore, for the present to the enlightenment of public opinion—on the intellectual plane, and materially to such modified realisation of freedom as the economic environment permits. (27)

The *Adult* was thus characterized by at least two conflicting ideological threads: an individualist critique of marriage, where free lovers are self-sufficient individuals for whom personal desire is paramount, and a socialist critique of marriage, where free love is the sexual analogue of communism.

This second position was often taken in the journal under Bedborough's editorship, as in his reflections on "Monopoly and Jealousy": "The monopolistic instinct of mankind—nowhere more reprehensible than in the relations of the sexes, needs to be deprecated in all such directions. The sense of right to exclusive possession, with its corollary of envy, hatred, jealousy, and all uncharitableness, must be steadily discountenanced" (June 1897: 4). Bedborough saw an intrinsic link between capitalism and marriage laws and argued for the abolition of both. Similar arguments were made by other socialist journals that advocated free love, as in "A Free Love Movement" from *Home Links*: "'Free Love' has become a disreputable epithet in every commercial country and will necessarily remain disreputable as long as economics are allowed to have any influence between the sexes. . . . If you hold private property, you cannot hold 'Pure Love.' And if you would have 'Pure Love' indeed you must, first of all, renounce private property" (24 May 1898: 57).

Many radical writers, however, were averse to such associations between free love and socialism, sensing that they would hurt socialism's chance among the working classes. In March 1885, when George Bernard Shaw sent an article titled "The Future of Marriage" to William Morris to be included in the *Commonweal,* Morris was loath to touch the issue. Shaw's article was not a defense of free love—in fact, it compared "Free Love" to "Free Contract," which had resulted in freeing employers of duties to workers (104)—but Morris's response shows his hesitancy to get into the marriage debate at all: "I think we of the [Socialist League] must before long state our views on wedlock quite plainly and take the consequences . . . but I think we had better leave the subject alone till we can pluck up heart to explain the ambiguities [in our] manifesto. Please to pity the sorrows of a poor editor" (*Collected Letters* 2B: 404). When the League did revise their statement on the issue in October of that year, the revised manifesto did not advocate free love but was ambiguous enough to be tarred with the free love brush: "Under a Socialistic system contracts between individuals would be voluntary and unenforced by the community. This would apply to the marriage contract as well as others" (*Manifesto of the Socialist League* 12). While not calling for the abolition of marriage altogether, the manifesto went far enough to alienate some readers. A letter in the 15 October 1887 issue of the socialist paper *Common Sense* objected to the position on marriage in the League's new manifesto. The writer, R. S. C. of Plymouth, said he read it "with a feeling akin to terror" and was hesitant to call himself a socialist precisely because of such statements (83–84). Under the circumstances Morris's editorial timidity with respect to the marriage question is not surprising.[8]

After the launch of the *Adult,* however, Bedborough actively sought connections with the socialist press. He sent copies of the journal to key editors, such as Keir Hardie (*Labour Leader*) and Robert Blatchford (*Clarion*), hoping to enlist their support, but their response echoed Morris's reply to Shaw's article: "Mr. Keir Hardie and Mr. Robert Blatchford write in almost identical terms and [in] the words of the latter . . . 'I think the relations of the sexes are unsatisfactory, but I have my hands full enough, without meddling with such a difficult matter'" (September 1897: 19). Whether or not socialist leaders agreed on the need for a radical change in the social bases of sex and marriage, taking a definite position on such matters in print was considered politically risky, especially because, as Morris put it in his letter to Shaw, "abolishing wedlock while the present economical slavery lasts would be futile." After the socialist revolution, Morris implied, the sex problem would take care of itself.

Despite Morris and others' certainty that changes in sex and marriage would follow an economic revolution, socialism itself was subject to dispute in the *Adult*, because the idea of state socialism conflicted with free love's ostensible ideological grounding in laissez-faire principle. Some *Adult* contributors were anarchist socialists, antistatist but economically collectivist; others were socialists who sought less state involvement in sexuality; still others were promarket libertarian anarchists who imagined that an invisible hand would govern free sexuality just like the free market. After Bedborough's arrest, the editorship of the *Adult* was taken over by Henry Seymour, an individualist anarchist who had edited the *Revolutionary Review* and who tended to emphasize the laissez-faire link between free print and free love. Even before Seymour took over the *Adult*, Leighton Pagan (the pen name of John Badcock Jr.) was a frequent contributor, and he too was an antisocialist, promarket, individualist anarchist. His lecture "The Judgment of Paris, Up to Date," printed in the November 1897 issue of the *Adult*, argued that free love would be a boon to free enterprise: "When a man's amours run smoothly, all the world is benefitted. He and his inamorata . . . work with a will, and are consequently able to spend prodigally" (59). What we might now call consumer confidence has, to Babcock, a biopolitical basis.

The Free Love Novel and the Radical Press

Free print was a shared passion for socialist and individualist free love advocates alike. Both groups saw literary discourse as leading the movement of sexual reform and as instrumental in forming the public that the *Adult* addressed. Leighton Pagan's "Judgment of Paris, Up to Date" comments on the "number of recent books that have been published for the purpose of discussing sex questions": "Novelists and dramatists have taken the subject up, and . . . a complete change has come over the spirit of the drama. . . . So is art a great revolutioniser, ever luring us on to taste forbidden fruits from the tabooed trees of knowledge" (71–72). Elsewhere the trend was reported in less tantalizing terms, as in Edmund Gosse's 1896 review for *Cosmopolis*: "A sheaf of 'purpose' stories on the 'marriage question' (as it is called) have just been irritating the nerves of the British Patron" (rpt. in Cox 264). Chief among these stories were Grant Allen's *The Woman Who Did* and Thomas Hardy's *Jude the Obscure*, both published in 1895 and both instantly infamous. The two novels were subjects of constant discussion in the *Adult*, where they were considered galvanizing texts for the free love movement. An article titled "To the Obscure Judes and Distracted Sues" by Leighton Pagan (aka John Badcock) addressed itself to real-life readers grappling with marriage and sex questions such as those raised in Hardy's novel (June 1897: 6).[9] Pagan was also a great admirer of Allen's novel, which he considered "the finest thing I've read on the subject. I fall in absolutely with Herminia Barton's ideas" (Dawson 236).

Although Allen's and Hardy's novels were perceived as groundbreaking in the *Adult*, they actually drew on radical literature of the previous decade in formulating a radical sexual politics. In defending her own anti-marriage position, Allen's heroine Herminia Barton uses Shaw's description of moral "pioneers" in *The Quintessence of Ibsenism*: "For whoever sees the truth . . . must be a moral pioneer, and the moral pioneer is always a martyr" (Allen 44). Herminia likewise references Shelley as the ultimate radical sexual pioneer, as Shaw and others had done in the 1880s (see Chapter 3): "I can never admire Shelley enough, who, in an age of slavery, refused to abjure or to deny his freedom, but acted unto death to the full height of his principles" (75). Likewise, in Hardy's novel Sue's husband, Phillotson, considers Jude and Sue to be "Shelleyan": "They remind me of—what are their names—Laon and Cythna" (243). Later, Sue herself quotes from *The Revolt of Islam*, the revised version of *Laon and Cythna* (301); elsewhere, she entreats Jude, "Say those pretty lines . . . from Shelley's 'Epipsychidion' as if they meant me!" (257). The July 1898 issue of the *Adult* would likewise reproduce a section from "Epipsychidion" under the heading "Shelley on Free Love" (184).

On the basis of his novels, Hardy was approached by the *Adult* as a leading theorist of free love, a characterization he rejected in a letter printed in the January 1898 correspondence column: "Dear Sir,—I am much obliged to you for drawing my attention to the Legitimation League, and its practical endeavours in respect of the tragedies of life that form the subject of some of my novels: though, as a mere observer and recorder, I am personally limited to the representation of these tragedies as faithfully as possible, without bias, or what is called 'purpose'" (134). This denial of purpose was somewhat disingenuous, considering Hardy's description of Jude and Arabella's wedding, for example: "Standing before the aforesaid officiator, the two swore that at every other time of their lives till death took them, they would assuredly believe, feel, and desire precisely as they had believed, felt, and desired during the few preceding weeks" (56).

Grant Allen was also approached by the *Adult*, and his response—more game than Hardy's but still cool—appeared in the March 1898 correspondence column: "Dear Sir—The question of sexual freedom is in abeyance just now; the public still remains in its reactionary mood; and I believe it is best to give them time to recover" (32). He went on to acknowledge his novel's centrality within the *Adult*'s pages: "Thanks for your kind references to 'The Woman Who Did.' My only addition would be to say that those who think the unhappy end an argument against similar unions ought to remember that it was brought about by existing public opinion." As Allen notes, despite the importance of his novel within free love discourse, some contributors to the *Adult* found the novel politically regressive because of Herminia's suicide at the end, an interpretation with which most recent critics have agreed.[10] After Herminia's daughter calls off her engagement, telling her mother, "While *you* live, I couldn't think of marrying him. I couldn't think of burdening an honest man with such a mother-in-law as you are!" (Allen 138), Herminia poisons herself with prussic acid for her daughter's sake. Hardy's novel has an even bleaker ending. One of Jude and Sue's children kills the other two and commits suicide—leaving the ghastly note, "Done because we are too meny" (Hardy 355)—and Sue penitently leaves Jude to return to the husband she does not love. Neither novel offers anything close to a happy resolution for their free love pioneers, who only suffer for their struggles against marriage.

Two women's voices in the *Adult* complained that the problem with these endings is that neither Allen nor Hardy could imagine free womanhood in their vision of free love. Emma Wardlaw Best, in a speech reported on in the *Adult*, objected to the "fallacies" of *The Woman Who Did*: "It is only the *free* woman . . . who can stand any chance at all of happiness" (January 1898: 139). Best, a woman who publicly declared her own free union (see Figure 31), took exception to Herminia's outcome in Allen's

ARTHUR WASTALL and EMMA WARDLAW BEST,
WRITERS ON FOOD AND SEX REFORMS,
Who recently formed an autonomistic alliance, without the usual sanctions of Church or State.

Figure 31. Emma Wardlaw Best (*Labour Annual*, 1898: 153).

novel.[11] Lillian Harman made similar objections in "Cast Off the Shell!" from the same issue of the *Adult*: "Such books as *Jude* and *The Woman Who Did* have an important place in the literature of radicalism, and are doubtless useful in their lessons of life," but "they seem ignorant or regardless of the fact that there are women . . . who live their lives in freedom, calmly ignoring conventional commands, without suffering any of the agonies of self-reproach and renunciation portrayed by these authors" (149). The article was followed by a reprinted section from *The Woman Who Did*.

Allen's novel did not originally appear in the radical press, but sections of it were reprinted not only in the *Adult* but also in the November 1896 issue of the anarchist paper *Freedom*, under the heading "Herminia's 'Marriage'" (Figure 32), and in the popular socialist paper *Clarion*, under the title "Patriotism and Property" (20 June 1896: 194).[12] Allen's and Hardy's novels were treated in the radical press not as mere imaginative novels but as potential prompters of sociosexual change. George Bedborough wrote in the June 1897 issue of the *Adult* that literature had preceded scientific discourse in raising the question of free love: "The recent development of advanced opinion on the sex question, as expressed in modern

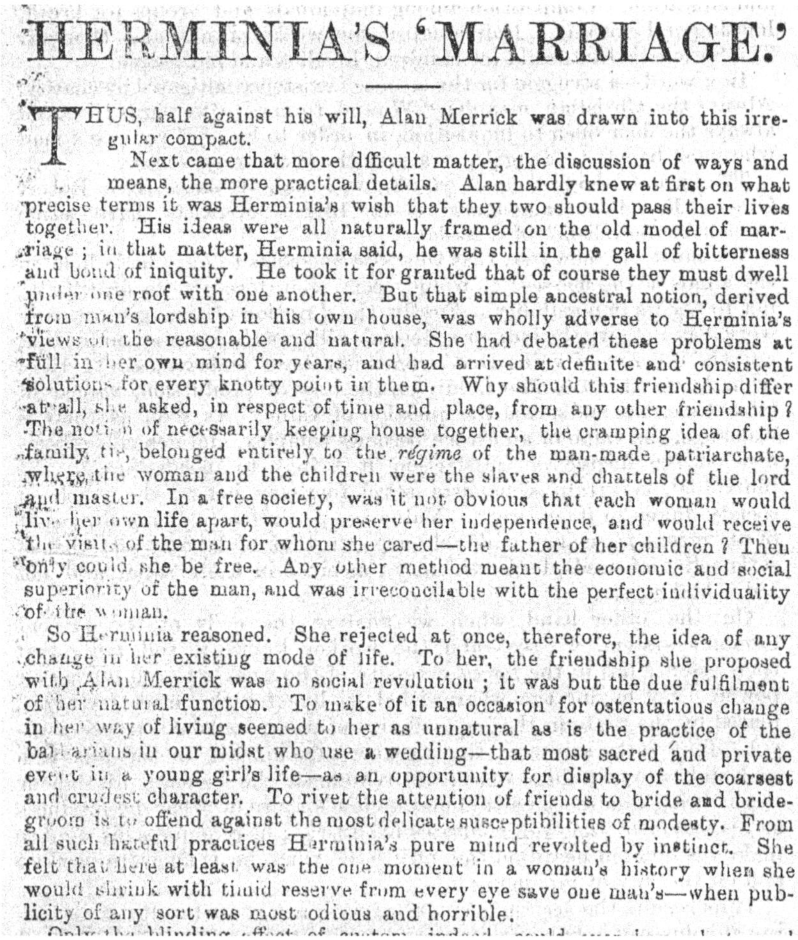

HERMINIA'S 'MARRIAGE.'

THUS, half against his will, Alan Merrick was drawn into this irregular compact.

Next came that more difficult matter, the discussion of ways and means, the more practical details. Alan hardly knew at first on what precise terms it was Herminia's wish that they two should pass their lives together. His ideas were all naturally framed on the old model of marriage ; in that matter, Herminia said, he was still in the gall of bitterness and bond of iniquity. He took it for granted that of course they must dwell under one roof with one another. But that simple ancestral notion, derived from man's lordship in his own house, was wholly adverse to Herminia's views of the reasonable and natural. She had debated these problems at full in her own mind for years, and had arrived at definite and consistent solutions for every knotty point in them. Why should this friendship differ at all, she asked, in respect of time and place, from any other friendship ? The notion of necessarily keeping house together, the cramping idea of the family tie, belonged entirely to the *régime* of the man-made patriarchate, where the woman and the children were the slaves and chattels of the lord and master. In a free society, was it not obvious that each woman would live her own life apart, would preserve her independence, and would receive the visits of the man for whom she cared—the father of her children ? Then only could she be free. Any other method meant the economic and social superiority of the man, and was irreconcilable with the perfect individuality of the woman.

So Herminia reasoned. She rejected at once, therefore, the idea of any change in her existing mode of life. To her, the friendship she proposed with Alan Merrick was no social revolution ; it was but the due fulfilment of her natural function. To make of it an occasion for ostentatious change in her way of living seemed to her as unnatural as is the practice of the barbarians in our midst who use a wedding—that most sacred and private event in a young girl's life—as an opportunity for display of the coarsest and crudest character. To rivet the attention of friends to bride and bridegroom is to offend against the most delicate susceptibilities of modesty. From all such hateful practices Herminia's pure mind revolted by instinct. She felt that here at least was the one moment in a woman's history when she would shrink with timid reserve from every eye save one man's—when publicity of any sort was most odious and horrible.

Only the blinding effect of custom indeed could ever have

Figure 32. Selection from *The Woman Who Did*, reprinted in *Freedom* (November 1896). Labadie Collection, University of Michigan.

novels, plays, poems, newspaper correspondence, and in fact wherever a free expression of thought is possible, may be taken as evidence that the time has come for some systematic consideration of a branch of science which is as important as human happiness itself" (2). Literature is ahead of science at the forefront of this social movement because it is a domain in which "free expression of thought is possible"—again, sex radicalism is closely tied to the cause against literary censorship.

Connecting the dots between free love and free print was fairly straightforward in the case of Allen's and Hardy's novels, which had aroused censorship, book burning, and a firestorm of protest in the mainstream press. Hardy's novel was bowdlerized in its original serial edition, and when printed in volume form in 1895, it was "burnt by a bishop—probably in his despair at not being able to burn me," as Hardy recalled in his 1912 preface (xxxvi). Margaret Oliphant attacked both novels together in her January 1896 review "The Anti-Marriage League" for *Blackwood's Magazine*, and she, like the *Adult*, saw in these novels the onslaught of a radical social movement. Hardy's novel, she said, was an "assault on the stronghold of marriage" (141), and she positioned both Allen's and Hardy's novels in the vanguard of "the crusade against marriage now officially organised and raging around us" (144), expressing amazement that they "should have attained a kind of success, testified apparently by sale . . . with the general public" (148). Allen's novel in particular sold remarkably well, going into nineteen editions in a single year (Warne and Colligan 21). Oliphant attributes this to the fact that novels are read "chiefly by women" and "the majority of women are still . . . quite untrained" and thus are easily "dazzled" by Allen's pseudo-intellectualism (148–49). She fears that the literary "school" represented by Allen and Hardy might take on "the force of a popular movement" (149).

Oliphant's fear was the hope of sexual radicals: that the literature of free love might serve as the testing ground for real sociosexual change. It is not surprising that the novel in particular would take on this role in the sphere of sex radicalism, even though, as we saw in Chapter 2, it had been deemed a reactionary literary form by many socialist writers. As we have seen, the death grip that the marriage plot held on the realist novel served as an impediment for Shaw in his attempts to write a socialist—not individualist—novel, yet the prominence of the marriage plot and of themes of courtship, love, and sexuality in the nineteenth-century novel meant that it was an obvious place for the interrogation of values within this sphere of life. Emma Brooke, a Fabian socialist and novelist, attributed the affinity of sex radicalism for the novelistic form to another cause: The novel had become the nucleus of this discourse, she thought, because there was so little radical consensus on the issue. Brooke thought that because there was "no unity of opinion," most socialists "came tacitly to assume that the best way of treating the Sex Question, is by representation" in fiction (qtd. in Daniels 154).

The novel was also central to free love discourse in another journal published by the University Press, *The University Magazine and Free Review*, which covered a wider range of topics than the *Adult* but likewise advocated free love in friction and in harmony with free print and socialism. These issues are at stake in Edith Ellis's novel *Seaweed: A Cornish Idyll*, which was serialized in the *University Magazine* in 1898 and published later that same year as a freestanding book by the University Press.[13] (Two years later Ellis was selling the novel from her home, according to an advertisement in the 1900 *Labour Annual* [67].)[14] Edith Ellis was married to Havelock Ellis and is remembered today as one of the anonymous lesbian case studies in her husband's book *Sexual Inversion*. But she was also a prolific writer in her own right who lectured on the socialist platform, wrote for the radical press, and penned novels as well as plays.[15] *Seaweed*, her first novel, can be read as a literary intervention into the vexed discursive context around sex radicalism, stitching together free love, free print, and a socialist analysis of class. *Seaweed* tells the story of Kit Trenoweth, a Cornish miner partially paralyzed in a mining accident. Kit comes to believe that his wife, Janet, should take a lover, given his own sexual disability. As Kit comes to reason out this position in the course of the novel, Janet has in fact already taken a lover, but she renounces him in the end in response to Kit's sexual magnanimity, after Kit proposes that they might all three live together. Despite the ménage-à-deux resolution, the novel is a free love polemic that makes the case for nature's management of sexuality and for the clumsiness of exterior social controls. Kit, the narrator says, "had to endure a cripple's life with its physical drawbacks and sexual disabilities. The virile lover was laid aside, and Nature, as if in revenge for her thwarted plan, had pressed the subtler spiritual laws of love-life into the foreground" (28). "Nature" leads Kit to a free love philosophy.

The novel's dialogue is written in a strongly flavored Cornish dialect that aligns the work with working-class social protest narrative, as does the mining accident that precipitates the plot.[16] In fact, a notice in the 1900 *Labour Annual* describes the novel as "deal[ing] with Social conditions among the poor in an out-of-the-way corner" (145) with no mention of its free love theme. The use of dialect also lends a naturalist cast to the proceedings, as does the subject matter; indeed, a review of the novel in the June 1898 *University Magazine*—a review that strangely appeared in the very journal serializing the novel before the serialization was complete—evinced as proof of *Seaweed*'s "realism" the novel's "coarseness of language," "graphically and dramatically told" story, and "dialogues largely in good Cornish dialect" (334–35). Clearly, the journal was at pains to associate Ellis's novel with the naturalist principles of Émile Zola, who was notorious in Britain for his novels' treatment of sexuality but who had become a cause célèbre for the anticensorship crowd after the 1888 prosecution of Henry Vizetelly for publishing Zola's *La Terre* in English. As discussed in Chapter 2, Zola's naturalism purports to cast a detached scientific light on unseemly subjects—to express the unspeakable in plain, precise narration—but his brand of naturalism was also accused of objectifying lower-class characters.

In Ellis's novel the working-class characters themselves struggle to address sex with plain objective speech. As Kit says to the local parson: "I reckons that i' this spring weather [Janet] do feel a want that's natural and right. . . . I'm no more use to she i' this job nor a eunuch, and that's plain speakin'!" (77–78). The middle-class parson tries to suppress such speech: "These matters are very delicate. . . . They scarcely bear talking over under any circumstance" (79). Ellis puts the language of enlightened sexual free thought in the mouths of her working characters, not in the mouths of middle-class reformers, which aligns free love with radical class discourse. The pastor's attempt to check Kit's heretical speech accords with a broader narrative of middle-class suppression of working-class dissent in the interest of preserving the status quo. When Kit appeals to the parson "whether her oughtn't to have another man, one as 'ud be a strong sweetheart to she and not a putty man like I be," the parson responds, "If such preposterous actions were countenanced by law, what on earth do you think would become of the family—the foundation of our Nation's happiness and prosperity?" (83). Kit cleverly turns this platitude on its head: "We ain't got no family, sir, that's the touchy bit in it all, don't 'ee see?" The Parson's argument against sociosexual change resonates with the slippery-slope language used by antireformist defenders of the class system throughout the nineteenth century: "These courses of conduct that you suggest will assuredly undermine all family purity and domestic peace" (90).

We can identify in Ellis's novel the hereditary traces of free print rhetoric in nineteenth-century radical history. By the end of the century such rhetoric, having originated in class radicalism, sat easier in the domain of sex radicalism, which kept alive a lingering radical vision of liberal Enlightenment values. Despite her novel's conventional form, we can also identify Ellis, as Jo-Ann Wallace does, with the emergence of literary modernism: "Early modernists like Edith Ellis used relatively conservative literary forms, like the novel of marriage . . . to argue for social and sexual experimentation" (33). Wallace argues that the connections between Ellis's class radicalism and her sex radicalism have "largely been repressed by a cultural history emphasizing the rise of a cynical, though heroic, high modernism devoted to formal experimentation and difficulty as a way of safeguarding genuine culture against the encroachments of mass culture" (16). In other words, Ellis's experimental attitude toward the representation of sexuality is recognizably modernist, even if her socialism is not—but the two are more connected than most histories of modernism would suggest.[17]

Of course, Ellis was not the only turn-of-the-century socialist who attempted to suture socialism with sex reform.[18] Many other socialist advocates of free love, however, sought to reclaim the phrase from laissez-faire principle and negative conceptions of freedom, associating truly "free" love with the absence of commercial pressures on sexuality rather than with Nature's invisible hand or the abolition of state interventions. These socialists often used the term *free love* to refer to a future state of love after the socialist revolution—love that was unimpeded by the economic and class interests that played such a determinant role in marriage and courtship. As early as 1885, Edith Nesbit was writing in *Justice* that only when women were financially independent could we "hope to see the last of the horrible, degrading, brutalizing traffic in which a woman sells herself body and soul to a man of whom she knows absolutely nothing, or whom she may actually detest, while parents and guardians smile approval" (4 April 1885: 4). The *Workers' Cry*, which aimed at an audience of working-class readers, imagined in "The Social Revolution and After" that everything, even sex, would be better after the revolution: "Then will lads and lasses make love and mate free from and unhindered by sordid thoughts of gain. Class convenience will not mar their mating" (20 June 1891: 19). Years later, Harry Quelch argued in the 8 August 1907 issue of the *Social Democrat*, "Socialism does mean Free Love, but only in the sense that men and women being free, there will be no coercion to force either man or woman into relations which are repulsive, or to unwillingly suffer the embraces of another" (462). Socialist poet Fred Henderson elaborated a similar idea in "Free Love," from his 1888 volume *Love Triumphant*: "Love that is bought is lust, and I would know / The love that springeth freely from true hearts, / . . . Free Love, which after many years will hold / Its first delight, nor ever can grow cold" (15).[19]

Reproduction, Birth Control, and the State

Whether referring to the absence of economic pressures on love or to the abolition of state controls over marriage and sexuality, free love was not the only biopolitical issue that brought fin de siècle radicals to the cause of sexual expression under the auspices of free print. As discussed in Chapter 5, Annie Besant and Charles Bradlaugh's trial for obscenity, after publishing *The Fruits of Philosophy*, established birth control as another key nexus of sex radicalism and anticensorship activism. Birth control, or neo-Malthusianism, was initially more likely to be associated with secularist advocates such as Bradlaugh (and Besant before her socialist conversion) than with socialism; as Coolsen has argued, "Most English socialists had little use for the neo-Malthusianism which had found a home among many members of the National Secularist [*sic*] Society in the early 1880's" (99). Growing socialist interest in reproduction, however, is evident in the *Clarion*'s women's columns that began to appear in the 1890s and were directed toward working-class women readers; these columns, discussed later in this chapter, suggest that birth control was emerging as a distinctly feminist cause within the socialist movement. The development drew on early nineteenth-century radical discourse in its rhetorical echoes of the free print cause but represented a major political shift, because birth control had for the most part been deeply unpopular among early nineteenth-century working-class radicals (Thompson, *English Working Class* 742).[20]

Not all socialists were pro-Malthusianism. Besant, as discussed in Chapter 5, abandoned her advocacy of birth control when she became a theosophist, which was especially significant because she, along with Bradlaugh, had provoked an important court decision on the circulation of birth control literature by printing Charles Knowlton's *Fruits of Philosophy* in 1877. In the preface to that volume, Besant and Bradlaugh claimed they were publishing the pamphlet largely to test the Obscene Publications Act of 1857: "The pamphlet which we now present to the public is one which has been lately prosecuted under Lord Campbell's Act, and which we republish in order to test the right of publication" (v). Their motivation, as explained in the preface, was the general defense of free print principles rather than the defense of birth control in particular: "We republish this pamphlet, honestly believing that . . . fullest right of free discussion ought to be maintained at all hazards. . . . Progress can only be made through discussion. . . . We claim the right to publish all opinions, so that the public . . . may have the materials for forming a sound judgment" (vi).[21] Importantly, to make this point about free discussion, Besant and Bradlaugh turned to the realm of the biopolitical and away from the sphere of religion and free thought that had hitherto occupied them.[22] Sex was the new domain of suppressed speech. Although the Knowlton pamphlet was somewhat outdated, having originally been published in 1832, its Enlightenment rhetoric perfectly served such ends: "I hold the following to be important and undeniable truths: That every man has a natural right both to receive and convey a knowledge of all the facts and discoveries of every art and science. . . . That a physical truth in its general effect cannot be a moral evil. That no fact in physics or in morals ought to be concealed from the enquiring mind" (9).

After converting to theosophy, however, Besant changed her position on birth control and began to advocate celibacy, in accordance with the theosophical platform. This new position was satirized in a short utopian story titled "At Low Street Fleece Court: A Free-Lover's Dream of A.D. 2898" in the November 1898 issue of the *Adult*. The story depicts a future free love Utopia in which a group of offenders are prosecuted for "conspiring against the sexual-freedom laws of the country," having published a book advocating celibacy "as well as a certain journal, to wit, 'The Fruits of Theosophy,' with intent to corrupt the morals of the commonwealth" (305). The allusions to celibacy, theosophy, and *The Fruits of Philosophy* make it clear that Besant is the target of the satire.

Published in the immediate wake of Bedborough's arrest, the story aligns Besant—traitor to the cause of sexual freedom—with those responsible for seizing and censoring Havelock Ellis's book and the journal *Adult*.

Beatrice Webb was another socialist leader opposed to birth control, because it "meant setting personal ease and inclination above the duty to produce children for the social good" (Caine 41).[23] Her husband, Sidney Webb, held the same position; his 1907 pamphlet *The Decline in the Birth Rate* summarized a Fabian statistical study that found the use of birth control "among at least one-half, and probably among three-fourths, of all the married people in Great Britain of reproductive age" (15).[24] Webb found it a cause for alarm that "the production of children is rapidly declining, and this decline is not uniform, but characteristic of the more prudent, foreseeing and self-restrained sections of the community" (15). Those communities not taking measures to limit births were prohibited religiously or were simply careless and in either case did not fit Webb's vision of ideal British parenthood: "Children are being freely born to the Irish Roman Catholics and the Polish, Russian and German Jews, on the one hand, and to the thriftless and irresponsible—largely the casual laborers and the other denizens of the one-roomed tenements of our great cities—on the other" (17). For Webb the situation was an argument for wider economic security by means of socialism, which would mitigate against prudent couples' will to regulate reproduction: "Once set free from the overwhelming economic penalties with which among four-fifths of the population is at present visited, the rearing of a family may gradually be rendered part of the code of the ordinary citizen's morality. The natural repulsion to interference in marital relations will have free play" (19). The Fabians were generally inclined to constructivist reasoning rather than to arguments premised on the natural, but even they believed that sexuality could be regulated by "natural repulsion" and "free play" under socialism.

As the opinions of Beatrice and Sidney Webb suggest, different ideas about the role of the state had a great deal of bearing on how and to what extent radical reformers took up questions of free love, sexual reform, and birth control.[25] Webb's position that "the rearing of a family may gradually be rendered part of the code of the ordinary citizen's morality" places him at the authoritarian end of a continuum of radical positions on sexuality and the state. By contrast, Edward Carpenter advocated a form of anarchist communism that allowed a great degree of individual latitude, and although not an advocate of birth control, he promoted the legitimation of homosexual love in part on the basis of its potential for reducing the birth rate. His 1894 pamphlet *Homogenic Love, and Its Place in a Free Society* argues:

It has probably been the arbitrary limitation of the function of love to child-breeding which has (unconsciously) influenced the popular mind against the form of love which we are considering. That this kind of union was not concerned with the propagation of the race was in itself enough to make the people look askance at it . . . from far-back times when the multiplication of the tribe was one of the very first duties of its members. . . . Nowadays when the need has swung round all the other way it is not unreasonable to suppose that a similar revolution will take place in people's views of the place and purpose of the non-child-bearing love. (33–34)

Carpenter makes the case for homogenic love on the basis of social health but stresses an accord between individuals' inherent desires and the interests of society at large, whereas the Webbs emphasize the suppression of individual desire in service of social ends. Carpenter argues that homogenic love has a "special function in social and heroic work, and in the generation—not of bodily children—but of those children of the mind, the philosophical conceptions and ideals which transform our lives and those of society." For a society to suppress such love might cause "considerable danger or damage to the common-weal" (42–43). Freed of the "*impedimenta* of family life," same-sex lovers "can supply the force and liberate the energies required for social and mental activities of the most necessary kind" (44). The argument of the pamphlet is that freedom to pursue one's independent sexual desire is actually the best avenue toward the social good.

John Badcock, aka Leighton Pagan, represented another brand of individualism—one that was strictly libertarian rather than communist in principle. He went further than many radical thinkers of the day in supporting the legitimation of abortion, not just birth control, calling for "a protest against the heavy penalties that now attend bigamy, adultery, abortions, and so on" (*Adult,* January 1898: 111). His views on the state and the individual were the reverse of the Webbs' and were quite distinct from Carpenter's. In his 1894 pamphlet *Slaves to Duty*, from a lecture at the South Place Junior Ethical Society, he argues stridently against the ethical constraints of duty, which he portrays as moral superstition: "In place of duty I put—nothing. Superstitions never want replacing, or we should never advance to freedom" (28). His pamphlet *When Love Is Liberty and Nature Law*, based on an 1893 lecture, argues: "No allegiance is due to any law or custom, as such; but that conformity need be given only to what the unfettered individual mind sees the reasonableness of, or attractiveness of" (4). We can connect Badcock's ideas with other 1890s attacks on the principle of social duty, such as Oscar Wilde's "Lord Arthur Savile's Crime: A Study of Duty" (1891) or Shaw's *Quintessence of Ibsenism* (1891), but what distinguishes Badcock's attack is that he uses it to make an explicit case against a certain brand of socialism, epitomized by the Fabian view of reproduction as a duty to the state: "The MOTHER is often held up as the pattern example of duty and self-sacrifice," he says, but this example fails "unless the typical mother comes up to the Fabian-Socialist's ideal, by being willing to endure that keenest of anguish: the sacrifice of her infant for the good of the community, because it happens to be club-footed, or has a birth-mark, or experts say it is not up to the regulation weight" (*Slaves* 29–30).

This characterization obviously exaggerates the eugenic measures favored by the Fabians, but Badcock's contention usefully illustrates the range of positions on reproduction and the state that we find in the radical press; on one end is Badcock's libertarian individualism, and at the other end is the Webbs' authoritarian socialism. Badcock articulates a critique of duty and a critique of marriage, imagining individuals (including child-bearing women) as self-sufficient agents; for Badcock this position extends from an ideological basis in laissez-faire individualism. The Fabians, meanwhile, emphasize an individual's sexual duty to the common good with respect to eugenics and reproduction. Because they imagine that all children's welfare might be secured through state accommodations, the Fabian position also enables a critique of marriage. Most radical thinkers of this era were somewhere in between Webb and Badcock; such is the case with the *Clarion*, which I will turn to next.

Sexuality and the Clarion

The *Clarion* was a popular mass-oriented socialist paper unaffiliated
with any particular group but favoring a democratic, decentralized
socialist state and a great deal of personal liberty. Perhaps because it
aimed at an audience of working-class readers, it tended to be relatively
conservative on sex questions. Indeed the *Clarion* introduces another
vector—class—into a continuum of radical perspectives on the state
and sexuality, for Webb and Badcock were equally middle class in their
opposing views. Sheila Rowbotham identifies *Clarion* editor Robert
Blatchford as "hostile to any connection of socialism with sexual radicalism," because he feared it would hurt socialism popularly (Rowbotham
and Weeks 116). Blatchford's 1907 utopian novel *The Sorcery Shop* depicts a socialist future where "the custom of strict monogamy" remains
entrenched (46), where the "foundation and pattern of [the] State . . .
is the family," and where "the heart of the family is the woman—the
mother" (45). Beyond Blatchford the *Clarion's* regular all-male staff
expressed many of the same traditional prejudices.

Still, as noted earlier, a section from *The Woman Who Did* was printed
in the 20 June 1896 issue of the *Clarion*, and in the 22 February 1896 issue Blatchford defended Grant Allen and Thomas Hardy against charges
of immorality. Referring specifically to Oliphant's diatribe against their
novels—"Here is one in 'Blackwood's' declares that not from the hand of
any master have we had books more impious, more disgusting, or more
foul in detail than those of Thomas Hardy and Grant Allen"—Blatchford
argues that the best means of combating corrupt literature is to "let the
spread of pure literature be free" (58). This includes, to his mind, these
two novels. Likewise, in the 11 January 1896 issue of the *Clarion*, the essay "Morals and Fiction" by "Dangle" (A. M. Thompson) drew on *Jude
the Obscure* as an example of moral art: "At this moment some of the noble
army of critics are assailing Thomas Hardy's works on the ground of
'immorality.' We are told that in 'Jude the Obscure' Hardy has 'indulged
an eccentric taste.'" But Hardy, Dangle says, has in fact "described nineteenth century humanity. Therefore his stories have a moral" (13).[26]

In a socialist paper allegedly opposed to sex radicalism, these excerpts
may seem surprising, but they suggest how the socialist press in general
flocked to cases of free print like moths to flame. They also suggest the

complexity of the *Clarion's* account of sexuality. For example, Carpenter was much beloved in its pages, if not always agreed with, as a review of his book *Sex Love, and Its Place in a Free Society* suggests.

> Whether or not the time has yet arrived for dealing with so difficult and delicate a matter as Sex Love is a question we are not prepared to answer. Evidently Mr. Carpenter thinks the time has arrived, and he is quite as capable of judging as we can be. . . . With most of what the author says . . . we are in accord. Where we cannot quite see as he sees . . . our failure may be due to the fact that Mr. Carpenter knows more, or has thought more, about the subject than we have. . . . This very question has been shelved by us; not only on account of its difficulty, but also because, with so many hard nuts to crack for present use, we were loth to injure our teeth by cracking nuts for future generations. 'Sex Love' is a wholesome and logical argument in favour of a more sensible, natural, and really *chaste* conduct of the relations between the sexes . . . and yet after reading it, we can sympathise with the feelings of the old-fashioned Tory or Radical who has just been decoyed into a perusal of the *Clarion.* Perhaps we ourselves are less free from conventional ideas and insular prejudices than we supposed. . . . However, if Edward Carpenter finds it necessary to flee from the wrath of Mrs. Grundy, he shall be afforded safe refuge in the *Clarion.* (3 February 1894: 8)

The last few lines of the review suggest how the adversarial, oppositional stance of Carpenter's work on sexuality was, virtually alone, enough to earn it "safe refuge in the *Clarion,*" despite the paper's acknowledgment of its own sexual conservatism.

The *Clarion's* conception of literature and journalism was on the whole less provocative and more appeasing than other radical papers; its specialty was to present socialism as everyday common sense, not to hazard the strongly oppositional stances on which other radical papers premised their identity. Blatchford took issue with a literary critic who complained about the public appetite for "second and third rate literature," arguing in his typically populist tone: "This seems to me to be hardly fair to the poor old public," a public that "is not rich, and is busy" and "is perforce obliged to open its mouth and shut its eyes and take what the cheaper houses send it." This public, he says, "reads not, as the cultured and leisured classes read, for information and refined enjoyment, but by way of relaxation, of respite from care, or escape from worry and the sordid scramble and moiling of the modern work-a-day world. Its poor dear head is too weary for subtle and fine irony, humour, reasoning" (13 March 1897: 81–82). With such a conception of its readership, it is no surprise that the *Clarion* avoided controversial accounts of sexuality. What is surprising is that the paper included women columnists who diverged from this editorial approach.

If the *Clarion* as a whole was not very bold in its approach to sexual questions, it was committed to the principle of free expression and included space for a feminist socialist perspective that departed from the paper's dominant voice.[27] The presence of women writers in the space of the paper was itself oppositional, as was apparent from the friendly jibes exchanged between the paper's regular staff and its occasional female contributors. On 10 March 1894, for example, Blatchford criticized a Margaret McMillan article from the week before, jokingly portraying McMillan as an interloper on the all-male staff's print domain: "Is a lady to come into our columns and calmly tell us that our birds and brooks and winds are not musical? This comes of the higher education of women. Did I not warn the delegates at the Labour Conference that the emancipation of women would lead to trouble?" (8). A discussion of Friedrich Nietzsche in the 22 August 1896 "Book Notes" column occasioned more teasing of the women contributors: "Mrs. Julia Dawson, Miss Margaret McMillan, and Miss Enid Stacy" are requested to consider "the following ideas of Master Nietzsche on women: '. . . Everything in woman is a riddle, and everything in woman hath one answer: its name is child-bearing'" (267).

A January 1895 face-off between Enid Stacy, who often contributed to the *Clarion*, and Dangle, one of its regular staff members, touched precisely on this question of whether women should have a social role outside the domestic sphere. Stacy objected to a recent piece by Dangle, arguing that the "Labour party inscribes Adult Suffrage [including women] on its political programme; but in the mind of several of its masculine members there is a curious half-defined instinctive antipathy to it—an antipathy often but half conscious of its own entity, which nevertheless eagerly picks up and exhibits any item of news which is supposed to tell against the 'New Woman'" (12 January 1895: 10). Dangle responded the next week: "Miss Stacy mistakes me when she takes me for an op-

ponent of Female Suffrage. . . . Decidedly, I agree with Miss Stacy. Our
wives should be allowed to go to Parliament—or further. . . . It is, unfortunately, a fact, however, that if you give a woman an inch she is apt
to make it an ell." As evidence, he adduces the case of a woman fighting
to join the police force in Bogotá, Colombia: "'Tis a dropsy of the mind
that still increases while we give drink to quench it. Make [women]
policemen: the unappeasable lust of power will carry them on till they
perish or they burst" (19 January 1895: 24). The exchange points to the
broad ideological gap on feminist issues between the paper's regular
male staff and its minority of women writers.

As a result, dedicated women's columns in the *Clarion* defined their
space in the paper as a separate corner independent of Blatchford, Dangle, and the regular staff.[28] When Eleanor Keeling of Liverpool (wife of
Joseph Edwards) began "Our Woman's Column" on 9 February 1895,
she wrote: "Herein we women may settle down to a cosy gossip about
our own affairs and what we say will be no business of the other sex.
. . . Now we women have got a column all to ourselves in the *Clarion*
and I hope we shall make good use of it" (43). Keeling's column did not
last long—its last appearance was April 1895—but Julia Dawson, one
of the most important figures in the *Clarion* movement, began writing
her more successful women's column, "Our Woman's Letter," in the
5 October 1895 issue of the *Clarion*.[29] Her first installment presents the
column's space as separate and oppositional within the paper: "I am told
that few women read the *Clarion*, and that, therefore, it will be very up-
hill work to make a Woman's Column popular" (320). One reader wrote
in, pessimistically predicting that, although "it is nice to think that we
women are to have a little corner of our own, there is not much chance
of our making ourselves heard amidst Nunquam's Clarion note, clear
and penetrating" (19 October 1895: 336). But Dawson's vision for the
column remained steady: "I want to swell the ranks of the women readers
of the *Clarion*. Most of us have aspirations, many of us have grievances.
Can we not mutually help each other to realise the one, and to remove
the other? Let us use this column to this end" (12 October 1895: 328).

The idea that women might form a unified block of interest within
the socialist movement was complicated by class issues evident in the
paper's columns for women. Perhaps overcompensating, the *Clarion*'s

middle-class women writers interpellated their women readers as working class rather than middle class, although both groups read the paper. Katharine St. John Conway, for example, wife of Bruce Glasier, expressed disdain for middle-class female malaise in "The Middle-Class Woman": "The typical middle-class woman, not yet touched by the spirit of Socialism, accepts the training of her mind and sense to the appreciation of the beautiful . . . *as a class privilege*, entailing on society the duty of providing her enlarged and refined desires with their fullest satisfaction" (*Clarion*, 16 February 1895: 56). Here, the biopolitical became the grounds for interclass conflict among women. Conway observes, "Often even a working-class mother's milk is stolen from her baby to preserve a rich woman's offspring that he may grow up the stronger to oppress" (56). The comment, its source unacknowledged, references George Moore's *Esther Waters*, a controversial novel published less than a year earlier in March 1894. In Moore's novel of an illiterate kitchen maid's struggle to raise an illegitimate son, the eponymous heroine turns her newborn over to a baby farmer so she can work as a wet nurse for the wealthy Rivers family for 15 shillings a week. When she learns, however, that the babies of the Rivers' two previous wet nurses had both died under the sort of care her own child is receiving, she realizes that "the children of two poor girls had been sacrificed so that this rich woman's child might be saved. Even that was not enough: the life of her beautiful boy was called for . . . and, as in a dream darkly, it seemed to this ignorant girl that she was the victim of a far-reaching conspiracy" (146).

Conway's piece in the *Clarion* positions *Esther Waters* and its treatment of wet nursing within the domain of socialist biopolitical argument. The novel had been banned by the circulating libraries and subject to the moral disapproval of critics on the basis of its frank treatment of sexuality, but as with *Jude the Obscure* and *The Woman Who Did*, the socialist press enthusiastically championed the novel. The *Labour Leader* declared that *Esther Waters* was "written in a democratic spirit" (12 May 1894: 3) and was "the best novel of the last two years" (19 May 1894: 14).[30] Conway's allusion to Moore's novel in the *Clarion* again suggests the wide overlap between the radical press and the cause of free print, the advanced novel, and open sexual expression, but it also aligns the paper with working-class women's biopolitical interests. Margaret McMillan was another *Clarion* contributor whose pieces spoke to working-class women's biopolitical concerns. As Carolyn Steedman has shown, in short fiction such as "Ann" and "Lola," both of which were published in the *Clarion*, McMillan popularized new theories of child development for a wide audience of readers (97). "Lola," the story of a workhouse girl, allowed McMillan to examine through fictional form "the influence of childhood experience on psychosexual development," "the notion of the unconscious mind," and "the psychological effect of deprivation in childhood" (69–70).

Julia Dawson, Birth Control, and Pastoral New Journalism

Like Katharine St. John Conway and Margaret McMillan, Julia Dawson was another woman writer for the *Clarion* who addressed working-class women's biopolitical interests, especially in her campaign for birth control launched in the *Clarion*'s women's column in 1895. Dawson sought to interpellate working-class women readers individually by means of the pseudopersonal voice of New Journalism that was the *Clarion*'s stock-in-trade, and such a voice was crucial to her birth control campaign. Already by this time Dawson had generated an intimate conversational rapport with readers. From her earliest columns she urged them to write to her: "Every letter will interest me . . . whether it comes from cot or castle, from factory or work-room, office or shop. But if I *must* confess to a partiality. My warmest sympathies go with those of my sisters who are struggling on as units amongst the thousands in our vast fields of labour, and leading a life of wearying toil" (5 October 1895: 320). Factory girls, shop girls, and waitresses were directly appealed to in the opening weeks of her column. Later, she professed, "I am so glad that I am not a lady, in the 19th century sense of the term. It is so much more honourable to be a working woman" (19 October 1895: 336).[31]

The emphasis on letters from readers and the effort to create an intimate, interactive print environment were tricks of New Journalism, indicating the extent of the *Clarion*'s reliance on the discursive techniques of the popular media sphere. Dawson used her distinctively New Journalist voice to draw readers closer, presenting the obstructive medium of print as a barrier to be overcome, so that antiprint rhetoric actually functioned in her column to reinforce the new print mode of New Journalism: "It is quite a new experience for me to feel so closely in touch with such a large number of you whose sympathies are running so warmly alongside my own, and I do count it a privilege to have found so many loyal and loving friends. Here is my hand, and I wish that I could have the pleasure of actually feeling the warm clasp of yours" (19 October 1895: 336). This was a familiar rhetorical move for Dawson—the expressed desire to transcend the distancing print media interface and to interact physically with readers. Metaphors of touch and temperature describe the desired relation, prohibited by print.

I should love to split myself up into a thousand Julias, and take a peep at you all by your own firesides, but alas I cannot, and this cold sheet of *Clarion* paper is of necessity my only means of communication with you. When you read it, therefore, will you try to believe that I am there in the flesh and blood, talking to you, and that I shall feel horribly repulsed and left out in the cold if you never have a word to say to me? (16 November 1895: 368)

Dawson actually used a pen name in her column—her real name was Mrs. D. J. Myddleton-Worral (Barrow and Bullock 157)—so her expressed desire for warm, intimate exchange with readers apart from the "cold" world of print was itself the affectation of a print persona.[32] When a reader requested that she include a photograph of herself at the head of her column, Dawson balked at the request; she affected to do so out of modesty, but given her use of a pen name, it is clear that maintenance of print pseudonymity was also at stake: "I do not think many people would feel that my Column would be improved if my photograph appeared at the head of it! I should dearly love to see you in your little study, and to give your hand a right good grip" (21 December 1895: 408). While declining to include her photograph with her words—a move that would have associated her column with her "real" bodily person—Dawson conveys a wish to clasp the reader's hand, interpreting the photograph request as an expression of frustration with the print barrier, not a desire to pin down authorial identity.

Interestingly, the *Labour Leader*'s women's column had by this time already shown that visual depiction of a columnist's image would not necessarily be taken as proof of authorial authenticity. The column, "Matrons and Maidens," was written under the pen name Lily Bell and included an illustration of its purported writer at the head of the column (see Figure *33*). But a letter to Bell in the 1 September 1894 issue indicates that some readers found the portrait and its accompanying persona suspect: "Dear Lily Bell—I met some bright youths last night who said they had been led to believe that 'Matrons and Maidens' was written by a man" (7). Critics today still dispute whether the column was written by a woman or a man: either Isabella Bream Pearce, president of the Glasgow Woman's Labour Party, or Keir Hardie, editor of the *Labour Leader*.[33] When Hardie introduced Bell to the paper's readers on 31 March 1894, he called her "a Scotch lassie, with a warm heart and a clear, strong brain" (2). Despite the use of her picture and the inclusion of this "warm" description, the reader's letter shows that Lily Bell was known not to exist, and rumors circulated that the column's writer was not a woman at all.

Dawson's column had a far more personal tone than "Matrons and Maidens" and seems to have been more popular, given that Bell often complained of a lack of correspondents, whereas Dawson was flooded

MATRONS AND MAIDENS.

Figure 33. Illustration of "Lily Bell" from the weekly *Labour Leader* column "Matrons and Maidens."

with letters from readers. Still, in Dawson's column print was often constructed as an impediment rather than an aid to interpersonal contact, demonstrating again how New Journalism ironically appealed to an antiprint sensibility. The delay between the writing and the reading of a column was often a source of complaint: "As I am writing this you are probably just having your first glance at my last week's 'column.'" Print disrupts the natural conversational flow for which Dawson yearns: "Nunquam must have his matter in hand so many days before he can turn it out ship-shape in the form of our beloved *Clarion*. The printer must set up all the 'copy' in type, and after sundry corrections and revisions of proofs carried out under the eagle eye of our Editor, the proofs are made up into columns. . . . All this takes time" (12 October 1895: 328). The limited space allotted to the column was another source of complaint, always described in terms of a conflict with the editor. When Dawson first convinced Blatchford to give a little extra room to "Our Woman's Letter," so she could include more letters and responses to readers, she reported his reply: "Understand my one stern and unalterable editorial *law*! You may have three columns in which to do your best . . . *but* beyond that limit not one inch must you trespass" (26 October 1895: 344). On 8 August 1896, however, Dawson announced that "my third column is going to be taken away from me" (256). Next month she complained, "Every week the printer sends me a long strip of 'over-matter.' 'Answers to Correspondents' and other paragraphs are being held over week by week, till they are almost out of date" (26 September 1896: 312).

Apart from this fight for space, however, Dawson felt free within the column to manage its content: "In our own respective corners we members of the *Clarion* staff are all allowed to say just exactly what we like, without any tiresome editorial interferences. . . . Owing to this freedom, I know that I am writing to friends . . . I think I may say, intimate friends, [who] feel ourselves at liberty to approach each other without the slightest formality" (17 October 1896: 336). This freedom from interference and the space that it creates for "intimate" exchange formed the discursive ground for Dawson's birth control campaign.

Dawson first began to stridently advocate birth control in the 14 December 1895 issue of the *Clarion*. In a customary rhetorical move for the column, she affected to have been driven to this decision by the trials and tribulations of her reader correspondents.

One writes that her husband . . . has been out of work for months, and they are often without food. Another has a large family, husband earning 10s. weekly. . . . She has scarcely a rag to put on her baby when it comes. . . . Another is a mother of ten, expecting her eleventh, and in dire poverty and distress. . . . What is the moral to which all these tales of . . . misery and want point? Is it not that people should restrict their families to the number they can comfortably keep? I look upon it as nothing more nor less than a *crime* to deliberately bring into the world innocent, helpless little children, when we know that we can neither give them bread to put into their mouths nor clothes to put on their backs. (400)

The passage appears to blame poor parents who bring children they cannot afford into the world, but the next paragraphs suggest that the real crime lies with those who would prevent such families from knowledge of birth control: "Now, dear friends who read this, and are poor, and have large families, do not think I am blaming you. If the knowledge how to limit the number of your children is withheld from you, how can you help yourselves?" (400). The underlying rhetorical context here is the long tradition of nineteenth-century radical print and its basic premise that more information and knowledge is always of public benefit in the promotion of self-help measures.

Dawson goes on to advocate use of *The Malthusian Hand Book*, which normally sells for 8 pence, but which she has arranged with the Malthusian League to be supplied to *Clarion* readers at half-price. A few weeks later, in her 28 December 1895 column, she recommends an even cheaper (2d.) print volume on the subject, brought to her attention by a reader. Other readers were

kind enough to send donations for the free distribution of Malthusian literature. I cannot find words to express my gratitude to all of you who have thus so kindly not only stood by me to uphold me in the somewhat difficult position in which I placed myself, but also come forward with your generous help to poor overburdened sisters. I am therefore sending straightaway for a supply of Malthusian books, and I shall be glad to send a copy to any friends who have not the means to buy for themselves. (416)

Dawson's difficult position in advocating for birth control was initially a matter of great anxiety—anxiety that was inflected by her minority position with respect to the *Clarion* staff. When she first raised the issue of birth control on 14 December 1895, she confessed, "I have been told that I—a young married woman—must be courageous almost to the degree of being bold and brazen to take up a subject of this sort in the columns of a widely read newspaper like the *Clarion*. Well, be it so" (400). Dawson's allusion to her own married life took on added weight because she herself, as she sometimes mentioned in the column, had only one daughter. Was the implication that Dawson herself used Malthusian methods? Later in the same column, she declares, "Nearly all the middle and richer classes are Malthusians." These subtle hints create the illusion of personal confession in a column that was actually written under a pen name.

Dawson presented herself as nervous about launching a birth control campaign—a move she made only a few months after starting the column in October 1895—but the response from readers apparently justified her decision.

Ten thousand thanks, and more, to all my sisters and brothers who have so kindly written to express their appreciation of last week's Letter. When I sent that letter off to the printers, I tried to feel brave, and as though I did not care what people thought of me or said of me, so long as I could show some of my poor weak sisters an easy way of escape from many of their miseries. . . . But now the cloud is banished from my brow. (28 December 1895: 416)

On 11 January 1896 Dawson reported that many readers who could not otherwise afford *The Malthusian Hand Book* wrote to request a free copy: "The remittances kindly sent me for the free distribution of Malthusian books have enabled me to send away hundreds, and I am pleased to say that readers have not been backward in sending for them" (16). These hundreds accounted only for those readers who could not purchase the discounted handbook themselves; altogether, it is apparent that thousands of handbooks circulated among *Clarion* readers as a result of Dawson's efforts: "I am pleased to hear from the secretary of the Malthusian League that owing to my notice in the *Clarion* of December 14th he has sent out about 2,000 copies of the Handbook. In addition, I have personally sent over 200 copies of the book. . . . May the reading of these books stem one of our most mischievous and misery-bringing tides" (18 January 1896: 24). Even these numbers do not account for sales of the 2d. handbook that Dawson recommended from another publisher or other such handbooks purchased in response to her column.

The topic was one that Dawson returned to often. In a column against the "Temporary Insanity" judgment in suicide cases (which she saw as a way of evading the hardships behind such cases), Dawson took the opportunity to subtly argue again for birth control: "A mother, with a family of eight and another coming, looks in her cupboard . . . and reflects how it will be in another week, when there will be still another mouth to feed. . . . That night she seeks the solace of the dark river" (12 September 1896: 296). In the "Answers to Correspondents" section of her column, she advises A. B. of Manchester, "You can obtain Malthusian books from the *Clarion* office," and warns "Collier Laddie," "Yes, marry, lad, marry, and enjoy all the love and happiness you possibly can. . . . Bear in mind, however, that although two can manage to live on your wages, with strict economy, if this number is doubled, you will all be half starved" (28 November 1896: 384). She counsels W. A. A. of Halifax, "Keep up your heart, if you can. I know it's hard. I am *so* sorry that your family has increased. If you let this happen again I shall have no more sympathy for you or your husband either" (17 April 1897: 128). Although such free reference to birth control was for the most part confined to the women's column of the *Clarion*, advertisements for Malthusian handbooks began to appear in the paper after Dawson took up this issue, such as on 19 December 1896, suggesting that her efforts were having a wider impact on the socialist discourse around birth control.[34] Eventually, by 1907, Beatrice Hastings would declare in the pages of the *New Age* that "in the future babies will only come when they are invited. Women are at last beginning to realise that they need not have so many" (27 June 1907: 132).

Birth control was not the only biopolitical issue into which Dawson's column ventured. She did not advocate free love, believing that marriage laws were a necessary protection for women, but she was often a voice for "fallen" women and she railed against social prejudice toward unwed mothers: "What has the girl done that all hearts are steeled against her, and she is branded as an outcast, a shameless hussy, neither fit to live nor to die? Her chief fault is that she is too loving, too trustful, that in the innocence of her heart she has put too much faith in man's honour" (*Clarion*, 22 February 1896: 64). At the end of her column Dawson printed notices intended to pair needy readers with socialists who might help them, often including notices for fallen women: "Will anyone befriend a so-called 'fallen' sister, 19, anxious to begin a new life? In Liverpool at present" (11 January 1896: 16). She also used the column to arrange adoptions, printing pleas from parents—often newly widowed—looking for new homes for babies and older children they could not afford to keep. The result of Dawson's efforts was "a new species of baby now to be found in various parts of the country, for which the *Clarion* must be held responsible! These interesting little specimens of humanity are called 'Clarion Babies'" (8 August 1896: 256). Dawson describes one such Clarion baby, adopted by a Yorkshire family and thriving under their care: "I well remember the poor widow writing to me from Keighley, saying that she had been left with seven children, one a baby, and that she herself was delicate and unable to work hard enough to support them all. Now I am glad that a good home has been found for the little one. . . . This is only one of the martyr-mothers of Merrie England of which the world learns all too little" (256).

In addition to arranging adoptions, Dawson also flirted with arranging marriages among socialist readers, at one point even contemplating starting a full-fledged "Matrimonial Agency" for socialists, with the hope that it would result in happy marriages among like-minded readers, providing a familial foundation for the making of more socialists. This was taking biopolitical socialist activism to a new level, for Dawson often wrote in her column of the importance of socialists marrying socialists and creating socialist homes. In her "Answers to Correspondents" she even dissuaded some readers from marrying nonsocialist sweethearts. Readers, Dawson said, were much in favor of the idea of the matrimonial agency: "Some hundreds of my sisters and brothers are anxious to see what I shall have to say further about the Matrimonial Agency. An overwhelming majority of my correspondents are heartily in favour of my taking means to bring together, through the *Clarion*, men and women who seem suited to link their lots together for life." Although

she decides that the "work involved would be more than I could undertake" (7 March 1896: 80), she advises readers that they may run personal
advertisements in her column, which they did: "Socialist, 35, Widower,
fair position, with one little boy, aged 10, Wishes to Correspond, with
view to Marriage; all letters will be replied to," or "Socialist, 26 (Midlands), Wishes to Correspond with Working Woman about same age,
with view to Marriage" (21 March 1896: 95).[35]

Dawson's ostensibly personal involvement in the reproductive and
romantic lives of individual readers exemplifies her pastoral approach
to socialist journalism, which we can link to the broader socialist turn
toward sex radicalism and biopolitics as the new site of free print activism. Foucault has described a "pastoral modality of power" emerging in modern Western societies as an "individualizing power," a set of
"techniques oriented toward individuals and intended to rule them in a
continuous and permanent way" ("Omnes" 227). Dawson did not seek
to "rule" her readers, but her column does establish biopolitical norms
for the *Clarion*'s working-class socialist public, and there are important
parallels between her pastoral overtures in the biopolitical realm—
tending to readers' sexuality, reproduction, marriage, and bodily well-
being—and what Foucault has described as the "strange technology"
within Western societies of "treating the vast majority of men as a flock
with a few as shepherds" (231). Pastoral power is characterized by gathering together "dispersed individuals" through individualized attention:
"The shepherd sees that all the sheep, each and every one of them, is
fed and saved" (229). To effect pastoral power "is to constantly ensure,
sustain, and improve the lives of each and every one" (235)—a modality of power uniquely suited for the democratic, liberalized socialism of
the *Clarion* and uniquely well served by Dawson's ostensibly personal
New Journalist print voice.

Although Dawson did not actually launch the matrimonial agency
that she contemplated forming, her very consideration of it suggests
the extent of her involvement in pastoral care of her readership. In the
"Answers to Correspondents" section at the end of her column, she offered individual readers advice on everything from love to underwear:
"E. B.—You will find a nice pattern for knickers in 'Weldon's Journal'
for October (1d.). They are most comfortable as underwear, and far more

hygienic than heavy, trailing petticoats" (23 November 1895: 376). However, Dawson's pastoral care of readers' bodies for the most part steered clear of the conventional domain of women's columns, for she was conscious of avoiding typical topics such as dress or cookery. When she did address such matters, it was always with qualification: "Here is a sensible little paragraph out of a Fashion Paper! 'Wheelmen and wheelwomen are now finding the benefit of sandals for cycling. They allow perfect freedom of movement, and keep the feet delightfully cool.' . . . I never have brought articles of dress and fashion into these columns, and don't intend to begin now: but it was so refreshing to read of such wholesome reform" (29 August 1896: 280). Dawson's problem with most women's journalism was that it threatened to confine women to the domestic sphere: "If we women continue to look in 'Ladies' Papers' for advice in the matter of dress, dinners, and house decorations . . . the day of our emancipation from domestic slavery will never never come. Necessary domestic work is all right. . . . It is the unnecessary work which makes us slaves" (3 April 1897: 112).

Dawson, like the other women writers for the *Clarion*, walked a thin line between encouraging women to limit their time devoted to domestic labor and not appearing to deprecate home life in any way—a move believed by many socialist women to be fatal to the cause. Eleanor Keeling, in her women's column, described the difficult balancing act socialists faced when addressing matters of sex and familial reform.

Though several of us in the *Clarion* have repeatedly expressed our reverence for the tender influence of Home, we are freshly attacked whenever any Socialist . . . advocates the idea of the communal home for children. . . . The marriage question brings kindred trouble. . . . It has always appeared to me that the shortest road towards the effectual emancipation of women was through the establishment of Socialism. Let the women be first assured of decent, independent conditions of existence, and then . . . the marriage question might very well arrange itself. (13 April 1895: 117)

Like Morris and Blatchford, Keeling professes to be waiting for socialism to see real changes in the area of sex, gender, and marriage; in point of fact, however, Keeling, Dawson, and the other women writers for the *Clarion* were constantly advocating a changed attitude in women readers toward their sexual and familial roles. Even Dawson's birth control

campaign, aimed at encouraging smaller families among socialist readers, fell into a larger effort on the part of the *Clarion*'s women writers
to reduce domestic labor for their female readers, leaving more time for
public and political engagement.

Dawson's effort to radicalize her flock of readers in the spheres of
sex and reproduction was not the paper's first move in this direction,
but she did go further than other woman writers in the *Clarion* by venturing into birth control as part of her efforts at socialist pastoralism.
In her advocacy of this issue, print retained its radical promise. Apart
from discussions of sexuality, Dawson constructed print as an inconve-
nient barrier to interpersonal intimacy, but sex still occupied an insecure
position within the domain of print; thus in advocating birth control,
Dawson could little afford such insouciance toward the medium and
pushed *The Malthusian Handbook* for all it was worth. At the same time,
Dawson adopted a New Journalistic voice to build a sense of intimacy
with readers, affecting to transcend the print barrier and to address each
reader individually; such a voice resonated with the emergence of pastoral modalities of power in the era of modern biopolitics and was also a
means of counteracting an increasingly anonymous mass print sphere.

Dawson's column is just one example of how sex radicalism became
the principal site for free print and print enlightenment rhetoric at the
end of the nineteenth century, whether among working-class women
readers of the *Clarion* or in the discursive print community that formed
around 1890s free love journals such as the *Adult*. We are accustomed
to considering the inward turn toward questions of sex and sex psychology in literature of this era as protomodernist, but efforts on the part of
such writers as Julia Dawson and Edith Ellis to connect the burgeoning
sex question to the traditional radical domain of working-class agitation suggest an alternative lineage for this discursive development. In
this view, threads of modernism emerge from radical literary discourse
at a moment when radical discourse is losing its rhetorical coherence
around the issue of class. At this moment the enduring radical working-
class discourse of free print and free expression fastened easily to the
biopolitical domain of sexuality, now the central arena for censorship
activity. Despite the efforts of working-class-oriented sex activists such
as Dawson and Ellis, the shift I want to emphasize here is that the free

print argument was, on the whole, redirected *away* from class-oriented agitation and *toward* sex and marriage reform. The domain of biopolitics had become, as Foucault suggests, increasingly central to liberal governance, and as the century came to a close, radical writers turned toward the biopolitical as the new site where radical agitation in its traditional sense could still function coherently.

Conclusion

I SUGGESTED IN THE INTRODUCTION that a consideration of slow print would offer a significant challenge to received notions of literary culture from 1880 to 1910. As we lift our heads from the radical press archive, the landscape of modern literature will look decidedly less familiar. In this brief conclusion I want to summarize the ways in which close attention to this overlooked body of radical print might unbalance some of our dominant ideas about literary modernism in particular. Ann Ardis and Patrick Collier have wondered whether the field of modernist studies, as currently constituted, "is prepared to accommodate what we find when we focus our inquiry on the more anonymous, more collaborative, less coherent authorial environments of magazines" (Introduction 7). Lucy Delap and Maria DiCenzo have similarly posited that modernism may be "too selective and distorting a framework" to adequately conceptualize magazine culture of the era (49). Yet modernism remains the dominant critical paradigm for early twentieth-century literary culture, and throughout this study we have seen how ostensibly modern literary qualities were manifested in turn-of-the-century radical print culture. Without in any way reducing radical literature to an unsung herald of modernism or delimiting its significance and interest to its protomodernist elements, I want to consider here how the literary culture of late Victorian slow print might bear on our conceptions of modernism and the genealogy of modern literature.

Over the last few decades the idea of modernist literature as a kind of marketing strategy has become a critical commonplace. Volumes such as Kevin J. H. Dettmar and Stephen Watt's *Marketing Modernisms*

(1996), Mark Morrison's *Public Face of Modernism* (2001), and Aaron Jaffe's *Modernism and the Culture of Celebrity* (2005) have emphasized the promotional strategies and shrewd marketplace management engaged in by modernist editors and writers, arguing that, as Jaffe puts it, "modernist value capitalizes" (10). This strain of criticism has been an important corrective to earlier versions of modernist studies, which saw modern writers as supposedly uninterested in the marketplace, and my book is companionable with such work in our mutual emphasis on archival sources and the materiality of print culture. And yet, looking ahead to modern literature from the vista of the late nineteenth-century radical print archive, it seems that such approaches can exaggerate the market orientation of aspects of modernist literary style. I find in radical print culture a reminder that a rejection of capitalist modes of print production and circulation was just as constitutive of the modernist moment as was an appeal to niche markets and readerships. Forming a separate literary and print culture was not simply a savvy response to a fragmenting marketplace; it was a gesture with a radical political history, a *recent* radical political history. Little magazines and private presses have a political form that was, at the turn of the century, still associated with anticapitalist dissent. Our understanding of the cultural rupture effected by modernist print is poorer if we do not see this rupture as connected to a history of aggressive political protest against market capitalism such as we see in the late Victorian radical press.

Critics interested in modern periodicals have recently been asking how investigations of print counterpublics might reframe our understanding of modernism. For example, in her work on William T. Stead and the *Pall Mall Gazette*, Laurel Brake finds continuities between modernism and New Journalism and asks "whether historical accounts of modernism err by associating it entirely with high culture forms such as literature and the visual arts, or whether a popular art such as journalism . . . may be located within the broader parameter of the new modernisms" ("Journalism" 158). Barbara Green similarly suggests that attention to the turn-of-the-century feminist press might produce a "productive decentering of the term 'modernism'" and that "current work on feminist periodicals conducted by literary critics continues the project of unsettling dominant definitions of literary modernism" ("Feminist Periodical Press" 198).

Attention to the radical press likewise produces "decentering" and "unsettling" effects, offering an alternative genealogy to aspects of modernist literary culture that have long been viewed as elitist—specifically, its oppositional stance toward the culture of mass production. The hostility toward the capitalist print marketplace that we see in the annals of modernist literary culture, such as Virginia and Leonard Woolf's Hogarth Press or D. H. Lawrence's and James Joyce's challenge to obscenity standards, looks different when we consider it as the tail end of a slow print revolution that began as an effort on the part of radical writers, editors, and printers to seize the means of print production. Such a perspective would challenge, for example, Joyce Wexler's argument about Joyce and Lawrence that "the marketing genius of modernist authors inspired them to defend erotic fiction as art and sell it as smut" (91). If we read "obscene" modernists in the context of changing rhetoric around free print, such as I describe in Chapter 6, the turn toward sexually outré topics seems to follow a shift of emphasis from class radicalism to sexuality in mechanisms of state suppression. Even if recognizing this genealogy does nothing to change the politics of individual modernist texts, it is a reminder of how easily resistance to capitalism can transmute—or be transmuted—into antipopulism and how part of capitalism's strength is to render the anticommercial as the antidemocratic.

Reviewing some of the major features of slow print literature discussed in this book, we find evidence of an alternative genealogy for an emerging modernist aesthetic. In tracking a shift from Victorianism to modernism, for example, one key development is the rejection of nineteenth-century realism; as Martin Hewitt puts it, "The replacement around 1900 of the Victorian physiognomic mode with a new psychological mode . . . helped tilt the balance away from realist projects and toward literary modernism's assault on the tyranny of fact" (419). Virginia Woolf argues in her seminal modernist essay "Mr. Bennett and Mrs. Brown" that the "transitional" writers of the turn of the century resisted realism precisely in reaction against Victorian aesthetics: "I think that after the creative activity of the Victorian age it was quite necessary, not only for literature but for life, that someone should write the books that Mr. Wells, Mr. Bennett, and Mr. Galsworthy have written," for to ask these writers "how to create characters that are real," she says, would be "like going to a bootmaker and asking him to teach you how to make a watch" (326). As discussed in Chapter 2, radical periodicals evinced suspicion of the realist novel even before the careers of these three writers discussed by Woolf; this suspicion was evident both in the kind of works radical journals printed and in their reviews of contemporary fiction. Socialist novels such as William Morris's *News from Nowhere* (serialized in the *Commonweal*) and George Bernard Shaw's *An Unsocial Socialist* (serialized in *To-Day*) ironize the "realism" of Victorian novels as a decidedly unrealistic, bourgeois fantasy.

Likewise, in Chapter 4 I suggest that poetry of the radical press prefigures modernist literary culture despite the fact that it represents a completely different aesthetic approach. Radical press poetry is traditional in its form and diverges from modernism in its conception of the politics of form, but it is thematically dominated by the notion of historical rupture, typically by means of the trope of revolution; it formulates a poetics of political rupture that precedes modernism's aesthetic rupture. In Chapter 5 I suggest that one unusual example of late Victorian radical poetry, Edward Carpenter's *Towards Democracy*, expresses the move toward esoteric complexity, ambiguity, and difficulty in modern poetry. Carpenter's interest in theosophy and Eastern religion became the grounds for an abstruse and inaccessible aesthetic approach, as would also happen with modernist artists and writers such as Wassily Kandinsky and W. B. Yeats.[1] At the same time the alternative models of authorial subjectivity offered by theosophy, evident in the work of Annie Besant and Alfred Orage and discussed in Chapter 5, could be said to prefigure what Jaffe has called the imprimatur of the modernist author, where "detached, disembodied reputations have the visionary appearance of bodily agency and textual form" (10).

Finally, in Chapter 6 we find a radical precedent for the modernist inward turn toward questions of sexuality and sex psychology in literature by looking at late Victorian free love journals and the discourse around sexuality in the radical press. At a time when radical discourse was losing its rhetorical coherence around the issue of class, sexuality emerged as a discursive site where early nineteenth-century radical arguments about censorship, free print, and print enlightenment continued to be effective. Sexuality would also become a locus of anti-authoritarian activism for modernist writers who challenged print censorship, and we can find a prehistory for this development in the turn toward sexuality and biopolitics in late Victorian radical discourse.

All these examples show elements of modernist aesthetics emerging in the radical sphere, but we can also see conventional critical ideas about modernism emerging in this same discursive space. A long critical tradition has read aesthetic modernity, or modernism, as a reaction against the technological and social forces of modernity.[2] In the October 1891 issue of *Seed Time*, we see the radical press beginning to make this argument about Morris's antirealist novel *News from Nowhere*. Reviewing Morris's novel, Percival Chubb describes a split between a writer like Edward Bellamy, who "accepts modern developments . . . the modern habit of doing things on a large scale, of large cities, large buildings, highly developed mechanical methods," and the "Morrisian," who "is a resolute enemy of these things. . . . He sees in large organisations foes of freedom and individuality" (2). Chubb's emphasis on scale is key, because it underscores what I see as the crucial move of radical literary culture and slow print: the rejection of large-scale forms of reproduction, metonymically represented by print reproduction, on the grounds that they do violence to our humanity. Such was the originating ideology of slow print projects such as the Kelmscott Press, and although it may well be difficult to divorce such a project from the elite audience it ended up attracting, it would certainly be a misreading of Kelmscott to argue that it was motivated by a savvy appeal to a niche market in luxury consumption.

Arguably, all periodical literature presents a challenge to the idea of the individual writer and a reminder that authorship always emerges from a milieu and a context. Perhaps attention to the radical press archive will remind us that literary movements coalesce not merely around the collective work of a group of individual writers but around a print context that shapes literary production both materially and culturally. I certainly do not intend to argue in this conclusion for a kind of modernist exceptionalism, wherein a late nineteenth-century radical print subculture is primarily of interest in the extent to which it is preparatory for or redolent of early twentieth-century modernism. Instead, my hope is to suggest that the recovery of a largely forgotten print subculture is interesting both for its own sake *and* for its connections with adjacent histories, print cultures, and literary movements. Mark Wollaeger has argued for the value of modernist literary aesthetics "in a world in which dependable facts in public discourse have become elusive, in which language is carefully engineered by public relation experts and market researchers to trigger specific emotional responses" (265). If we consider modernism as emerging, in part, in reaction to the crisis in media and information that Wollaeger describes, we can thank the late Victorian radical press for bringing an awareness of this crisis into literary discourse and into the materiality of print production.

Reference Matter

Notes

Introduction

1. A tradition of Marxist critique continues to link a culture of overprint with the production of capitalist ideology. For example, in 1971 Fredric Jameson, in *Marxism and Form*, discussed "the canons of clear and fluid journalistic writing taught in the schools" and asked, "What if, in this period of the overproduction of printed matter and the proliferation of methods of quick reading, they were intended to speed the reader across a sentence in such a way that he can salute a readymade idea effortlessly in passing, without suspecting that real thought demands a descent into the materiality of language and a consent to time itself in the form of the sentence?" (xiii).

2. This period is sometimes called the socialist revival and is at other times considered the first flowering of socialism in Britain. The difference depends on whether or not early nineteenth-century Owenism is considered a socialist movement; according to Barbara Taylor, Owenism had come to be called socialism by the late 1830s (118).

3. By the 1880s, for example, "the development of chemical and mechanical methods of preparing wood pulp helped satisfy the demand for a paper suitable for cheap books and periodicals" (Altick 306), a change that "utterly transformed the printing industry" (McGann, *Black Riders* 7).

4. In an authoritarian communication system "the purpose of communication is to protect, maintain, or advance a social order based on minority power" (Williams 131). Censorship and governmental control over media outlets, by means of licensing or taxes, are means of maintaining such power. By contrast, a commercial communication system is allegedly free but is actually subject to commercial rather than governmental constraints: "Works are openly offered for sale and openly bought, as people actually choose" (132), but the available choices are determined by "individuals or groups whose main, if not only, qualification will be that they possess or can raise the necessary capital" (133).

5. According to Harrison et al.'s *Warwick Guide to British Labour Periodicals*, between 1850 and 1879 there were 251 papers "produced by an organised body consisting wholly or mainly of wage-earners or collectively dependent employees" or "produced in the avowed interest of the working class . . . 'on the side of Labour' as against Capital" (xiii). Between 1880 and 1909 there were 868 such papers. The *Warwick Guide* is

by no means a complete record of the papers of interest here, but it demonstrates the broad trend.

6. Shaw, for example, describes with some exaggeration Ruskin's minimal influence on late-century socialism: "Here and there in the Socialist movement workmen turned up who had read Fors Clavigera or Unto This Last. . . . But Ruskin's name was hardly mentioned in the Fabian Society" ("On the History" 278).

7. According to Negt and Kluge, "Between 1800 and 1840 there develops [in England] something equivalent to a proletarian form of communication independent of commodity production, which in part integrates, refashions, and redirects elements of popular culture with a view to the constitution of the proletariat as a class" (187). However, this "autonomous communication network, which is independent of bourgeois forms of the public sphere" (188), does not last. After Chartism there is a shift toward "particularism": "Throughout the subsequent phase, the forms of struggle are trade unionism, Fabianism, and the shop steward movement" (199). As we will see in the following chapters, forms of struggle at the end of the century are far more diverse than Negt and Kluge suggest, yet these two writers are correct in their conclusion that "there is no longer an attempt to create a public sphere embracing the whole nation" (197). In *Slow Print* I will investigate why this change occurred, considering the question from the perspective of literature and media production.

8. Late nineteenth-century radical writers were not as rigid as Marshall McLuhan in connecting print's form with its ideology, but they anticipated many of his observations. McLuhan views print as "fostering habits of private property, privacy, and many forms of 'enclosure.'" He points to the rise of authorship in print culture: "Manuscript culture did not foster any grand ideas in this department. Print did" (131). And he notes that "printed books, themselves the first uniform, repeatable, and mass-produced items in the world, provided endless paradigms of uniform commodity culture for sixteenth and succeeding centuries" (163). W. B. Worthen describes these elements of literary print culture as peaking in the late nineteenth century; he argues that "the rise of print has tended to articulate certain values—standardization (of letterforms), regularization (of spelling and punctuation), formalization (of distinct genres, each with its own conventions of layout, design, marketing), repeatability and reiteration," and he claims that the late nineteenth century was the moment "when print culture might be said to have reached its zenith, still unrivalled by other means of mass communication" (*Print* 5).

9. As this suggests, my findings differ significantly from those of Mark Morrison, who argues that the "publicity and mass publication techniques that made wealthy men of publishers like Harmsworth, Pearson, and Newnes . . . were quickly adapted, in varying degrees, by suffragist, socialist, and anarchist groups" and that these "radical groups influenced modernist authors and editors to adapt commercial culture to the needs of modernist literature" (6). Although some modernist writers doubtless had an "optimism about markets, and . . . did not believe that commercial culture is a monolithic and totalizing phenomenon," this was certainly not the case for the radical antecedents that Morrison sees them as borrowing from (7). Morrison's argument works best with respect to the suffragist press, which was not explicitly anticapitalist, but it misrepresents the socialist and anarchist press. My own survey reveals a sense

of embattled anticommercialism among late nineteenth-century radical writers and journals, prompting diverse efforts to build an anticapitalist counterculture.

10. The radical press tended to be suspicious of *Reynolds's Newspaper*, although they sometimes found common cause, especially on liberal issues such as free expression. Where they were at odds was over questions of radical economic or political reform, such as the formation of a new party. As the *Labour Elector* put it, "We are sorry, but not surprised, to see that *Reynolds's Newspaper*, once a sturdy champion of the British Democracy, is doing all it can to discredit and damage the Independent Labour party" (14 January 1893: 7). *Justice*, the Social Democratic Federation paper, sums up the radical press's view of *Reynolds's*: "We don't place much reliance on the capitalist press or journals supported by capitalist advertisements and run for profit. But we are bound to admit that *Reynolds' Newspaper* and the *Star* did admirable service among the workers during the late election for the County Council. . . . Let us never forget, however, that no newspaper can be trusted permanently which is not in the hands of the workers, or their direct representations" (26 January 1889: 1).

11. Bradlaugh was an atheist and a democrat, but he believed in free enterprise, became a Member of Parliament, and strongly believed in the parliamentary political system as an agent of reform.

12. This focus on class-oriented social protest means that my analysis does not extend to the turn-of-the-century feminist press. Although there are important continuities between the emergence of radical slow print and the emergence of a feminist press, exploring these continuities is, regrettably, beyond the scope of this book. Turn-of-the-century feminism incorporated a wide variety of ideological perspectives; my analysis does not extend to feminisms that were not specifically anticapitalist, although I do discuss feminist socialism and anarchism in Chapters 5 and 6. A significant body of work on the feminist press of this era already exists; see, for example, Beaumont ("Influential Force"), Bland, Delap and DiCenzo, Green ("Feminist Things"), Joannou, Schuch, and Youngkin. See Green ("Feminist Periodical Press") for an overview and summary of all recent work in this field.

13. Wilson's notes on the history of *Freedom* are held in the *Freedom* Archive at the International Institute of Social History (4338/4/2).

14. Some papers operated their own presses, which they often lent or rented out for the printing of other radical papers and pamphlets (e.g., *Commonweal* and the *Torch*). Other papers were printed at left-wing houses such as the Modern Press in London or the Labour Press Society in Manchester (e.g., *Justice* was originally printed at the Modern Press until obtaining its own press after difficulties with Henry Hyde Champion at the Press). Still others were printed at regular printing firms, sometimes leading to problems over the treatment of the workers, as I discuss later in the introduction. The Labour Press Society, to give one example of a leftist printing hub, was founded in 1893, and according to a notice in the 1896 *Labour Annual*: "Its first plant was a small hand platen machine and a few ounces of type. . . . Now it occupies extensive premises in Tib St. [Manchester], possessing facilities for turning out newspapers, pamphlets, and books at very short notice. . . . It keeps a shop, where a large stock of advanced literature can always be inspected. . . . The society is an encouraging example of workmen's cooperative effort" (23–25). The 1897 *Labour*

Annual noted that the press "employs 30 people, and turns over £5,000 yearly. Best wages are paid, and 8-hr day was pioneered by them in Manchester district. . . . Sold in four years a million and a half pamphlets, half a million of which have been their own publications" (246).

15. The Social Democratic Federation was a Marxist socialist group; its paper, *Justice*, was founded in 1884 and ran into the 1930s (changing its name to the *Social Democrat* in the 1920s). Despite its foundational influence within the era's radical press, complaints did appear in other papers about *Justice*'s antagonistic rhetoric. Henry Hyde Champion wrote in his paper, *Common Sense*, "I have often said myself, and have heard it said by others, that if you wish to make a man a Socialist you should not let him read *Justice*" (15 September 1887: 69). Correspondents in future issues agreed; Henry Ellis of Camberwell wrote, "I am in cordial agreement with . . . your condemnation of the style in which *Justice* is conducted. To anybody who values decent controversy, and recognizes the fact that mere vulgar abuse is a long way from being sound argument, there cannot be a doubt that your cause is heavily handicapped by the advocacy of such a journal" (15 November 1887: 109–10).

16. Indeed, a notice in the *Labour Annual* for 1895 advertised the services of "Romeike and Curtice Press Cutting and Information Agency," which employs "over one hundred hands reading thousands of Newspapers, Periodicals, Magazines, and Reviews, and extracting from them each week over **100,000** cuttings" (92). A surfeit of print required these kinds of services merely to keep up with the mass press.

17. Whether or not a paper should reprint "stereo" (cut-and-paste items from other publications) was another subject of dispute in the radical press, and *Justice* went back and forth on this. The 16 January 1886 issue declared that the paper would give up printing stereo (such as a humor column and "Bits of Fun") and advertising: "After this week we shall give up printing any 'stereo' or advertisements in JUSTICE. We have received so many remonstrances on this subject that we have decided to waste no more money in providing our readers with matter which they do not want" (5). (The reference to advertisements here does not refer to regular capitalist advertisements but to announcements pertaining to other radical publications.) *Labour Leader* proclaimed its quality on the basis of its lack of stereo, describing its aim to be "as bright and readable as the best brains in the movement, encouraged by generous pay, and aided by clear type, and good paper and printer's ink can make it. There will be no stereo about it; every letter will be set for the *Leader* and for it alone" (November 1893: 5–6). Payment of writers was another controversial issue in the radical press, because some thought it would compromise political purity, but the *Leader* depicts payment as a mark of quality.

18. The late-century advertising boom had likewise created a situation in which it was difficult for new publications to capture attention without advertising. As J. L. Joynes wrote to Shaw of the early socialist journal *Christian Socialist*, "We find our great difficulty is to make the paper known without incurring heavy expense in advertising. . . . There ought to be enough people who would sympathise to make it a success, if we only knew where to find them" (22 June 1883; British Library ms 50510, f. 81).

19. *Justice* also relied on gifts from benefactors: "A generous friend, who, though no Socialist, has aided the [Social Democratic Federation] from time to time since its

foundation in January, 1881, has advanced £50 to buy type. [This refers to Edward Carpenter.] Miss Helen Taylor has given a press and the wooden type necessary to print the contents bills, which has cost about £32. . . . The Voluntary Compositors have subscribed among themselves sufficient money to provide column rules for the paper" (28 March 1885: 4).

20. Indeed, mechanized typesetting was just around the corner. In 1886 Ottmar Mergenthaler developed the Linotype, in which "all the operations of casting, composing, justifying, and eventually distributing, were combined in one machine" (Clair 222).

21. Oz Frankel writes that in the nineteenth century the "key concept of 'public opinion' served to efface political mediation, to fill the gap between the public and its substitutes—elected representatives—by supposedly endowing all citizens of an opinion-based polity with a voice in national decision making" (16). The term *public opinion* was also used to efface the gap between the public and its newspapers. It produced what Negt and Kluge describe as the bourgeois public sphere's "illusory synthesis of the totality of society. . . . This aspect of the public sphere has to manufacture the appearance of a collective will, of a meaningful context that embraces the entire world, along with the illusion of participation on the part of all members of society" (56).

22. For more on Chartism's emphasis on reading and self-education, see, for example, Vicinus's *Industrial Muse.*

23. Radical writers William Morris and George Bernard Shaw similarly worked to defamiliarize the print interface, as I will discuss in Chapters 1, 2, and 3. Shaw had marveled at Tucker's paper, which "appeared to be in verse because the lines of print were not 'justified'" (*William Morris* 23). He eventually published his essay on Max Nordau in *Liberty* and was loathe to reprint it elsewhere, claiming to "intensely enjoy making people swallow Liberty & the blank verse printing & so on" (*Collected Letters* 1: 561).

24. Readers had grown wearily accustomed to this pattern. An old Owenite named John Frearson wrote to subscribe to the *Commonweal* on 21 December 1885, recalling all the other papers he had subscribed to which had folded: "This is another adventure—one of many in my time—and so far I have not been very fortunate. . . . And now for the 'Commonweal'—will it continue? Or will it cease to be?" (Socialist League Archive, f. 1463).

25. See Brake ("Journalism") and Weiner for more on New Journalism.

26. According to Lyons, writing in 1910, "The little book was issued in various forms, at prices ranging from five shillings down to a penny. Seven hundred and fifty thousand (750,000) copies of the penny edition were sold at the first rush. Its sale in this country and America has since exceeded two million copies. If one states that this book alone has made more converts to English Socialism than all other Socialist publications combined, one is putting the case conservatively" (99).

27. The *Clarion Cyclist's Journal*, a spin-off publication directed toward the Cycling Clubs, humorously described in its first issue how the social aspects of the clubs sometimes overcame the socialist imperative.

A certain good man [Blatchford] conceived that he had a message to the people of these islands, the knowledge of which would enable them to banish poverty and its attendant evils from the land. . . . Then behold, there arose certain young men who possessed bicycles, and they said to the bearer of the message: "Lo, behold, here are we! Strong, healthy, young, energetic, and intelligent! We will take the Message of Peace to the uttermost parts of the country, and that the messengers shall be identified with the message, we will call our organizations 'Clarion Cycling Clubs.'" ... Now it came to pass that after the message had been taken, with more or less success to *more than three places*, the messengers began to faint by the way side, so that they required refreshments and dances immediately [after] they arrived at their destination. (August 1896: 7) In addition to the *Clarion Cyclist's Journal*, see Pye for more on the Clarion Cycling Club.

28. See Stephen Yeo or Chris Waters (*British Socialists*) for more on British socialists' attempt to build such an alternative culture.

29. Projected films were not shown in Britain until 1896, but as recent work on the "prehistory" of cinema has established, cinema-like visual experiences proliferated in the years immediately preceding film. Peepshow devices such as the Kinematoscope and Thomas Edison's Kinetoscope along with projecting apparatuses such as the zoopraxiscope and the magic lantern augured a new era of visual media years before the explosive popularity of cinema. For more on this topic, see Charney and Schwartz or Crary (*Suspensions* and *Techniques*).

Chapter 1

1. Both of these images appeared regularly in the *Workman's Times*.

2. The quotations about art for its own sake compare with Wilde's vision of socialist aestheticism in "The Soul of Man Under Socialism": "With the abolition of private property, then, we shall have true, beautiful, healthy Individualism" (1178). But Wilde emphasizes socialist leisure above socialist labor, perhaps drawing on Paul Lafargue's *Right to Be Lazy*, which was serialized in English translation in *Justice* beginning with the 13 February 1886 issue. Lafargue's essay, at odds with a Ruskinian or Morrisian theory of labor, sparked debate in the paper; James Blackwell defended it, arguing that it "was meant to be an ironical reply to the advocates of work for the proletariat, work for those whom work has demoralized, physically and mentally" (*Justice*, 14 August 1886: 4).

3. See also Diana Maltz's *British Aestheticism and the Urban Working Classes*, which describes the rise of "missionary aestheticism," a middle-class reform doctrine of "faith in the elevating potential of the beautiful" for the poor and working classes (16).

4. Norman Kelvin claimed in 1996 that critics "have made less effort to see Morris synchronously with other figures who shaped the [1890s]" (425). Since 1996 Regenia Gagnier has identified continuities among Morris, Ruskin, and Wilde, arguing that all three write for "freedom, equality, and toleration" (*Insatiability* 152). Linda Dowling has also brought Morris into line with his aesthetic contemporaries, but whereas Gagnier achieves this by conceptualizing aestheticism as more politically engaged than it is usually considered to be—a big tent incorporating productivist and consumerist strains ("Productive Bodies, Pleasured Bodies")—Dowling identifies an essential conservatism in Morris's thought. She argues that an "ideal of aristocratic sensibility unrecognized as such" lies "at the heart of the vision of aesthetic democracy inspiring Ruskin and Morris," that Morris "repressed" this ideal, and that this repressed ideal corresponds with "Pater's emergent and Wilde's wholly developed aesthetic elitism" (xii–xiii).

5. Ruth Livesey, for example, argues that Morris's socialist aesthetics are "at odds with the aestheticism through which Wilde defined his own work at the time" (*Socialism* 1), even though he was "co-opted" as an aesthetic (4).

6. An obvious example is Morris's "Society of the Future," which originally appeared in the *Commonweal* (30 March 1889). His "Useful Work Versus Useless Toil," which was originally printed as a Socialist League pamphlet in 1885, looks forward to the "happy day" when "we shall no longer be hurried and driven by the fear of starvation" (99). In "How We Live and How We Might Live," which originally ran in the *Commonweal* (4–11 June 1887), Morris claims that all humans are entitled to surroundings "pleasant, generous, and beautiful; that I know is a large claim, but this I will say about it, that if it cannot be satisfied, if every civilized community cannot provide such surroundings for all its members, I do not want the world to go on; it is a mere misery that man has ever existed" (153).

7. This polarity characterized the controversy over Thomas Paine's *Rights of Man* and other radical pamphlets of the 1790s as well as the 1830s debates surrounding the growth of the penny press. Evangelical reformers were somewhere in the middle, advocating print of the "healthy" censored sort for the masses. (For more on the relation of religious movements to literacy and print, see Altick or Vincent.) Morris's ideas emerged from a strain of left-wing social protest constituted by radicalism, Chartism, secularism, and (later) Marxism—a strain that had traditionally advocated unrestrained, plentiful print.

8. William S. Peterson has argued that because of Morris's prejudices against print, the Kelmscott Press "was undertaken by Morris almost grudgingly. His heart always lay with the manuscript rather than the printed book. Among the proofs and trial pages from the Press that are treasured today in library special-collections rooms, there are numerous little scraps of paper that betray Morris's secret hankering to abandon the printing press in favour of the pen" (*Kelmscott Press* 64).

9. As an active collector of fifteenth-century incunabula (the earliest printed books), Morris could be said to fetishize print produced at this stage in its history, and he struggled to reconcile his love for expensive medieval books with socialist, egalitarian values. In an 1891 interview with the *Pall Mall Gazette*, Morris argued that rare books were not antidemocratic so long as they were held in public libraries: "If we were all Socialists things would be different. We should have a public library at each street corner, where everybody might see and read all the best books, printed in the best and most beautiful type. I should not then have to buy all these old books, but they would be common property, and I could go and look at them whenever I wanted them, as would everybody else" ("Poet" 92).

10. Even earlier, while at university, Morris had edited the short-lived *Oxford and Cambridge Magazine*. See Demoor for more on this publication.

11. Among Morris's contemporaries, see, for example, Annie Besant's *Our Corner*, which frequently comments: "Among my Socialist contemporaries, I note the *Commonweal* as the best weekly" (July 1886: 58). Among more recent critics, see, for example, Thompson, *William Morris* 391–92, or Coolsen 80–82.

12. In his notes for remarks at the *Commonweal*'s semiannual conference in January 1886, H. Halliday Sparling (Morris's son-in-law-to-be who subedited the paper) reported that in its first year the average issue sold about 3,500 copies, cost about £15 to produce, brought in about £7 in receipts, and had a debt of about £4 (Socialist League Archive, f. 15). After its first year the paper became a weekly rather than a

monthly, and its circulation dropped accordingly. Morris wrote in a July 1887 letter that "with the present circulation of say about 2800 we are losing £4 per week" (*Collected Letters* 2: 679). In March 1889 circulation was "going up, but too slowly" (3: 42); and in December 1889 Morris wrote that "sale of the paper has fallen off" (3: 132). Distribution was mainly through subscription and a small number of sympathetic dealers, and delivery to these dealers was by voluntary League labor.

13. We can also see this argument in Morris's attack on the Royal Academy in "Individualism at the Royal Academy" in the 24 May 1884 issue of *Justice*: "Grievous indeed that art should be used as a stalking horse for such proceedings; unbearable to an artist, if we did not see revolution beyond it, and a clean sweep of all that folly." The revolution, he believes, "will sweep the sham art away and give us good hope of a new art arising from a society founded on the equality of labour" (4).

14. Letter from Oscar Wilde, 29 October 1887, Socialist League Archive, f. 3230.

15. This is an old debate, and although critics such as Gagnier (*Idylls*) and Eltis have reclaimed Wilde as a politically engaged writer, counterclaims persist, as in Guy and Small.

16. Matthew Beaumont suggests that the Commune had been figured in British discourse as a utopian event that "ruptured the bourgeois faith in progress," which suggests the aptness of Crane's image for the particular context of the *Commonweal* (Beaumont, "Cacotopianism" 467). However, the extent to which working-class readers would have had a positive association with the Commune is not clear. In a 26 September 1885 letter to Sparling, George King (a League member from Dublin) wrote of a fundamentally different conception of the Commune among Irish workers: "Fancy a lecturer . . . here saying a word in favour of the Paris Commune. . . . The one fact that the average Dublin working man knows about the Commune is that during the struggle the Archbishop of Paris was shot and he holds all communists guilty of the murder of an Archbishop" (Socialist League Archive, f. 1877).

17. In their use of abstracted female figures, Crane's cartoons exemplify the lingering idealist tradition within the *Commonweal*'s utopianism. As Moi describes, idealist aesthetics required the artwork to transcend the carnal, the animal, and the sexual; thus "poetry and painting need to idealize [women] far more intensively than they do men" and "the figure of the *pure woman*" became "an icon of idealist aesthetics" (80). Crane's cartoons reproduce this gendered idealist iconography. By contrast, as Kristina Huneault describes, Crane's design work for women's trade unions "moved away from the more allegorical personae that women usually assumed in the artist's socialist imaginary" (157).

18. Morris was reluctant to do even a paper of this scale. After he resigned as editor of the *Commonweal*, his comrade Glasier proposed a new paper, to which Morris responded, "I don't like papers; and we have after a very long experiment found out that a sectional paper cannot be run" (*Collected Letters* 3: 244). According to Shaw, Morris's work on the paper was always grueling: "Another grievous task for him was to keep *The Commonweal*, the weekly paper of the League, going from number to number with topical paragraphs. Some of the stuff thus produced went to the rock bottom truth of the situation; but it did not come easily and happily" (*William Morris* 51–52).

19. Monotype was invented in the United States around 1890; by 1918 it "could provide a composition very similar to one typeset by hand" (Genet 28).

20. The same has been said of Morris's late romances, but Plotz has recently argued that their lack of realistic particularity is a political strategy based in socialist egalitarianism, not an "excursion into indulgent fantasy" ("Nowhere" 938).

21. Morris also made this argument in "The Dull Level of Life" from the 26 April 1884 issue of *Justice* (4).

22. It was through Morris, Barringer argues, that *The Nature of Gothic* took "its place amongst the founding texts of British socialism, enshrining at its core a linkage between aesthetics and the ethics of labour" (255).

23. Although the *Commonweal* sold for only a penny—much less than Ruskin's pamphlets—it struggled on the fringes of commercial print to find a sustainable readership; the Kelmscott books, meanwhile, were quite expensive but sold very well. Morris defended the high prices of Kelmscott books by referencing their high quality and handmade materials, but he also ensured that their prices would *remain* high for time immemorial by preserving their scarcity. After Morris's death, his Kelmscott executor Sydney Cockerell wrote: "All the woodblocks . . . have been sent to the British Museum, and have been accepted with a condition that they shall not be reproduced or printed from for the space of a hundred years. The electrotypes have been destroyed. In taking this course, which was sanctioned by William Morris when the matter was talked of shortly before his death, the aim of the trustees has been to keep the series of Kelmscott Press books as a thing apart, and to prevent the designs becoming stale by constant repetition" (86). We might view this gesture as a means of permanently prohibiting mass-produced aesthetics from taking hold at Kelmscott Press through "constant repetition," yet it also appears that Morris understood and accepted that Kelmscott trafficked in aura and that the books' aura emanated from their inaccessibility and rareness.

24. Morris bought Kelmscott's first Albion press on 26 November 1891 for £42 10s. 0d. "During the printing of the Chaucer another press was added and the two were almost continuously at work" (Clair 245).

25. In establishing the configuration of labor at the press, Morris drew on his experience in moving the firm (Morris & Co.) to Merton Abbey in 1881. There, "Morris was able to preside over a workshop that seemed to offer a modern equivalent of the guild structure that had nurtured and protected the craftsman ideal" (Barringer 295), although some scholars have argued that the Abbey's workers "had rather less creative freedom than the Gothic ideal would require" (297).

26. C. R. Ashbee launched the Essex House Press in 1898, T. J. Cobden-Sanderson and Emery Walker founded Doves Press in 1900, and Lucien and Esther Pissarro launched Eragny Press in 1894. For more on these and other fine presses, see Clair, Genz, *In Fine Print*, Cave, or Stratton. Cobden-Sanderson had been a major influence on Morris in his thinking about print; Stansky notes that Oscar Wilde reported anonymously in the *Pall Mall Gazette* on Cobden-Sanderson's 22 November 1888 talk on bookbinding at the Arts and Crafts Exhibition Society and that Wilde quoted him as saying, "Before we have really good bookbinding we must have a social revolution" (222).

27. *Labour Leader*, the Independent Labour Party newspaper, also periodically announced the release of new Kelmscott books, as in the 27 October 1894 issue: "Mr. William Morris's romance, 'The Wood Beyond the World,' has just been issued from the Kelmscott Press. From the press notices of it we gather that in every sense it maintains Mr. Morris's reputation as an artist. The book itself is a delight to the eye" (11).

28. Holzman ("Encouragement") describes Morris's use of historical accounts and sources in *John Ball*.

29. This was, of course, a difficult argument to accept if one's consumption was already severely restricted, and it went against long-standing tenets of working-class radical thought. As Hollis notes, many papers from the 1830s working-class press had developed an "under-consumption" theory—the theory that if workers were paid higher wages, they could afford to buy more goods, which would be good for them *and* for the capitalists. Of course, not all working-class radicals bought this theory, but its legacy compounded the difficulties for a socialist argument against overconsumption (237).

30. In between the *Commonweal* and Kelmscott editions, the novels were published in freestanding cheap editions. As Thompson notes, the cheap edition of *News from Nowhere* sold extremely well—far more than any of Morris's other socialist writings (*William Morris* 602). See Liberman for more on textual changes to the novel in these editions.

31. This effect in the drawing appears to have been of Morris's design; critiquing an early version of the illustration in a December 1892 letter to Gere, Morris writes, "The stone path up to the porch might be drawn with more literality" (*Collected Letters* 3: 482).

32. *News from Nowhere* can also be said to naturalize a gendered division of labor. Even though the women of the future society have full equality with the men, most continue to choose domestic and service roles out of "natural" preference. Morris is not inattentive to feminism in the novel: *News* puts forth a standard Marxist-feminist argument that sexual inequality under capitalism comes from the devaluing of women's labor in the home, which is not paid labor (107). The women in *News* exhibit a great deal of sexual agency, and some choose less "feminine" occupations, but gender essentialism remains a problematic aspect of the book. For more on women in *News*, see Boos and Boos or Mineo. For discussions of Morris and masculinity, see Livesey (*Socialism*) or Jan Marsh.

33. Longtime friends, Burne-Jones and Morris had been planning to collaborate on an illustrated volume for more than twenty years, but *John Ball* was the first Morris book to include a Burne-Jones illustration. See Dunlap for more on their failed mutual project of the 1860s. Later, with the Kelmscott Chaucer, they would undertake a more monumental collaboration.

34. William Peterson provides a detailed description of the negotiations involved in transforming the *John Ball* image from Burne-Jones's illustration to Hooper's woodblock engraving (*Kelmscott Press* 147–52). Hooper was "an experienced craftsman who had produced wood-engraved illustrations for publications such as *Punch* and *The Illustrated London News* and who came out of retirement to work for the Kelmscott Press" (*In Fine Print* 42).

35. Morris makes a similar point in *A Dream of John Ball* by continually singling out "the lawyers" as the most egregious offenders of the feudal order.

36. This depiction may reflect Morris's own frustration with the direction of the *Commonweal* at the time of *News from Nowhere*'s publication. In 1890 the Socialist

League was wracked with dissent, and the future of its newspaper was uncertain. In the midst of *News from Nowhere's* ten-month serialization, Morris was forced to relinquish the paper to the anarchists. See Holzman ("Anarchism") or Thompson (*William Morris*) for a comprehensive discussion of Morris's departure from the Socialist League and the *Commonweal.*

37. Characters who manifest a taste for reading are often somewhat eccentric. Robert, the weaver, who has "literary" interests and enjoys "grubbing into those idiotic old books about political economy," is said to "scarcely know how to behave" around others and to "trample down all good manners in the pursuit of utilitarian knowledge" (Morris, *News* 66–67). See also "the Grumbler," whom I discuss later in the chapter. A few characters do present reading in a more positive light. The unnamed woman who works in the guesthouse says she "began to read a pretty old book yesterday" (69). Likewise, the unnamed brother and sister who tend the tobacco shop are reading when Guest enters (84–85).

38. It should be noted that this second song was in the Kelmscott but not the *Commonweal* edition of the novel; Morris added it to the first book edition in 1888. See Salmon for a detailed account of Morris's revisions, mostly minor, to *John Ball.*

39. Shakespeare's plays also endure in *News from Nowhere* (97), despite Morris's personal dislike of them (he calls them "really a very bad form of drama" in an 1885 letter to Fred Henderson [*Collected Letters* 2: 507]). Drama of course is a visual and oral genre more than a written one.

40. Discussing different aspects of the novel, Brantlinger ("News") and Donaldson have also suggested that *News from Nowhere* prefigures Brechtian techniques of alienation. Arata has argued that Morris's literary work, especially his poetry, purposefully cultivates readers' inattention: "Morris consciously endeavored to produce works that could be read without effort or concentration" (203). We might also view this quality as an alienation effect, a way to prevent readers' immersion in the text.

41. It should be said that *News from Nowhere* makes a great many digs at contemporary art and literature, and although some of these align with aesthetic critique— such as the attack on realism at the end of Chapter 16—others target aestheticism, such as when Oxford and Cambridge are referred to as "the breeding places of a peculiar class of parasites, who called themselves cultivated people . . . but they affected an exaggeration of cynicism in order that they might be thought knowing and worldly-wise. . . . They were laughed at, despised—and paid. Which last was what they aimed at" (117).

42. That Morris was thinking about flatness and depth in relation to verisimilitude when he turned to print production is apparent in a lecture on pattern design that he gave at the Working Men's College on 10 December 1881: "By the word pattern-design, of which I have to speak to you tonight I mean the ornamentation of a surface by work that is not imitative or historical at any rate in its essence: such work is often not literally flat, for it may be carving or moulded work in plaster or clay or pottery, but *whatever material relief it may have, is given to it for the sake of the beauty or richness thereby obtainable, and not for the sake of imitation* or of telling a fact directly" (my emphasis; British Library ms Add 45331). The lecture was reprinted in *The Architect* (17 December 1881): 391–94 and 408–10.

43. Likewise, in response to a reader's report for his first novel, *Immaturity*, Shaw wrote to Macmillan that "the flatness of the novel" was part of its "design" (*Collected Letters* 1: 27).

44. The proliferating forms of late Victorian visual media are discussed in the notes to the Introduction.

Chapter 2

1. Maguire's poem was originally published in *Labour Leader* (5 January 1895: 4) and then in his posthumous volume, *Machine-Room Chants* (32–33). For more on Maguire, see Chapter 4.

2. Keating says this changed with the publication of Tressell's *Ragged Trousered Philanthropists* in 1914—an event that has been viewed by critics working in the area of socialist fiction as the real birth of the novel in socialist form. David Smith's *Socialist Propaganda in the Twentieth-Century British Novel* finds almost nothing of interest before its publication: "*The Ragged Trousered Philanthropists* stands, in fact, in this pre-thirties period, not in isolation, but certainly as a lonely peak in a sparsely mountained country" (4).

3. Shaw's earliest novel, *Immaturity*, was the only one that did not appear in the socialist press and, in fact, was not published for fifty years.

4. W. T. Stead, a liberal reform journalist, was the intrepid reporter behind the Maiden Tribute series of 1888, and one of the era's preeminent practitioners of the New Journalism style. Shaw went back and forth in his support for Stead; at times he lauded Stead as a journalistic hero, whereas at other times he attacked his puritanical grandstanding (Marshik 325). Shaw thought Stead a bit of a philistine; in a 16 June 1894 letter, he teased him to attend a performance of *Arms and the Man*: "Now you were brought up to believe in God, but not in Mozart and Beethoven, whereas I was brought up to believe in Mozart and Beethoven but not in God. . . . I think you ought to occasionally try the influence of art, just to see what it is like" (W. T. Stead Papers, STED 1/64).

5. This first edition was followed by an 1886 Sonnenschein edition that featured a misprinted title as well as a misspelling of the publisher's name, among other errors (Loewenstein 11).

6. The first book edition of *Cashel Byron's Profession* was printed and "hurled on the market" by Champion in a "misshapen shilling edition," as Shaw put it ("Novels" 8).

7. Shaw called Annie Besant an "incorrigible benefactress" (qtd. in Holroyd 1: 168), and indeed paying him for his work was an act of kindness outside the conventions of the radical press. In discussing the terms for *Love Among the Artists*, Besant wrote to Shaw: "My dear Bernard, I have been going over my arrangements for the autumn and winter, and I find that I can offer you somewhat better terms than I have hitherto done for your literary work. The leading reduces the amount of matter in a page, the printer tells me, about one-third. I propose 7/6 per page of leaded matter, not less than 10¾ pp (4£) to go in each month. I *may* put in more, but cannot bind myself to do so. I don't say now that this is adequate pay for work like yours, but it is a little less inadequate" (11 June 1887, British Library ms 50529, f. 62).

8. Recent critics have made the same point about many other late nineteenth-century middle-class authors' attempts at writing a socialist novel. For example,

Chris Waters argues that Isabella Ford and Katharine Bruce Glasier, in attempting to make over the New Woman novel into a socialist literary form, "failed to address the concerns of the working-class movement to which they were both dedicated" ("New Women" 39). Ford's novel, *On the Threshold* (1895), is in fact better read as a satire of the socialist novel, despite its author's committed socialism. The novel focuses on two young women who move to London and take up lodgings—the classic New Woman novel plot—but their clumsy attempts to "improve" a young servant girl who is prone to prostitution and who shows a serious disinclination to work reveal their naïve understanding of the working classes they hope to raise.

9. Clarke owed his start as a writer to essay contests in popular papers and to George Newnes's magazine *Tit-Bits*, which suggests that New Journalism did have some democratizing effects in the literary market: "Lancashire journalist Allen Clarke (b. 1863), the son of a Bolton textile worker, avidly read his father's paperback editions of Shakespeare and ploughed through the literature section . . . of the public library. With that preparation, he was winning prizes for poems in London papers by age thirteen. In 1881 he bought the first issue of *Tit-Bits*, where he began publishing verses and humorous sketches" (Rose 419).

10. See Nord for more on this context in Harkness's and Webb's lives.

11. Annie Besant's socialist magazine *Our Corner* took issue with *A City Girl*'s realism from another direction in an 1887 review of Harkness's novel: "'A City Girl', by John Law, will be a little handicapped by its sub-title 'A Realistic Story', for the word 'realistic' carries with it a suggestion of Zola to many readers, and is therefore terrifying to genteel British respectability. There is, however, nothing Zolaistic in the story, save in so far as observation of facts may be regarded as characteristic of the French master" (1 August 1887: 120). The underlying suggestion here is that "Zola" and "realism" signify to many British readers at this time nothing so much as bluntness of sexual expression.

12. Much of the material in this article was reproduced in a chapter titled "On Realism" in Blatchford's 1900 book, *My Favourite Books*.

13. On fears that literary accounts of foreign poverty might be counterrevolutionary among British readers, *Justice* claimed, for example, that Ouida "has been writing harrowing accounts of the condition of the peasantry on the continent, contrasting it with the wealth in which the British peasant is reveling. The moral inculcated by the capitalist press is that a poor man should think himself well off if others can be found poorer still" (12 December 1885: 5).

14. The *Clarion* also expresses doubt about Zola in the article "Fiction and Morals," but again, legal suppression of Zola's work seems to have won him some measure of approval in the radical press: "A correspondent writes to ask whether Ibsen and Zola are 'immoral.' Ibsen 'immoral'! Ye gods! . . . As to Zola, well . . . I should hesitate to call him immoral, but I would describe much of his work . . . as exceedingly unpleasant. . . . Is Zola 'immoral'? If we answer affirmatively, many noble works may come under the same ban. The Handsworth Free Library Committee have already decided to cast out and burn Hardy's 'Jude the Obscure'" (14 March 1896: 86).

15. For more on Harkness, see Ledger (*New Woman*), Livesey (*Socialism*), Nord, or Von Rosenberg.

16. Harkness also published "Girl Labour in the City" (3 March 1888: 4–5) and "Home Industries" (25 August 1888: 2) in *Justice*. The first essay details the hours and wages for various occupations for young women in the city, and the second describes the exploitation of women workers in "home industries," especially those shut out by the victory of the match girls in the famous strike against Bryant and May. Both articles are aimed at educating middle-class consumers who unwittingly contribute to such exploitation. "Home Industries" states, "I am sure if the public knew what the hours of work are for these unfortunate women, and their pay, people would shudder to think of the price in blood and flesh that is paid by the workers in order that the rich may congratulate themselves on bargains."

17. *A Working Class Tragedy* is discussed at length by Mutch ("Intemperate Narratives"). As she notes, the identity of Bramsbury is a mystery, but many critics have thought the novel was written by Henry M. Hyndman.

18. For another view of the late nineteenth-century utopian novel, see Beaumont (*Utopia*), who suggests that the attraction to the genre among socialists and radicals only expresses how far from revolutionary change Britain actually was. Far from undermining the novel's allegiance to bourgeois capitalism, in his analysis "state-socialist utopias exemplify the petty-bourgeois temperament" (46). He regards *News from Nowhere* as an exception, however.

19. The novel's "aggressive atheism" grated on Quelch: "So long as men recognise the material economic facts of Social Democracy, it is a matter of little moment from the socialist point of view whether they swear by Jesus Christ or Karl Marx or both" (*Justice*, 2 June 1888: 2). The novel also received a negative review in Besant's *Our Corner* (1 June 1888: 388–89).

20. During the months when Shaw's novel *An Unsocial Socialist* was serialized in *To-Day*, the journal ran poetry by such writers as Walt Whitman and W. J. Linton, the important Morris essay "Art Under Plutocracy," and reviews of literary works by authors such as Amy Levy, Michael Field, and George Gissing.

21. Shaw's 1896 article "Socialism for Millionaires" exhibits a similar tongue-in-cheek reflexivity about minority publics. The essay pretends to target the overlooked public of millionaires, who have hitherto been ignored by political propagandists, advertisers, and other hunters of the "mass" audience: "The millionaire class, a small but growing one, into which any of us may be flung to-morrow by the accidents of commerce, is perhaps the most neglected in the community. As far as I know, this is the first Tract that has ever been written for millionaires. In the advertisements of the manufactures of the country I find that everything is produced for the million and nothing for the millionaire" (391).

22. As William St. Clair notes, in the 1820s and 1830s alone "over 500 men went to prison for selling unstamped newspapers" (310).

23. Trefusis has left his wife after concluding that the world needed dedicated socialist propagandists more than besotted husbands, but at the end of the novel, he ends up marrying Agatha Wylie.

24. This was an aspect of modern literature to which the *Clarion*, more artistically conservative than other socialist papers, objected: "One short generation ago, the personages of the English novel still wore hearts under their ample waistcoats. . . .

Now . . . as for hearts, tut, tut! they are gone clean out of fashion: the men and women of the New Novel wear internal electric batteries in the place of those obsolete appliances" (17 April 1897: 123).

25. Shaw created a similar effect in *Cashel Byron's Profession.* When Lydia Carew first sees the title character, she "at first [takes him] to be a beautiful statue. . . . His broad pectoral muscles, in their white covering, were like slabs of marble. Even his hair, short, crisp, and curly, seemed like burnished bronze" (58). The image of a statue presents Byron, like Trefusis, as empty of interiority.

26. Just as Brantlinger labels *News from Nowhere* an "anti-novel," Eileen Sypher calls *An Unsocial Socialist* an "anti-novel" and points to its satirical parody of Jane Austen novels (246).

27. Shaw's attacks on the realist novel might seem ironic to drama critics such as W. B. Worthen, who argues in *Modern Drama and the Rhetoric of Theater* that Shaw's adherence to theatrical realism made his dramas far less politically effective than they might have been.

28. A review of *An Unsocial Socialist* in the May 1887 issue of Annie Besant's *Our Corner* emphasized its innovative approach to the novel form: "Opinions may differ as to the ultimate literary practicability of the line [Shaw] is marking out for himself, but none can question the originality of his method nor the many admirable qualities of his style" (313).

29. Griffith claims that in the course of the 1890s, Shaw came to believe that "politics could not be conceived as the simple pursuit of instrumental rationality. Behind the veil of Fabian realism he glimpsed a deeper reality where the political arena was a place of conflicting illusions, or a madhouse of ignorant enthusiasm" (56).

30. The Fabians even developed a magic lantern show to promote socialism visually and orally rather than through print: "A series of Fabian Lantern Lectures has proved very effective for purposes of political propaganda. The pictures emphasize the spoken word. They attract audiences which, without the incentive of lantern slides, would never attend political meetings or receive any kind of political instruction" (*Labour Annual,* 1897: 245–46). Why British socialists did not make more political use of the new visual media technologies of the era—most obviously, cinema—is an interesting question; radical aversion to commercial culture produced a particular bias against visual media like cinema, which at this time was utterly commercialized.

31. Later, in 1913, the Fabians did launch a newspaper, the *New Statesman,* "a platform for the reformist middle class" that was to be a "truly Fabian enterprise" (Holroyd 2: 318–22), but it was for the most part driven by Beatrice Webb's desire to create a rival publication to the *New Age,* which was being run by apostate Fabians (see Chapter 5).

32. With similar surprise, Shaw notes that the first edition of *Facts for Socialists* "actually brought us a profit," which was virtually unheard of for socialist print forums of the day (*Fabian Society* 19). The Fabian Society itself published the first edition of *Fabian Essays,* as Pease relates, after initial arrangements with a publisher "broke down because he declined to have the book printed at a 'fair house'" (88).

33. Recognizing Shaw's reaction against utilitarian notions of print, here and elsewhere, offers a challenge to those critics who read Shaw as oppositional to Morris's brand of aesthetic socialism; for example, Ruth Livesey argues that Shaw advocated

"a break from the generation of Victorians who had devoted themselves to the distinctively aesthetic politics of socialism in the 1880s," such as Morris, Edward Carpenter, and Walter Crane ("Socialism" 127). And yet Shaw's aesthetic concern with print's form, apart from its status as a conveyor of information, demonstrates his continuity with these socialists too.

34. This was the Fabian strategy, but of course it did not mean that individual members would not launch their own papers with their own goals. Annie Besant ran *Our Corner* and *The Link* while active in the Fabian Society, and Thomas Bolas and W. K. Burton launched *The Practical Socialist*, which, like *Our Corner*, included Fabian news and a cover design by Walter Crane.

35. Shaw was leery of such approaches and advocated in an 1887 essay a "policy for developing our existing institutions into socialistic ones, and not a catastrophic policy for simultaneously destroying existing institutions and replacing them with a ready-made Utopia" ("New Radicalism" 31).

36. As Davis notes, the Fabians thought that the domain of art and entertainment "was a necessity and should be provided with reliable quality at the lowest possible cost, rather like water and sanitation. It was not necessary to bludgeon the working classes with entertainment that portrayed the Fabians' political utopia. . . . Instead they called for removing art from the exigencies of a commercial system while retaining heterogeneity" (21).

37. Shaw claimed, for example, that the Fabians had influenced the *Clarion*, but Blatchford, the editor of the *Clarion*, angrily wrote to Shaw on 14 August 1892: "The Fabian Society had no more to do with the Socialism of the *Clarion* than the man in the moon. The *Clarion* was founded by four Socialists on purpose to advocate Socialism. The Fabian Society never had a word in it. Why should they?" (Fabian Society Archive, A 6/3). Alexander has recently argued that Shaw's claims for influencing the *Star* in this direction are equally exaggerated (88–89).

38. Morris's *Dream of John Ball*, for example, includes a warm, lively depiction of a simple, hearty meal shared with stories and political conversation in a thirteenth-century pub.

39. Griffith claims that Fabian policy under the leadership of Beatrice and Sidney Webb was "underpinned by a suspicion of democracy, based on the view that ordinary people" were "fundamentally irrational and incapable of enlightenment" (64). Ian Britain recently suggested that the Fabians' reputation as authoritarian socialists is overstated; he argues that the Webbs' influence has been exaggerated and that the democratic influence of founder Thomas Davidson has been largely ignored (38). Shaw was much less of an authoritarian than the Webbs, but over time a Webbian tendency did pervade his political thought, such as in his sympathetic view of Soviet Russia in the 1930s and his flirtation with dictators during the same era.

Chapter 3

1. *Workers' Herald* was an Aberdeen socialist newspaper. John Howard Crawford was the author of *The Brotherhood of Mankind: A Study Towards a Christian Philosophy of History* (1895). Although not an avowed socialist, his ideas aligned with the Christian Socialist movement of the day.

2. The working-class Clarionettes did form a few dramatic societies, but these were a decidedly small part of the Clarion movement (see Pye 51–52). Other socialist groups also organized amateur theatricals for fun and for a purpose but only sporadically (*Clarion*, 26 September 1896: 312).

3. Shaw's and Ibsen's dramas were often performed by workers' theaters and Clarionette drama societies in the early twentieth century. According to Pye, "Shaw's plays tended to dominate production lists" of the Clarion dramatic societies (52), and Samuel notes of the long-running People's Theatre of Newcastle that nine of its first twelve dramas were Shaw's "and it was the performance of Shaw which made the group's local reputation" (Samuel et al. 18). Likewise, Ness Edwards's *Workers' Theatre* (1930), the "most systematic case for class struggle drama" at the time, "pa[id] tribute to Ibsen and Shaw" but "argue[d] that the new workers' drama . . . must 'present problems in class rather than personal terms'" (Samuel et al. 36).

4. Horniman, in addition to funding the Gaiety in Manchester and the Abbey Theatre in Dublin, provided financial backing for the first public performance of a Shaw play, *Arms and the Man*, in 1894; it ran with a one-act opener by Yeats, *The Land of Heart's Desire*. The Gaiety prospectus, like the other documents produced for the theater, not only emulates the Kelmscott Press but also bears the trace of Horniman's membership in the occultist Hermetic Order of the Golden Dawn. The prospectus features an esoteric symbol that was incorporated into many of the Gaiety's documents, and an article in the Manchester *Evening News* explained that the figure combines the symbols for the sun, Venus, Mercury, and the moon ("Miss Horniman's Symbol," 9 May 1908). The use of this complex esoteric symbol perfectly captures the air of exclusivity that surrounded late Victorian radical theater. The Gaiety prospectus, titled *Miss Horniman's Company*, is held in the John Rylands Library, Annie Horniman Papers, AEH/2/2.

5. Morris's utopian, pastoral *Tables Turned* likely influenced the development of Yeats's political drama, but for all the political vigor of the Abbey Theatre, Yeats himself ended up advocating "an 'aristocratic' theater and not a popular one, a small chamber and not an arena for the assembled *populus*. In his notorious 'A People's Theatre: A Letter to Lady Gregory' (1919–23) . . . [he drew] the following conclusion: 'I want to create for myself an unpopular theatre and an audience like a secret society where admission is by favour and never too many'" (Puchner 138).

6. Walter Scott published the first edition of *Quintessence*, in an edition of 2,100, with a price of 2s. 6d. (Kelly 34).

7. Other private radical theater groups relevant to this study include the Playgoers Society, which emerged from and quickly outgrew the Leeds Arts Club, and the Clarion theater groups mentioned earlier. There were also theater appreciation groups such as the Church and Stage Guild, a Christian Socialist group (*Clarion*, 6 February 1892: 3).

8. The Roycroft Press, an American firm founded by Elbert Hubbard in emulation of Morris's Kelmscott Press, printed a Shaw essay as one of its first publications, suggesting that Shaw (at least for Hubbard) was associated with the Morrisian print socialist movement. The volume, *On Going to Church*, was published in 1896 and used paper, font, inks, and botanical designs in the Kelmscott style.

9. An early staging of Ibsen's *Pillars of Society*, a one-off Wednesday matinee on 15 December 1880, had been organized by William Archer. This was the first Ibsen

performance in England, but in Archer's words it "failed to make any impression on the English public" (qtd. in Franc 80).

10. See, for example, MacKenzie and MacKenzie (168).

11. In 1892 the *Clarion* expressed uneasiness at the prospect of a *Cenci* revival on the stage (13 February 1892: 7). The paper also did not like Wilde; exemplifying many anti-Wilde statements is a review of *Lady Windermere's Fan*: "There is not absolutely one real Human touch in the whole piece. From beginning to end it is unreal and bizarre" (27 February 1892: 2).

12. This article sparked a dispute between Shaw and Blatchford in the pages of the *Clarion*. Shaw wrote to Blatchford in the next issue: "You will never be worth your salt as a reviewer of high-class literature until you learn to face the world without imposing your trumpery little moral system on it. . . . You cannot review poetry and philosophy of the first class with a little frame of red and blue ideals" (13 February 1897: 49). Responses flew back and forth.

13. The quotation is from an 1871 letter from Ibsen to George Brandes (*Letters* 208).

14. Shaw thought at this time that a national theater would need to be privately funded rather than state funded. On this issue, unlike other Fabians, he did not trust the state to be an effective arbiter of culture (Britain 265).

15. Under Morris's editorship the *Commonweal* never printed Shelley poems, although it did print William Blake's poetry. (In 1892, after Morris had left, the *Commonweal* did reprint Shelley.)

16. In a study of socialist songbooks from the era, Waters notes that Fabian songbooks contained a higher portion of Romantic authors than other socialist groups, suggesting how Shelley veneration went along in some sense with Fabian appeals to English tradition (*British Socialists* 112).

17. See St. Clair for more on the publication history of the poem.

18. See, for example, William Michael Rossetti's and William Sharp's important 1880s biographies of the poet, which helped position Shelley in the late Victorian literary left. *Prometheus Unbound* was the subject of many lectures and discussions among the radical intelligentsia: Alfred Orage lectured on it to the York branch of the Independent Labour Party (Steele 32), and W. J. Jupp lectured on it to the Fellowship of the New Life (*Seed Time*, January 1893: 15).

19. For examples of such songbooks, see *Songs for Socialists* (1912), *Socialist Songs* (1896), or *Chants of Labour* (1888). Chris Waters notes that two-thirds of turn-of-the-century socialist songbooks included "Men of England," making it one of the one most commonly printed socialist songs (*British Socialists* 111).

20. Todhunter was an Irish poet and playwright living in London at the time.

21. A 12 April 1881 letter from Dante Gabriel Rossetti to Lucy Rossetti, William's wife, suggests that William had familial as well as occupational pressure to modulate his political expression: "Several of William's truest friends, no less than myself, are greatly alarmed at the tone taken in some of his sonnets respecting 'tyrannicide,' Fenianism, and other incendiary subjects. It occurs to me and to others that the consequences are absolutely and very perilously uncertain, when an official (as William is) of a monarchical government, allows himself such unbridled licence of public speech. The prosecution against the editor of the *Freiheit* seems very ominous to us and per-

fectly just. . . . My object in writing this letter is to awaken your mind to the clear possibility of absolute ruin . . . for my dear brother and his family whom he loves so well" (British Library ms Ashley A4152).

22. In a letter to Shaw, Rossetti wrote: "I brought the Chicago petition before the Committee of the Shelley Society last evening, but found my colleagues decidedly disinclined to move in the matter: a vote was taken, and it was adverse. So I posted back last night the petition to Dr. Aveling, bearing my signature. I am sorry for this result but couldn't help it. . . . My feelings go along with yours in the matter" (10 November 1887, British Library ms 50511, f. 355).

23. This was in contradistinction to the critical aestheticism of, for example, John Addington Symonds, who "insisted on a separation between Shelley's wonderful lyrical gifts and his moral and social theories, theories 'that could not but have proved pernicious to mankind at large.'" Thus he presented Shelley "as both excellent and innocuous" (Kearney 63–64). Symonds had written to Rossetti that he might join the Shelley Society in an honorary capacity but not as a regular member (Rossetti, *Selected Letters* 482).

24. For more on Furnivall, see Peterson (*Interrogating*).

25. See the lecture program for the Shelley Centenary, British Library ms 50701.

26. Curran claims (incorrectly, to my mind) that the "political undercurrents of *The Cenci*" were "ignored by the Shelley Society" (209).

27. Shelley, of course, was infamous for leaving his wife, Harriet Westbrook, to run off with Mary Godwin and her half-sister Claire Clairmont; to have relations with a wife's sister was legally considered incest at the time, because incest laws operated by the logic of affiliation rather than consanguinity. The nature of Shelley's relations with Clairmont was a source of gossipy interest for members of the Shelley Society. For example, William Michael Rossetti wrote to Anna Steele on 28 March 1896: "I don't consider that Shelley ever 'made love' to Miss C—tho no doubt he expended upon her, as upon other women, some of his superabundant sentiment." Steele disagreed, and the epistolary debate went on for months (John Rylands Library, GB 133 Eng MS 1277). Shelley was also guilty of incest by association, because his close friend Byron had left England amid revelations of a relationship with his own half-sister. Rumors circulated that Shelley and Byron, exiled abroad, constituted a "league of incest," where both men were conducting affairs with the sisters Mary and Claire at once. (See Holmes for more on this topic.) In addition, Shelley's poem *Laon and Cythna*—later revised and toned down as *The Revolt of Islam*—had depicted its title characters as brother and sister lovers.

28. In his novel *Love Among the Artists*, originally serialized in Annie Besant's socialist magazine *Our Corner*, Shaw presents Shelley as forever beyond public appreciation and approval. In the novel, Owen Jack, a brilliant ultramodern composer, sets Shelley's *Prometheus Unbound* to music, and the performance elicits "a partly hysterical mixture of hand clapping and protesting hisses" (244), prompting one character to note, "Commerce is the ruin of England. It renders the people quite anti-artistic" (247).

29. Quotations from *The Cenci* refer to the Norton edition.

30. Puchner's notion of "the epistemology of the closet drama" is relevant here—"Such an epistemology would be devoted to tracing the forms of deviance, including but not limited to sexual deviance, that find their place in the closet drama" (90–91)—although it is important to remember that Shelley had not intended the play as a closet drama.

31. This was Shaw's spin for the authorities. In a 1916 effort to get the play licensed, he wrote to the censor's office that he wanted to "shew the objection to what was called politely (by 'advanced' people) Group Marriage" and "to shew what was the real character of what is now called the White Slave Traffic" (8 October 1916, British Library ms. L.C.P. Corr. 1924/5632).

32. Recent critics have tended to take at his word Shaw's stated purpose: that incest illustrates the social perils of prostitution. Petra Dierkes-Thrun, however, has recently argued that incest functions in the play to reveal "the victimization of young women and girls, not just in brothels but also in private lives" (294). This interpretation fails to fully acknowledge, however, that Mrs. Warren, in moving from prostitute-laborer to brothel-owning capitalist, herself becomes a capitalist predator preying on women's bodies. Ultimately, Shaw's play, like *The Cenci*, makes a systemic argument about the way social organization directs all individual human behavior: Shelley's play exposes the corruption of autocratic power, whereas Shaw's reveals the corruption of capital. Even Vivie, the New Woman, does not escape this corruption. Choosing a career as an actuary, she makes her living by turning human beings into numbers and statistics; she becomes the agent of a capitalist system that persistently objectifies human beings. Prostitution serves throughout the play as an allegory for this broader capitalist logic of instrumentalization and dehumanization.

33. Shaw's later plays continue this theme of calling our attention to what cannot be stated viva voce. Perhaps the most legendary example is *Pygmalion*, which famously stoked controversy by using the word *bloody*, a curse considered so shocking that audiences were abuzz with its presence in the play even before opening night.

34. Byzantine copyright laws meant that if a play was published before it was staged, the author would lose all performance rights to the drama. To get around this problem and secure his copyright, Shaw staged a "mangled and mutilated three-act version" in which Mrs. Warren was a female thief rather than a prostitute (Conolly 55).

35. *Mrs Warren* was not actually staged, even in private, until the Stage Society mounted a production in January 1902. Shaw had originally written the play for Grein's Independent Theatre, with the idea that Mrs. Theodore Wright and Janet Achurch would play the two leading parts, but Grein thought it was too controversial even for the private theatrical sphere (Mander and Mitchenson 30). The first public performance was in New Haven, Connecticut, in 1905, and it was promptly shut down; a New York production launched shortly thereafter ran for fourteen performances. The first public performance in England did not occur until 1925. Conolly offers a detailed description of the production history of *Mrs Warren's Profession* and the long fight to have it licensed.

Chapter 4

1. "Sending to the War" (part 3 of *The Pilgrims of Hope*) was first published in the *Commonweal* in May 1885. Morris's friend Bruce Glasier was, according to Janowitz, the first to call the poem a "proletarian epic" (221).

2. As Janowitz has described in her reading of *Pilgrims of Hope*, the poem draws on a hodgepodge of traditional verse modes: "the narrative teleology of the ballad tradition and the depth psychology of the inward lyric" (197), the alliterative Anglo-Saxon tradition, and the hexameter of international classical epic mode (225).

3. W. B. Yeats and Ezra Pound, Bristow notes, bear much responsibility for this "selective manner in which memories about the 1890s were passed down to the next [literary] generation" (27).

4. Herbert Tucker briefly discusses *The Pilgrims of Hope* in his book *Epic*. Janowitz offers a detailed analysis of the poem, focusing on how *Pilgrims* blends epic and lyric forms to make an argument about individuality and collectivity (225). Boos has also examined the poem ("Banners" 33–34).

5. According to Quail, the Russian and German governments pressured Britain to prosecute Most, and his "arrest and sentence caused something of a stir in London Radical and socialist circles" (12). Joll notes that Most's paper came to be "suspected of fomenting assassinations of all kinds, and when Lord Frederick Cavendish was murdered in Dublin by Irish nationalists who had nothing to do with the anarchist movement and of whose aims Most would have thoroughly disapproved, *Freiheit* was again raided and two of its printers arrested" (121).

6. Joynes, also discussed in Chapter 2, was a key writer, editor, and activist in the early socialist movement. With Henry Salt, he had been an Eton master before being dismissed for his opinions. "As masters at Eton," E. P. Thompson writes, the two men were "under suspicion as Radicals, free-thinkers and possessors of tricycles" (*William Morris* 290).

7. Of nineteenth-century efforts to collect oral ballads in Scotland, Vincent writes: "It has been estimated that of the material painstakingly recorded from elderly traditional singers in remote corners of Britain in the late nineteenth and early twentieth centuries, as much as four-fifths had once appeared in printed broadsides" (93). "What was recovered," William St. Clair notes, "was not an oral and performative popular tradition stretching back into the mists of time, but a continuous privately owned print tradition" (346).

8. W. C. Bennett, a radical poet who published a few poems in the *Commonweal*, published *Contributions to a Ballad History of England* in 1879, arguing for the power of traditional ballads as a medium in contemporary working-class politics. A review of this book in the 6 November 1880 issue of the *Common Good* was skeptical: "At present, what with defective education, and the absorbing devotion of the whole nation to newspaper reading . . . we confess that the prospects of success are not encouraging" (76).

9. Glasier's letters to the *Commonweal* suggest his sense of humor about his poetry and that he would not have scrupled to use flawed form for comic effect. An 18 September 1885 letter reads: "Dear Comrade, If the enclosed verses are worthy of a place in *Commonweal* I shall feel pleased—if you put them in the waste basket, they will only go where many of my 'hopes have gone before' and I shall bear the calamity with, I trust, becoming socialistic fortitude" (Socialist League Archive, f. 1532). Another letter reads: "If you think the enclosed suitable for *Commonweal*, put it in—if you think it unsuitable bury it decently in your waste paper basket. It is somewhat *free and easy* in spirit—a quality somewhat needed I think. . . . The majority of socialist songs in this country are serious in character and laden with propaganda—the one enclosed, you may think, might be better if it followed the rule. You are judge, jury, and jailor in this matter—condemn if you will" (9 May 1887, Socialist League Archive, f. 1540).

10. Elsewhere the *Clarion* made fun of this Romantic ideal of poetry: "A correspondent, one John W. Milton, wants to know if I can tell him 'how to make poetry.' . . . Get

some nice clean paper, a box of pens, and a pint of ink. Then have something for supper that doesn't agree with you very well; then go and roost on the back fence, and gaze at the stars till some particularly idiotic notion finds birth in your brain. Then go into the house and write it down in short length; make the last words rhyme—if possible. . . . Only be careful about one thing . . . it must not be sense, or it won't be poetry" (4 April 1896: 105).

11. The *Clarion* did print poems from readers at least occasionally. For example, the 2 January 1897 issue included the poem "A Sister's Yule-Tide" by L. Hird with the headnote: "A Bradford correspondent sends us the following verses" (2).

12. Carpenter continued to add to the poem over the years. The 1883 version became Part I when Carpenter added a second part in 1885. He published Parts III and IV in 1892 and 1902, and the complete edition in 1905. According to Tony Brown, 16,000 copies of the 1909 pocket edition had been sold by 1916.

13. This is not to say that these poems never appeared therein. A section of *Towards Democracy* ran in the October 1888 issue of Annie Besant's magazine *Our Corner*, under the title "Democracy" (208–9). *Our Corner*, as discussed in Chapter 5, was a Fabian journal aimed at a middle-class audience, which tended to be elitist in its view of art and culture. A few years earlier, the magazine's review of *Towards Democracy* said that the book is "not to be swallowed at a sitting like a pill, but to be read bit by bit with pauses between for thinking. The rhythm is of Walt Whitman . . . do the yearnings of the new Democracy towards the higher life flow naturally into this mould of expression?" (April 1886: 249–50). Poems from *Towards Democracy* also appeared in *Justice* (16 April 1892: 4) and the *Labour Leader* (13 November 1897: 371).

As for Whitman, "Resurgemus" appeared in the September 1884 issue of *To-Day* (230–32); "The Foil'd European Revolutionaire" ran in the *Commonweal* on 19 July 1890; and the *Labour Leader* printed two Whitman poems in August 1893. John Trevor, editor of the *Labour Prophet*, was an intensely fervent fan of Whitman, and in the April 1892 issue he printed numerous passages of Whitman's poetry followed by his own reflections.

14. Sixsmith began another, later lecture on *Towards Democracy*, "Edward Carpenter, Poet and Prophet," by situating Carpenter's volume against the capitalist culture of overprint and the "democratic" mass print readership. His notes for the lecture begin: "Books published 1912. 11,778 . . . British Museum Library, nearly 3 million books. 50/60 miles of shelves. . . . How are we to get at the real live books amid the mazes and mountains of ephemeral books?" (Sixsmith Collection, 1171/3/3). He presents Carpenter's esoteric text as unfit for a culture of mass print: "For a long time it was scarcely known and only understood and appreciated by a very few choice souls." Eventually, he says, the book made its way by word of mouth rather than advertising.

15. For examples of Gilbert and Sullivan parodies in the *Commonweal*, see "The Individualist Apologises" (21 April 1888: 123) or "A Gilbertian Perversion" (20 July 1889: 227).

16. For example, the *Labour Leader* ran a special "Diamond Jubilee Number" on 19 June 1897, running the parodic poem "God Save the Queen" by "Gleaner" on its front page:

A fulsome blare is in the air,

And forth from tower and steeple

Resounds abroad once more, I ween,

That ancient cant God Save the Queen,

While democrats chip in between

With—Reason Save the People. (1)

17. The poem was printed again in the March 1897 issue of the *Social Democrat.*

18. Of the 309 poems published in the *Commonweal,* 13 were published in 1885, 42 in 1886 (the paper switched from a monthly to a weekly on 1 May), 53 in 1887, 59 in 1888, 64 in 1889, 35 in 1890 (Morris left the paper in the fall after a dispute with Socialist League anarchists), 12 in 1891 (the paper returned to a monthly format and then switched back to a weekly but with only four pages per issue), 11 in 1892 (publication was suspended from 4 September 1892 to 1 May 1893), 11 in 1893, and 9 in 1894.

19. Anonymity does not necessarily signify sloppy editing, but in this case it does coincide with more careless handling of the journal's poetry after 1890. In one case the same poem was printed twice under different titles: "The Anarchist's Hope" (4 June 1892) and "The True Reformer" (1 May 1893). The respected anarchist poet Louisa Sarah Bevington did, however, publish several poems in the *Commonweal* after its anarchist turn.

20. Some poems may have been reprinted without being credited; my numbers include those that are identified as reprints or are quite obviously so (e.g., poems by William Blake).

21. Peter Scheckner's *Anthology of Chartist Poetry* attributes this poem to *The Northern Star and National Trades Journal* (9 May 1846).

22. Henderson received little support from the socialist literary elite. He published poems in the *Commonweal, Our Corner,* and other radical journals, but Morris discouraged him from writing poetry: "Pray don't be down-cast because you have tried to write poetry & failed" (*Collected Letters* 2: 472). Edward Carpenter wrote a lukewarm review of Henderson's *By the Sea and Other Poems* for the December 1892 issue of the *Labour Prophet.* The review notes "the present overstocked condition of the poetry market, where 'over-production' holds high revel" and offers subdued praise for the 24-year-old socialist's work: "The author has a good faculty for language, and when he keeps the expression sincere and clear, and well pent in the bounds of poetic form, produces some passably substantial work" (89–90). Carpenter himself had transgressed "the bounds of poetic form" in his Whitmanesque *Towards Democracy,* but he implies here that an inferior poet such as Henderson must rely on form in a way that Carpenter need not.

23. *Scout,* a spin-off publication of the *Clarion,* even offered a prize contest in its October 1895 issue for the best musical accompaniment to a socialist song: "It is generally admitted that one of the great needs of the Socialist cause is good original Socialist songs, choruses, and anthems. We therefore offer a prize of ONE GUINEA *or* its value in any other form preferred; also A 'CLARION' CERTIFICATE, signed by the members of the Board, for the best musical setting of the words given below, or any others of Socialist flavour which the competitor may select from the works of any recognised poet" (184). The winning entry, by "G. von H.," offered music for William Morris's "All for the Cause," from the 16 March 1889 issue of the *Commonweal.*

24. Most of the *Commonweal's* poems are quite short; Morris's *Pilgrims of Hope* and Joynes's *Lord of Burleigh* are the only long serial works. These two writers were

prominent members of the socialist movement known for literary learnedness; thus they were afforded unusual space and time to publish these poems.

25. Twenty-two (11 percent) of the journal's poems, not including translations and reprints, were sonnets.

26. All of the verse in *Machine-Room Chants* was originally printed in the *Labour Leader*, and most of the poems in *Tom Maguire, A Remembrance* are identified as reprints from various radical periodicals. (Among those not identified as reprints, at least one, "The Lay of a Loose Essence," I know to have appeared in the *Workman's Times.*) Bessie Ford reported in a letter to the *Clarion* that some of the verses in the latter volume had been found in manuscript after Maguire's death (13 July 1895: 221).

27. Florence Boos, for example, notes that "Critical attention to working-class poetry as a genre has suffered for many years from a tendency to ignore these works' original publication history. It is easy to comment once again on the stereotypical qualities of a few readily accessible volumes of verse, but difficult to canvass thousands of unindexed pages of long-expired and barely extant periodicals, in search of working-class poets' original audiences, contexts, and modes of expression." She continues, "Most working-class poets sent their work to local newspapers or journals, and many saw their poems 'in print' in penny-newspapers and journals. Few seriously hoped to see them in hard covers" ("Homely Muse" 255).

28. For more background on Maguire, see Maguire, *Tom Maguire, A Remembrance*; "Tom Maguire," in the 1896 *Labour Annual*, 211; Battle; Kershen; or Barnard.

29. After the publication of this review, Wilde went further in his assistance to Skipsey, writing to W. T. Stead: "Joseph Skipsey, the Tyneside poet . . . has asked me to forward the accompanying volume of his poems to you. I reviewed him for the P. M. G. last year and he seems to have been much pleased with the notice. There is much in his work that is good and fine—and some of the little lyrics are delightful in their freshness and freedom" (n.d., W. T. Stead Papers).

30. Maguire often wrote to the paper's editors with intelligent advice on how the paper might be improved; the Socialist League archive is full of long letters from Maguire demonstrating his range of ideas and his creativity in thinking about everything from organization to procedure to layout and font size. He wrote in an 1885 letter, addressed to "Comrade Editor": "I see that a fine distinction is drawn in the setting of the *C.* in that the best-written article gets the larger type. This seems to me scarcely Socialistic. . . . There should be no mincing of contributing articles" (Socialist League Archive, f. 2124). Another letter, dated 15 March 1885, suggests that "the *illustration* that decks the London manifesto . . . could be put to valuable use. You could get a large poster with that engraving attached thereto and with the following subjoined: 'The Commonweal. The Workingman's Friend. Should be read by all Workers' etc. Also it would be a fine thing to flourish on a banner at all open-air meetings" (f. 2128).

31. The *Clarion* also used the motif of circuses, freak shows, and so on to depict politics as absurd, as in the 13 February 1892 poem "The Political Show":

> Hi hi! Hi hi! walk up! walk up!
>
> Step forward, ye sharps and flats;
>
> Come plank down your money

And laugh at the funny

Political acrobats. (1)

32. The *Labour Champion*, like the *Clarion*, sometimes made nationalist appeals to a sense of racial community among working-class white British and Irish-British readers. Its most egregiously racist article is in the second issue (21 October 1893) and refers to the "Canoe Indians" (a misspelling of "Canu") as the "Ugliest People on Earth" (5).

33. See Deborah Mutch's *English Socialist Periodicals* for lists of Tom Maguire's and Bardolph's contributions to a select group of socialist periodicals.

34. For more on the tailoresses' strike, see Kershen or Katrina Honeyman.

35. Discussing Maguire's relation to nationalism and internationalism, Anne Kershen notes that he "spoke out in favour of controls on pauper alien immigration" but "was sympathetic to the cause of those who, having settled in England, were then used and abused by middlemen and masters" (67).

36. By way of Carpenter's collection, these two songs by Maguire also made it into American socialist songbooks, such as *Socialist Songs with Music*, compiled by Charles Kerr in 1901.

37. Carpenter had worked to make this volume as inclusive as possible; a notice in the 3 September 1887 issue of *Justice* called on readers to send contributions: "Our comrade Edward Carpenter is preparing a Socialist Song Book . . . and will be glad to receive contributions in the shape of good words matched to good tunes. . . . Songs in actual use among Socialist bodies will be specially welcome" (3). H. W. Hobart reviewed the volume in the 19 May 1888 issue of *Justice* and thought that it "partially supplied" a "want that has long been felt," but he complained of ill-fitting tunes for some of the songs (2).

Chapter 5

1. *Our Corner* did not formally align itself with Fabian socialism until 1886, but the socialist interests of the journal are clear from early on. Within the first few months of its publication in 1883, *Our Corner* printed an article by J. L. Joynes, one of Britain's most prominent socialists, titled "Leading Socialist Theories." From 1883 to 1884, Edward Aveling, a prominent leader in the early socialist movement, wrote the journal's "Art Corner" column (which George Bernard Shaw, another prominent socialist, would take over in 1885). In 1884 the journal printed a series about the American economist Henry George, whose book *Progress and Poverty* had an enormous influence on 1880s British socialism. In its 1 August 1885 issue *Justice* (the Social Democratic Federation paper) used passages from *Our Corner* to formally announce that Besant had "pledged herself to Socialism."

2. Besant's *Commonweal*, published in India and launched in 1914, extended the Socialist League's international version of the "commonweal," which was primarily focused on the dissolution of class, to a "Commonweal of the World," which focused on the dissolution of ethnic and racial division (2 January 1914: 5). "The Commonweal of the World" describes a "geographical division of the one earth into separate, unrelated, or at most slightly related parts," but also "another division of our planet which was not geographical but mental. People were classed as civilised and barbarian, as compatriots and 'foreigners,' as familiar and 'outlandish.' This was mainly an ethnic and racial division" (5).

3. Maguire included more favorable references to theosophy in his socialist paper, *Labour Champion*—a sign of theosophy's prominence in the radical Leeds community that his paper served. The paper included advertisements for Theosophical Society meetings and ran an article titled "What Is Theosophy? An Interview with Mr. E. S. Pickard." Representing the Theosophical Society, Pickard says that the aim of theosophy is to "bring about a common understanding between all known religions" (4 November 1893: 4).

4. *Autobiographical Sketches* does appear to have produced the sort of response in readers that Besant was aiming to effect. Edith Nesbit wrote to Shaw in an 18 October 1886 letter, "I've just been reading Mrs. Besant's autobiography. It made me long to rush off and do something for her and to scratch the faces of everyone who has ever been unkind to her" (British Library ms 50511, f. 220).

5. As noted earlier, *Our Corner* did not formally align with Fabian socialism until 1886, but from its beginning the journal expressed interest in socialism and included socialist content.

6. Bloody Sunday refers to a 13 November 1887 demonstration in Trafalgar Square that was violently suppressed by the police, resulting in one fatality and many injuries.

7. Besant's anticolonial activism in India culminated in a three-month prison term in 1917; the British Raj had asked her to censor support of Indian home rule in her newspaper, *New India*, and she refused. Recent critics, however, have qualified the extent to which Besant can be viewed as a hero of Indian nationalism. Viswanathan argues, "All the time that she courted arrest . . . Besant always stressed that she opposed the British government for failing to live up to the principles it stood for, and not because she sought the destruction of empire itself. Her plea for Indian self-government *within* the empire was not quite the same thing as a call for Indian independence from Britain, which more radical Indian nationalists were seeking" (203–4). For more on Besant's long career in Indian nationalism, see Bevir, Paxton, Anne Taylor, or Viswanathan.

8. For biographical accounts of Besant's life, see Bevir, Dixon, Nethercot, or Anne Taylor. Also see the introduction and appendixes in Carol Mackay's Broadview edition of *Autobiographical Sketches*. See Linda Peterson for more on the "classic, hermeneutic" Victorian autobiographical subject (ix).

9. Like Mackay in *Creative Negativity*, I focus on Besant's series of "deconversions," to use Mackay's term, but I come to a different conclusion regarding their effect. Mackay finds in Besant's autobiography a structural arch and a unity of purpose, centered around deconversion itself, whereas I read the deconversions as mitigating against such a cohesive representation of self.

10. I discuss the Knowlton pamphlet and trial at greater length later in this chapter and in Chapter 6.

11. Scott was a pamphleteer for whom Besant wrote on free thought, religion, education, and other matters. Besant signed her first writings for him "by the wife of a beneficed clergyman," because, as Besant says, "My name was not mine to use, so it was agreed that any essays from my pen should be anonymous" (*Autobiography* 114–15). Ironically, it was not until after she separated from her husband that Besant felt free to sign her writings with her married name. In this case, Besant's use of her husband's name signified freedom rather than bondage.

12. Many anonymous and pseudonymous pieces were printed in the radical press, but many socialist papers nevertheless made an effort to eschew print anonymity. *Justice* declared, "No notice will be taken of anonymous contributors" (19 January 1884: 4). The *Workers' Herald* made the same pledge on 12 December 1891 (6). Suspicion of print anonymity had a long history in nineteenth-century radical discourse, as Gilmartin describes (35–36). Nevertheless, the socialist journal *To-Day* claimed it would "use the shield of anonymity for the rightful purpose of protecting its writers against the attacks of prejudice and spite" (14 April 1883: 3), and when the anarchist journal *Freedom* was launched, its editors made a concerted decision to print articles unsigned in the spirit of collectivist values (Thomas 11). Likewise, Fabian Society pamphlets were usually unsigned, because they were meant to be "collective works, in that every member was expected to assist in them by criticism and suggestion" (Pease 83) (although most of the early pamphlets were initially drafted by Shaw or Sidney Webb).

13. The exceptions are the opening chapters of the volume, which depict Besant's life before she became a writer and thus are not as dense with quotations as the other chapters. Yet even here Besant reproduces sections of prayers that she composed during her intensely religious adolescence. A few quotations from these early prayers also appear in *Autobiographical Sketches*, but in *Sketches* they are the only example of Besant quoting from an earlier piece of writing with which she no longer agrees (whereas she does this often in *An Autobiography*).

14. Besant does excerpt quotations from other authors, such as Bradlaugh, in *Autobiographical Sketches.*

15. As noted earlier, the one exception to this in *Autobiographical Sketches* is Besant's short reference to the prayers she wrote as a fervently religious adolescent.

16. Throughout her career, Besant put such dialectical intertextuality to intellectual use. Both autobiographies describe how she first began to doubt the Bible when she outlined the four Gospels and discerned their discrepancies. Her 1882 pamphlet *Blasphemy* likewise juxtaposes a series of biblical quotations with illegal quotations to prove the "artificial" nature of the offense.

17. This idea persists in more recent accounts, such as that of Norman and Jeanne MacKenzie, who argue that each of Besant's conversions "was personified in an attachment to a new male idol," because "her temperament seemed to demand a masculine partner whom she could both admire and patronize" (45–46).

18. Besant publicly reclaimed her support for birth control in 1927 (Paxton 342).

19. This theosophical notion of thought forms had an important influence on modernist artists and writers, as I discuss in the Conclusion.

20. Ivan Kreilkamp argues along similar lines that Joseph Conrad's *Heart of Darkness* (1899) "draws on new representational possibilities suggested by the phonograph," but in this case "to represent a grave danger to human agency and authorship" (182). Besant's autobiography registers no such danger.

21. Besant and Bradlaugh's Freethought Publishing Company had published an homage to Paine (*Oration on Thomas Paine*, by Colonel Robert G. Ingersoll) in 1877. The pamphlet demonstrates the secularist sense of debt to an old school radical tradition that heavily emphasized free print. But the decreasing role that censorship and

controls on speech played in radical political discourse meant that Paine's relevance for modern socialism was diminishing.

22. See Viswanathan for more on secularists' interest in Eastern religion. For many the study of non-Christian religions served primarily as a means of undermining the authority of the Christian tradition; but others were genuinely interested in the epistemological and/or spiritual bases of Eastern religions.

23. Orage was deeply influenced by Besant and Carpenter in his early socialist career, but he later turned against them. In the 5 October 1916 issue of the *New Age*, for example, he argued, "Edward Carpenter has contributed very little to modern life and thought; like Mrs. Besant, he has only made publicly accessible trends of thought rather than ideas" (545–46).

24. As Pierson notes, most of the funding for the Labour Churches came from wealthy and middle-class socialists, but the membership "was predominantly working class" ("John Trevor" 468).

25. In Orage and in his work for the *Labour Leader*, the Leeds Art Club, and the *New Age*, Steele identifies "three main strands" of late Victorian socialism: (1) "nineteenth century 'cultural criticism' articulated in various ways by Ruskin, Carlyle and William Morris," (2) "late nineteenth-century spiritualism, which combined elements of translated eastern mysticism, the theosophy of Blavatsky, [and] Annie Besant," and (3) "Nietzsche and high German romanticism" (263). These three avenues, along with Fabianism, formed Orage's idiosyncratic version of socialism from which the *New Age* would later emerge.

26. Publication of the *Reformers' Year Book* (formerly the *Labour Annual*) was taken over in 1909 by the New Age Press, which was operated by Orage and associated with the *New Age* journal. With the 1909 volume the *Year Book* moved away from its earlier, more neutral perspective to a partisan voice under the New Age Press. In discussing the Social Democratic Party (formerly the Social Democratic Federation), for example, the *Year Book* declared: "Most of the English Socialist leaders have been members of the S.D.P. in their earlier days, but have left it owing to its rigid and uncompromising adherence to all the teachings of Karl Marx and its disinclination to take part in practical social progress" (148). Although many historical accounts of the Federation would echo this conclusion, its tone was a departure for a publication that had previously striven to draw together, not divide, England's various radical organizations.

27. Orage, in initially proposing the Arts Group to the Fabian Society, emphasized "the relation of the handicrafts and craft guilds to Socialism. . . . The Arts and Crafts movement had entrusted its politics to socialists" (qtd. in Britain 170). But the politics of the Arts and Crafts movement, if it could be said to have a politics, offered a far more decentralized vision of the socialist state than the Fabians. By this time Orage had already begun to move toward "guild socialism," the type of socialism that would eventually dominate the *New Age*; guild socialism called for the replacement of capitalist control of industry "not by full State control, administered through schemes of municipal collectivism or nationalization, but, rather, by the control of the industrial workers themselves, organized into a network of communal associations based on the present trade unions" (Britain 11). "It was rather disingenuous of Orage," Britain

argues, "to suggest in public that Guild Socialist ideals could simply be hitched on to the Fabians' concerns when in private he was stressing the incompatibility of those ideals with Fabian collectivism as currently formulated" (171).

28. As Martin describes, the purchase came about when "Jackson applied to Shaw for financial help. The latter indicated that he would give them some of the royalties from *The Doctor's Dilemma*, which was then enjoying financial success in the West End; he suggested, however, that they 'raid the City first', as others would be more willing to help if they did not know of his offer. Meanwhile, Orage was doing just that. One morning early in 1907, their post contained letters from Lewis Wallace, a merchant banker whom Orage had met in Theosophical circles, and Shaw, each offering to contribute five hundred pounds towards the purchase and operation of *The New Age*" (24).

29. As explained earlier in the notes to this chapter, guild socialism called for the capitalist control of industry to be handed over to the industrial workers themselves, not the state.

30. My analysis focuses on the paper's early years so as to maintain a rough chronological synchronicity with the other works under study in this book.

31. Yeats and Farr would later work together to formulate a system of uniting music and poetry, intermingling spoken verse with musical notes. See Johnson or Morrison for more on this effort and its consequences for modernist poetry and drama.

32. This is not to present theosophy or occultism as adequate avenues to empowerment for women leaders like Besant. Although many politically engaged women did find voice, authority, and influence by way of spiritualist movements (see Despard's *Theosophy and the Woman's Movement*), these fringe groups could also distract from more overt forms of activism and public engagement, because, as Alex Owen puts it, they offered "a compromised understanding of power" (242).

Chapter 6

1. Allen believed in "free love as the thing closest to natural selection. Individuals need to be free to act on impulsive desire and form spontaneous sexual unions" (Cameron 290). Allen, along with other socialists interested in sexuality, such as Olive Schreiner, Edward Carpenter, Havelock Ellis, and Karl Pearson, was influenced in this belief by the work of Herbert Spencer, which helped them "imagine a new theory of human beings' sexual reproduction as part of the larger, natural forces of social evolution" (282).

2. The subtitle of the *Adult* varied from "An Unconventional Journal" to "The Journal of Sex," to "A Journal for the Free Discussion of Tabooed Topics."

3. Bax, when not occupied with Marxist theory, was fond of penning antifeminist propaganda, such as *The Fraud of Feminism* (1913), *The Legal Subjection of Men* (1908), and "Outraged Feminism" (*Social Democrat*, April 1901: 100–4), a predilection that has baffled many historians, given Bax's close ties to staunch socialist feminists such as Eleanor Marx. See Karen Hunt (*Equivocal Feminists*) for more on this topic.

4. Bedborough, in pleading guilty to the charges, was viewed by many as having betrayed the cause of free expression and the opportunity that his trial presented. The 1899 *Labour Annual* argued: "One of the strongest committees in defence of the freedom of the Press that has ever been got together was organized. . . . A very con-

siderable agitation had been carried on. . . . The Free Press Defence Committee had brought the case in sight of certain victory, and had collected about £500 for the defence, when Bedborough and the police effected a compromise behind the backs of the committee" (80).

5. *Home Links* was an ethical socialist journal edited and published by A. Gottschling, and even though it was not as thoroughgoing as the Legitimation League or the *Adult*, the journal claimed in its debut issue that in the society of its imagining "women will mutually and harmoniously devise the terms for Sexual Unions and their progeny; and room there will be none for any dictates from the man-Bishops and man-Parliaments that have proved unfair and unjust to the cause of women and children" (February 1897: 10). The journal reported regularly on free love, the Bedborough case, and the cause of free speech; it was another site within the radical press for the intermingling of socialist, free love, and free print principles.

6. Carpenter's pamphlet "An Unknown People" garnered praise in the December 1897 issue of the *Adult*: "Like most of Mr. Carpenter's work it is strikingly readable, tantalizingly reticent, and seductively encouraging to deeper study of the subjects he discusses. *An Unknown People* are 'Urnings,' or homosexualists" (74). Carpenter's *Love's Coming of Age* was reviewed in the *Adult* at greater length by "Sagitarrius" in February 1898. The review was positive, but Sagitarrius complained that Carpenter confused "sex-cell hunger" with love: "The prime duty of the sex reformer to-day is . . . to rescue that 'sex-cell hunger' from the obloquy which has been cast upon it, to enforce that fact that all appetites and functions of the body are clean and wholesome" (13). Sheila Rowbotham's biography of Carpenter describes his careful balancing act as a writer who tried to depict his radical sexual ideals in as user-friendly a manner as possible for greatest potential impact; this moderated tone diminished Carpenter's ideas for a reviewer like Sagitarrius. The April 1898 issue of the *Adult* included a notice of Wilde's "Ballad of Reading Gaol": "Mr. Wilde has signed the ballad by the name he bore during those terrible months of suffering—needless suffering—suffering which had neither justice nor sense for its excuse" (89).

7. Emil Ruedebusch was an American advocate of free love and the author of *The Old and New Ideal*, for which he was tried for obscenity.

8. Popular association of socialism with free love was rooted in misconceptions about early nineteenth-century Owenism (see Barbara Taylor). As a radical secularist, Charles Bradlaugh had been tarred with the free love brush in 1875, even though, as Annie Besant noted, his "views on marriage were conservative rather than revolutionary" (*Our Corner*, December 1884: 329). Years later, radicals continued to be vulnerable to the free love charge, as was abundantly evident in the fall 1907 election in the working-class district of Kirkdale, when the candidate John Hill—not a socialist but a Labour candidate with strong socialist support—was undone by his links to the socialist movement. His opponents used his socialist support against him, painting him as an advocate of free love and state custody of children (Pierson, *British Socialism* 153–54). Earlier that year Victor Grayson had successfully overcome such tactics in a Colne Valley election, but Harry Quelch's article "Socialism and Sex Relations" in the *Social Democrat* warned against escalating use of such tactics: "Good, orthodox people are warned off with the cry that Socialists are Atheists and advocates of 'Free Love,'

and that the victory of Socialism means the dethronement of God and the abolition of the institution of marriage" (8 August 1907: 457–58).

9. Badcock expanded on this point in a speech reported in the January 1898 issue of the *Adult*: "If we attract to our midst the obscure Judes and discarded Sues of society, we should do them a great deal of good" (111).

10. Warne and Colligan offer a summary of critical response to Allen's novel since the 1970s and claim, "Without exception, recent critics express dissatisfaction with the gender politics of Allen's novel" (22).

11. A brief biography of Emma Wardlaw Best and her partner, Arthur Wastall, appeared in the 1898 *Labour Annual*: "Their recent 'Free Union' will interest many of our readers. They left England a few months ago. . . . Before their departure they issued to their friends 'A Marriage Protest and Free Union Declaration.' . . . They enter the relationship with the intention of a life-long partnership, but entirely free of any bond save love, and that failing, the union will be dissolved" (209–10).

12. The novel was originally published in the Keynotes Series, "a group of ideologically progressive texts published by John Lane for Bodley Head in the 1890s" (Warne and Colligan 21).

13. *Seaweed* was serialized from March to August 1898, but the serialization was not complete. No part was published in the September 1898 issue, the last monthly issue of the journal to appear. The cessation of the journal was explained on the issue's back cover: "The University Press, through the persistent and systematic boycott, of which we have informed our readers in the last three numbers, is compelled to discontinue the publication of the UNIVERSITY MAGAZINE as a monthly periodical. . . . Of booksellers in the country about fifty per cent have yielded to the threat contained in an anonymous letter, which has been forwarded to them from a person or party interested in the suppression of this Magazine, and therefore our means of distribution have been reduced to such an extent that the further publication . . . would cause a very considerable loss to the proprietors."

14. The novel was later published in the United States under the title *Kit's Woman*.

15. The October 1893 issue of *Seed Time* reports on two of Edith Ellis's lectures: "Democracy in the Kitchen" and "A Noviciate for Marriage." In the latter lecture Ellis "pleads very strongly for a much more thorough knowledge of each other's habits and idiosyncrasies than the present conventional engagement can afford the affianced couple" (14). A biography of Ellis in the 1895 *Labour Annual* states that she "has lectured for 8 years on social subjects; in general sympathy with Fabian standpoint and New Fellowship ethics, but emphasises need for making life beautiful as well as simple and for living closer to nature; has devoted special attention to sex questions; monogamist; . . . advocates some preliminary sexual experience before entering into the binding contract of marriage" (169).

16. Ellis toned down the Cornish dialect in a later edition of her novel, but it is quite strong in the 1898 edition published by the University Press.

17. Ellis's novel, in its later incarnation as *Kit's Woman*, was reviewed in the 21 November 1907 issue of the *New Age*, a socialist paper and key journal of early literary modernism discussed in Chapter 5, but the unsigned review aligned the book with a feminized culture of novels rather than with a virile new literary movement: "Novels

dealing with extreme examples of sex psychology and morality are written almost exclusively by women for women. Certainly we should not expect to find a story like this written by a man" (76).

18. Somewhat later, H. G. Wells was another socialist who tried to link socialism with sex reform, as we see in his free love novels *Ann Veronica* (1909) and *In the Days of the Comet* (1906). In *Ann Veronica* the title character elopes with her married science instructor, and *Days of the Comet* depicts a free love society in a future socialist utopia. By the end of the first decade of the twentieth century, Wells had become a focal point for those who sought to damage socialism by associating it with free love. Despite the drift of his novels and his own penchant for seduction, Wells—somewhat disingenuously—fought back against the association in the pages of the *New Age*. He wrote in the 17 October 1907 issue, "My name is frequently given by the Anti-Socialists as an advocate of 'free love' . . . I have never advocated 'free love'" (392).

19. Some of the poems in this volume originally appeared in the radical press, but not this poem, as far as I have found.

20. The legacy of radical anti-Malthusianism is still evident at the end of the century, however, in works such as Robert Blatchford's pamphlet *Imprudent Marriages*, which objects to the idea that "a great deal of the poverty and misery of the poor is caused by 'imprudent marriages'" (3).

21. Later, Besant would defend birth control out of feminist (not just free print) principle, but the emphasis in the trial was on freedom of information. In the 1 August 1885 issue of *Our Corner*, Besant would claim: "If the burden of maternity which weighs on women had to be borne by men, the whole of the prejudice against preventive checks would promptly vanish" (98).

22. The trial and imprisonment of G. W. Foote, editor of *Freethinker*, for blasphemy in 1883 essentially severed the bond between secularism and free print agitation, as Joss Marsh describes in *Word Crimes*. At the third trial in the case, "Lord Coleridge handed down a ruling . . . that fundamentally changed the definition of the crime of blasphemy" (154): "I now lay it down as law that, if the decencies of controversy are observed, even the fundamentals of religion may be attacked without a person being guilty of blasphemous libel" (qtd. in Marsh 160). Foote brought about this ruling by arguing convincingly in court that blasphemy laws were primarily enforced out of political motivations and class interests.

23. Among feminists, too, birth control was a controversial issue, and free love and sexual radicalism were generally looked on with disfavor: "The leaders of the more militant [Women's Social and Political Union] in the 1900s were . . . suspicious of sexual radicalism. Christabel Pankhurst was prepared to use direct action but she had no sympathy for a growing current in the feminist movement that was asserting active female sexuality" (Rowbotham and Weeks 17). See Bland for more on feminist opposition to birth control.

24. Pease describes how this sensitive survey was carried out, in terms that may lead us to question its findings: "Carefully drafted enquiry forms were sent out to all members of the Society except unmarried women" (161). Webb initially published his findings in the *Times* "to secure the most generally impressive publicity" (162).

25. Sexuality was a key site of conflict during a time that saw deep tensions on the left between liberalism and state socialism. The broad contours of this conflict

are especially apparent in the "New Liberalism" journal *Progressive Review,* founded in 1896, which stated in its first issue: "To the cause of political, industrial, religious, and educational freedom . . . [the Liberal Party] has rendered many and illustrious services." But its negative conception of freedom "will not enable it to carry to completion the task of securing genuine economic freedom, still less . . . to secure the material and moral welfare of the people" (October 1896: 4). The journal calls for a "fuller and more rational conception of the State as an instrument for social progress" (7).

26. The *Clarion* writers, despite their apparent populism, were more bothered by cheap, popular, sensational literature than by highbrow novels about sex. The article "Fiction and Morals" in the 14 March 1896 issue (not to be confused with "Morals and Fiction" in the 11 January 1896 issue) argued: "The popular sensation novels—written, we regret to say, for the most part by women—are most pernicious trash. So are the profitable 'shilling shockers.' . . . These stories . . . create a false standard of conduct in the weak heads of their readers" (86).

27. Most of the *Clarion's* female writers would not have labeled themselves feminist, because that term was thought by many socialists to have an individualist connotation, but they nonetheless fitted more recent conceptions of the term.

28. For more on women's columns across the socialist press, see Hunt and Hannam. Among socialist papers, the *Clarion* was an early adopter of the women's column. "Fabianne" authored the paper's first stab at a "woman's letter" ("'Woman's Letter' from the Mountains") on 5 January 1895 (8).

29. Dawson's column would run until 1911, when she left the *Clarion* as a result of political differences with Blatchford (Hunt and Hannam 179). Her prominence in the Clarion movement is due not only to her work on the women's column but also to her idea to start the Clarion Van, a repurposed horse-drawn soup caravan staffed by a few women Clarionettes and aided by a young boy. On summer tours the women in the Clarion Van would travel around various English districts, holding speeches, rallies, and lectures and distributing literature to advocate for socialism. Dawson first proposed the idea of the van in "Our Woman's Letter" (*Clarion,* 29 February 1896: 72).

30. The *Labour Leader* had little patience for the detractors of *Esther Waters:* "The feature of this book, that has caused so much public comment, is the plain speech used in reference to the great question of sex. . . . We would be lacking in our sense of duty to our readers, if we did not condemn most thoroughly, the spirit that could place such a stupid censorship over a book that deserves the esteem of all those who can appreciate good and conscientious work" (19 May 1894: 14).

31. Keeling also reported a lively epistolary response to her women's column and described letters from poor women "sadly in need of many necessary things of life" and letters from middle-class women seeking "to relieve the monotony of a life spent amidst highly respectable and well-to-do surroundings" (*Clarion,* 16 March 1895: 82).

32. Dawson's real name is variously spelled in the literature as "Mrs. D. Middleton Worrall" (Hannam and Hunt 75; Hunt and Hannam 171).

33. Recent work by Hannam, Karen Hunt, and Livesey attributes the column to Pearce, but other critics, such as Brake and Demoor, Collette, Hopkin, and Steedman, have attributed it to Hardie.

34. The *Clarion* did not, however, run advertisements for abortifacient patent medicines, although such ads were common in the late Victorian press. In general, patent medicines were among the worst offenders of capitalist puffery, but ads for abortifacient medicines did run in the *Labour Leader*, typically near the woman's column.

35. Dawson did charge for most of these ads, so she did not run them entirely out of biopolitical philanthropy. She explains her policy on this in the 17 October 1896 issue of the *Clarion*: "Many who send advertisements for my columns are forgetting that the charge is 18 words for 6d., except in the cases of young women wanting work who really cannot afford to pay anything. Only these are inserted free" (336).

Conclusion

1. Modern abstract painter Kandinsky was deeply influenced by theosophy and the theosophical notion of thought forms. As Materer notes of Kandinsky's "On the Spiritual in Art," "Besant's and Leadbeater's *Thought-Forms* influenced Kandinsky's theory that emotions were vibrations that can be expressed visually. Kandinsky's ideas reached the vorticists through Edward Wadsworth's translation of 'On the Spiritual,' which appeared in BLAST No. 1 (1914). Pound borrowed from Kandinsky freely and without acknowledgment for his BLAST statement (entitled 'Vortex') about vorticist art" (34).

2. See Amanda Anderson for more on the critical tendency to read aesthetic modernity as an oppositional reaction to Enlightenment modernity.

Works Cited

Archives and Collections

British Library ms	British Library manuscripts, London
Fabian Society Archive	Fabian Society Archive, London School of Economics
John Rylands Library	John Rylands Library, University of Manchester
Sixsmith Collection	C. F. Sixsmith Edward Carpenter Collection, John Rylands Library, University of Manchester
Socialist League Archive	Socialist League Archive, International Institute of Social History, Amsterdam
W. T. Stead Papers	Churchill Archives Centre, Churchill College, Cambridge

Radical Periodicals

The Adult
The Alarm
The Anarchist (Glasgow)
The Anarchist (London)
Christian Socialist
Clarion
Clarion Cyclist's Journal
Common Good
Common Sense
Commonweal
The Conference Record
Daily Herald
The Dawn
Democrat
Fabian News
Fiery Cross
Free Exchange
Freedom
Freiheit

Hammersmith Socialist Record
Home Links
Justice
Labour Annual
Labour Champion
Labour Elector
Labour Journal
Labour Leader
Labour Prophet
Liberty
The Link
New Age
New Statesman
Notebook of the Shelley Society
Our Corner
The Practical Socialist
Progressive Review
The Radical
Radical Leader
The Reformers' Yearbook
Revolutionary Review
Scout
Seed Time
Social Democrat
To-Day
The Torch
University Magazine and Free Review
Workers' Cry
Workers' Herald
Workman's Times

Books, Articles, and Pamphlets

Adamson, Glenn. *Thinking Through Craft*. Oxford: Berg, 2007.

Agresti, Olivia Rossetti. *The Anecdotage of an Interpreter*, unpublished memoir (1958). Housed in the Oral History Collection, Columbia University.

Alexander, James. *Shaw's Controversial Socialism*. Gainesville: UP of Florida, 2008.

Allen, Grant. *The Woman Who Did*. Oxford: Oxford UP, 1995.

Altick, Richard. *The English Common Reader: A Social History of the Mass Reading Public, 1800–1900*. 2nd ed. Columbus: Ohio State UP, 1998.

Anderson, Amanda. "Victorian Studies and the Two Modernities." *Victorian Studies* 47.2 (2005): 195–203.

Anderson, Benedict. *Imagined Communities: Reflections on the Origin and Spread of Nationalism*. London: Verso, 1983.

Arata, Stephen. "On Not Paying Attention." *Victorian Studies* 46.2 (2004): 193–205.

Ardis, Ann L. "The Dialogics of Modernism(s) in the *New Age*." *Modernism/Modernity* 14.3 (2007): 407–34.

———. *Modernism and Cultural Conflict, 1880–1922*. Cambridge: Cambridge UP, 2002.

———. "Staging the Public Sphere: Magazine Dialogism and the Prosthetics of Authorship at the Turn of the Twentieth Century." *Transatlantic Print Culture*. Ed. Ardis and Collier. Houndmills, UK: Palgrave, 2008. 30–47.

Ardis, Ann, and Patrick Collier. Introduction. *Transatlantic Print Culture*. Ed. Ardis and Collier. Houndmills, UK: Palgrave, 2008. 1–12.

———, eds. *Transatlantic Print Culture, 1880–1940: Emerging Media, Emerging Modernisms*. Houndmills, UK: Palgrave, 2008.

Arnold, Matthew. "Shelley." *The Complete Prose Works*. Vol. 11. Ed. R. H. Super. Ann Arbor: University of Michigan Press, 1977. 305–27.

Arscott, Caroline. "William Morris: Decoration and Materialism." *Marxism and the History of Art: From William Morris to the New Left*. Ed. Andrew Hemingway. Ann Arbor: U of Michigan P, 2006. 9–27.

———. *William Morris and Edward Burne-Jones: Interlacings*. New Haven, CT: Yale UP, 2008.

Aveling, Edward, and Eleanor Marx Aveling. *Shelley's Socialism*. 1888. London: Journeyman, 1979.

Badcock, [John]. *Slaves to Duty*. London: William Reeves, 1894.

———. *When Love Is Liberty and Nature Law*. Lecture read before the Walthamstow Library Institute on March 3, 1893. London: Reeves, 1893.

Barish, Jonas. *The Antitheatrical Prejudice*. Berkeley: U of California P, 1981.

Barnard, Sylvia M. *To Prove I'm Not Forgot: Living and Dying in a Victorian City*. Manchester, UK: Manchester UP, 1990.

Barringer, Tim. *Men at Work: Art and Labour in Victorian Britain*. New Haven, CT: Yale UP, 2005.

Barrow, Logie. "Socialism in Eternity: The Ideology of Plebeian Spiritualists, 1853–1913." *History Workshop Journal* 9 (1980): 37–69.

Barrow, Logie, and Ian Bullock. *Democratic Ideas and the British Labour Movement, 1880–1914*. Cambridge: Cambridge UP, 1996.

Battle, John. *Tom Maguire: Socialist and Poet*. Leeds: Ford Maguire Society, 1997.

Beaumont, Matthew. "Cacotopianism, the Paris Commune, and England's Anti-Communist Imaginary, 1870–1900." *ELH* 73 (2006): 465–87.

———. "Influential Force: *Shafts* and the Diffusion of Knowledge at the *Fin de Siècle*." *19: Interdisciplinary Studies in the Long Nineteenth Century* 3 (2006): 1–19.

———. "*News from Nowhere* and the Here and Now: Reification and the Representation of the Present in Utopian Fiction." *Victorian Studies* 47.1 (2004): 33–54.

———. *Utopia Ltd.: Ideologies of Social Dreaming in England, 1870–1900*. Leiden: Brill, 2005.

———. "William Reeves and Late-Victorian Radical Publishing: Unpacking the Bellamy Library." *History Workshop Journal* 55 (2003): 91–110.

Besant, Annie. *Annie Besant: An Autobiography*. London: T. Fisher Unwin, 1893.

———. *Autobiographical Sketches*. 1885. Serialized in *Our Corner* (1 January 1884 to 1 June 1885).

———. *Autobiographical Sketches.* Ed. Carol Hanbery MacKay. Peterborough: Broadview, 2009.

———. *Blasphemy.* London: Besant & Bradlaugh, 1882.

———. *Communication Between Different Worlds.* 1909. 2nd ed. Adyar, India: Theosophical Publishing House, 1913.

———. "How London Amuses Itself." *Our Corner* July 1886: 13–23 and August 1886: 107–16.

———. "Why I Am a Socialist." *Our Corner* 1 September 1886: 157–63.

Besant, Walter. *All Sorts and Conditions of Men.* London: Chatto & Windus, 1883.

Bevir, Mark. "A Theosophist in India." *Imperial Objects: Essays on Victorian Women's Emigration and the Unauthorized Imperial Experience.* Ed. Rita S. Kranidis. New York: Twayne, 1998. 211–27.

Birch, Dinah. Introduction. *Fors Clavigera: Letters to the Workmen and Labourers of Great Britain.* By John Ruskin. Edinburgh: Edinburgh UP, 2000. xxxiii–xlix.

Black, Clementina. *An Agitator.* 1894. New York: Harper, 1895.

Bland, Lucy. "Heterosexuality, Feminism, and *The Freewoman* Journal in Early Twentieth-Century England." *Women's History Review* 4.1 (1995): 5–23.

Blatchford, Robert. *Imprudent Marriages.* Chicago: Charles H. Kerr, 1899.

———. *Merrie England.* London: Clarion, 1893. Rpt. London: Journeyman, 1976.

———. *My Favourite Books.* London: Clarion, 1900.

———. *The New Religion.* London: Clarion, n.d.

———. *The Sorcery Shop: An Impossible Romance.* London: Clarion, 1907.

Blavatsky, Helena Petrovna. *The Secret Doctrine: The Synthesis of Science, Religion, and Philosophy.* Vol. 1. 1888. Adyar, India: Theosophical Publishing House, 1962.

Boos, Florence S. "'The Banners of the Spring to Be': The Dialectical Pattern of Morris's Later Poetry." *English Studies* 81.1 (2000): 14–40.

———. "The 'Homely Muse' in Her Diurnal Setting: The Periodical Poems of 'Marie,' Janet Hamilton, and Fanny Forrester." *Victorian Poetry* 39.2 (2001): 255–85.

Boos, Florence S., and William Boos. "*News from Nowhere* and Victorian Socialist-Feminism." *Nineteenth-Century Contexts* 14.1 (1990): 3–32.

Boos, Florence S., and Carole Silver, eds. *Socialism and the Literary Artistry of William Morris.* Columbia: U of Missouri P, 1990.

Brake, Laurel. "Journalism and Modernism, Continued: The Case of W. T. Stead." *Transatlantic Print Culture.* Ed. Ann Ardis and Patrick Collier. Houndmills, UK: Palgrave, 2008. 149–66.

———. *Print in Transition, 1850–1910: Studies in Media and Book History.* Houndmills, UK: Palgrave, 2001.

Brake, Laurel, and Marysa Demoor, eds. *Dictionary of Nineteenth Century Journalism.* London: British Library, 2009.

Brantlinger, Patrick. "'News from Nowhere': Morris's Socialist Anti-Novel." *Victorian Studies* 19.1 (1975): 35–49.

———. *The Threat of Mass Literacy in Nineteenth-Century British Fiction.* Bloomington: Indiana UP, 1998.

Bristow, Joseph. Introduction. *The Fin de Siècle Poem: English Literary Culture and the 1890s.* Ed. Bristow. Athens: Ohio UP, 2005. 1–46.

Britain, Ian. *Fabianism and Culture: A Study in British Socialism and the Arts c. 1884–1918.* Cambridge: Cambridge UP, 1982.

Brown, Tony. "Edward Carpenter and the Waste Land." *Review of English Studies* 34.135 (1983): 312–15.

Buzard, James. "Ethnography as Interruption: *News from Nowhere,* Narrative, and the Modern Romance of Authority." *Victorian Studies* 40.3 (1997): 445–74.

Caine, Barbara. "Beatrice Webb and the 'Woman Question.'" *History Workshop Journal* 14 (1982): 23–44.

Cameron, Brooke. "Grant Allen's *The Woman Who Did*: Spencerian Individualism and Teaching New Women to Be Mothers." *English Literature in Transition* 51.3 (2008): 281–301.

Carpenter, Edward, ed. *Chants of Labour: A Song Book of the People with Music.* London: Swan Sonnenschein, 1888.

———. *Homogenic Love, and Its Place in a Free Society.* "Printed for Private Circulation Only." Manchester, UK: Labour Press Society, 1894.

———. "Memoir." *Tom Maguire, A Remembrance.* By Tom Maguire. Manchester, UK: Labour Press Society, 1895. ix–xiii.

———. *Towards Democracy.* 2nd ed. Manchester, UK: John Heywood: 1885.

Carpenter, Edward, and George Barnefield. *The Psychology of the Poet Shelley.* London: Allen & Unwin, 1925.

Cave, Roderick. *Fine Printing and Private Presses: Selected Papers.* London: British Library, 2001.

Charney, Leo, and Vanessa R. Schwartz, eds. *Cinema and the Invention of Modern Life.* Berkeley: U of California P, 1995.

Chesterton, Gilbert K. *George Bernard Shaw.* New York: John Lane, 1909.

Clair, Colin. *A History of Printing in Britain.* London: Cassell, 1965.

Clarke, C. Allen. *The Knobstick.* 1893. Blackpool, UK: Ellis, 1906.

Cockerell, Sydney. "A Short History and Description of the Kelmscott Press." *A Note by William Morris on His Aims in Founding the Kelmscott Press: Together with a Short Description of the Press.* By William Morris. London: Kelmscott, 1898. Rpt. in *The Ideal Book.* By Morris. Berkeley: U of California P, 1982. 79–88.

Collette, Christine. "Socialism and Scandal: The Sexual Politics of the Early Labour Movement." *History Workshop Journal* 23 (1987): 102–11.

Conolly, L. W. "*Mrs Warren's Profession* and the Lord Chamberlain." *Shaw* 24 (2004): 46–95.

Coolsen, James Gordon. "The Evolution of Selected Major English Socialist Periodicals, 1883–1889." Diss. American University, 1973.

Cox, R. G. *Thomas Hardy: The Critical Heritage.* London: Routledge, 1979.

Crane, Walter. *An Artist's Reminiscences.* London: Methuen, 1907.

———. *Cartoons for the Cause, 1886–1896.* London: Twentieth Century Press, 1896. Rpt. London: Marx Memorial Library, 1976.

———. Introduction. *The Easter Art Annual for 1898: The Work of Walter Crane with Notes by the Artist.* Extra issue of *Art Journal* (1898): 1–32.

———. *William Morris to Whistler: Papers and Addresses on Art and Craft and the Commonweal.* London: G. Bell & Sons, 1911.

Crary, Jonathan. *Suspensions of Perception: Attention, Spectacle, and Modern Culture.* Cambridge, MA: MIT P, 2001.

———. *Techniques of the Observer: On Vision and Modernity in the Nineteenth Century.* Cambridge, MA: MIT P, 1992.

Curran, Stuart. *Shelley's Cenci: Scorpions Ringed with Fire.* Princeton, NJ: Princeton UP, 1970.

Daniels, Kay. "Emma Brooke: Fabian, Feminist, and Writer." *Women's History Review* 12.2 (2003): 153–68.

Davis, Tracy C. *George Bernard Shaw and the Socialist Theatre.* Westport, CT: Greenwood, 1994.

Dawson, Oswald, ed. *Bar Sinister and Licit Love: The First Biennial Proceedings of the Legitimation League.* London: Reeves, 1895.

Delap, Lucy, and Maria DiCenzo. "Transatlantic Print Culture: The Anglo-American Feminist Press and Emerging 'Modernities.'" *Transatlantic Print Culture.* Ed. Ann Ardis and Patrick Collier. Houndmills, UK: Palgrave, 2008. 48–65.

Demoor, Marysa. "In the Beginning, There Was *The Germ*: The Pre-Raphaelites and 'Little Magazines.'" *The Oxford Critical and Cultural History of Modernist Magazines.* Vol. I. Ed. Peter Brooker and Andrew Thacker. Oxford: Oxford UP, 2009. 51–65.

Derrida, Jacques. *Dissemination.* Trans. Barbara Johnson. Chicago: U of Chicago P, 1981.

———. *Of Grammatology.* Trans. Gayatri Chakravorty Spivak. Baltimore: Johns Hopkins UP, 1976.

Despard, C. *Theosophy and the Woman's Movement.* London: Theosophical Publishing Society, 1913.

Dettmar, Kevin J. H., and Stephen Watt, eds. *Marketing Modernisms: Self-Promotion, Canonization, and Rereading.* Ann Arbor: U of Michigan P, 1996.

Dierkes-Thrun, Petra. "Incest and the Trafficking of Women in *Mrs. Warren's Profession*: 'It Runs in the Family.'" *English Literature in Transition* 49.3 (2006): 293–310.

Dietrich, Richard Farr. *Bernard Shaw's Novels.* Gainesville: UP of Florida, 1996.

Dixon, Joy. *Divine Feminine: Theosophy and Feminism in England.* Baltimore: Johns Hopkins UP, 2001.

Donaldson, Laura. "Boffin in Paradise, or the Artistry of Reversal in *News from Nowhere.*" *Socialism and the Literary Artistry of William Morris.* Ed. Florence S. Boos and Carole Silver. Columbia: U of Missouri P, 1990. 26–37.

Dowling, Linda. *The Vulgarization of Art: The Victorians and Aesthetic Democracy.* Charlottesville: UP of Virginia, 1996.

Dunlap, Joseph R. *The Book That Never Was.* New York: Oriole, 1971.

Eagleton, Terry. "The Flight to the Real." *Cultural Politics at the Fin de Siècle.* Ed. Sally Ledger and Scott McCracken. Cambridge: Cambridge UP, 1995. 11–21.

Eisenstein, Sergei. "Dickens, Griffith, and the Film Today." *Film Form.* Ed. and Trans. Jay Leyda. San Diego: Harvest, 1977. 195–256.

Ellis, Edith. *Seaweed: A Cornish Idyll.* London: University Press, 1898.

Ellis, Havelock. *A Note on the Bedborough Trial.* London: University Press, 1898.

———. Preface. *The Pillars of Society and Other Plays.* By Henrik Ibsen. London: Walter Scott, 1888.

————. *Sexual Inversion: Studies in the Psychology of Sex.* Vol. 1. London: University Press, 1897.

Eltis, Sos. *Revising Wilde: Society and Subversion in the Plays of Oscar Wilde.* Oxford: Oxford UP, 1996.

Engels, Friedrich. Letter to Margaret Harkness, London, April 1888. Rpt. in *Manchester Shirtmaker.* By John Law. West Yorkshire, UK: Northern Herald Books, 2002. 83–85.

Foot, Paul. *Red Shelley.* London: Sidgwick, 1980.

Ford, Isabella. *On the Threshold.* London: Edward Arnold, 1895. (Facsimile edition printed by the British Library Historical Print Editions.)

Foucault, Michel. *The Birth of Biopolitics: Lectures at the College de France, 1978–79.* Ed. Michel Senellart. Trans. Graham Burchell. Houndmills, UK: Palgrave, 2008.

————. *The History of Sexuality: An Introduction.* Vol. 1. Trans. Robert Hurley. New York: Vintage, 1990.

————. "Omnes et Singulatim: Towards a Critique of 'Political Reason.'" *The Essential Works of Foucault, 1954–1984.* Ed. Paul Rabinow and Nikolas Rose. New York: New Press, 2003. 180–201.

Franc, Miriam A. *Ibsen in England.* Boston: Four Seas, 1919.

Francis, Pat. "Socialism and the Art of Printing." *History Workshop Journal* 23 (1987): 154–58.

Frankel, Oz. *States of Inquiry: Social Investigations and Print Culture in Nineteenth-Century Britain and the United States.* Baltimore: Johns Hopkins UP, 2006.

Frye, Northrop. "The Meeting of Past and Future in William Morris." *Studies in Romanticism* 21.3 (1982): 303–18.

Gagnier, Regenia. *Idylls of the Marketplace: Oscar Wilde and the Victorian Public.* Stanford, CA: Stanford UP, 1986.

————. *The Insatiability of Human Wants: Economics and Aesthetics in Market Society.* Chicago: U of Chicago P, 2000.

————. *Subjectivities: A History of Self-Representation in Britain, 1832–1920.* Oxford: Oxford UP, 1991.

Gandhi, Leela. *Affective Communities: Anticolonial Thought, Fin-de-Siècle Radicalism, and the Politics of Friendship.* Durham, NC: Duke UP, 2006.

Garnett, Edward. *The Paradox Club.* London: T. Fisher Unwin, 1888.

Genet, Jacqueline. "The Artistic Background." *The Book in Ireland.* Ed. Jacqueline Genet, Sylvie Mikowski, and Fabienne Garcier. Cambridge: Cambridge Scholars Press, 2006. 2–47.

Genz, Marcella D. *A History of the Eragny Press.* London: Oak Knoll, 2004.

Gilmartin, Kevin. *Print Politics: The Press and Radical Opposition in Early Nineteenth-Century England.* Cambridge: Cambridge UP, 1996.

Gissing, George. *The Nether World.* 1889. Ed. Stephen Gill. New York: Oxford UP, 1992.

Glasier, John Bruce. *J. Bruce Glasier: A Memorial.* Ed. Wilfrid Whiteley. Manchester, UK: National Labour Press, [1920].

————. *William Morris and the Early Days of the Socialist Movement.* 1921. Bristol, UK: Thommes, 1994.

————. *Working Men Indeed!* Aberdeen, UK: James Leatham, 1890.

Green, Barbara. "The Feminist Periodical Press: Women, Periodical Studies, and Modernity." *Literature Compass* 6.1 (2009): 191–205.

———. "Feminist Things." *Transatlantic Print Culture.* Ed. Ann Ardis and Patrick Collier. Houndmills, UK: Palgrave, 2008. 66–79.

Grein, J. T. Preface. *Widowers' Houses.* By George Bernard Shaw. Independent Theatre Series of Plays. London: Henry & Co., 1893. v–vi.

Griffith, Gareth. *Socialism and Superior Brains: The Political Thought of Bernard Shaw.* London: Routledge, 1993.

Guy, Josephine, and Ian Small. *Oscar Wilde's Profession.* Oxford: Oxford UP, 2000.

Habermas, Jürgen. *The Structural Transformation of the Public Sphere.* 1962. Trans. Thomas Burger. Cambridge, MA: MIT P, 1989.

Hammond, Mary. *Reading, Publishing, and the Formation of Literary Taste in England, 1880–1914.* Aldershot, UK: Ashgate, 2006.

Hannam, June. "Women and the ILP, 1890–1914." *The Centennial History of the Independent Labour Party.* Ed. David James et al. Krumlin, Canada: Ryburn, 1992. 205–28.

Hannam, June, and Karen Hunt. *Socialist Women: Britain, 1880s to 1920s.* London: Routledge, 2002.

Hardy, Thomas. *Jude the Obscure.* Oxford: Oxford UP, 1985.

Harrison, Royden, Gillian B. Woolven, and Robert Duncan, eds. *The Warwick Guide to British Labour Periodicals 1790–1970.* Hassocks, UK: Harvester, 1977.

Haywood, Ian. "Encountering Time: Memory and Tradition in the Radical Victorian Press." *Encounters in the Victorian Press: Editors, Authors, Readers.* Ed. Laurel Brake and Julie F. Codell. Houndmills, UK: Palgrave, 2005. 69–87.

———. *The Revolution in Popular Literature: Print, Politics, and the People, 1790–1860.* Cambridge: Cambridge UP, 2004.

———. *Working-Class Fiction: From Chartism to Trainspotting.* Plymouth, UK: Northcote, 1997.

Helsinger, Elizabeth K. *Poetry and the Pre-Raphaelite Arts: Dante Gabriel Rossetti and William Morris.* New Haven, CT: Yale UP, 2008.

Henderson, Fred. *By the Sea and Other Poems.* 2nd ed. London: T. Fisher Unwin, 1892.

———. *Love Triumphant: A Series of Sonnets.* London: Jarrold & Sons, 1888.

Hewitt, Martin. "Why the Notion of Victorian Britain Does Make Sense." *Victorian Studies* 48.3 (2006): 395–438.

Hollis, Patricia. *The Pauper Press: A Study in Working-Class Radicalism of the 1830s.* Oxford: Oxford UP, 1970.

Holmes, Richard. *Shelley: The Pursuit.* Rev. ed. New York: New York Review Books, 2003.

Holroyd, Michael. *Bernard Shaw.* 5 vols. London: Chatto & Windus, 1988–1992.

Holzman, Michael. "Anarchism and Utopia: William Morris's *News from Nowhere.*" *ELH* 51.3 (1984): 589–603.

———. "The Encouragement and Warming of History: William Morris's *A Dream of John Ball.*" *Socialism and the Literary Artistry of William Morris.* Ed. Florence S. Boos and Carole Silver. Columbia: U of Missouri P, 1990. 98–116.

Honeyman, Katrina. *Well Suited: A History of the Leeds Clothing Industry, 1850–1990.* Oxford: Oxford UP, 2000.

Hopkin, Deian. "The Left-Wing Press and the New Journalism." *Papers for the Millions.* Ed. Joel H. Weiner. Westport, CT: Greenwood, 1988. 225–41.

Horkheimer, Max, and Theodor W. Adorno. *Dialectic of Enlightenment.* 1944. Trans. John Cumming. New York: Herder & Herder, 1972.

Houston, Natalie M. "Newspaper Poems: Material Texts in the Public Sphere." *Victorian Studies* 50.2 (2008): 233–42.

Hughes, Linda K., and Michael Lund. *The Victorian Serial.* Charlottesville: UP of Virginia, 1991.

Humpherys, Anne. "The Journal That Did: Form and Content in *The Adult* (1897–1899)." *Media History* 9.1 (2003): 63–78.

Huneault, Kristina. *Difficult Subjects: Working Women and Visual Culture, Britain 1880–1914.* Aldershot, UK: Ashgate, 2002.

Hunt, Karen. *Equivocal Feminists: The Social Democratic Federation and the Woman Question, 1884–1914.* Cambridge: Cambridge UP, 1996.

Hunt, Karen, and June Hannam. "Propagandising as Socialist Women: The Case of the Women Columns in British Socialist Newspapers, 1884–1914." *Propaganda: Political Rhetoric and Identity, 1300–2000.* Ed. Bertrand Taithe and Tim Thornton. Stroud, UK: Sutton, 1999. 167–82.

Hunt, Lynn, ed. *The Invention of Pornography: Obscenity and the Origins of Modernity, 1500–1800.* New York: Zone, 1993.

Ibsen, Henrik. *Ghosts. The Complete Major Prose Plays.* Trans. Rolf Fjelde. New York: Farrar, Straus, Giroux, 1978. 197–277.

———. *The Letters of Henrik Ibsen.* Trans. John Nilsen Laurvik and Mary Morison. New York: Fox, Duffield, 1905.

———. *The Pillars of Society and Other Plays.* Ed. Havelock Ellis. London: Walter Scott, 1888.

In Fine Print: William Morris as Book Designer. Catalog of an exhibition held at the William Morris Gallery & Brangwyn Gift, London. London: London Borough of Waltham Forest, Libraries and Arts Department, 1976.

Ingersoll, Robert G. *Oration on Thomas Paine.* London: Freethought, [1877].

Jaffe, Aaron. *Modernism and the Culture of Celebrity.* Cambridge: Cambridge UP, 2005.

Jameson, Fredric. *Archaeologies of the Future: The Desire Called Utopia and Other Science Fictions.* London: Verso, 2005.

———. *Marxism and Form: Twentieth-Century Dialectical Theories of Literature.* Princeton, NJ: Princeton UP, 1971.

———. *The Political Unconscious: Narrative as a Socially Symbolic Act.* Ithaca, NY: Cornell UP, 1981.

Janowitz, Anne. *Lyric and Labour in the Romantic Tradition.* Cambridge: Cambridge UP, 1998.

Joannou, Maroula. "The Angel of Freedom: Dora Marsden and the Transformation of *The Freewoman* into *The Egoist.*" *Women's History Review* 11.4 (2002): 595–611.

Johnson, Josephine. *Florence Farr: Bernard Shaw's 'New Woman.'* Gerrards Cross, UK: Colin Smythe, 1975.

Joll, James. *The Anarchists.* 2nd ed. London: Methuen, 1979.

Kearney, Anthony. "Reading Shelley: A Problem for Late Victorian English Studies." *Victorian Poetry* 36.1 (1998): 59–73.

Keating, Peter. *The Haunted Study: A Social History of the English Novel, 1875–1914.* London: Secker & Warburg, 1989.

Kelly, Katherine E. "Imprinting the Stage: Shaw and the Publishing Trade, 1883–1903." *The Cambridge Companion to George Bernard Shaw.* Ed. Christopher Innes. Cambridge: Cambridge UP, 1998. 25–54.

Kelvin, Norman. "Morris, the 1890s, and the Problematic Autonomy of Art." *Victorian Poetry* 34.3 (1996): 425–32.

Kennedy, Dennis. "The New Drama and the New Audience." *The Edwardian Theatre: Essays on Performance and the Stage.* Ed. Michael R. Booth and Joel H. Kaplan. Cambridge: Cambridge UP, 1996. 130–47.

Kershen, Anne J. *Uniting the Tailors: Trade Unionism Amongst the Tailoring Workers of London and Leeds, 1870–1939.* Ilford, UK: Cass, 1995.

King, Andrew, and John Plunkett, eds. *Victorian Print Media: A Reader.* Oxford: Oxford UP, 2005.

Knowlton, Charles. *Fruits of Philosophy: An Essay on the Population Question.* 1832. Ed. Annie Besant and Charles Bradlaugh. London: Freethought, [1876].

Kreilkamp, Ivan. *Voice and the Victorian Storyteller.* Cambridge: Cambridge UP, 2005.

Kropotkin, Peter. *Memoirs of a Revolutionist.* Boston: Houghton Mifflin, 1899.

Law, John [Margaret Harkness]. *A City Girl: A Realistic Story.* 1887. New York: Garland, 1984.

———. *A Manchester Shirtmaker.* 1890. Brighouse, UK: Northern Herald Books, 2002.

Ledbetter, Kathryn. *Tennyson and Victorian Periodicals: Commodities in Context.* Aldershot, UK: Ashgate, 2007.

Ledger, Sally. "Ibsen, the New Woman, and the Actress." *The New Woman in Fiction and in Fact: Fin de Siècle Feminisms.* Ed. Angelique Richardson and Chris Willis. Houndmills, UK: Palgrave, 2001. 79–93.

———. *The New Woman: Fiction and Feminism at the Fin de Siècle.* Manchester, UK: Manchester UP, 1997.

Liberman, Michael. "Major Textual Changes in William Morris's *News from Nowhere.*" *Nineteenth-Century Literature* 41.3 (1986): 349–56.

Livesey, Ruth. "Morris, Carpenter, Wilde, and the Political Aesthetics of Labor." *Victorian Literature and Culture* 32 (2004): 601–16.

———. "Socialism in Bloomsbury: Virginia Woolf and the Political Aesthetics of the 1880s." *Yearbook of English Studies* 37.1 (2007): 126–46.

———. *Socialism, Sex, and the Culture of Aestheticism in Britain, 1880–1914.* Oxford: Oxford UP, 2007.

Loewenstein F. E. *The History of a Famous Novel.* Privately printed in London, 1946.

Lord, Henrietta Frances. "Life of Henrik Ibsen." Introduction to *Nora.* By Henrik Ibsen. London: Griffith, 1882.

Lukács, Georg. "Realism in the Balance." *Aesthetics and Politics: The Key Texts of the Classic Debate Within German Marxism.* Ed. Ronald Taylor. London: Verso, 2002. 28–59.

Lyons, Neil A. *Robert Blatchford: The Sketch of a Personality: An Estimate of Some Achievements.* London: Clarion, 1910.

Mackay, Carol Hanbery. *Creative Negativity: Four Victorian Exemplars of the Female Quest.* Stanford, CA: Stanford UP, 2001.

MacKenzie, Norman, and Jeanne MacKenzie. *The Fabians.* New York: Simon & Schuster, 1977.

Maguire, Tom. *Machine-Room Chants.* London: Labour Leader, 1895.

———. *Tom Maguire, A Remembrance: Being a Selection from the Prose and Verse Writings of a Socialist Pioneer. With Memoirs.* Manchester, UK: Labour Press Society, 1895.

Maidment, Brian. "Readers Fair and Foul: John Ruskin and the Periodical Press." *The Victorian Periodical Press: Samplings and Soundings.* Ed. Joanne Shattock and Michael Wolff. Leicester, UK: Leicester UP, 1982. 29–58.

Maltz, Diana. *British Aestheticism and the Urban Working Classes, 1870–1900.* Houndmills, UK: Palgrave, 2006.

Mander, Raymond, and Joe Mitchenson. *Theatrical Companion to Shaw: A Pictorial Record of the First Performances of the Plays of GBS.* London: Rockliff, 1954.

"Manifesto of the Socialist League." *Commonweal* 1.1 (February 1885): 1.

Manifesto of the Socialist League. 2nd ed. London: Socialist League, 1885.

Marsh, Jan. "William Morris and Victorian Manliness." *William Morris: Centenary Essays.* Ed. Peter Faulkner and Peter Preston. Exeter, UK: U of Exeter P, 1999. 185–99.

Marsh, Josh. *Word Crimes: Blasphemy, Culture, and Literature in Nineteenth-Century England.* Chicago: U of Chicago P, 1998.

Marshik, Celia. "Parodying the £5 Virgin: Bernard Shaw and the Playing of *Pygmalion.*" *Yale Journal of Criticism* 13.2 (2000): 321–41.

Martin, Wallace. *The New Age Under Orage: Chapters in English Cultural History.* Manchester, UK: Manchester UP, 1967.

Marx, Karl, and Friedrich Engels. *The Communist Manifesto.* 1848. Rpt. in *Selected Writings.* By Karl Marx. Ed. Lawrence H. Simon. Indianapolis: Hackett, 1994. 157–86.

———. "Marx and Engels on the British Working Class Movement, 1879–1895," part IV. *Labour Monthly* (February 1934): 120–26.

———. "Marx and Engels on the British Working Class Movement, 1879–1895," part VII. *Labour Monthly* (May 1934): 308–13.

Materer, Timothy. *Modernist Alchemy: Poetry and the Occult.* Ithaca, NY: Cornell UP, 1995.

Mattison, Alf. "Memoir." *Tom Maguire, A Remembrance.* By Tom Maguire. Manchester, UK: Labour Press Society, 1895. xiii–xvi.

McCormack, Jerusha. "Engendering Tragedy: Toward a Definition of 1890s Poetry." *The Fin de Siècle Poem: English Literary Culture and the 1890s.* Ed. Joseph Bristow. Athens: Ohio UP, 2005. 47–68.

McGann, Jerome. *Black Riders: The Visible Language of Modernism.* Princeton, NJ: Princeton UP, 1993.

———. *The Textual Condition.* Princeton, NJ: Princeton UP, 1991.

McLaughlin, Kevin. *Paperwork: Fiction and Mass Mediacy in the Paper Age.* Philadelphia: U of Pennsylvania P, 2005.

McLuhan, Marshall. *The Gutenberg Galaxy: The Making of Typographic Man.* Toronto: U of Toronto P, 1962.

Menke, Richard. *Telegraphic Realism: Victorian Fiction and Other Information Systems.* Stanford, CA: Stanford UP, 2008.

Mineo, Ady. "Beyond the Law of the Father: The 'New Woman' in *News from Nowhere.*" *William Morris: Centenary Essays.* Ed. Peter Faulkner and Peter Preston. Exeter, UK: U of Exeter P, 1999. 200–206.

Moi, Toril. *Henrik Ibsen and the Birth of Modernism,* Oxford: Oxford UP, 2006.

Moore, George. *Esther Waters.* Oxford: Oxford UP, 1999.

Morley, John. "Anonymous Journalism." *Fortnightly Review* (September 1867). Rpt. in *Victorian Print Media: A Reader.* Ed. Andrew King and John Plunkett. Oxford: Oxford UP, 2005. 287–92.

Morris, William. "Art Under Plutocracy." University College, Oxford. 14 November 1883. Printed in *To-Day* (February/March 1884). Rpt. in *Political Writings.* 57–85.

———. *Collected Letters of William Morris.* Ed. Norman Kelvin. 4 vols. Princeton, NJ: Princeton UP, 1984.

———. *A Dream of John Ball.* 1888. *Three Works by William Morris.* Ed. A. L. Morton. New York: International Publishers, 1986. 33–114.

———. "The Early Illustration of Printed Books." London County Council School of Arts and Crafts. 14 December 1895. Summary printed in *British Colonial Printer and Stationer* (9 January 1896). Rpt. in *The Ideal Book.* 15–24.

———. "How I Became a Socialist." *Justice* (16 June 1894). Rpt. in *Political Writings.* 241–46.

———. "How We Live and How We Might Live." Hammersmith Branch of the Social Democratic Federation, Kelmscott House, London. 30 November 1884. Printed in *Commonweal* (4–11 June 1887). Rpt. in *Political Writings.* 134–58.

———. *The Ideal Book: Essays and Lectures on the Arts of the Book.* Ed. William S. Peterson. Berkeley: U of California P, 1982.

———. "'Master Printer Morris': A Visit to the Kelmscott Press." *Daily Chronicle* (22 February 1893). Rpt. in *The Ideal Book.* 95–98.

———. "Mr. William Morris at the Kelmscott Press." *English Illustrated Magazine* (April 1895). Rpt. in *The Ideal Book.* 98–106.

———. *News from Nowhere.* 1890. Ed. Stephen Arata. Peterborough, Canada: Broadview, 2003.

———. "A Note by William Morris on His Aims in Founding the Kelmscott Press." *Modern Art* 4 (winter 1896). Rpt. in *The Ideal Book.* 75–78.

———. "Poet as Printer." *Pall Mall Gazette* (12 November 1891). Rpt. in *The Ideal Book.* 89–95.

———. *Political Writings of William Morris.* Ed. A. L. Morton. New York: International Publishers, 1973.

———. Preface. *The Nature of Gothic: A Chapter of the Stones of Venice.* By John Ruskin. London: Kelmscott, 1892. i–v.

———. "The Society of the Future." Hammersmith Branch of the Socialist League, London. 13 November 1887. Printed in *Commonweal* (30 March 1889). Rpt. in *Political Writings.* 188–204.

———. "Some Thoughts on the Ornamented Manuscripts of the Middle Ages." *The Ideal Book.* 1–6.

———. *The Tables Turned, or Nupkins Awakened.* Athens: Ohio UP, 1994.

———. "Useful Work Versus Useless Toil." Hampstead Liberal Club. 16 January 1884. Printed as Socialist League pamphlet, 1885. Rpt. in *Political Writings*. 86–108.

Morrison, Mark S. *The Public Face of Modernism: Little Magazines, Audiences, and Reception, 1905–1920*. Madison: U of Wisconsin P, 2001.

Morton, A. L. Introduction. *The Political Writings of William Morris*. By William Morris. New York: International Publishers, 1973. 11–30.

Mutch, Deborah. *English Socialist Periodicals, 1880–1900: A Reference Source*. Aldershot, UK: Ashgate, 2005.

———. "Intemperate Narratives: Tory Tipplers, Liberal Abstainers, and Victorian British Socialist Fiction." *Victorian Literature and Culture* 36 (2008): 471–87.

Negt, Oskar, and Alexander Kluge. *Public Sphere and Experience: Toward an Analysis of the Bourgeois and Proletarian Public Sphere*. Trans. Peter Labanyi, Owen Daniel, and Assenka Oksiloff. Minneapolis: U of Minnesota P, 1993.

Nethercot, Arthur H. *The First Five Lives of Annie Besant*. Chicago: U of Chicago P, 1960.

Nord, Deborah Epstein. *Walking the Victorian Streets: Women, Representation, and the City*. Ithaca, NY: Cornell UP, 1995.

Oliphant, Margaret. "The Anti-Marriage League." *Blackwood's Edinburgh Magazine* 159 (January 1896): 135–49.

Ong, Walter. *Orality and Literacy: The Technologizing of the Word*. London: Routledge, 1982.

Orage, A. R. *Consciousness: Animal, Human, and Superhuman*. 1907. New York: Weiser, 1974.

Owen, Alex. *The Darkened Room: Women, Power, and Spiritualism in Late Victorian England*. Philadelphia: U of Pennsylvania P, 1990.

Paxton, Nancy L. "Feminism Under the Raj: Complicity and Resistance in the Writings of Flora Annie Steel and Annie Besant." *Women's Studies International Forum* 13.4 (1990): 333–46.

Pease, Edward R. *The History of the Fabian Society*. 1918. London: Cass, 1963.

Peterson, Linda. *Traditions of Victorian Women's Autobiography: The Poetics and Politics of Life Writing*. Charlottesville: UP of Virginia, 1999.

Peterson, William S. *Interrogating the Oracle: A History of the London Browning Society*. Athens: Ohio UP, 1969.

———. *The Kelmscott Press: A History of William Morris's Typographical Adventure*. Oxford: Clarendon, 1991.

Pierson, Stanley. *British Socialism: The Journey from Fantasy to Politics*. Cambridge, MA: Harvard UP, 1979.

———. "John Trevor and the Labor Church Movement in England, 1891–1900." *Church History* 29.4 (1960): 463–78.

Plato. *Phaedrus*. Trans. Alexander Nehamas and Paul Woodruff. *Plato: Complete Works*. Ed. John M. Cooper. Indianapolis: Hackett, 1997.

———. *Republic*. Trans. C. D. C. Reeve. Indianapolis: Hackett, 2004.

Plotz, John. "Nowhere and Everywhere: The End of Portability in William Morris's Romances." *ELH* 74 (2007): 931–56.

———. *Portable Property: Victorian Culture on the Move*. Princeton, NJ: Princeton UP, 2008.

Plunkett, John. *Queen Victoria: First Media Monarch*. Oxford: Oxford UP, 2003.

Preston, Sydney E., ed. *Notes on the First Performance of Shelley's Cenci*. Printed for private circulation, London, 1886.

Price, Leah. "From Ghostwriter to Typewriter: Delegating Authority at Fin de Siècle." *The Faces of Anonymity: Anonymous and Pseudonymous Publication from the Sixteenth to the Twentieth Century.* Ed. Robert J. Griffin. New York: Palgrave, 2003. 211–32.

Prins, Yopie. *Victorian Sappho.* Princeton, NJ: Princeton UP, 1999.

Puchner, Martin. *Stage Fright: Modernism, Anti-Theatricality, and Drama.* Baltimore: Johns Hopkins UP, 2002.

Pye, Denis. *Fellowship Is Life: The National Clarion Cycling Club, 1895–1995.* Bolton, UK: Clarion, 1995.

Quail, John. *The Slow Burning Fuse: The Lost History of the British Anarchists.* London: Granada, 1978.

Reiman, Donald H., ed. *The Romantics Reviewed: Contemporary Reviews of British Romantic Writers.* Part C: *Shelley, Keats, and London Radical Writers.* Vol. II: *Gentleman's Magazine—Theological Inquirer.* New York: Garland, 1972.

Robson, Catherine. "The Presence of Poetry: Response." *Victorian Studies* 50.2 (2008): 254–62.

Rose, Jonathan. *The Intellectual Life of the British Working Classes.* New Haven, CT: Yale UP, 2001.

Rossetti, William Michael. *A Memoir of Shelley.* London: Shelley Society, 1886.

———. *Selected Letters of William Michael Rossetti.* Ed. Roger W. Peattie. University Park: Pennsylvania State UP, 1990.

Rowbotham, Sheila. *Edward Carpenter: A Life of Liberty and Love.* London: Verso, 2008.

Rowbotham, Sheila, and Jeffrey Weeks. *Socialism and the New Life: The Personal and Sexual Politics of Edward Carpenter and Havelock Ellis.* London: Pluto, 1977.

Royle, Edward. *Radicals, Secularists, and Republicans: Popular Freethought in Britain, 1866–1915.* Manchester, UK: Manchester UP, 1980.

Rubery, Matthew. *The Novelty of Newspapers: Victorian Fiction After the Invention of News.* Oxford: Oxford UP, 2009.

Ruskin, John. *Fors Clavigera: Letters to the Workmen and Labourers of Great Britain.* Ed. Dinah Birch. Edinburgh: Edinburgh University Press, 2000.

Salmon, Nicholas. "The Revision of *A Dream of John Ball.*" *Journal of the William Morris Society* 10.2 (1993): 15–17.

Salt, Henry S. *Shelley as a Pioneer of Humanitarianism.* London: George Bell, 1902.

———. *Shelley's Principles: Has Time Refuted or Confirmed Them? A Retrospect and Forecast.* London: William Reeves, 1892.

Samuel, Raphael, Ewan MacColl, and Stuart Cosgrove. *Theatres of the Left, 1880–1935: Workers' Theatre Movements in Britain and America.* London: Routledge, 1985.

Scheckner, Peter. *An Anthology of Chartist Poetry: Poetry of the British Working Class, 1830s–1850s.* Madison, NJ: Fairleigh Dickinson UP, 1989.

Schuch, Elke. "'Shafts of Thought': New Wifestyles in Victorian Feminist Periodicals in the 1890s." *Nineteenth-Century Feminisms* 4 (2001): 119–35.

Sharp, William. *Life of Percy Bysshe Shelley.* London: Walter Scott, 1887.

Shaw, George Bernard. *Agitations: Letters to the Press, 1875–1950.* Ed. Dan H. Laurence and James Rambeau. New York: Ungar, 1985.

———. "Annie Besant's Passage Through Fabian Socialism." *Dr. Annie Besant: Fifty Years of Public Work.* Ed. David Graham Pole. London, 1924. 3–8.

———. *Candida.* [1898]. *Plays Pleasant.* 91–160.

———. *Cashel Byron's Profession.* London: Penguin, 1979.

———. *Collected Letters.* 4 vols. Ed. Dan H. Laurence. New York: Viking, 1985–1988.

———. "Epistle Dedicatory to Arthur Bingham Walkley." *Man and Superman.* 1–28.

———, ed. *Fabian Essays in Socialism.* London: Fabian Society, 1889.

———. *The Fabian Society: Its Early History.* Fabian Tract No. 41. London: Fabian Society, 1892. Rpt. 1914.

———. "Freedom and the State." [1888?]. *The Road to Equality.* 37–54.

———. "The Future of Marriage." [1885]. Rpt. in *Shaw* 16 (1996): 101–104.

———. "How to Become a Man of Genius." [1894]. *Selected Non-Dramatic Writings.* 341–46.

———. "The Illusions of Socialism." [1896]. *Selected Non-Dramatic Writings.* 406–26.

———. *The Irrational Knot.* New York: Brentanos, 1905.

———. "The Late Censor." *Saturday Review* (2 March 1895). Rpt. in *Our Theatres in the Nineties.* Vol. 2, 48–55.

———. *Love Among the Artists.* New York: Viking, 1962.

———. "Mainly About Myself." *Plays Unpleasant.* 7–27.

———. *Man and Superman.* New York: Bantam, 1963.

———. *Mrs Warren's Profession.* Peterborough, Canada: Broadview, 2005.

———. "The New Radicalism." *Road to Equality.* 19–36.

———. "Not Worth Reading." *Saturday Review* (24 April 1897). Rpt. in *Our Theatres in the Nineties.* Vol. 3, 111–15.

———. "Novels of My Nonage." *Cashel Byron's Profession.* 5–20.

———. *On Going to Church: Being the Preachment Which Treats of Church-Going, Art, and Some Other Themes.* East Aurora, NY: Roycroft, 1896.

———. "On the History of Fabian Economics." *The History of the Fabian Society.* By Edward Pease. 1918. London: Cass, 1963. 273–80.

———. *Our Theatres in the Nineties.* 3 vols. London: Constable, 1932.

———. *The Philanderer.* [1898]. *Plays Unpleasant.* 97–177.

———. *Plays Pleasant.* New York: Penguin, 2003.

———. *Plays Unpleasant.* London: Penguin, 2000.

———. Preface. *Fabian Essays in Socialism.* iii–iv.

———. Preface. *Irrational Knot.* vii–xxvi.

———. *Pygmalion.* [1912]. *George Bernard Shaw's Plays.* 2nd ed. Ed. Sandie Byrne. New York: Norton, 2002. 286–360.

———. *The Quintessence of Ibsenism.* [1891]. *Selected Non-Dramatic Writings.* Ed. Dan H. Laurence. 207–306.

———. Review of *The Importance of Being Earnest. Saturday Review* (23 February 1895). Rpt. in *Oscar Wilde: The Critical Heritage.* Ed. Karl Beckson. London: Routledge, 1970. 194–95.

———. *Selected Non-Dramatic Writings of Bernard Shaw.* Ed. Dan H. Laurence. Boston: Houghton Mifflin, 1965.

———. "Shaming the Devil About Shelley." [1892]. *Selected Non-Dramatic Writings.* 315–22.

———. "Socialism for Millionaires." [1896]. *Selected Non-Dramatic Writings.* 391–405.

————. *An Unsocial Socialist*. New York: Norton, 1972.

————. "Who I Am, and What I Think." [1901]. *Selected Non-Dramatic Writings*. 446–55.

————. *Widowers' Houses*. Independent Theatre Series of Plays. London: Henry & Co. 1893.

————. *Widowers' Houses*. [1893]. *Plays Unpleasant*. 29–96.

————. "William Morris as Actor and Dramatist." *Saturday Review* (10 October 1896). Rpt. in *Our Theatres in the Nineties*. Vol. 1, 209–16.

————. *William Morris as I Knew Him*. New York: Dodd, 1936.

————. *You Never Can Tell*. [1898]. *Plays Pleasant*. 209–316.

Shelley, Percy Bysshe. *The Cenci*. *Shelley's Poetry and Prose*. Ed. Donald H. Reiman and Sharon B. Powers. New York: Norton, 1977. 237–301.

————. *The Cenci: A Tragedy in Five Acts*. London: Published for the Shelley Society by Reeves & Turner, 1886.

Sigel, Lisa. *Governing Pleasures: Pornography and Social Change in England, 1815–1914*. New Brunswick, NJ: Rutgers UP, 2002.

Skoblow, Jeffrey. "Beyond Reading: Kelmscott and the Modern." *The Victorian Illustrated Book*. Ed. Richard Maxwell. Charlottesville: UP of Virginia, 2002. 239–58.

Smith, David. *Socialist Propaganda in the Twentieth-Century British Novel*. London: Macmillan, 1978.

Snyder, Carey. "Katherine Mansfield and the *New Age* School of Satire." *Journal of Modern Periodical Studies* 1.2 (2010): 125–58.

Stansky, Peter. *Redesigning the World: William Morris, the 1880s, and the Arts and Crafts*. Princeton, NJ: Princeton UP, 1985. Rpt. Palo Alto, CA: Society for the Promotion of Science and Scholarship, 1996.

St. Clair, William. *The Reading Nation in the Romantic Period*. Cambridge: Cambridge UP, 2004.

Stead, W. T. Introduction. *Side Lights*. By James Runciman. London: T. Fisher Unwin, 1893. xxi–xxix.

Steedman, Carolyn. *Childhood, Culture and Class in Britain, 1860–1931*. London: Virago, 1990.

Steele, Tom. *Alfred Orage and the Leeds Arts Club, 1893–1923*. Aldershot, UK: Scolar Press, 1990.

Stoddart, Judith. *Ruskin's Culture Wars: Fors Clavigera and the Crisis of Victorian Liberalism*. Charlottesville: UP of Virginia, 1998.

Stratton, Mary Chenoweth, ed. *Printing as Art: William Morris and His Circle of Influence*. Lewisburg, PA: Appletree Alley, 1994.

Strychacz, Thomas. *Modernism, Mass Culture, and Professionalism*. Cambridge: Cambridge UP, 1993.

Sypher, Eileen. "Fabian Anti-Novel: Shaw's An Unsocial Socialist." *Literature and History* 11.2 (1985): 241–53.

Taylor, Anne. *Annie Besant: A Biography*. Oxford: Oxford UP, 1992.

Taylor, Barbara. *Eve and the New Jerusalem: Socialism and Feminism in the Nineteenth Century*. Cambridge: Harvard UP, 1993.

Tennyson, Alfred. *Poems*. Vol. 3. 2nd ed. Ed. Christopher Ricks. Berkeley: U of California P, 1987.

Thirlwell, Angela. *William and Lucy: The Other Rossettis*. New Haven, CT: Yale UP, 2003.

Thomas, Matthew. *Anarchist Ideas and Counter-Cultures in Britain, 1880–1914*. Aldershot, UK: Ashgate, 2005.

Thompson, E. P. "Homage to Tom Maguire." *Essays in Labour History*. Ed. Asa Briggs and John Saville. London: Macmillan, 1967. 276–316.

———. *The Making of the English Working Class*. New York: Vintage, 1966.

———. *William Morris: Romantic to Revolutionary*. New York: Pantheon, 1955.

Tressell, Robert. *The Ragged Trousered Philanthropists*. Oxford: Oxford UP, 2005.

Tucker, Herbert F. *Epic: Britain's Heroic Muse, 1790–1910*. Oxford: Oxford UP, 2008.

Veblen, Thorstein. *Theory of the Leisure Class*. 1899. Harmondsworth, UK: Penguin, 1979.

Vicinus, Martha. *The Industrial Muse: A Study of Nineteenth Century British Working-Class Literature*. London: Croom Helm, 1974.

Vincent, David. *The Rise of Mass Literacy: Reading and Writing in Modern Europe*. Cambridge, UK: Polity, 2000.

Viswanathan, Gauri. *Outside the Fold: Conversion, Modernity, and Belief*. Princeton, NJ: Princeton UP, 1998.

Von Rosenberg, Ingrid. "French Naturalism and the English Socialist Novel: Margaret Harkness and William Edwards Tirebuck." *The Rise of Socialist Fiction, 1880–1914*. Ed. H. Gustav Klaus. Sussex, UK: Harvester, 1987. 151–71.

Walkowitz, Judith. *City of Dreadful Delight: Narratives of Sexual Danger in Late-Victorian London*. Chicago: U of Chicago P, 1992.

Wallace, Jo-Ann. "The Case of Edith Ellis." *Modernist Sexualities*. Ed. Hugh Stevens and Caroline Howlett. Manchester, UK: Manchester UP, 2000. 13–40.

Wallace, J. W. Memoir and Preface. *On the Road to Liberty: Poems and Ballads*. By J. Bruce Glasier. Manchester, UK: National Labour Press, [1921]. vii–xvii.

Warne, Vanessa, and Colette Colligan. "The Man Who Wrote A New Woman Novel: Grant Allen's *The Woman Who Did* and the Gendering of New Woman Authorship." *Victorian Literature and Culture* 33 (2005): 21–46.

Waters, Chris. *British Socialists and the Politics of Popular Culture, 1884–1914*. Manchester, UK: Manchester UP, 1990.

———. "New Women and Socialist-Feminist Fiction: The Novels of Isabella Ford and Katharine Bruce Glasier." *Rediscovering Forgotten Radicals: British Women Writers, 1889–1939*. Eds. Angela Ingram and Daphne Patai. Chapel Hill: U of North Carolina P, 1993. 25–42.

Webb, Sidney. *The Decline in the Birth-Rate*. Fabian Tract No. 131. London: Fabian Society, 1907.

Weiner, Joel H., ed. *Papers for the Millions: The New Journalism in Britain, 1850s to 1914*. Westport, CT: Greenwood, 1988.

Wells, H. G. *Ann Veronica*. London: Penguin, 2005.

———. *In the Days of the Comet*. New York: Berkley Highland, 1967.

Wexler, Joyce. "Selling Sex as Art." *Marketing Modernisms: Self-Promotion, Canonization, and Rereading*. Ed. Kevin J. H. Dettmar and Stephen Watt. Ann Arbor: U of Michigan P, 1996. 91–108.

Whiteley, Wilfrid, ed. *J. Bruce Glasier: A Memorial*. Manchester, UK: National Labour Press, [1920].

Wiens, Pamela Bracken. Introduction. *The Tables Turned, or Nupkins Awakened: A Socialist Interlude.* By William Morris. Athens: Ohio UP, 1994. 1–29.

Wilde, Oscar. *Complete Works of Oscar Wilde.* New York: Harper Collins, 2003.

———. "The Critic as Artist." *Complete Works.* 1108–55.

———. "The Decay of Lying." *Complete Works.* 1071–92.

———. *An Ideal Husband.* [1895]. *Complete Works.* 515–82.

———. *The Importance of Being Earnest.* [1895]. *Complete Works.* 357–419.

———. "Lord Arthur Savile's Crime." *Complete Works.* 160–83.

———. "Miner and Minor Poets." *Pall Mall Gazette* (1 February 1887). Rpt. in *Reviews.* 123–27.

———. *The Picture of Dorian Gray.* New York: Pearson, 2007.

———. "Poetical Socialists." *Pall Mall Gazette* (15 February 1889). Rpt. in *The Soul of Man.* 17–19.

———, *Reviews.* London: Methuen, 1908.

———. "The Soul of Man Under Socialism." *Complete Works.* 1174–97.

———. *The Soul of Man Under Socialism and Selected Critical Prose.* Ed. Linda Dowling. London: Penguin, 2001.

Williams, Raymond. *Communications.* 3rd ed. London: Penguin, 1977.

Wollaeger, Mark. *Modernism, Media, and Propaganda: British Narrative from 1900 to 1945.* Princeton, NJ: Princeton UP, 2006.

Woolf, Virginia. "Mr. Bennett and Mrs. Brown." *Collected Essays.* Ed. Leonard Woolf. London: Hogarth, 1966. Vol. 1, 319–37.

Wordsworth, William. Preface to *Lyrical Ballads.* 1802. *William Wordsworth: A Critical Edition of the Major Works.* Ed. Stephen Gil. Oxford: Oxford UP, 1984. 595–615.

Worthen, W. B. *Modern Drama and the Rhetoric of Theater.* Berkeley: U of California P, 1991.

———. *Print and the Poetics of Modern Drama.* Cambridge UP, 2005.

Yeo, Stephen. "A New Life: The Religion of Socialism in Britain 1883–1896." *History Workshop Journal* 4 (1977): 5–58.

Youngkin, Molly. *Feminist Realism at the Fin de Siècle: The Influence of the Late-Victorian Women's Press on the Development of the Novel.* Columbus: Ohio State UP, 2007.

Zola, Émile. *Germinal.* Trans. L. W. Tancock. Harmondsworth, UK: Penguin, 1954.

Index

Page numbers in italics indicate illustrations.

utopianism: of *Commonweal*, 40–51; of
Kelmscott Press, 54–55, 56, 58, 62;
of Morris, 36–37, 313n6; negative
political connotations of, 50–51; as
politically revolutionary, 36; in socialist aestheticism, 35; of Wilde, 45
utopian novels. *See also A Dream of John
Ball* (Morris); *News from Nowhere*
(Morris); socialist novels: radical
attraction to, 320n18; *vs.* naturalist
novels, 104

Veblen, Thorstein, 53
"Vicissitudes of Queen Mab, The"
(Forman), 156
"Victim, A" (Maguire), 213
Victoria (queen of England), jubilees of,
191, 193, 328n16
Victory Web Perfecting Machine, 17
Villiers, Roland de, 261
violence, in naturalist novels, 101, 103
visual media: in late-nineteenth century,
30, 312n29; Morris on, 80–81
"Vive la Commune" (Crane), 46–47, *48*
Vizetelly, Henry, 96, 100
volunteers, in newspaper production,
15–16, 310n19

"Wagner, Millet and Whitman" (Car-
penter), 186–187
Wallace, Lewis, 223
Wastall, Arthur, *271*, 337n11
Waters, Chris, 25, 180, 198, 312n28,
318n8, 324n16, 324n19
Webb, Beatrice, 96, 127, 132, 249, 279–
280, 319n10, 321n31, 322n39
Webb, Sidney, 127, 132, 249, 250, 279–
82, 333n12, 338n24
Wells, H. G., 1–2, 120, 250–251, 338n18
wet nursing, 286
"What Is the Right Word?," 173
Wheeler, J. M., 240
Whelen, Frederick, 133–134
"When Labour First in Strength
Awoke," 198–199

When Love Is Liberty and Nature Law
(Babcock), 281
Whitman, Walt, 181, 184, 185, 186, 187,
320n20, 328n13
"Why I Am a Socialist" (Besant), 241
Widowers' House (Shaw), 130–133, 251
Wilde, Oscar: aestheticism of, 44–45,
312n2; as apolitical, 314n15; flat-
ness in works of, 79–80; Morris's
influence on, 35, 44–45; on popular
culture, 180; utopianism of, 45; on
working-class poetry, 207–208,
330n29
Wilhelm I, death of, 40
"William Morris as Actor and
Dramatist" (Shaw), 123–124
Williams, Raymond, 2, 168, 307n4
Wilson, Charlotte, 9, 191
Woman of No Importance, A (Wilde), 79
Woman Who Did, The (Allen), 257, 269–
273, *272*, 282, 337n10
women: *The Cenci* (Shelley) and, 158–159;
at *Clarion*, 284–286, 339n27–2829;
in free love, 270–271; in idealist art,
314n17; in Maguire's poetry, 213–
217; in *News from Nowhere* (Morris),
316n32; in sex radicalism, 284–287;
in theosophy, 253–254, 335n32;
unwed mothers, 293–294
Wood, Esther, 105–106
wood-block illustrations, in Kelmscott
editions, *64*, 65–66
Woolf, Leonard, 301
Woolf, Virginia, 301
"Workers' Claims and 'Public Opinion,'"
The (leaflet), 19–20
Workers' Cry, 142, 185, 197, 276–277
Workers' Herald, 20, 122–123, 322n1
"Worker's Share of Art, The" (Morris),
44
Workers' Theatre Movement, 123
working-class, use of term, 9
Working Class Tragedy, A (Bramsbury),
102–103, 105
Working Men Indeed! (pamphlet), 19